W9-AHN-843

My Mother
Wears Combat Boots

A Parenting Guide for the Rest of Us

My Mother Wears Combat Boots

A Parenting Guide for the Rest of Us

Jessica Mills

AK PRESS

EDINBURGH · OAKLAND · WEST VIRGINIA

My Mother Wears Combat Boots
© 2007 Jessica Mills

ISBN 1904859720
ISBN-13 9781904859727

Library of Congress Control Number: 2007928385

AK Press
674-A 23rd Street
Oakland, CA 94612
USA
www.akpress.org
akpress@akpress.org

AK Press
PO Box 12766
Edinburgh, EH8 9YE
Scotland
www.akuk.com
ak@akedin.demon.co.uk

The above addresses would be delighted to provide you with the latest AK Press distribution catalog, which features the several thousand books, pamphlets, zines, audio and video products, and stylish apparel published and/or distributed by AK Press. Alternatively, visit our website for the complete catalog, latest news, and secure ordering.

Printed in Canada on acid free, recycled paper with union labor.

Cover by Cristy Road
Interior design and layout by ZB

Table of Contents

3 Years Old

4 Years Old

5 Years Old

Acknowledgments

Thanks for help big and small, without you this book wouldn't have happened: My family and my parents Bob and Abby Mills, Ramsey Kanaan, Arwen Curry and *MRR* coordinators, Karoline Collins, *Clamor*, Mamaphiles, Vikki Law, China Martens, Jessica and Lynne and the Gainesville Midwives Cooperative, Debbie Marin, Adriana Algeri, Janice Heller, Ann Marie Rian Wanzeck, Citizen Fish, Subhumans, Molotonic, Placenta, Kaile Adney, Mona Harris, Elizabeth Bonet, Tracey Kenyon Milarsky, Cristy Road, Chris Boarts-Larson, Amber Rae Kelly and Laurie Reisman and the Gainesville Childcare Cooperative, Gainesville Street Skool, Village Cooperative Skool, Jenny Brown, GWL and Gainesville Area NOW, Samantha Jones, Anna Bryant, Charles Weigl, Joy Rabinni, Andrea Mass, Lisa Heeg, Jacinta Bunnell, Darlene Martinez, Sarah Campbell, Christian Pugmire, Rosa Maria DiDonato, Andy Submission Hold, Angelina Drake, Jason Straw, Erik Davis, Rahula Janowski, anarchist parenting listserv mamas and papas, Darby and the Anti-Authoritarian Babysitting Collective, Tomas Moniz, the AK Press collective, and the hugest I-couldn't-have-done-it-without-you-thanks to my editor, Ellen Cavalli.

This book is for Ernesto, Emma-Joy, and Maya-Rae.

Visit the author's blog at MyMotherWearsCombatBoots.blogspot.com

Preface

When *Maximum Rock N Roll* (*MRR*) zine announced they were putting out a "punks having kids" theme issue, I didn't hesitate to send in a little written something along with a picture of my newly protruding preggo belly. By the time that issue came out, my newborn Emma-Joy was with me and I couldn't have devoured fast enough the words the other punks with kids had to offer.

In July 2000, I sent in my first column for *MRR*, titled "My Mother Wears Combat Boots." My new mama friend Kaile gave me the idea for the title after I told her I'd chosen a "punk parent" theme for it, though I had free reign to write about any topic. Being a new parent, I couldn't think about anything more immediate that I needed or wanted to write about. Ideally I thought, I'd be helping myself navigate these new mama waters by writing about it and at the same time, sharing experiences with and getting in touch with other punk parents. You know, building community.

In the first year, the column got me in touch with a slew of other parents through letters, email, and phone calls, too. Some offered their words as column contributors. Due to requests from some others who didn't get their hands on *MRR* as often as they'd liked, I compiled the first year's worth of columns into zine format, putting it out as *Yard Wide Yarns* #8, the zine I'd been doing since 1993.

It was then, in late 2001, that I first thought it would be great to some day write a book. My initial idea was to wait to compile what would be the "best of" the first five year's worth of columns. In July 2005, when I sat down to sketch out an outline of what the book would and wouldn't contain, the project started taking on a life of its own.

What you hold in your hands now contains very little original column writing; those columns make up maybe just half the book's skeleton. And two chapters,

"Pregnancy: Month by Month, Inside and Out" and "When Birth Doesn't Go As Planned" originally appeared in *Clamor* magazine as a three part series in their first three issues; here they have been edited and updated from their original versions. The rest of the book is all new writing, carefully balancing personal anecdote, practical advice, and political analysis.

The book itself is a dream come true. Once the opportunity to do it came, having worked hard to make a dream come true, I was scared of it. Scared enough to almost convince myself that it was too much for me, that I should just let it go. But then a different internal voice told me that if I didn't take the opportunity to make a dream come true, I'd be a flat out loser.

So I started juggling. Finding the space and time to do it, between work and kid, between getting pregnant again, having a new baby in 2006, moving cross country, stealing away sleep time even after I'd hired a babysitter, I can't believe I pulled it off. Though the book ends with Emma-Joy in kindergarten, I didn't finish writing it until the new baby, Maya-Rae was sixteen months old and Emma-Joy was seven, just finishing the first grade.

You hold here a journey. In many ways, writing a book was like being pregnant and giving birth all over again.

I sincerely hope this book will add to the generations of mama voices before mine and to my own generation's collection of mama voices so that the new mamas and papas searching for ideas on "how to do it" will feel a bit of solidarity in the ranks. I hope it will serve as sort of an instruction manual—the one I searched for when I became a new mama, but couldn't find.

In the book, I've also set out to debunk some myths. Among them, that hospital birth is the only choice, that only "stay-at-home" moms can successfully breastfeed, that it takes a shit ton of money to have a child, the supermom myth, that it's time to "settle down", and that you can't do certain things anymore (like go on tour with your band) once you have a kid.

And oh yeah, to remind you, too, that you have to keep your sense of humor.

Though this book is written from a partnered parenting perspective, it is not meant to exclude single parents, same-sex parents, step-parents, extra parents, or any other nontraditional families. I hope you will be able to translate my standard language to fit your family type.

For those of you who are not mamas or papas yet: though NO amount of reading other's stories of parenthood will prepare you for what parenthood is REALLY like, hopefully this book will show you that though your life certainly changes beyond comprehension, it doesn't end. Quit the opposite. Life parenting a child is new and there's never a dull moment. Though things do get tired and broken, it keeps changing, evolving, recreating meaning, and redefining ideas. It's the hard-est thing ever and worth it. Read with an open mind, but not so open that you take everything in. Just take what resonates with you and leave the rest. Don't subscribe to any one style. Be selective in learning about and developing your own style that fits you, your kid, and your family. Recognize your privileges as well as your limita-tions; what your circumstances dictate that you have to work with and work with it! Parenting demands lots of responsibility and hard work. No matter what you have or don't have, do things as close to how you want and think they should be. Above all, think and make conscious choices instead of being purely reactionary and parent (or not parent as the case may more often be) the same way you were parented.

For those of you who are already parents, may you find solidarity in the ranks, may these stories help you out like others' stories have helped me. It's always nice to know you're not alone when you feel like you are, and with parenting, knowing you're not alone is necessary. Be patient with yourself as much as you need to be with your kid—figuring out how parenting and ideals mesh together isn't a no-brainer. It's a rather large task to find the balance between your own and your kid's desires and needs. Consider these comforting words from Erik W. Davis, a fellow parent on the anarchist parenting listserv, "Listen to yourself. Be brave about your doubts, but don't punish yourself for some ideal of 'perfect parenting.' There are no perfect parents, and the sooner we all realize that, the better we'll actually be as real parents... Go for your ideals as hard as you can, but keep in mind that perfec-tion is not possible, and kindness to yourself may occasionally mean not pursuing an ideal in favor of your own or your child's best interests." Shit happens and you will make mistakes. But don't despair. Kids get over it, the world doesn't end and kids are forgiving, especially when you've established trust and a history of sincere apology when necessary. Learn from your mistakes and do better next time.

For those of you who haven't yet decided if kids are for you, may you neither be scared away nor pulled in—the answer to your kid or no-kid question can only be found by taking a look inward.

For those who have decided that kids are most definitely not for you, may this book give you insight into the world of the parents and kids in your life and com-munity, as well as courage to be an ally and recognize that supporting choice goes both ways. It goes for those who've chosen not to become a parent and for those who have. And that, as cliché as it sounds, it really does take a village to raise a child, and you can be a part of that village-wide effort. You'll benefit, too.

Parenting is living a life of daily revolution.

Pregnancy and Birth

1.

Pregnancy: Month by Month, Inside and Out

Month 1: Inside

Egg, meet sperm. Sperm, meet egg. Out of the 140 to 350 million sperm released in the one payload called *ejaculation*, only one—if it's lucky—is allowed the victory of entering the egg wall and causing *fertilization*. The sperm's chromosomes determine the sex of the baby (X is female, Y male) at the moment of fertilization, and cell division begins. When the cells reach about 100 in number—about four or five days after fertilization—they form a ball about the size of a pin head—the *blastocyst*. (For all you punks without a name for your band, try Blast-O-Cyst.) This cell ball has two layers. The outer layer will become the *placenta*, and the inner, the *embryo*. Embryonic stem cells (ES cells) are stem cells derived from this inner cell mass of the blastocyst. They are pluripotent, meaning they are able to differentiate into all derivatives of the three primary germ layers: ectoderm, endoderm, and mesoderm.

When the cells reach about 150 in number, they divide into three layers of tissue, called *germ layers*, which will develop separately. The inside layer will become the liver, pancreas, urinary bladder, tonsils, thyroid, and breathing and digestive organs. The middle layer is going to develop into bones, cartilage, muscles, circulatory system, spleen, kidneys, and sex organs. The outside layer will become the baby's hair, skin, nails, tooth enamel, pituitary gland, mammary glands, sweat glands, and nervous system—including the brain. The total size of the embryo at this stage is between one-quarter and half the size of a lowercase letter "o" on this page.

Halfway through the first month, the embryo attaches itself to the wall of the uterus, its home for the nine months (average thirty-seven to forty-two weeks) of gestation. Some preliminary tissues also transforms from a ball of cells into a tubular, folded structure called the *neural tube*, one end of which will become the baby's brain, and other end the spinal cord.

By the end of the month, the approximately 0.08 to 0.16 inch (2 to 4 mm) embryo looks like a tadpole, with the rudimentary beginnings of arms and legs. The *optic vesicles*, a pocket of embryonic tissue that is the beginning of an organ, and lenses in the eyes are also forming. Although the heart is located on the outside of the body, not yet inside the chest cavity, it is beginning to beat. Fetal heart rate tends to vary with gestational age in the very early parts of pregnancy.

This is the beginning of the *embryonic period*, an extremely important time of development when the embryo is most susceptible to factors that can interfere with its development. Most malformations originate during this critical period.

THINGS TO AVOID DURING PREGNANCY

Beyond the obvious—don't drink alcohol, use drugs, or smoke—here are some activities that should be avoided during pregnancy because they can result in embryonic developmental problems, pregnancy complications, or even miscarriage.

1. Douching: This is a bad idea anyway, but especially so in pregnancy because it can cause vaginal infections.

2. Starting an unfamiliar sport or one that could cause injury. Do you need a broken whatever from skating a vert ramp? Stumping around in a cast is gonna make being pregnant much less fun, and you won't want to take the pain meds.

3. Raising your core temperature to about 102° F. Overheating can cause developmental problems. Stay out of the sauna and hot tub. Regular bathing is OK but water should not be hotter than about 101° F for prolonged soaking.

4. Lifting over thirty-five pounds. The hormones that relax your joints make you more prone to injury, so be sure to use correct body mechanics when lifting, especially later in pregnancy.

5. Taking over-the-counter medicines. Check with your provider before taking anything—and try and avoid anything in your first twelve weeks. For example, Ibuprofen and Aspirin are not recommended during pregnancy because of the chance of bleeding.

6. Inhaling chemical fumes, including household cleaners. These fumes are toxic.

7. Sitting or standing for prolonged periods—especially in late pregnancy. As mentioned above, your joints are more prone to injury, and swelling can occur in your legs, feet, arms, and hands.

8. If in doubt, check with your care provider, and use common sense!

Month 1: Outside

It was late May 1999, and Ernesto and I had both just quit our jobs (mine as an after-school tutor/teacher, his as a cook at Our Place Café in Gainesville, Florida) and hit the road for a two-month whirlwind of a journey. I think, subconsciously, I knew I'd be getting pregnant during our trip. Up until then, my daily routine had been hectic: picking up the Food Not Bombs and Free Fridge donations, working on the Free Radio Gainesville logistics, working on my zine, teaching part-time, and going to band practice and shows. Once I had let go of those things, my body seemed to have relaxed enough to become fertilized. We hadn't been trying to get pregnant in the sense that we were charting ovulation and timing sex. But we had stopped using condoms because we did want to have a baby together. After about ten months, we were tired of the monthly mystery and kind of settled more into a "whatever" mindset—letting go as much as we could of the anxiety to conceive.

According to some licensed midwives and friends of mine who claim this is how they got pregnant, there is a general feeling that fertilization often occurs when there's a change in your schedule that induces relaxation. There is some limited information available about this with regard to infertility treatments combined with acupuncture and massage. However, in the world of ruthless consumerism, some travel companies are now promoting the "babymoon"—a vacation taken by a couple with the express intent of conceiving, away from all the stresses and strains of everyday life. Little did we know that our idea could be marketed, but on a rather more upscale level than hopping freight trains, sleeping under highway overpasses, and eating a freegan dumpstered diet of whatever!

This trip was our last chance to get out of town for a while because Ernesto had decided to go back to school in the fall. Our routines were also killing both of us. We needed to shed all responsibility and just go...

The beginning of the trip was pretty intense. Although it was only the middle of my cycle, I was moodier than when I have PMS. Actually, I was downright fierce. We'd been so looking forward to our two months off, yet we were coming apart at the seams. We had individual travel agendas, but our plans didn't mesh with each other's. He wanted to be in the mountains away from cities and bands and people, I wanted cities and bands and people.

We eventually compromised, but I practically didn't speak to him for a couple days. When it came time to catch that first freight train, I agreed that we needed to be friends again.

For the rest of the month, we were back in love as usual, and happily riding trains and hitchhiking through the Northwest states, hiking part of the Olympic Peninsula and all over British Columbia, including Vancouver Island. Sometimes we hiked through a city and other times a forest. We met up with friends, took rides from strangers, and were alone quite a bit, too. I even got to see my friend's band, on tour from San Francisco, play in Missoula, Montana at J's Tavern.

Month 2: Inside

At the beginning of this month, the embryo's backbone is forming, with five to eight vertebrae laid down. By the end of the month, all the backbone will be laid down and the spinal canal closed over, although the lower part of the back will still be undeveloped. There is quite a long rudimentary tail, which is an extension of the spinal column. The embryo is growing in a curved seahorse shape because the blocks of tissue in the back of the embryo grow more quickly than those in front.

All of the major organs—heart, brain, lungs, kidneys, liver, and intestines—are in place, although not yet fully developed. The heart is now inside the body, beating with enough strength to circulate blood cells through the blood vessels. The head is starting to form and eyelid folds are developing on its face. Internal and external ears are forming. The embryo's mouth can open, with lips and tongue visible. The appendix is now present, as is the pancreas, the tip of the nose, elbows, and toes. The arms are as long as a printed exclamation point (!). The embryo looks like an extremely small human being, but it still may be impossible to distinguish a male from a female as external organs of the male and female appear very similar at this stage in the game and will not be distinguishable for another few weeks.

Nerve and muscle work together for the first time now and the embryo has reflexes, moving its body and limbs. The first true bone cells begin to replace cartilage. This is the end of the embryonic period. The *fetal period* begins. The embryo is now clinically called a *fetus*. Rapid growth and maturation of the tissues follow; a critical part of the fetus's development is ending.

And talk about an incredible growth spurt! During the first week of this month, the fetus grows from 0.16 to 0.20 inches (4 to 5 mm) to 0.43 to 0.51 inches (1.1 to 1.3 cm)—about the size of a green pea. The second week of the month, it will be the size of a pinto bean. By the end of the month, the fetus is a little more than one inch (2.5 cm) long and weighs in like a small plum, just under 0.04 ounces (1.1 g). Normal heart rate at six weeks is around 90 to 110 beats per minute (bpm), and at nine weeks is 140 to 170 bpm.

Month 2: Outside

I found out I was pregnant at the very beginning of July. At first, I attributed my late period to the tribulations of travel, sleeping in abandoned houses and eating gruel-like couscous with instant black-bean flakes. I was choosing to ignore that my boobs were extremely sore, and the fact that even when my period was a little late in the past, it had never been this late. It's probably closer to the truth to say that I didn't want my hopes to be built up and then dashed if I found out a little one wasn't taking hold inside me.

We went to a Planned Parenthood in Bozeman, Montana, I peed in a cup, and the test came back positive. Ernesto said he already knew I was pregnant just by looking at me. Funny how he can tell those things. He could probably tell I was ovulating when his sperm fertilized my egg, too, but he just forgot to remind me. He's always been more in touch with my cycle than I have been, probably because he's the one who witnesses my cyclical shifts in hormones, as I naturally remain oblivious.

Our heads floating in the clouds, we had to take turns figuring out how to turn the doorknob to let ourselves out of the Planned Parenthood office. Once outside, we emptied our back pockets of their packs of Export A cigarettes, Ernesto committing to quit with me. I entered the first used bookstore I saw, purchased a book about pregnancy, and dove in.

I called a toll-free Healthy Pregnancy hotline to ask if the four times I had imbibed alcohol while unknowingly pregnant would be of any consequence. They assured me things would be OK and explained that during the first few weeks following fertilization, the developing baby is just a floating ball of cells not yet hooked up to the uterus and therefore wasn't in the direct line of fire. My fear of accidentally damaging my baby subsided.

Later that month, we crossed the country from Montana to Virginia and went to my family's reunion in the Appalachian Mountains. When I told my mom our news, she squealed with excitement. The rest of the family was, of course, congratulatory and full of questions. After the reunion, Ernesto and I hit the Appalachian Trail with my parents for four days. The temperatures were reaching over 100° F, water and food were not available in ideal quantities, and the actual hiking was sometimes excruciating. I later read that this was probably not the best situation I could have been placing myself in, but everything turned out just fine.

Ernesto and I spent the rest of the month gallivanting leisurely all over New Brunswick, Prince Edward Island, and Nova Scotia. I was determined, either wisely or not, to see this trip through to the end. Camping out wherever we happened to wind up every night was fun. Nutrition was my only concern, so I cut out dumpster-diving for food and we made it a point to seek out a decent health food store every other day. I got myself a bottle of prenatal vitamins and all was well, although our trip became a bit more expensive now that I was taking care of myself for the sake of someone else.

Oh yeah, the only music I had with me for the two-month trip was a Subhumans tape. Aawww, baby's first lullabies.

Month 3: Inside

At the beginning of the month, the fetus's fastest growth is in the limbs, hands, and feet. Nail beds on the fingers and toes are forming for eventual nails.

Due to rapid brain growth, the head is almost half the entire length of the baby. (At birth, the baby's head is only one-fourth the size of its body.) The eyes, which were at the sides of the head, are moving to the front. The ears also come to lie in their normal position on the side of the head. Taste buds appear now and the vocal cords are developing. Tooth buds are present. The fetus can swallow, suck, and chew. It swallows amniotic fluid and urinates it back into the amniotic fluid in which it floats.

The heart is beating 120 to 160 bpm. At this stage, heart rate can often be heard with a Doppler, a special listening device that looks like a microphone. (Don't worry if you can't hear it though. Your healthcare provider may order an ultrasound just to check.) The umbilical cord has fully formed and blood is circulating through it. The liver is producing bile.

Few, if any, structures in the fetus are formed after the twelfth week of pregnancy, the end of the third month. By the end of the month, it can curl its toes, bend its elbows, rotate its wrists, and form tight fists. The neck continues to get longer and the chin no longer rests on the chest. It can make facial expressions like pressing its lips together and frowning. It weighs between 0.5 and 0.9 ounce (14.5 to 25.5 g) and measures about 4.5 inches (11.4 cm), the size of my fist.

Month 3: Outside

There was never a doubt in my mind that I would seek out a midwife instead of a hospital-based obstetrician. Midwives are specially trained in assessing and taking care of normal, healthy, low-risk pregnancies and aiding natural birth. Obstetricians are specially trained in dealing with high-risk pregnancies and birth complications. As far as I could tell (which was later confirmed by my midwife), I was experiencing a normal, healthy, low-risk pregnancy. I had no breakthrough bleeding or cramping. I was not underweight or overweight, and had no history of high blood pressure, heart disease, or chronic illness. And aside from normal fatigue and nausea associated with early pregnancy, I felt good. Therefore, the first place I visited the day we returned home was the Gainesville Birth Center. The birth center was situated in an old house less than a mile from where we lived and was run by two midwives who offered the option of giving birth there or in your own home. A midwife gave me a free orientation, an appointment to begin prenatal care, and information on how to apply for Medicaid and WIC (Women, Infants, and Children Nutrition Program).

I began telling friends that I was pregnant and was surprised when they said they had expected the news. While I was gone traveling, one of my bandmates had even suggested to the others, "I know Jessica is gonna come back pregnant."

PREGNANT AND WANT TO TOUR?

1. Think it through.
2. Check with your provider.
3. Talk to your partner(s).
4. Trust yourself to make the right decision.
5. There is not a one-size-fits-all answer to most of this stuff; as they say, if the shoe fits...

At my first prenatal appointment, the midwife thought, based on the size of my expanding uterus, that I was a month farther along than I believed I was. (This is possible because some women experience hormone-related bleeding early in their pregnancies, which they might confuse with a menstrual period.) She scheduled me to have an ultrasound to determine if that was the case or if I was carrying twins. I was happy to find out that I was only twelve weeks along. Ernesto was the happiest to find out that I wasn't carrying twins, so happy, in fact, that he danced a little jig in the corner of the room.

I explained to the midwife that had I been sixteen weeks along instead of twelve, the first month would not have been anywhere near substance-free because I had been in California recording an album with my band. She said, "The way I look at it is this: you live in a college town where lots of people are partying all the time, probably half of the pregnancies happen under the influence of alcohol, women don't usually discover they're pregnant until they're six to eight weeks along, and you don't see all the kids running around retarded, do you?" I felt a bit better. She said the ideal situation, though, is a planned pregnancy where all the things you would quit during pregnancy have already been stopped well in advance of conception. However, since fully 50% of pregnancies are unplanned, the best thing to do is quit *as soon as you think you might be pregnant.*

I also began looking for a job without telling any of the potential employers I was pregnant. I didn't think anyone would hire a pregnant person, even though such employment discrimination is illegal. They quickly bored me with their barely above-minimum-wage offerings while asking for a two-year commitment, so I went back to the place I had been teaching and tutoring part-time. Ernesto started school and a work-study library job. We were poor, but happier than ever.

Just when I started back at my old job, I got a call from my friend Richard, a roadie for Citizen Fish. He said the band needed a horn player for their month-long U.S. tour and asked if I was interested. My midwife gave me the thumbs-up. She said that going on tour, as with any activity, requires common sense. She asked me to consider the following questions: Will you be able to take care of yourself and your unborn baby? Will it be possible to eat enough of the right kind of food, have enough water, get enough rest? Is the environment going to make it difficult to maintain your drug-free, sober life? Are you able to meet the physical demands of whatever you are doing? I was able to confidently answer yes, yes, no, and yes, respectively, so I decided to go for it. Ernesto's biggest concern was that since this might be the only time I'd ever be pregnant, he didn't want to miss any of it, especially if I started to "show" while away on tour.

I'm addicted to travel, touring especially, and I did not want to pass on this opportunity. I got the ball rolling immediately. With the help of my ol' bandmate Karl, I learned the songs in ten days, got my tickets to travel, and was set! I told my employer, "I'm going to be working out of town next month. I'll call you when I get home."

For the rest of the month until I left for tour, I tried to take it easy and finish the new issue of my zine, *Yard Wide Yarns #7*. This wasn't so hard to do since I had toned down my activities with Food Not Bombs and Free Radio Gainesville to one day a week, as a way to purposely create open time and space for this new life growing inside me.

The only time it could be said that I wasn't taking it easy was when I wrecked on my bike. Although the handlebars lodged themselves firmly into my gut and knocked the wind and tears out of me, the baby was fine. I called my midwife to ask her if it was OK for me to keep riding my bike as my means of transportation. I also asked her what physical activities I should avoid. She said that the list of things to avoid is potentially endless and that it comes down to common sense. She advised me to ask myself: Is this something you have always done and are good at? Does it have a huge potential for injury? She said that if I had been riding a bike for years, that I could probably keep doing it, but that this is not the time for a novice rider to decide to start biking everywhere.

She added that scuba diving was out, and so was bungee jumping, skydiving, skiing, horseback riding, bull riding, playing rugby—you get the picture! Also, jogging was a bad idea because of the potential for joint injury as hormones loosen joints—stick with brisk walking. She said that anything that raised my heart rate and breathing to the point that I could no longer talk was working me too hard; it's best to back it down a little so you can carry on a conversation.

I found myself going to fewer shows than usual. This wasn't because I was consciously making that decision, but because of the natural fatigue of pregnancy and some hormonal shift that was summoning my mama-like nesting urges, the same hormonal shift that now had me crying at movies when a kid would be shown hurt. When I did go to shows, however, I'd come home all wound up, amped, and talking a mile a minute, instead of flopping down on the bed, still wearing my boots. Let's hear it for hormones—more addictive than speed and more fun than weed! Plus, I was confident that going to shows wasn't hurting me or my resident baby. Passive smoke inhalation would be a concern if I had been exposed to a lot of it for long periods of time, but I wasn't. My common sense made sure of that. And at this stage of development, the baby cannot yet hear, it just feels vibrations, so I wasn't concerned that the noise would hurt its ears.

Month 4: Inside

A word about the placenta: The placenta is an organ created by the mother's body to nourish the fetus and excrete its waste products. By now it is both fully formed and operational. It looks like a large, round-ish liver and is attached on one side to the uterus and on the other side to the fetus's umbilical cord. It is the fetus's lifeline to the mother: blood, oxygen, and nutrients all reach the fetus through a fine membrane into the placenta. The placenta functions like a sieve, passing oxygen, food, and protective antibodies from mother to fetus (although harmful elements can also filter through). The fetus gets rid of its waste products by filtering them through the placenta into the mother's bloodstream, allowing the mother to excrete them. The blood from which the fetus has already taken oxygen comes back through an artery in the umbilical cord into the placenta.

This month marks the beginning of the second trimester, the time when the fetus does most of its growing and when its organs mature. In these weeks, the fetus is moving actively and can even turn somersaults, although the mother probably won't feel these movements yet. Fat begins to form, and is important in heat production and metabolism. The fetus's heartbeat is almost twice as fast as the mother's; its head now moves freely on its body; hair has begun to grow, including fluff on the head, eyelashes, and eyebrows. *Lanugo* has also grown. This is a fine, downy hair that appears all over the fetus's face and body, keeping its temperature constant. Most of this hair will disappear before it is born and whatever is left will fall out soon after birth.

Because the three tiny bones of the middle ear are the first bones to harden, the fetus can probably hear by now. From now on, the mother is what the fetus will be listening to! Through the amniotic fluid, the fetus can hear the mother's heart beating, stomach rumbling, and the sound of her voice. However, the auditory centers in the brain have not yet fully formed and are unable to process the information.

Certain sounds from outside the womb can also reach the fetus. If a loud sound is made next to the uterus, the fetus will raise its hands and cover its ears. Very loud sounds have been known to startle a fetus enough to make it jump inside the mother.

During the fourth month, the fetus quadruples in weight and doubles in height. It now weighs about 7 ounces (198.4 g) and is 6 inches (15.2 cm) long.

Month 4: Outside

Before I left for tour at the beginning of the month, I found out that one of my oldest friend's partner, Kaile, was pregnant. Perfect timing! A big priority for Ernesto and me was to build community with other punks and activists who had—or would be having—kids.

I escaped the entire first trimester with only one incidence of morning sickness (just so happened to be the day Frank and Kaile were getting hitched down at the courthouse and I was bummed to have to miss it) and continued to feel absolutely great throughout the tour. It was definitely a big kick for me to be pregnant and still touring. It was also definitely different from any tour I had done before; out of fifteen tours, this was my first sober one! This was also the first tour I've ever been on that was fast food-free. (If you tour and want to eat well, get yourself a copy of *Healthy Highways: The Traveler's Guide To Healthy Eating*, by Nikki and David Goldbeck, available from AK Press. It will let you know where there are decent groceries, delis, and restaurants.)

On tour, I found myself hanging out less and sleeping more. If people were just drinkin' and smokin' on the porch, then I was usually the first one to crash. Urges to partake were not hindering my desire to stay awake; it was more the fact that making a baby is physically draining. The books I've read say that it's comparable to the daily energy exerted by a mountain climber.

The tour itself was absolutely a dream. The road crew, Richard, Karoline, and Paige, were incredible. Most of the band members were in the Subhumans, the very first punk band I'd ever heard and I totally love them. They made me feel welcome, as if I were a regular band member, and on the few occasions when a kid or two would ask us to sign something, they'd chuckle at my "Jessica +1" signature.

One occasion with Richard stands out in my mind because it showed how my pregnancy had a positive effect on others. He'd had a vasectomy and wasn't too down with the idea of having kids. During our conversation, though, he told me that being around me during my pregnancy made him feel differently about people in our "community" deciding to have kids. He said that hearing me talk about what Ernesto and I had learned so far about natural childbirth and some of our goals, dreams, and plans in terms of conscientiously parenting a free child, made him happy. I was beaming.

Karoline, too, really made me feel great about being pregnant. She was not only supportive, but extremely helpful, playing mommy to me, the mommy-to-be. I was always alerted to where I could find good things to eat. She got me drinking pregnancy tea every day, something I would never have done on my own, even though it was really helpful stuff. There are several different blends of pregnancy tea, but

HERBS TO AVOID DURING PREGNANCY

This is a very long list, and changes frequently, depending on which source you trust. Therefore, before using any medicinal herbs, check with your practitioner and/or a good herb reference book, such as *Wise Woman Herbal for the Childbearing Year* by Susun S. Weed.

they all tend to contain raspberry leaf, which has been used traditionally as a uterine tonic and toner. Some also have herbs that are high in iron and other nutrients. One really safe blend is red raspberry leaf, peppermint, oatstraw, nettles, and chamomile. She was the only other nonsmoker and nondrinker on the tour, so it was nice to have the sober camaraderie, too.

I had the first of three pregnancy dreams. I was lying on my back in a field of grass under a beautifully bright shining sun. Sitting playfully on his mama, my two-year-old boy had a huge and radiant toothy smile; bronze, sun-kissed skin; and a head full of sun-bleached curly locks. His name was Ernesto, but we called him Che.

Not everyone was understanding and supportive of my decisions. When we were loading out after the Philadelphia show, some young boys who had just seen the show were standing around our van, attempting small talk. I was stacking the book and CD crates in the back, and they said something that prompted me to respond, "Not bad for a pregnant woman, huh?" They asked, "Pregnant? Shouldn't you be at home then? Shouldn't you not be out on tour and lifting crates?" I gave them a lengthy tongue-lashing about the stereotype of a pregnant woman belonging at home with her feet up being bullshit. It was for my fourth month of pregnancy, anyway. Plus, I was adhering to the weight-lifting limits my midwife advised—nothing heavier than thirty-five pounds. (Note about lifting while pregnant: Be sure to use good body mechanics, especially later in pregnancy. Bend your knees and lift with your legs, not your back, to avoid straining your already overworked back and abdominal muscles.)

On the night of our first anniversary, I called Ernesto from a pay phone in the middle of an Arizona desert. I let him know that I wasn't "showing" yet and that I'd be home in a week and a half.

Two days after I got home, my belly finally poked out. Ernesto was quite pleased and joked, "That's right, already listening to your papa, not showing yourself until I was there to see you."

Month 5: Inside

The fetus's skin is transparent, appearing red because the blood vessels are visible through it. By the end of the fourth month, the fetus has a bottom layer (*hypodermis*), a middle layer (*dermis*), and a surface layer (*epidermis*). What is significant about this time in development is that the epidermis has achieved all five of its sublayers and assumes the structure of adult skin. The epidermis contains *epidermal ridges*. They are responsible for patterns of surfaces on fingertips, palms, and soles of the feet and are genetically determined. The dermis forms *dermal papillae*, which push upward into the epidermis. These projections contain a small blood vessel (capillary) or a nerve. This deeper layer also contains large amounts of fat.

The skin has begun to develop *vernix*, a white coating like cream cheese that protects the fetus's skin from the increasing concentration of its urine in the amniotic fluid. By the time the fetus is ready to be born, most of the vernix will have dissolved. However, some vernix will still be there to lubricate the fetus's journey down the birth canal during labor and delivery.

At this stage, the fetal digestive system has developed enough to allow the fetus to swallow quite a lot of amniotic fluid; its stomach begins to secrete gastric juices, enabling its body to absorb the salts and nutrients found in the amniotic fluid. After the fluid is absorbed, the fetus's kidneys filter the fluid and excrete it back into the amniotic sac. The amniotic fluid swallowed by the fetus contributes only a small amount to the caloric needs of the fetus, but researchers believe it may contribute essential nutrients to the developing fetus.

Both sexes develop nipples and underlying mammary glands. The external genital organs have now developed sufficiently for the fetus's sex to be detected by ultrasound.

The fetus's muscles are now almost fully developed, including the chest muscles, which are beginning to make movements similar to those that it will use for respiration later on. Tiny air sacs, known as *alveoli*, which the fetus will need later in order to breathe, are forming inside the tiny developing lungs.

Buds for permanent teeth begin forming behind those that have already developed for its baby teeth.

This month, the fetus grew about an inch a week, putting it at about 10 inches (25.4 cm) and weighing about 12 ounces (340.2 g).

Month 5: Outside

After I got home from tour in October, my appetite swung into full force. I really hate it when I fit perfectly into a stereotype, but it was true this time—I was a pregnant woman with amazing food cravings. I was obsessed with food. I'd be eating something filling while thinking about what my next meal would be.

I started feeling the baby-to-be moving at the very beginning of this month. Ernesto got in the habit of rolling over and putting his hand on my belly as soon as he awoke in the morning. By the end of the month, not only could I feel movements, but I could also see it moving. It's quite weird the first time you witness your own mid-section having what looks like a seismic tremor.

I also started feeling my uterus having growth spurts! There are two ligaments that span either side of the uterus and, ouch, they hurt when they're stretching! Typically they will hurt when you get up quickly, especially if you turn sideways as you get up—like jumping out of bed first thing in the morning to pee. Warm compresses, baths, or a hot water bottle can help alleviate a ligament that is sore or pulled. After they have reached their maximum stretch, they stop complaining. I would sleep a marathon one night, have sore and tight ligaments the entire next day, and then bounce back full of energy the day after that.

Other than a couple of sore days, I felt phenomenal. Given my personality and lifestyle, I never would have guessed I would actually really like being pregnant, but I did. On several occasions people told me, "You're glowing!" and it was kind of funny that I found myself feeling like people didn't suck as bad as I used to think they did.

For Halloween, some girlfriends and I played as Bikini Kill at a party where Minor Threat, Black Sabbath, and X also made Halloween cover appearances. At this stage of development, the nerve endings in the baby's ears that enable it to hear sounds are not connected, so all it really heard of the night were vibrations…but they were punk-rockin' vibes!

I started going to a weekly gentle/prenatal yoga, class so I could learn how to relax and breath—two absolutely important factors when labor strikes. I could have done without the meditative chanting we did at the beginning and end of each class. Hearing a bunch of out-of-tune women chanting words that I didn't understand did the exact opposite of relax me. I just tried to tune them out and think about what food I was going to eat after class.

Complete strangers started to ask me when I was due and if I were having a boy or girl. Very few people were able to fathom the idea that I would not find out the baby's sex before it was born. One woman asked me, in all seriousness, "If you don't know if it's a boy or girl, how are you going to know how to decorate?" I was too stunned to even be able to laugh at the question. Most people couldn't comprehend that we didn't want to know the sex prior to its birth because we were hoping to avoid the gender color-coding crap that we'd have to rally against anyway after the baby was born.

Month 6: Inside

Last month the fetus's skin was transparent; now it becomes opaque. The skin is extremely wrinkled, almost as though the fetus hasn't grown into it, because there aren't any fat deposits beneath the skin yet.

Its body has started to produce white blood cells. These are essential in order for it to be able to combat disease and infection.

This month, the face and body assume more of the appearance of an infant at birth. The tongue is also fully developed now.

Measuring a little over 1 foot long (30.5 cm) and weighing almost 2 pounds (0.9 kg), the fetus would have a chance of surviving if it were delivered at this time. No one wants a baby to deliver this early, as survival is very difficult for an infant this premature, but new technology could keep it alive. The baby would probably have to spend several months in the hospital, with risks of infection and other possible complications.

Month 6: Outside

My hormonal nesting urges were still in full effect as I chose to not go to even more shows. One day I even broke out the sewing machine and made a shoulder bag and two little pillows out of fake fur and Subhumans and Hot Water Music patches. Every now and then I stopped and asked, "What's wrong with me?" My friend Samantha reminded me, "You're pregnant!" Oh, yeah, the baby would need little pillows.

The times I went to some shows, I was amazed to feel my resident baby start kicking as the band started playing. I wised up at the Born Dead Icons show and stood behind the amps. Fewer amniotic waves that way, I was sure, because the rib-kicking subsided. I was also amazed that while riding my bike to the show, dumb-ass guys would still holler at an obviously very pregnant woman, "Hey baby! Yow, what's up?" I mean really, give me a fucking break!

Speaking of bikes, I had another wising up and traded my hafta-bend-over-to-ride-it mountain bike for Samantha's get-to-sit-up-straight, cushy-seat beach cruiser bike.

I'd been wising up book-wise, too. I felt such inspiration and empowerment by reading some really incredible firsthand accounts, written both by midwives and mothers who have delivered naturally (see the Resources section). Small percentages of births do have their complications that dictate that it would be wise to seek an obstetrician's hospital services. Some examples of these complications might include twins, breech, diabetes, high blood pressure, placenta previa, and prematurity. Most pregnancies, if adequate prenatal care has been received, are classi-

OB-Assisted Versus Midwife-Assisted Birth Statistics

If you choose obstetrician care right off the bat, don't be surprised if your OB doesn't let you know what some reputable mainstream journals published recently—that studies show midwife-assisted out-of-hospital births are as safe, if not safer, than OB-assisted hospital births for both mother and baby.

A 2003 study in the *American Journal of Public Health* found that midwife-assisted birth centers provided the same level of safety as hospitals for both mothers and babies in normal, low-risk deliveries. However, only 8.4% of the birth-center group received labor induction, compared to 14.7% of the hospital group. Episiotomy rates were 13.1% for the birth-center group and 37.8% for the hospital group. Only 10.7% of the birth-center group had cesarean sections, a percentage that falls within the target range put forth by the World Health Organization (WHO), compared to 19.1% of the hospital group.

The largest study of U.S. and Canadian home births attended by Certified Professional Midwives, published in 2005 in the *British Medical Journal*, revealed that planned home birth is safe for low-risk women and involves fewer interventions than hospital births. In the study group, which tracked the home births of 5,418 women, the rates of maternal and neonatal mortality of the home-birth group were consistent with those of similar hospital deliveries. Other statistics are telling: 2.1% of the home births required induction of labor, while 21.0% of hospital births were (seemingly needlessly) induced. Episiotomy rates also varied widely: 2.1% of the home births compared to 33.0% of hospital births. The most remarkable difference was in the rate of cesarean sections: 3.7% of home births compared to a staggering 19.0% in hospital births!

Not only are midwife-assisted out-of-hospital births safe and less invasive for low-risk, normal deliveries, they are also in line with the recommendations of the WHO. First, the WHO recommends that pain-relief drugs during labor, like epidurals, be used non-routinely and only when medically necessary (compared to their routine use for U.S. births—80% in 2004); a 10% or less rate of induction of labor (compared to 21.2% for U.S. births in 2004); low/5% use of episiotomies (compared to 23.7%), and 10%–15% cesarean rate (compared to 29.1% in 2004).

For extensive information on midwifery and alternatives to hospital births, visit Citizens for Midwifery (www.cfmidwifery.org)... (cont'd)

fied as normal, healthy, and low-risk. A woman's body knows how to give birth and if allowed to do so at its own pace, without the obstetrical interventions of monitors, drugs, and incisions that usually cause more harm than they do help, it will yield an alert, healthy baby and an intact, empowered mother.

I had the second of three pregnancy dreams. I had given birth to a tiny, sticky, hairless kitten. I didn't know what to do because I had been expecting a human infant. I put it down on the table while I called my co-worker Karen to ask her what I should do. She said to not be embarrassed, that no one would judge me, and to go ahead and nurse it. When I picked it up off the table, its rear left foot had stuck to the table and had been partially pulled off. When I nursed my kitten, it grew instantly into a beautiful full-grown black cat, my seven-year-old pet kitty Boneless who I'd known since the day she was born.

Halfway through my pregnancy, it seemed as though corporations that sell baby things could smell my mailbox. I'd stupidly filed out a couple of postage-free postcards offering a free growth chart and a free insulated bag for storing pumped breast milk. I should have known better because I knew that companies sell and share marketing mailing lists. My mailbox began filling up with coupon packs, free offers, and complimentary issues of mainstream pregnancy magazines. I was totally repulsed by their attempts to hawk their bullshit goods to expectant women, preying on them during emotional and sen- *Midwifery Today* magazine's website (http://midwiferytoday.com), and *Mothering* magazine's website (www.mothering.com).

sitive months. Some mailers were blatantly pushing the consumer culture: "We've Got Everything You NEED for Your New CONSUMER," and "Your Dream Nursery for an Affordable Couple Grand!"

What really got me were some comments I read in one mainstream magazine while in the waiting room when I went for the ultrasound my midwife recommended: "Doctors generally like moms to take an active role in planning their births—so long as your hopes don't ossify into control-oriented demands, which may not be realistic." Oh, so it's OK to have hopes, but if you've come to trust your body and are empowered to have a natural birth and it takes more time than the doctor has, then it's not realistic? Clearly, statements such as this send a message that a woman taking control of her own birth experience is not accepted in the doctor-controlled hospital setting.

I discussed this issue with my midwife, along with my fear of having a ten-pound baby, and she reassured me that my body knows exactly what it's doing: "Your body isn't making a baby it can't handle."

Learning to trust my body was an incredible experience. Even the funny things were important parts of my overall enjoyment of being pregnant. My emotions got all crazy, as I found myself both laughing and crying in the same hour. People started to reach out and rub my belly, as if it were public domain. Even the stretching ligaments, lower back pain, leaky boobs, and pear-shaped body were OK by me. I thought my boobs looked huge in just my second month, and compared to my belly that still hadn't begun to protrude, they were. But at six months, when my baby belly looked like it had grown a watermelon, my boobs wound up looking dwarfed in comparison.

While I was home visiting for Thanksgiving, my dad must have made five attempts at the same fat joke in two hours. I asked him, "Can't you think of anything else to say?" He put his head on my shoulder and said sweetly, but almost pitifully, "It's just that you're my baby and I don't know how to act." My mom, my Grandmary, and my Aunt Lisa were all incredibly sweet. This baby would be the first of the next generation of my family, just as I had been twenty-nine years earlier.

I remained in awe, constantly reminding myself that every new day brought me closer to having this baby. Twelve or so weeks to go.

Month 7: Inside

This month, the beginning of the third trimester, the fetus's growth is slow and steady. Its body is fattening up, becoming plumper and rounder, and growing at a faster pace than its head, which until now has been disproportionately large. The fetus's body is getting long and thin, with fat deposits now building up under the skin.

Its hands are active now, and its muscular coordination has developed so that it's able to get its thumb into its mouth. Thumb-sucking calms the fetus and strengthens jaw and cheek muscles.

Although it's been able to hiccup for some time, by the beginning of this month, fetus has a new skill: the ability to cry!

The fetus also has rapid eye movement (REM) sleep, which means that the unborn fetus may be dreaming now. By the middle of this month, the eyelids begin to part. The fetus can open its eyes and blink and look around for the first time. The retina, which is at the back of the eye, is important in the reception of light images. Its normal layers are now developed. These layers are important in receiving light and light information, and transmitting it to the brain for interpretation. The fetus's world inside the uterus is not always dark. Bright sunlight and artificial light can filter through the uterine wall. The fetus now also has fully developed delicate eyebrows and eyelashes.

Also by the middle of this month, the brain forms characteristic grooves and indentions on the surface called the *gyri* and *sulci*. The amount of brain tissue also increases.

The fetus has put on more than a pound in this seventh month, for a total weight of about 2.5 pounds (1.1 kg). (In eleven weeks, the fetus has increased its weight by ten times!) The length has reached 15 inches (38.1 cm).

Month 7: Outside

It was December and I don't think I'd ever been calmer and more relaxed in my life. People hustling and bustling about with their holiday shopping and the explosive millennial celebration plans and the inescapable holiday advertisements annoyed me, but they didn't faze me. Rather, they couldn't faze me.

Even if I'd wanted to participate in the shop-'til-you-drop consumption of needless gifts, I had no money to do so. About to have a baby, I was concerned about the unknown number of months I wouldn't work after its birth. I was concerned about how we'd make ends meet, but I remained calm and relaxed.

In the middle of the month, the two bands I'd been playing with since 1997, Reina Aveja and Crustaceans, played at the two-day-long last show at the Hardback Café in Gainesville. Playing that show, twice, kept my musical hunger satisfied for quite a while. While the last band, Strikeforce Diablo, played, shit got crazy. The ceiling was nearly ripped down, and electrical wires swam and crackled in beer puddles around my feet. Newly broken pipes spewed water everywhere. A fire-breathing friend of mine who shall remain nameless spat flames in through the destroyed front door. Bottle rockets whizzed in every direction. After exchanging "Uh-oh" glances with my friend Var who was standing next to me, not thinking it would be too wise to stick around any longer, I slogged outta there.

A few days later, my mom accompanied me to one of my prenatal appointments with the midwife at the birth center. I showed her around the large old house, pointing out the two home-like birthing bedrooms. She most liked the upstairs room where the sunlight streamed in brightly through lightly curtained windows, but I reminded her that more babies are born late at night than in the daytime and besides, normal labors are many hours long, so the amount of potential sunlight in the room would probably not be a lasting comfort. I brought her down to my preferred birthing room, where there was a large tub right next to the bed and a kitchen right outside the door.

The midwife checked my blood pressure and measured my uterus. The part of the exam when the Doppler is used to listen to the fetal heartbeat was my favorite and it was my mom's, too. Hearing that strong little pump pound out its 120 to 160 beats per minute was reassuring and elicited uncontrolled smiles.

The rest of the appointment yielded information that my diabetes screening test results came back normal, I'd gained a total of twenty-three pounds so far, and the baby could come as soon as seven weeks or as late as twelve weeks and be considered a safe, normal time for its birth. The midwife had me increase my iron intake for the duration of my pregnancy since brain development during this last trimester is rapid.

Disgusted by the free mainstream pregnancy magazines that show up in my mailbox, I decided to invest thirty dollars for subscriptions to two magazines more my style, *Mothering* and *Hip Mama*. A friend also sent me a couple of issues of *The Radical Mother's Voice* that was mightily bad-ass!

My friend Leslie, who had trained to become a doula, lent me a video called *Gentle Birth Choices*. Ernesto and I watched it together and every time a baby was shown popping into the world, we both couldn't control the tears shooting out of our eyes. I don't know what I was expecting an out-of-hospital, natural birth to look like, but I was left overwhelmed for a week. The images our society shows in

TV and movie birth situations are obviously overly dramatized. This fact should be obvious, so why was I amazed to see that birth is really an extremely calm and slow, gentle process? I don't know, but the calmness and slowness translated into my head as an extremely intense experience! When it comes down to it, the woman and baby are birthing together and in control of their own experiences; monitors and drugs and sterile hospital personnel shouldn't be dictating their experiences for them.

I felt confident in my choice to have an out-of-hospital birth and the research convinced me that a licensed midwife-attended out-of-hospital birth is just as safe as—if not safer than—an OB-attended hospital birth. I'm a pretty stubborn person, but not so stubborn that I would refuse to be transported to the hospital if it came down to taking a risk with the baby's or my own well-being. That's what they're there for: to deal with emergencies. If I ended up there, fine. I just knew it was not the right place for me to start out. I knew no labor would be easy, no matter what environment had been chosen. I was just choosing where I would be most comfortable mentally, physically, and emotionally. I know some mamas who were more at peace with a hospital birth. Research shows that fear impedes labor, so if someone has reservations about an out-of-hospital birth that they cannot reconcile before labor starts, then they most certainly should be where they will be most comfortable. That's what informed choice is all about.

Month 8: Inside

The fetus can hear even more by this stage; previously it could mainly hear vibrations, but now the nerve endings in its ears are connected, enabling it to hear sounds. It can hear voices now, which researchers claim to know because the fetus's heart rate increases when its mother or father speaks. Also, the fetus can hear music now, although it has to be played quite loudly since its ears are plugged by water and vernix. When a newborn hears music played before birth, he may show he recognizes it by becoming less active while he listens.

During this time, the air sacs inside the fetus's lungs become lined with a layer of cells that produce a liquid called *surfactant*. This material prevents the air sacs from collapsing when the baby first begins to breathe after birth.

Brain growth continues to be great at this time. And as the fetus grows plumper, the wrinkles in the skin fill out and it appears smoother. Both the lanugo and vernix that cover its skin begin to disappear around this time.

By the end of the month, the fetus weighs about 4 pounds (1.8 kg) and its total length is about 19.5 inches (49.5 cm).

Month 8: Outside

We'd spent our New Year's Eve around a campfire at our friend's house near a lake, after sharing a potluck supper. We sang old labor, civil rights, antiwar, and women's liberation songs with those who'd been organizers in SDS, SNCC, GWL (Gainesville Women's Liberation), Redstockings, and VVAW, and in the streets fighting for social change before we were born. Two had even been to Spain to fight with the Abraham Lincoln Brigade in 1936–1937.

Though my evening had been alcohol-free, I began the "new millennium" sick as shit. I actually thought I'd be the only one up and about on January 1st not feeling hung over, but noooooo, I had to join the puking ranks. My stomach was pressed high up into my ribs as a result of my upwardly expanding uterus. The heartburn I felt the first of this month was so painful that I thought I was having a heart attack. Luckily, I was only sick for a day, bringing my total sick days of the pregnancy to three.

During my appointment with my midwife at the beginning of the month, I learned that the fetus's head was already down, just as it should have been. I could feel definite feet and knee shapes when I pressed around my belly, and the kicks and rolls were packing a wallop those days!

Also at the beginning of this month, Ernesto and I started attending birth classes. They were held one evening a week at the birth center and offered us all the best parts of the Lamaze and Bradley methods, along with our birth educator's personal experiences. At the start of the six-week series, I found myself taking notes without pause as the instructor gave us all sorts of information about the different stages of labor. I had to remind myself that this wasn't a class where I'd be given a written test, and instead, I should just calm down and listen. My evaluation would come in the form of hands-on experience with labor, birth, and caring for my newborn.

It's true that babies don't come with an instruction manual—not that I ever read those things anyway—so I was hoping that some of those natural instincts I kept hearing about would kick in. I was getting nervous about little things, like how to give a baby a bath and put on a cloth diaper. I really needed the classes and looked forward to them. I never would have known seemingly simple things, like when bathing the baby, don't submerge its belly in water until the little umbilical cord stump has healed into a belly button.

I also started looking forward to my prenatal Kundalini yoga class every Thursday night. When I started four months earlier, the chanting and meditation exercises annoyed me. Although they were still my least favorite part, I had become a deep-breathing and relaxation junky.

By mid-month, it was time to take the ring out of my navel. Talk about stretched tight and sensitive! My midwife advised me to go ahead and take out my other unconventional piercings, too. Other discomforts increased a bit, but remained relatively minor, as my growth-spurt sleeping marathons followed by uterine-ligament soreness became more regular. Nighttime sleep started to become interrupted with mild lower backache, muscle pulling, and hip soreness. When I'd wake in the mornings, the joints in my fingers would feel arthritic, too.

Almost as soon as I started telling people I was pregnant, they wanted to know about a baby shower. Truthfully, I thought it was something we wouldn't do. I didn't want to be the center of attention where people would just heap gifts upon me, making me feel all awkward, thinking my thanks would come off as not genuine. Ernesto wanted to discourage the entire notion of "must consume."

But my dear friend and ol' bandmate Samantha pulled it off for us beautifully. She hand-made the little invitations, promoting the shower as a BYOJ (Bring Your Own Juice) affair. I really enjoyed having a small gathering of friends who genuinely wanted to wish us the best and lend a hand in the way of giving us useful and practical gifts, including babysitting and night-out-on-the-town coupons. Margaret, one of my bandmates and a fellow mom, upped the DIY baby clothes ante by dying up a batch of black, newborn-sized onesies, complete with the classic "circle A" and "Reina Aveja" (the band we were in together) batik designs on the front. An added bonus was that Ernesto's sister and her family came to town for it, as did my parents, who brought us my old baby furniture, all repainted. It was definitely fun that night after the shower to fill the little dresser drawers with baby clothes and blankets.

After filling the drawers, we headed down a few blocks to the Fugazi show. Now that I knew the baby's ears were formed enough to hear more than just vibrations, it was my motherly duty to make sure it got to hear good music, especially since its hearing cannot be damaged as it is protected by my body and its personal protective bubble of amniotic fluid. (The structural components of the ear are completed by twenty-four weeks; this correlates to the evidence that most fetuses can hear by this time. However, sounds from the outside are muffled by sounds from the inside—maternal circulation, digestion, and voice—as well as the exterior barriers of the amniotic fluid and uterus.) My little one also heard some of her mama's favorites, Hot Water Music and Cavity.

There were other shows I missed because I was just feeling so pregnant. I wanted so bad to go see bands play, had shows written on my calendar for weeks, but when it came time to go, I just couldn't. My heart's desire was there, but my body's comfort demanded that I be propped up reading. I thought I should be taking advantage of still being able to go, because once the baby came, I wouldn't even have the luxury to choose to go or not. Breast-feeding would really keep me attached (pun intended) for the first however many months!

So, how was I doing this far along? Just fine. No complaints, really. I was up a total of thirty-two pounds and could be caught giving into the "nesting" urges that I had read about in my pregnancy books. While wearing hideous pink and white polka-dotted pajamas, I taped up old show flyers I had been saving, and framed and hung some pictures I had taken of some of my favorite bands over the years. Sometimes at work, while tutoring a student in geometry, my brain would just shut off mid-problem. And guests who stayed longer than three days would get me all unraveled. I was pregnant, I liked it, and I just wanted to be able to get comfy wherever and whenever without having to divert my attention away from my task at hand, incubating this little one.

I had the third of my three pregnancy dreams. I was inside my uterus with my baby boy. We were curled up together in there, snuggled side by side like twins. I was much bigger than he was. His eyes were closed but he had a content smile pressed across his lips. Bubbles were floating all around us in the amniotic fluid.

Month 9: Inside

The fetus's lungs are almost fully developed now, although their development won't be complete until just before birth. It's probably trying to practice breathing using its lungs, but since no air is available, it swallows amniotic fluid into its windpipe, which can give it frequent hiccups.

The body is still on the thin side at the beginning of the month, but from now until birth, it will continuously accumulate fat deposits beneath the skin to the tune of up to a pound a week. The fetus needs to get plumper to prepare itself for life on the outside. Fat cells are important for the baby to be able to regulate a warm-enough body temperature after birth.

The uterus has filled up the mother's pelvis and most of her abdomen, all the way up to the lower tip of her sternum. The fetus is running out of room to move around in there and sometimes, its feet get caught under the mother's ribs. The toenails and fingernails have grown to the tips of its toes and fingers.

In this last trimester of pregnancy, the fetus has received antibodies from the mother and has gotten short-term protection from whatever illnesses the mother has had, from measles to the common cold, or any diseases she has been immunized against, like polio or smallpox. It may weigh anywhere from 6 to 11 pounds (2.7 to 5.0 kg). Average length is 18 to 22 inches (45.7 to 55.9 cm) at birth.

The baby is ready to be born.

A Note About Birth Plans

A birth plan is a good way to open up dialogue with your partner and healthcare provider about the decisions surrounding the birth. It gives you a chance to do your own research on topics such as episiotomy, delayed cord clamping and cutting, and positions in labor. You will be able to explore your feelings and ideas, which sets you up to make an informed decision about your preferences. Most importantly, the development of a birth plan is not to be a rigid structure of how things will unfold, but rather an idea of the possibilities. Identifying your desires and then being flexible usually produces a positive birth experience. *Obstetric Myths Versus Research Realities: A Guide to the Medical Literature* by Henci Goer is a great book to help you develop a birth plan and facilitate conversation with your healthcare provider.

Is Circumcision Necessary?

While circumcision—the surgical removal of a newborn boy's foreskin—is uncommon or even nonexistent in most of the world, many in the United States continue to regard this as standard procedure. The fact is, circumcision is *not* medically necessary. The American Academy of Pediatrics' policy states, "Scientific studies show some medical benefits of circumcision. However, these benefits are not sufficient for the American Academy of Pediatrics (AAP) to recommend that all infant boys be circumcised." The American Medical Association (AMA) agrees with the AAP.

Among the few potential benefits of circumcision are reduced chances of urinary tract infections in infants (1 in 1,000 chance for circumcised infants, versus 1 in 100 in intact infants), lower risk of getting cancer of the penis (thought the AAP emphasizes that "this type of cancer is very rare in both circumcised and uncircumcised males"), and easier genital hygiene. The risks of circumcision—both short and long term—outweigh any potential benefits: tight circumcision, infection, excessive bleeding, postoperative pain, and future sexual dysfunction. And besides, circumcision is not always performed with anesthetics, and cutting a newborn's sensitive penis tissue is definitely painful. Did you know that medical professionals used to...(cont'd)

Month 9: Outside

At my thirty-six-week appointment this month, my midwife asked me, "Have you chosen a pediatrician?"

"Uh... no" was my honest reply.

It seemed that my usual one-step-at-a-time way of dealing with life wasn't going to hold up anymore. I'd been so focused on the pregnancy that I'd forgotten to consider some pretty important things, like what tests I'd consent to be performed on my newborn and what pediatrician to take the baby to for its twenty-four to seventy-two hour checkup.

It had also been suggested to me that I take a tour of the hospital "just in case" and write up a birth plan. A birth plan is a way of setting down on paper your preferences for labor and birth. It can be a good tool for discussion with your care provider—you should give them a copy well in advance of your due date so that compromises can be negotiated if necessary. I really have no idea why I didn't do either.

We'd also been advised to have the car seat strapped in the car from here on out; clean the house; and launder the clothes, blankets, and diapers we'd gathered. There was so much to think about now, it seemed like the only thing we'd decided on is that if we had a boy, we would not have him circumcised.

Another thing we were committed to was the idea of the family bed. It didn't make a whole lot of sense to either Ernesto or me that we would put the baby down to sleep in a separate "nest." Ernesto called it his natural primal instinct to keep our little one close. To me, it was just a weird idea to carry this little baby inside me for nine months and then all of a sudden, have it sleep away from me (see "The Family Bed Controversy" chapter).

So we got ourselves a king-size bed. Our little bedroom was practically wall-to-wall bed now. The day we got it in the room and I made it up with a new sheet, I stood back and smiled the biggest and most satisfied smile. I was so in love with how our new nest perfectly fit three pillows across.

At my thirty-seven-week appointment, my midwife informed me that I had tested positive for Group B Strep (GBS). An exclamatory "SHIT!" was my response. It seems positive GBS screenings are the latest buzz in the medical legal community. Everyone wants to cover their asses, but is trying to do so at the expense of the mothers and newborns. Many pediatricians these days, if the mother has tested positive, call for the newborn to be hospitalized under observation for forty-eight hours following birth.

Here's the deal: GBS is a bacteria commonly found in the intestinal tract. Between 10% and 40% of pregnant women are colonized with it. Colonization is usually asymptomatic, but can

think that babies couldn't feel pain like we do? Research now indicates that not only do they feel it, but more intensely in relation to us because as we age, we become desensitized to some pain.

After carrying and caring for your baby for nine months in utero, why would you subject your newborn to an excruciating and medically unnecessary procedure? To give him that special masochistic "Welcome, honey pie, here's a little genital torture as a token of our love?" So father and son can have matching penises? Please, save the matching stuff, if you must do it at all, for sweaters and scarves. You gonna give your newborn a nose job to match daddy's nose, too? For cleanliness? If you really need help in that department, your pediatrician can show you easy steps for cleaning the foreskin, and your son can learn to do this for himself as he matures, just as he learns to bathe himself and brush his teeth. For religion? Perhaps someday all religions will leave the innocent genitals of babies alone. Even within the religious groups that ritually practice circumcision, Judaism and Islam, there are groups that are actively organizing against it, for example Jews Against Circumcision and the Islamic Intactivist Movement.

Parents around the country are increasingly realizing that it isn't worth the trauma that this elective surgery brings. In the 1970, the U.S. circumcision rate for hospital births was around 90%. By 1999, according to the U.S. Centers for Disease Control and Prevention, that rate was about 65%. More recent reports show that the rate is down to 60%. For the sake of your son, be sure to ask your pediatrician for all the facts and do your own research before choosing a circumcision. Make an informed choice!

For more information, visit the Circumcision Resource Center (www.circumcision.org), National Organization of Circumcision Information Resources Centers (www.nocirc.org), Doctors Opposing Circumcision (www.doctorsopposingcircumcision.org), and National Organization to Halt the Abuse and Routine Mutilation of Males (http://noharmm.org).

result in severe infection in newborns. Newborn infection, however, is a relatively low risk. Approximately 8,000 babies in the United States get GBS disease each year; 5% to 15% of these babies die. The current public-health prophylactic is that women who test positive are given intravenous antibiotics during their labors.

SEX DURING PREGNANCY

Sex is generally safe in pregnancy. If you have a history of miscarriages, you may want to take it easy in the first trimester. With a history of preterm labor, pelvic rest may be suggested by your healthcare provider. There may be times when intercourse and/or orgasm are not OK, as with threatened preterm labor and placenta previa, for example. You will both need creativity and a good sense of humor late in pregnancy. During intercourse, side-lying and woman-on-top positions can allow the woman to control the depth of penetration.

Libido can change for both the pregnant woman and the partner throughout the pregnancy. If your desires decrease or disappear, this is not serious nor long lasting. You can have intimacy with cuddling, massage, or other forms of physical contact. Women should check with their healthcare provider if they have questions and should not feel shy about doing so as most midwives and OBs have been asked very detailed questions!

Without the antibiotic, current statistics reflect a 1 in 200 chance of delivering a baby with GBS disease.

I had no symptoms as a result of being colonized with GBS and was considered at low risk for having a baby with GBS disease, however, I had been encouraged by a midwife to receive the antibiotics in labor. I decided that I would get them, but was still concerned that the pediatrician would want to have the baby hospitalized for observation to protect herself from liability. It was something I wouldn't agree to. My baby would be in better care with me attending to it than an anonymous nurse assigned a row of infants in the hospital nursery. Ten years earlier, women weren't even tested for GBS and I was willing to bet that ten years from then, the medical community would not be responding to positive test results with prophylactic antibiotics for the mothers and hospital observation for the newborns.

Two uptight and nervous days followed the news of my positive test result, but I dealt with it the most rational and intellectual way possible. After doing a little research and discussing it again with my midwife, I felt that everything was going to be just fine.

Everything *was* fine. People who looked at my belly let me know they didn't see a single stretch mark. To be honest, I didn't care if I did get some. I'd carry them as if they were inkless tattoos I earned. I was more short of breath those days due to my lungs being moved back out of the way of my upwardly expanding uterus. I reminded myself to just breath deep and relax, which is what I'd need to be good at during labor. I felt comfortable and satisfied, already looking back a few months at what a great feeling it'd been to be two, then three, four, five, six, seven, and eight months pregnant. I was addicted. I'd never felt better.

It was two weeks before my due date. The baby could come as soon as that day and up to four weeks later, and that's when my life and lifestyle as I knew them would change forever. This close to my due date, Ernesto and I accepted that the baby was already here. The little baby's head was now nestled lower into my pelvis and the only way out of the situation was birthing it through there.

Even at this late stage, I still rode a bike, went to work teaching kids, wrote for my zine and others, played music, volunteered at the nonprofit volunteer-run punk record store, took naps, and ate voraciously. Yes, having sex was still in there, too. Do you think any women would be into being pregnant for nine-plus months if sex was out of the question? Well, maybe a few would be, but how do you think I got this way?

2.

When Birth Doesn't Go as Planned

My due date came and went without even the slightest twinge of labor. In fact, several days came and went without any feelings that my baby was on the way. Every night before falling asleep, I'd wish to wake up in labor. A week and a half after my due date, I did begin to feel some mild contractions, but none of them ever developed into a regular pattern. Mild, irregular contractions teased me for days.

It's not every day that someone actually looks forward to the pains of childbirth, but I was starting to feel desperate. I was desperate not because I was uncomfortable, but because if I was still pregnant two weeks past my due date, I would not be able to deliver at the birth center. Florida law says my midwife would have to transfer me into the care of the birth center's backup obstetrician.

Ernesto and I were trying everything from nipple stimulation to orgasmic sex, walking to foot massage, cohosh to castor oil, and still no labor. My midwife even stripped my membranes to get things going, twice, but nothing put me into labor. I was set to kick the next person to recommend a fast, bumpy car ride down a dirt road.

I decided I had better go to a few shows. I hoped that the baby would be rocked out of me. Really. When Hot Water Music didn't do it one night, I went to see Strike Anywhere a few days later. Unfortunately, they didn't do it either, even though they tried.

Two weeks past my due date and still pregnant, my mom drove me down to the birth center where I was checked out again and found to be one to two centimeters dilated with no regular, intense contractions. No out-of-hospital birth for me. I was transferred to the care of the birth center's backup obstetrician and instructed to go to the hospital in a few hours for a routine nonstress test (NST;

for more information, see "Epilogue: Reflections on My Birthing Experience"), the same routine nonstress test I had taken a week prior. Ugh! How stressful!

I accepted that I'd deliver my baby in the hospital because I was assured that I'd be accompanied by a midwife and that everything would be fine. Transferring me was just a good safety measure—"protocol," they call it. I wasn't really thrown for a loop yet, even if for nine and a half months I had given zero consideration to the possibility of a hospital birth. A few months back, I had actually shrugged off my birth educator's idea of touring the labor and delivery ward of the hospital, just in case.

I learned my first lessons of motherhood before I even gave birth: there's no such thing as planning, and I should have listened to someone who has more experience than I do.

To the Hospital

My mom and I drove home from the birth center and then walked over to the hospital. She walked; I waddled. I was admitted at the outpatient counter and given a wheelchair for the ride up to the fourth floor. I can understand, given my extra-large appearance, how someone might think I would want a wheelchair, but I convinced them to let me walk when I told them I had just walked there from home. Walking is good for bringing labor.

Up in the fourth-floor triage unit, a nurse hooked me up to an electronic fetal monitor for the nonstress test. They needed thirty minutes of recorded regular baby movement to determine that everything was still fine and that the baby wasn't showing any signs of distress. Earlier that morning, however—in a last-ditch effort to throw myself into labor—I drank another four ounces of castor oil.

It wasn't until I got strapped up to the machine that the castor oil kicked in. My ass was exploding. For the next hour, I had to unstrap myself every five minutes and hustle my nine-and-a-half-months pregnant-self to the toilet. Ugh. I was pretty worried the one time I really needed the toilet and another extremely pregnant woman just beat me to it. The four-minute wait was a real test of rectal muscle control.

The obstetrician finally came to check out my situation, but wasn't able to determine much from the test because I had been unstrapped from the monitor so many times and didn't get a thirty-minute reading. Although I wasn't scheduled for a different test with him until the next afternoon, he decided to do it right then.

This test was a biophysical profile (BPP; for more information, see "Epilogue: Reflections on My Birthing Experience"), performed with an ultrasound. He found that I had plenty of amniotic fluid left and that the baby's heartbeat was strong. However, he judged that the baby's breathing pattern was not be as strong as he'd like. He said there also wasn't enough baby movement. I told him that I felt the baby moving often, but he said that didn't matter; he should have seen enough movement during that specific time frame. I told myself that I should have drunk a sugary beverage before the BPP—that would have awakened a napping baby.

He told me that I would be induced the next day. I told him okay, and thank you, and that I'd see him tomorrow, sincerely asking what time I should come back for that.

He laughed and said I wasn't going anywhere. I asked him why not, and he corrected himself by saying, "You're forty-two weeks and need to be monitored overnight. Going home against my advice is your own decision to make, but you don't want a dead baby, do you?"

I started to panic. Because my head was swirling, I don't remember specifics, but it amounted to me being admitted right there on the spot and being scheduled to be induced in the morning. I do remember other panic-inducing phrases like, "The baby could be really big" and "The baby's ready. It needs to come out."

I had just plummeted down the first of many slopes of what would be a two-day roller-coaster ride.

Settling In

I allowed myself to be wheelchaired up to my room. Ernesto rode his bike back to our house to fetch our bags that I had packed weeks before. My mom stayed with me to help me settle in. I was strapped to the electronic fetal monitor all night, except for the one time I unhooked myself to take a walk outside so I could sink my bare feet into the earth and get some fresh air. How I was expected to be good and rested for my big labor day the next day is beyond me. The damn thing's terribly uncomfortable—mentally more than physically.

My girlfriends started trickling in. Margaret brought a boom box, some CDs, and a big glass jar of freshly brewed cohosh. She made it extra strong and I drank it by the cupful, my last hope of getting into labor without having to be induced.

My midwife came with a bunch of just-picked flowers and the news that neither she nor the other midwife would be able to be present tomorrow, but I could pick which midwife student I wanted to come as my doula.

Samantha came with her sleeping bag to camp out on the floor at the foot of my bed. My friend Kristen just happened to still be in town on her visit from New York, and Mahlia came to give me encouragement and much-needed massage on my legs and feet. Ernesto's mom would be there first thing in the morning.

The powerful female presence quickly transformed the hospital-room atmosphere from strange, sterile, and stressful to relaxed, familiar, and jovial. We listened to music, chatted up a storm, burned incense probably against hospital rules, and I drank the batch of cohosh brew. I was determined to be strong, ready, and in labor by daybreak.

As my mom slept on the couch in the room, Ernesto and Samantha stayed up all night with me. In the wee hours, I started contracting more intensely and at more regular intervals. They were really coming on and feeling great, getting to be five minutes apart. I really enjoyed breathing through them, knowing my body was teaching itself to open up for my baby to pass through. Ernesto and Samantha were quietly cheering me on, and their presence really kept me going in a positive mental direction. But alas, the contractions only stayed with me for an hour or two, and when I woke early in the morning, I was not in labor.

Inducing Labor

In each other's arms, Ernesto and I sobbed uncontrollably, still trying to accept the fact that I would be induced and that I would not be having the noninterventive birth I had envisioned during my entire pregnancy. It was hard to let that go. Of course I wanted the baby to be born healthy and safely, but how that end would be achieved was scaring me. My mind reeled into worst-case scenario mode, replaying nightmarish birth stories I had read about, about how one intervention led to the next. What's worse was that I knew that the kind of fear that had a hold of me was the kind of fear that impeded labor.

The vibe we filled the room with was pretty intense. One moment, my mom was fine and the next, she was coming out of the bathroom sweating and pale. I started worrying about her more than myself. She later told me that our sobbing was so overwhelming, she almost fainted.

I remained tightly wound up until 9 a.m., when Lori arrived. She was the senior midwife student I had requested to act as my doula. She immediately sensed what was going on in the room and in my head, and got to work. She sat with me, stroked my head and arms, and spoke softly, reminding me that my body knew what to do and was going to do so beautifully. She gave me symbolic female amulets to hold and a framed picture depicting a birth at The Farm to gaze into. The Farm is an intentional community in Summertown, Tennessee, that began in 1971. It became well known for its natural childbirth and midwifery practice, thanks to Ina May Gaskin, often credited as being the pioneering spirit responsible for modern-day midwifery. My friendship with two sisters who were born on The Farm introduced me to the idea of natural childbirth and midwifery several years prior. Lori quickly realigned my vision towards the beautiful, empowering birth I believed in and unraveled the doubt that bound me. With scents and herbal remedies and oils and massage, she calmed me and I felt a sense of peace.

The doctor was scheduled to come break my bag of waters and induce me at noon. He showed up an hour and a half late, plenty of time for my anxiety to start creeping back in. He explained that first he was going to break my bag of waters, called rupturing the membranes, and depending on how the fluid looked, he would determine the next course of action. He cleared the room except for a nurse, Ernesto, and Lori.

I held my breath and summoned all the butterflies I could imagine into my belly. Please, please, please let the fluid run clear.

With a wand instrument with a little plastic hook at the end, he ruptured my membranes. What a gush! I remember the doctor saying something to the effect of, "Whoa, whoa," as I watched my pregnant belly deflate to half its size. I don't think the amount of fluid could be classified as polyhydramnios, too much amniotic fluid, but I am suspect that the amount of fluid was what kept my uterus from engaging in regular labor contractions. I suspect this because I felt my body beginning to contract right after my water was broken.

I also suspect that while the water poured out and my belly partially deflated, the baby must have done a little floating turn, her back now against mine instead of properly positioned with her belly side toward my spine. Thank goodness the umbilical cord did not wash down through the cervix. A prolapsed cord would have meant an emergency cesarean section.

I let my breath out with a very happy exclamation of relief once the doctor confirmed that my water ran clear and there were no signs of distress. Had there been meconium staining, the brownish-black protective substance in the baby's bowels before birth, sometimes discharged when the baby is under stress (as when lacking oxygen because of an aged placenta), I think I would have been given a cesarean section.

Even though I had started to contract right away without it, I was started on a slow IV drip of Pitocin, a synthetic copy of the natural hormone oxytocin that is responsible for, among other things, making the uterus contract. Because my water was broken and therefore, the baby's protective covering gone, I was on a time limit. Remembering what I had read about the situation, called artificial rupture of the membranes (AROM), I thought I'd have twenty-four hours to get the baby out. The doctor, however, had me on a different time schedule. He told me I'd be having the baby in twelve hours. I naively wondered how he knew that.

The Pitocin kicked me into definite labor. My body didn't have time to get its natural endorphin painkillers going, so the contractions were pretty intense and building quickly. I remember working through the first hour of them easily by using what I had learned about breath and breathing in my gentle/prenatal yoga class. My yoga teacher told us we can breath through anything, and I kept reminding myself of that. I also remember moving my arms around in weird snakelike motions and flexing my hands about as if I were grabbing hold of the energy, using it, and then throwing it to the air. Along with moving my arms and hands, shaking my head from side to side as if I were shaking the energy away helped me feel the natural high I had read about. I am thankful that no one had told me that Pitocin makes contractions feel more intense and painful. I just told myself to suck it up and deal with it because this is what labor feels like.

Just as I had planned an out-of-hospital birth, I had also planned who would be with me at the birth. When my location plan changed, so did my company. I think because I was in such a foreign environment, I welcomed the additional friends who joined me. My plan had been to have just three people with me, but there I was with seven. The additional mental, emotional, and physical support really helped me keep in a positive state of mind, something I think was crucial for my labor to progress.

There was one nurse, however, who was not part of my seven-person support, but who needed to do her job and pop in every once in a while. When the doctor was still in the room and she was following his orders to start my Pitocin, she was fine. But after he left, she seemed to be calling her own shots with managing my labor.

The first negative encounter with her happened when she came in the room and without explaining what she was doing, increased the amount of Pitocin I had been getting through the IV. She did this with complete disregard for the sign we had placed on the room door requesting that no personnel come in offering pain-relief medications or unwarranted interventions. Ernesto asked her what she was doing and requested that she not do anything again without first consulting with us. She immediately jumped into defensive mode, saying that what she was doing was ordered by the doctor.

I told her I didn't remember the doctor saying anything about the Pitocin being increased at set time intervals. I also told her that I could feel what was going on in my body and I was definitely opening up and didn't need an increase of Pitocin. She increased the Pitocin anyway.

I continued to labor with increasing intensity. In addition to being zapped into labor without time to build up my natural painkilling endorphins, I was having back labor, which happens when the baby's back is facing your spine. With every contraction, I needed Ernesto to counter the pressure by pushing on my lower back. Eventually, this became a two-person job, both Ernesto and Lori working up a sweat.

I was really working now, struggling for comfortable positions. I was in and out of the rocking chair, up and down off the floor, on all fours, draped over the birthing ball, and crouched hanging on to the end of the bed. I don't know how many positions I tried or how often I revisited some of them, but I do remember the maneuvering was sometimes tricky. I had an electrode wire for the electronic fetal monitor up in me, attached to the baby's head, and two different IVs, one for Pitocin and one for the antibiotics I had to have due to me testing positive for Group B Strep.

Enter the nurse again. She came to check my cervix to determine how far I was dilated, and asked me to get up off the floor and make it to the rocking chair or bed for her to check me. Was she fucking crazy? I was trying to get my labor on and she wanted me to accommodate her? I told her she'd have to get on her hands and knees if she wanted to check me; I wasn't moving. That she did and then made her diagnosis sound like my progression was no big deal, not fast enough. She even suggested I might be swelling on one ridge of my cervix. Argh. I requested that Lori check me for a second opinion. Of course, her diagnosis was positive; I was progressing fine and I needn't scare myself with the nurse's suggestion.

I labored longer and harder, working, working, working, breathing, gutturally groaning, and sometimes stupidly watching the clock. Hours went by. How much longer would I be able to work this hard? It was increasingly hard to keep going; I was really working up into a full-blown infernal ball of energy. I was glad Lori had covered up the electronic fetal monitor screen with a towel. It was a definite distraction watching what I was feeling inside up on a TV screen. I wanted my information to come from my body, not a monitor.

Not knowing how much longer I could keep working through the back labor and the still-mounting contractions and starting to feel the urge to push, I requested to have my cervical dilation checked again. The nurse came and checked me. Again, her prognosis was negative; she said I wasn't opening up fast enough and if I pushed at all before I was completely dilated, ten centimeters, I could swell my cervix to the point that I would have to have a cesarean. She recommended an epidural, a procedure in which pain-relieving drugs are injected into the epidural space in the spinal column.

Panic hit the room. I was losing it. I was at my most vulnerable point in my life and I was searching for help of any kind. Knowing vulnerability is a factor during labor was exactly why Lori had placed the sign on the door for no personnel to come in the room offering things like an epidural. I screamed for them to just go ahead and give me the damn epidural, although I knew it wasn't what I really wanted.

Lori took charge and cleared the room of everyone except Ernesto. The two of them came to my side calmly and spoke to me quietly. Lori reminded me that everything was of course my decision, but also reminded me of what I had read about epidurals: they more than likely slow down labor and because I wouldn't be able to feel myself pushing the baby out; it might result in the use forceps or vacuum extraction or even cesarean delivery. She assured me I was doing fine without it. Ernesto reminded me that as my advocate, my prelabor voice, he was obligated to remind me that it was my wish to have this baby with the least amount of interventions safety would allow.

That five minutes alone with them completely transformed the energy in the room and the panic I had felt. My mind was realigned and I was back in control. I knew I could and would do this.

I needed Margaret to keep me on track. I remembered how she told me she got through this, the hardest part of labor called transition. She locked eyes with her partner and he matched her vocalizations. That's what I needed her to do with me because she'd been through this before. Poor Margaret, five-months pregnant herself, and I'm gripping her arm with both of my hands practically pulling her into me, the pupils of my eyes burning through hers and moaning the most abdomen-rattling, loud animal sounds I've ever heard. She hung in there with me, and without her, I couldn't have made it through like I did.

The contractions were peaking, sometimes double peaking, so sharply and intensely that I'd feel every cell in my body choking, constricting, popping. Goddamn Pitocin! It was hard to catch a breath at all sometimes, let alone trying to breathe through them. Holding myself back from pushing and working through those Richter scale-quality contractions at the same time was impossible.

The baby was on the way.

I insisted that the doctor get there as soon as he could. Where was he? Was he on his way? How long until he'd be here to check me? Those thirty minutes it took for him to get there were ridiculously long. A new shift nurse told me not to push until he got there.

He finally made it and checked my dilation. Without hesitation, he told me I was completely dilated and that I could start pushing. I don't have the written words here to express how excited and happy I was! I checked with Margaret: Was pushing going to be harder than that last hour of contractions? She assured me it was the easy part and I got even more excited! I was having this baby!

Because the doctor didn't know how long I had been fully dilated—it could have been an hour, he guessed—he gave me one hour to push the baby out. If I weren't so excited by my complete dilation, I would have snapped his head off for making me wait like he did, holding back the cannonball express, when my natural urges were to let the baby out! He said that if I didn't have the baby out in an hour, he might have to offer me some help in the way of forceps or vacuum extraction. I set my eyes on that clock. It was 7:30 and I was going to have that baby out of me on time. I had just labored intensely for six hours on Pitocin without additional interventions like an epidural and wasn't about to blow my plan now.

I geared up for the excitement by requesting Reina Aveja and Immaculate Rejection on the boom box, playing air bass guitar between contractions.

I can honestly say that pushing was the most fun and pleasurable pain I have ever felt. When I'd feel a contraction coming on, I'd get ready with a deep breath. Then, while Ernesto counted out loud to ten, I'd push with all my might, take a gasping breath, and push for another ten count if I could. I was so into it, the contractions weren't coming quick enough—the same contractions that last hour I thought were going to kill me. I remember even being up to take a call from our friend Chuck who was out of town on tour with his band, calling to find out any baby news.

It was purely amazing and incredible feeling that little body, that little person, that baby moving down and through me. I was warned and had read about it, but I never had the feeling that my pelvic bones were going to break or my muscles were going to rip apart. The doctor was called back to the room.

There was the baby's head, ready to be born, after exactly one hour of being allowed to push. I thought my eyes had popped from all the pressure in my head from pushing, but I didn't care. I remembered that I should take it easy to get the head out and not push too quickly or forcefully because my perineum, the area of skin and muscle between the vagina and anus, needed time to stretch. I suddenly didn't care about tearing. I just wanted that baby out so bad, I pushed with all I had left.

I would have torn anyway because the baby's little hand was right there, alongside her 13.5-inch-round head. As soon as the doctor noticed I was starting to tear in several places, he gave me a shot to numb the area and then gave me a second-degree episiotomy. (Episiotomies are classified according to the depth of the incision. A first-degree episiotomy cuts through skin only. A second-degree episiotomy involves skin and muscle and extends midway between the vagina and the anus. A third-degree episiotomy cuts through skin, muscle, and the rectal sphincter.) With that and one more good push, I birthed the head. Because I'd been cut, I didn't feel the "ring of fire" that some women describe as the most intense and painful part of childbirth. With the next push, I birthed the rest of the baby's body.

Birth...and Emergency

The room cheered, "It's a girl!" Ernesto and I were really surprised. We thought for sure, based on the dreams I had while pregnant and older women's assessment of how my belly looked, it was going to be a boy.

The doctor couldn't have put her on my chest quick enough.

She sure was slippery! I held on to her carefully, clutching her seven pounds, twelve ounces to my chest. Oh wow, I had my baby! I couldn't believe she was here! She didn't have any signs of being postmature. She had plenty of vernix and lanugo, her fingernails weren't overgrown, and her skin wasn't cracked and peeling. Her first feature I noticed was her extra long eyelashes. She was the most perfect and beautiful thing I'd ever seen.

I looked into her eyes and thanked her for coming. Though she looked pissed, with her brow furled, I assured her she'd like it here with us. I told her about all the fun we're going to have and all the love we're going to share. I was absolutely ecstatic in Babyland. I locked onto Ernesto's happily sobbing eyes.

The nurse had recorded baby Emma-Joy's Apgar scores as 8 at one minute and 8 at five minutes. Babies score up to two points for each of the following: activity (muscle tone), pulse, grimace (reflex irritability), appearance (skin color), and respiration. The OB had recorded them at 9 and 10, respectively. It was her appearance (skin color) that did not score perfectly. Whether her scores were 8, 9, or 10, she was a healthy baby by all counts.

I had no idea that I was hemorrhaging and that my blood pressure plummeted. I thought whatever action was happening at the foot of the bed was standard procedure. I wasn't paying much attention; I had my perfect, beautiful baby in my arms.

But when the room started looking like an *ER* episode and the baby was taken from my chest, I realized something was up. Whatever it was, it couldn't be that bad; I felt fine. I leaned up to the frantically working doctor and told him so. He didn't hear me correctly and thought I said I felt faint. I told him again that I felt fine. He told me that that was because shock didn't hurt.

Shock? Oh, so that explained my head feeling thick and my hearing and vision sounding and looking weird, getting fuzzy. I thought I was just exhausted from pushing for an hour. The doctor tried to calmly explain to me what was going on.

My mental capacities weren't exactly sharp and I was barely getting any of what he was saying, but I did understand that I had just dumped a bunch of blood and we were on a time limit to get it under control and my placenta out, too.

The doctor snapped into lifesaving mode and was calling his shots quickly and orderly. The room was cleared of my mom, Ernesto's mom, and my friends except Kristen, and instantly filled with nurses, an anesthesiologist, a surgeon, and more I don't remember. They tried to get Ernesto to leave with the baby, but he told them they were crazy, that the baby was fine, and he wasn't leaving his bleeding partner's side. Needles were flying and scary words like "transfusion" landed in my ears.

I don't know exactly how it happened, but as soon as I heard the word "transfusion," I stopped bleeding. I knew I didn't want one. The doctor then started to work on getting my placenta out. I was jacked with a big zap of Pitocin to get my uterus to contract so I could birth the placenta. I remember looking down at my belly and it was quivering up and down with contractions I wasn't even feeling. My placenta wasn't budging. The doctor was pushing down, quite uncomfortably, all around my belly to get the placenta to move out of me. That wasn't working either.

I was shaking uncontrollably, but I wasn't cold. I repeatedly asked Lori if I was going to be OK and she assured me every time that I was. Kristen stayed by my side holding my hand while I hummed and shook my head back and forth as an attempt to distract myself from what was going on. I just wanted to nurse my baby.

The doctor determined that my placenta wasn't going to come loose from my uterine wall and decided he had to remove it manually. He had to cut me some more and reached in almost up to his elbow and grabbed it. To make sure there wasn't any of the tissue left inside me, he performed a manual D&C (dilation and curretage) with what looked like a scrub brush. Did I mention uncomfortable?

My pelvic floor muscles and my perineum were stitched up. I was cleaned off and hooked up to IVs to replace my fluids. My baby girl, Emma-Joy, was brought back to me and I lifted her to my breast.

3.

Epilogue: Reflections on My Birthing Experience

In the hours and days immediately after giving birth, the only thing that mattered to me was my healthy newborn baby. While still in the hospital the two days after her birth, I didn't have time to think about what had happened. I was only thinking about getting breast-feeding established, holding my baby, and getting much-needed rest in between visitors.

Once at home, I had plenty of time to replay my birthing experience over and over and over again in my head. My midwife recommended that I have three weeks of bed rest to fully recuperate. The inside of my uterus especially needed time to heal. To mentally recuperate would take much longer though I hadn't yet realized it would—it still hadn't dawned on me that what I'd been through had been traumatic. I'd bought the line that was fed to me: "Good thing I was in the hospital for that unforeseen emergency. I was exactly where I needed to be."

As the months wore on, I started to question what had happened and why, especially because what had happened was not common. I wanted to understand why I had hemorrhaged immediately after Emma-Joy was born, losing an estimated 1.4 liters of blood. Why was my placenta retained, needing to be manually removed, then resulting in a D&C? How had the nonstress test (NST), biophysical profile (BPP),

Initial Hindsight

I questioned the motivation behind such scary "dead baby" commentary from the OB. When I shared my story with midwives and other mothers, they suggested that he was out of line, only saying those things to either scare me into staying because he wasn't used to someone questioning his advice or because he was worried about his own liability. While the baby's breathing pattern was something that warranted monitoring, there were no signs of fetal distress. I had not eaten or drank anything for hours and as soon as I did, the baby's movement picked up as usual. I'd later learn that guessing, via ultrasound, how large a baby is that late in gestation is just that—a guess—as measurements after the 24th week have no predictive value. The doctor guessed ten pounds; she weighed in under eight.

the external electronic fetal monitor (EFM), hospital climate of fear, IV fluids and antibiotics (to treat my positive Group B Strep status), and amniotomy (AROM) combined with an internal EFM, Pitocin induction, and tightly scheduled labor result in what was essentially a vaginal cesarean?

Yes, what I'd been through was scary. But intellectually, I still knew that birthing didn't have to be scary. I still believed that birth as a natural process was proven to be safe, that out-of-hospital birth emergency transports to the hospital were rare among low-risk healthy pregnancies. Because of my due date and a questionable BPP, I was no longer treated as healthy and low risk, even though there was never evidence of distress or emergency. I still believed that natural childbirth had many benefits for both baby and mother, including feelings of empowerment for the mother. (See Month 6 in "Pregnancy: Month by Month, Inside and Out" for statistical information on the safety of out-of-hospital birth.)

I most definitely lacked feelings of empowerment. If anything, I was left with feeling a lack of confidence, uncertainty, and displeasure. And I felt like I'd been mistreated, like I had been punished for having a different vision of childbirth than the hospital personnel had. These feelings, coupled with my questioning what had happened and why, led me to investigate my birthing experience. I combed over the labor and delivery events with various midwives and my childbirth educator, did my own research, and even obtained my hospital records.

One midwife suggested that I start at the beginning—to look inward to find what had kept me from natural labor. I did and guessed that I'd been anxious and not as ready to become a mother as I'd thought. Maybe I was unconsciously scared of becoming a parent, and keeping her inside where I was confident she was safe. These thoughts, mixed with my own natural gestational needs (my own mother carried me forty-three weeks), could be why she did not come sooner than forty-two weeks.

She also suggested that I should have waited to go from the birth center to the hospital for my NST until after the effects of the castor oil had ended. I should have gone for the test with food and drink in my belly, not an exploding ass. She said that more than likely, a good, uninterrupted NST would have allowed me to go home instead of leading to me having the BPP right then. She said there's no way of telling, of course, but given the fact that I was having signs of early labor contractions after I was admitted, they might have continued into a better labor pattern that night peacefully and unbound by fear at home. She also said that going to a location that is independent from the hospital for the NST and BPP is a good idea because the "alarms" don't seem to go off as easily when not in the hospital triage environment. She also thought I'd been scheduled to be induced too soon.

BIOPHYSICAL PROFILE (BPP)

The BPP is a test that's done by fetal ultrasound to measure the baby's health. Five things are looked at: nonstress test (NST), breathing movement, body movement, muscle tone, and amniotic fluid volume (AFV). (Because my nonstress test was too interrupted by the effects of castor oil, the OB performed a BPP immediately rather than waiting, as is the usual practice.) For each measurement that is normal, two points are given. For each abnormal, zero points are given. A score of 6 to 8 is considered healthy, 4 to 6 means that you may need to be retested in twelve to twenty-four hours, and a score of 4 or less may mean the baby's having problems.

I scored a 6. NST, AFV, and muscle tone were all good. But the baby's breathing and body movement were not what the OB thought they should be in a thirty-minute period. Therefore, I was scheduled for induction the next day. A Doppler ultrasound or a contraction stress test could have been recommended for my abnormal BPP results, too.

Factors that were present during my test that could have interfered with the accuracy of the results include fetal position, low blood-sugar levels (I hadn't eaten in several hours), and possible (though it's rare) feces or air in the intestines or rectum (castor oil effects!).

According to *Oxorn-Foote Human Labor and Birth*, by Harry Oxorn (a standard medical text), "While prolongation of pregnancy beyond 42 weeks may have an adverse effect on neonatal outcome in some cases, fetal death is rare. Induction of labor does not improve the results. What the latter practice does achieve is an increase in the rate of cesarean section because of failed induction. An uncomplicated postterm pregnancy is not an indication for the induction of labor. Early delivery is necessary only when tests of fetal health show that deterioration is taking place."

I next learned that I should have gotten up out of that hospital bed when I was having that stretch of really nice early labor contractions the night before I was induced. I had been scared into not being unhooked from the EFM for too long, because after all, like the OB had said, I didn't want a dead baby, did I? Had I known then what I know now, I would have gotten up and moved with the contractions, sinking into each one with a nice long doorknob squat, perhaps urging them to keep coming with some nipple stimulation, too.

ARTIFICIAL RUPTURE OF MEMBRANES
(AROM)

This procedure is called amniotomy and is often performed to either start or speed labor. Research indicates it only saves you an hour or two on the total length of labor, which is not much benefit for the increased risk of infection, or the significantly increased risk of cord prolapse. Or the fact that my baby was swooshed into a posterior position, and with the water gone, was not able to move back into a good position.

Had I known then what I know now, in particular "The Pregnant Patient's Bill of Rights" and "The Pregnant Patient's Responsibilities," put forth by the International Childbirth Education Association (ICEA; see http://www.aimsusa.org/ppbr.htm), because I had begun contracting immediately upon my bag of waters being ruptured by the OB (artificial rupture of membranes, or AROM), I would have declined being further augmented with Pitocin. (As it was, I had not been informed by the OB of the risks and hazards associated with being treated with Pitocin.) I would have refused it until my body gave proof that I really needed it. According to my hospital records, my cervix was 100% effaced, bulging membranes, two centimeters dilated, and station high. Therefore, my cervix was soft, ripe, and ready.

Without the immediate Pitocin drip, my body would have been able to get its own natural endorphin painkillers as well as oxytocin, the body's natural hormone, secreted in bursts. Instead I was shocked into labor that had me suffering pretty good, pretty quickly. (Endorphins block the release of neurotransmitter molecules from the nerve terminal so that pain signals do not reach the brain. The endorphins, therefore, are said to have an analgesic effect and create a state of euphoria, also reducing stress. They have similar actions to opiate drugs.) Pitocin disrupts that natural physiological process of normal labor. According to the ICPA Research Foundation, "...when you are given pitocin you are placed on a regulated intravenous pump to regulate the amount of pitocin to a steady flow. Therefore, pitocin induced contractions are entirely different from your body's natural contractions, in both strength and effect." Further, one of the hazards associated with Pitocin is turbulent labor and tetanic contractions for the mother, which can lead to, among other things, post-birth hemorrhage.

There are also hazards associated with labor induction itself. For example, induction of labor involves the need for other interventions like IV drips, continuous EFM, and usually confinement to bed, all of which also can have adverse effects. I had all of those interventions. The hospital staff would have much preferred me to stay in bed. (Remember the nurse who wanted me to get up off the floor so it would be more convenient for her

INDUCTION OF LABOR

For information on the problems and hazards of inducing labor, you can read a Coalition for Improving Maternity Services (CIMS) fact sheet at www.motherfriendly.org/Downloads/induct-fact-sheet.pdf.

to check me?) It's easier for the staff to manage patients that way. But I just had to move, even though the EFM restricted me, and I was tethered to a pole of IVs. It was the only way to stave off the edginess of the Pitocin-induced contractions.

The more I learned about Pitocin from medical journals, the more I believed my labor had been over-managed. According to the nurse, she'd come in on doctor's orders (who'd disappeared for hours, having no idea how I was progressing), upping my Pitocin drip at set intervals. This effort to push my body into more active labor was too aggressive. The goal should have been to just give me enough to bring on contractions to help my cervix dilate, not to bring the too frequent, abnormally long and strong contractions. We tried to intercept this intervention, but again, we should have refused their protocol.

Another reason I believe my labor was over-managed was because of the time limit they'd imposed. Typically, with an AROM situation, twenty-four hours are allowed for labor. I was put on a shorter clock and allowed only twelve. Though the OB did not explain why, my investigation turned up the probable reason: my positive Group B Strep (GBS) status. This may also explain the overzealous Pitocin drip. (See Month 9 of "Pregnancy: Month by Month, Inside and Out" for a full discussion of GBS.)

AROM removes the protective barrier between the baby and any potentially infection-causing bacteria. After so many hours past AROM, the risk of infection increases significantly, and therefore the risk of emergency cesarean section. Although I was receiving the recommended IV antibiotics during labor, there was still a risk of infection. Add the fact that AROM carries with it the added bells and whistles of continuous EFM (I had both external and internal, an internal monitor attached to baby's scalp that actually creates a small scrape on baby's head where the bacteria can get into the bloodstream, therefore carrying a higher risk of infection), and a balancing act was created between the interventions increasing the risk of GBS infecting my baby and a shorter time limit on my labor.

Neither the AROM nor the internal monitor had been explained as carrying additional risks for infection. They, therefore, had only my ignorant consent. Not exactly the same as informed consent.

And what was up with having the urge to push but being told by a nurse to wait for the doctor? Of all the ridiculousities, that one took the cake. He was so concerned that I have this baby as quickly as possible that he took what felt like forever when I needed to push? Oh, the irony of him then putting me on a one-hour time limit because he didn't know how long I'd been fully dilated. He was obviously too busy to have my care in his hands.

Trying to understand more about the reasons why I had a postpartum hemorrhage and retained placenta, I am left with a similar answer to the question, "Which came first, the chicken or the egg?" After manually removing my placenta, the OB said that it had been healthy and intact. However, partial separation of the placenta (meaning that part of it detached while the rest remained attached to my uterus) was probably to blame for the postpartum hemorrhage. Reasons why partial separations happen are varied. Maybe the placenta was located in the lower section of the uterus and therefore had a harder time separating completely—the muscles there are not as effective at cutting off the spiral arteries that connect it to the uterine lining. Or maybe uterine atony was to blame—that is, the lack of or uneven postpartum contractions that normally separate the placenta from the uterine wall. One reason a uterus may contract in an uneven or spastic way is due to fundal massage before the placenta is out. The spots that are rubbed contract, the placenta separates there, but not the entire thing. Uterine atony is responsible for 80% to 90% of postpartum hemorrhage cases. Atony allows continued blood loss from the placental site because there is no contracting, clamping down, and constriction of the uterine blood vessels. I did learn, however, that risk factors for atony include fatigued uterus (for example, augmented labor overworking the uterus) and obstructed uterus (for example, retained placenta or malpresentation—my baby had been posterior with a compound presentation, her hand up by her face—making the uterus work harder to get her out).

Though I am critical of the way my postdate pregnancy and induced labor were managed, and suspect that it contributed to the postpartum emergencies, I remain grateful and impressed by how well the OB was able to get the postpartum hemorrhage under control and the placenta out in the time he needed to. As a result, I didn't have to have blood transfusions or emergency hysterectomy surgery.

Replaying the birth in my head, I could see that the hospital environment could have been more comforting and less hostile. (Even the next day, when I was up and walking down the hallway, a nurse still gave me attitude by saying that what had happened to me must not have been as bad as she heard it was, because if it had been, there was no way I'd have the energy to be up on my feet.) There could have been a lot done to create a comfortable, calm place instead of one that was "us versus them," argumentative, or fear inducing. (The hospital staff was well aware of my state of mind. Even on my Obstetric Admission Assessment form, the "Parent(s) appear: Anxious and Fearful" boxes were checked.) For example, the nurse who checked my dilation made her assessments sound negative, whereas my doula Lori's sounded positive. The nurse wanted me to accommodate her by getting up off the floor. Lori was more than willing to help me wherever I was. The nurse offered an epidural. Lori reassured me it wasn't necessary. Lori was my saving grace. I'm convinced that her presence allowed me to avoid the epidural and a probable cesarean section.

I wondered why in the world we'd bothered to place that sign on our door, asking that no one come in offering unwarranted interventions. Mine had been ignored. Or maybe it hadn't been. Maybe it had offended the hospital personnel and they worked harder to show me who was in charge. I started feeling like the hospital personnel had an agenda, wanting me to have a c-section because it would be a hell of a lot easier, faster, and predictable for them...doing all these risky things to me without my informed consent.

Working through the post traumatic stress by investigating what happened during Emma-Joy's birth, I experienced a shift in my feelings. At first, I regarded the OB as a lifesaver and bought the line he sold me, "It's a good thing you were here instead of at the birth center. If you had that postpartum hemorrhage there, you'd have been emergency transported and would've wound up with an emergency hysterectomy." I thanked him. I even had Ernesto's mom cook him some amazing food. But later, I thought more that I wouldn't have hemorrhaged if I'd been at the birth center. There, my labor wouldn't have been over-managed with all the interventions. My thinking shifted to view the hospital as a place of last resort. I'd gone there for help

WHAT'S WRONG WITH EPIDURALS?

Before I rail against what's wrong with epidurals, I'd like to point out that there are certainly instances when pain relief is warranted. All labors are intense and uncomfortable to varying degrees, and people certainly do have different pain thresholds. When a laboring woman is beyond exhausted and/or clearly suffering and is asking for relief for her suffering and the exhaustion/suffering is impeding labor progress, then pain-relieving medications can be more helpful than harmful.

With that said, I do believe that epidurals—often portrayed as completely safe—have risks that are undercommunicated to women, and true informed consent is not given. A general estimate of the overall complication rate of epidural anesthesia is 23%.

Some of the maternal risks include, but are not limited to: a drop in blood pressure, urinary retention and postpartum bladder dysfunction, nausea and vomiting, fever, incomplete or nonexistent pain relief, postpartum feelings of regret or loss of autonomy, and inability to move about freely on one's own. Some very serious and rare risks include convulsions, respiratory paralysis, cardiac arrest, allergic shock, nerve injury, epidural abscess, and death.

Labor side effects may include prolonged first stage of labor, increased malpresentation of baby's head, increased need for Pitocin augmentation, prolonged second stage of labor, decreased ability to push effectively, increased likelihood of forceps or vacuum-extraction delivery, increased likelihood of needing an episiotomy, and increased chance of cesarean section.

Baby's side effects may include fetal distress, abnormal fetal heart rate, drowsiness at birth, poor sucking reflex, and poor muscle strength and tone in the first hours.

Well before you expect to go into labor, talk to your midwife or OB about the pros and cons of epidurals. Consider how much of the birthing process you want to fully experience. And let you healthcare provider, your partner, your birthing coach, and others who will be around during your labor know exactly how you feel about epidurals, so that they can remind you of your decision during the vulnerable time of labor. Whether you have an epidural or not, make sure that is *your* choice, not a doctor's or nurse's.

BE PREPARED

Here are some things you can do to help prepare for any birthing eventuality—for when things don't go according to plan—so you don't become overrun with fear.

1. If you are planning a home or birth-center birth, go ahead and tour the hospital anyway. Tour one that has the best natural-birth reputation, not the one with the highest c-section rate in town.

2. Decide ahead of time under what circumstances you'd allow yourself to be admitted—firm up what your beliefs are and what your commitment is to natural birth.

3. Insist on informed consent.

4. Arm yourself with "The Pregnant Patient's Bill of Rights" and "The Pregnant Patient's Responsibilities."

5. Keep your health and your baby's health your focus.

but it was there that I was put through the wringer. I also got over the idea that my life being spared was a sign that I should have only one child, that 100 years ago I'd have been one of the mothers who died in childbirth. After my independent investigation, then going on to work as the director of the Hollywood Birth Center in Florida four years later, I learned and experienced what I needed to in order to help myself get past those limiting ideas, to understand birth better, and to heal.

In the end, it's true that the goal is a healthy mother and baby, but it's not the only thing that matters. Birth matters. And it can have lifelong implications for both mother and baby. So choose the place where you will be most comfortable birthing and wherever that place is, home, birth center, or hospital, insist on informed consent. And have a doula or other advocate with you.

Newborn (0-3 Months)

4.

Newborn Care

Part of my prenatal care with the midwives at the Gainesville Birth Center included a six-week childbirth education class that met once a week. Childbirth education classes are important not only to prepare for birth, but also to learn about newborn care; five classes were about labor and birth, one was about newborn care. It is well understood by biologists and psychologists that knowing how to care for a newborn is not an instinctual skill, but one that is learned.

I was a diligent note-taker. My diligence was out of fear of the unknown. I was scared that I wouldn't know what to do once Emma-Joy got here. In the weeks leading up to her birth, I reread my newborn-care notes many times, trying to commit them to memory. I recopied them in neater handwriting and kept them easily accessible in my ever-expanding notebook of baby information.

I trusted what our childbirth educator was teaching us because she wasn't teaching just one parenting philosophy or style. She was coming to us with lots of research-based information and personal experience, and was picking and choosing what she thought were the best bits from different styles. I liked that because, after spending some time at the library with the countless rows of parenting books, I was overwhelmed by not knowing which styles were utter crap, and which were worthwhile.

Twenty Things You Should Know

Behold my actual list of notes (though slightly updated) on newborn care that helped me over the newborn hurdles:

1. A well-attended baby is one whose basic needs are met quickly. A well-attended baby is one who is picked up within ninety seconds of crying starting.

Research confirms that indulging in the early dependency needs of your baby leads to independence. This responsiveness is associated with the unfolding of self-reliance. Independence cannot be taught; it's a natural state your child will grow into, but only after being allowed an opportunity to experience and outgrow dependency.

> ### A Note to New Parents
> The fact that babies do not cry because they are trying to manipulate you is contrary to what other parenting books may tell you. There is the school of thought that babies do cry to manipulate people and it will be espoused by grandparents, relatives, nosybodies on the street, neighbors, etc. Beware! You new parents may be bombarded with this type of "advice." And know, too, that crying is not a needed lung exercise.

2. Babies do not cry because they are trying to manipulate you. Manipulation just isn't there with a baby. They are nonverbal. Crying is their only way of telling you something is wrong, to communicate that they have a need for something. They are not doing it to drive you crazy, no matter how crazy the crying makes you. Never shake a baby out of frustration. Shaking a baby can cause serious harm, up to and including death. If you feel frustrated and there is no one to hand the baby over to, put the baby down, walk away, and take ten deep breaths.

3. Call the pediatrician if there's any fever in a baby under three months old. If anything is red, swollen, or oozing, that is a sign of infection. If there are red streaks, that's an emergency!

4. For bathing, get in the tub with the baby, but only after the umbilical cord stump has fallen off. Gently bathe with just a soft washcloth, scalp included—this will prevent the development of cradle cap. No soap required! Get a rubber-ducky thermometer for the tub. Between 90° F and 100° F is a good bath temperature. Bathing two or three times a week is fine. Not all babies love a bath. Use bath time to stroke, cuddle, and talk to your baby and it can be a special time for both of you. For added skin softness, add a cloth tea bag full of oatmeal to the bath water. Wet babies are slippery! To help you not lose the baby in the bath, sit baby on a washcloth on your lap.

5. Ask everyone to wash their hands before handling the baby up to thirteen-weeks old, which is when baby becomes immunocompetent.

6. Cut baby's nails, when needed, after the bath. Or do it when baby is in deep sleep, also called "limp limb time." Depress the bottom finger pad so you don't clip it along with the nail.

7. Don't use talc. (See "The Virtues of Cloth Diapers" for further discussion.)

8. Don't overdress the baby. If your baby is bundled and is crying and feels hot, take a layer off. Likewise, don't under-dress baby when going out. Check for chilly hands and feet.

9. Nurse the baby on demand, not on a schedule. Pay attention to signs of rooting, a searching-for-food reflex that subsides around four months. Crying is a late sign of hunger.

10. Check the baby's diaper every hour and change it often—as soon as it's wet or poopy. Let the baby's skin dry completely before putting on another diaper.

11. Eight to twelve inches is the distance that baby's vision is best, the distance between your face and the baby's during nursing. Make eye contact. Looking at human faces is the most interesting activity for a newborn. Parent faces are their favorite.

12. There are six stages of consciousness in the newborn infant: quiet alert, active alert, crying, drowsy, quiet sleep, and active sleep.

13. Pace yourself to the baby's cues during the quiet alert state. Disengage when they do or else you'll overwhelm them. For example, this isn't the time for continued clapping and singing or zooming around like an airplane. This state has little or no body movement. They can copy your facial expressions during this time. During this state is when learning takes place. This is the most rewarding experience time with a newborn. The quiet alert state is 10% of every twenty-four hours.

14. During active alert, there is frequent, rhythmic movement.

15. Quiet sleep is deep sleep. Active sleep is REM sleep. Put baby to sleep on his/her back. Newborns sleep well when swaddled. Sleep when the baby sleeps. If you don't feel tired, consider yourself lucky and use that time to do things that refresh and reenergize you. Read, write, catch up on mail, do things that you can't do with an awake newborn.

16. Talk to your baby often each day. Explain things you're doing. Describe things you see and sounds you hear. Imitate your baby's cooing and jabbering sounds. Language, along with eye contact, is what makes your baby's brain take shape, something important for their development. You don't have to keep things quiet all the time. Babies like hearing different noises—play music or white noise. But don't forget they need some quiet time to babble and learn.

17. Babies get bored lying around. Carry your baby around with you often. A sling is a great way to be able to carry your baby lots and lots. (See "Baby-wearing" for further discussion.) Smile at each other. Rock your baby in a rock-

ing chair, showing love by touching and talking softly. Sing to your baby. Babies thrive on loving attention.

18. Give baby tummy time each day so baby will lift his/her head. Encourage rolling over by slowly moving a favorite object from one side to the other.

19. Give baby bright colorful objects to look at. They love simple black-and-white designs. They like interesting shapes hanging from a mobile, as well as baby-safe mirrors.

20. Babies under six months old should spend very little time in the sun. Sunscreen is not recommended for babies under six months old. Use protective clothing instead.

Responding to Baby's Needs

Though I'd done my homework on newborn care, when it came time to take the test, I felt like I was flailing. Newborn care is constant care, it seemed. While she was doing her job being a newborn, adjusting the best she could to life on the outside (I later learned that the newborn months should be considered the fourth trimester), I was getting my on-the-job training. It took more than just having memorized a list of newborn-care notes. The patience I needed with myself was the same patience I needed to practice having for baby.

I knew that taking care of a newborn was a learned skill, but I still felt incompetent for the first six or seven months. It felt like not a shred of maternal instinct had kicked in while I struggled with learning her stages of consciousness, following her cues, and understanding the general order of operations. I had read in a few books about this mythical maternal instinct thing and I wanted it to help me! Where was mine?

Turns out, too, that I got the "hard" baby model, not the "easy" one. Some babies are born calm, as predictable nappers, and are easy to soothe. Others are colicky, fight their sleep, and need lots of extra help in the soothing department. (To help with colic, breast-feeding mamas could cut dairy from their diets. Dairy is known to be a contributor to colic.) My baby Emma-Joy was in this latter category: a "high-needs" baby is a term I later learned that applied to her.

She didn't want to be put down ever. And it wasn't enough to just hold her; she needed constant motion. When I was alone with her, it was hard for me to even get myself dressed or make myself a sandwich. Showering was out of the question. She wanted to nurse constantly and hung out on the breast even when she really wasn't hungry. If she fell asleep on me like that, she'd wake up if I tried to move her off of me. She preferred to sleep belly down on my or Ernesto's chest, instead of on her back in a bassinet or on a mattress. Some nights I spent in the rocking chair with

DON'T UNDERESTIMATE THE POWER OF
PARENTAL PATIENCE AND LACK OF SLEEP

It is a lot easier to model present and responsive
parenting behaviors when all is well. Lack of sleep
and patience are trying circumstances, ones that
beg outside support. But when support to help
alleviate fatigue and impatience are not available,
you have to do the best you can. If the baby needs
to be in motion but all you can manage is to hold
the baby while sitting still, you are still doing better
for baby than by doing nothing. Likewise, if baby is
telling you she needs to nurse but you don't have
the patience to do so right then because you are
hungry and need to eat first, then get yourself fed
first! Getting everyone's basic needs met—not just
baby's—is a constant balancing act.

her, sleepless exhausting nights for
both Ernesto and me as we took turns
rocking, walking, and soothing her.

It quickly became my pet peeve to
hear people talking about "good" babies
and "bad" babies. I knew that all babies
are good babies, it's just that some are
easy and some are hard. Simply, they
are unique individuals and individuals
have different needs.

Recognizing this helped us get
through the toughest first month. We
were proud that we'd made it through.
Then we got through the rest of the newborn months (to three months old) and
beyond that, take one month at a time. Slowly but surely, she was getting out of the
colicky funk and we were getting the hang of how to care for her.

Most of the newborn-care advice we'd followed focused on meeting basic
needs, but we found that it also incorporated nicely with our intent of raising a free
child, one who'd know justice, freedom, responsibility, and self-regulation by having learned and felt them firsthand through the ways she was cared for. We were,
even at such a young age, laying a foundation. Free-child parenting principles apply to newborns, too. The methods we'd adopted meshed well with key ideas we'd
identified as the heart of our parenting philosophy: cooperation, mutual respect,
mutual trust, freedom, and nonpunitive/gentle discipline.

We felt that by meeting our baby's basic needs in a timely, gentle manner—
whether they were easy or hard needs to meet, we were setting the stage for mutual trust and respect, ideals we both held. It was the first intersection we saw
where our ideals meshed with parenting in practical, instead of theoretical terms.
Plus, we knew that having basic needs met allows for the freedom to develop and
learn. For example, being hungry prevents a child from being able to engage in a
learning state. By feeding our baby when she was hungry instead of on a schedule,
she wouldn't be crying for an hour waiting for feeding time, an hour trying to
communicate her escalating need, instead of an hour potentially spent in an alert
state. We believed that following baby's cues is connected to respect, something
essential for both parent and baby—mutual respect.

Additionally, we believed that by being present and responsive, she would
learn to trust that her needs were going to be met quickly and in respectful ways.
If she cried, we were going to honor her attempt to communicate something to

us and help her, instead of ignoring her or letting her cry it out, which would have taught her that she cannot trust us to meet her needs. Even if our attempts to respond were incorrect—for example, offering to nurse when it's just that she wanted a change of scenery—we believed an incorrect response would be better than no response. She'd eventually recognize our care as patient, well-intentioned, and worthy of her trust. Even if our care wasn't always perfect because we were short on sleep, short on patience, or just at a plain loss for how to deal with certain situations, at least we'd be modeling respect as our guiding force.

She'd learn that good communication is worth it because we were acting open and responsive to her cries, further setting the stage for mutual respect, because being open and responsive are key active-listening skills crucial to mutual respect. We imagined that it would be unreasonable for us to expect good verbal communication from her down the road if we weren't good listeners to her nonverbal communication now. To not be an active listener to one with whom you are engaged in an intimate relationship, which a parent-child relationship most certainly is, is most disrespectful. One cannot reasonably expect to be respectfully listened to if one doesn't in turn respectfully listen.

Our goal was to be able to make her as comfortable as possible, whether by means of a full belly, suitable temperature, or stimulating environment, because being made comfortable when you're incapable of creating comfort for yourself is also a building block for trust and respect. We were modeling behavior that we believed she'd eventually grow to value, learn herself, and recognize in others. After all, children learn desired behaviors best by observing desired behaviors.

We knew better than to think our newborn baby was capable of thinking through these ideas of building trust and respect like we were, but believed that she would someday, and the sooner that she had experiences with feeling trust and respect to which she could later attach the words, the better. Starting this way, demonstrating respect toward her through the way we cared for her, she'd learn respect, thus mutual respect, toward everyone else, parents included. It was the closest we'd ever come in investing in the future. Her future and ours together.

5.

Breast-Feed Your Baby

I automatically knew I was going to breast-feed my baby just like I automatically sought my prenatal care from midwives at a freestanding birth center, rather than a hospital-based obstetrician. It seemed like a no-brainer; the idea that it was even a choice between breast-feeding and formula/bottle feeding didn't ever cross my mind. But what I didn't know automatically was *how* to breast-feed. And I didn't realize that I didn't know how until after I'd gotten a bright purple hickey-blister-bruise on my left nipple and a ridiculously excruciatingly sore right one.

Though some babies can temporarily have poor suck responses for a variety of reasons, breast-feeding is instinctual for all babies. A healthy newborn, when put on mama's chest or even mama's tummy, will usually find its way to the breast to begin nursing within the first hour of life.

While the desire to breast-feed may be instinctual for many mamas, the ability to do so is a learned art. Breast-feeding is a skill that needs patience, practice, and support to master.

I'd simply done what I assumed was simple—I just put the baby up to my breast and let her start sucking. When things didn't seem to be working as they should (it hurt, and the way her little lapping, Hoover-strength vacuum tongue was darting around out of her frantic, quivering lips just didn't look right), I thought I should just give it a few more seconds, that she'd get the hang of it in a jiffy. After several minutes, the second in which she got the hang of it still hadn't come. The only thing I got in a jiffy was a painful purple nurple and a crying urge to yell "Ouch!" and pull her off (the wrong way, I'd later learn), only to torture the other nipple with my same ignorance moments later.

Ernesto and I were alone with our brand-new baby Emma-Joy in the hospital delivery room; she'd been brought in to us so I could nurse her for the first time. The nurse handed her to me and asked if I knew what I was doing. I told her yes because I thought I did. She said OK and that she'd be back later to get Emma-Joy so I could rest. I really wish I'd had the foresight to know first, that breast-feeding is not an instinctual skill, and second, how to freakin' do it!

Not until the next day did the hospital's only part-time lactation consultant check in with me to see how breast-feeding was going. I showed her my left nipple. She grimaced, "Oh my, that looks dreadful," and got to work

> ### CORRECT LATCH-ON AND BREAKING THE BABY'S LATCH
>
> I did not know either of these things before I initiated breast-feeding Emma-Joy and wound up with nipples that felt like they'd been through a meat grinder.
>
> A correct latch-on is one that has a large part of the areola drawn into the baby's mouth; both of the baby's lips should be flared outward with no part of either lip sucked in under itself. Bring the baby to the breast, not the breast to the baby, and lose any timidity you may have about ramming that wide-mouthed baby onto the boob!
>
> Nip an incorrect latch in the bud! But don't just pull baby off your breast. You first must break the suction by sneaking a tip of your clean finger in between the baby's mouth and your breast.
>
> For more information, including latching videos and an animation illustrating asymmetrical latch technique, see "Latching and Positioning Resources" found at www.kellymom.com/bf/start/basics/latch-resources.html.

with us. She said that because of our incorrect start, she was afraid that it was still going to hurt for awhile, but promised that I'd at least have the hang of correct latch-on and breaking the baby's latch by the time we went home. There's nothing like having a complete stranger grab up your sore tit with one hand, compress it just so, and make your nipple tease the baby's mouth open wide enough for it to be smooshed onto the boob with her other hand. But yeah, she kept her promise, and after two days, although it still did hurt like hell, I did have a better hang of getting Emma-Joy latched on and off the boob. A better hang if it, but still a far from effortless one; I wasn't that good at it on my own yet, and was still lacking confidence.

Breast-Feeding from an Evolutionary Point of View

News flash: we humans are mammals. And what is the defining characteristic of the class Mammalia? You got it—the ability to produce milk that's designed specifically to nourish the young.

Author and professor Margaret C. Neville writes, "The provision of milk frees the mother from the necessity of providing a specialized environment for rearing of the young. It allows birth to occur at a relatively early stage of development and provides a time of intense maternal interaction with the newborn during early behavioral development. In addition the nutritional reserves of the mother may be

MILK SUPPLY: QUALITY AND QUANTITY

To produce adequate milk, breast-feeding mothers should continue taking prenatal vitamins and increase their caloric intake by 500–1,000 calories over their caloric intake while pregnant. You're still eating for two, and that baby is bigger now than when in utero! Two-thirds of milk production comes from mama's nutrition and one-third comes from your pregnancy's stored fat.

But even mothers lacking proper nutrition can make milk that will meet baby's needs. In her article "Constituents of Human Milk" in *Food and Nutrition Bulletin*, Ann Prentice writes, "In the past it was commonly believed that poorly nourished mothers had reduced lactational performance, in both the amount and the quality of breastmilk produced. This view has now been shown to be largely incorrect." The nutrients that are lacking in the mother's diet are then either made by the body itself or taken from the mother's stores. For example, if calcium is lacking in the diet, the calcium in breast milk comes from the mother's bones or teeth.

It is the very rare woman who cannot produce enough breast milk because her milk ducts never developed. If there is an instance when an insufficient milk supply cannot be alleviated by simply nursing more or correcting a latch-on or sucking problem, factors such as stress, fatigue, anemia, or cigarette smoking need to be looked at. Linda J. Smith writes in her article "How Mother's Milk Is Made" (published on the Bright Future Resource Centre's website, www.bflrc.com), that other significant inhibiting factors appear to be breast surgery, retained placenta, Sheehan's syndrome or pituitary shock, hormonal contraception, and insufficient glandular tissue. The following herbs have been known to boost milk supply: fenugreek, red clover blossoms, nettles, red raspberry leaf, blessed thistle, alfalfa, borage, fennel, and hops.

Two books—*A Medication Guide for Breast-Feeding Moms* and *Medication and Mother's Milk*—both written by renowned clinical pharmacologist Dr. Thomas W. Hale, are extremely helpful references should you have any questions about continuing breast-feeding while taking medications of any kind imaginable.

able to sustain the suckling through a period of famine. Milk composition is species specific."

Humans are the only species to drink milk of another species and the only ones to continue drinking another animal's milk after weaning. Let us not forget that lactation is the final phase of the reproductive cycle in mammals and is essential for optimum growth and development of the young mammals during early postnatal life.

The sugar and oils in breast milk come in a living, organic form, which also includes living enzymes, vitamins, hormones, and antibodies tailored to meet the needs of a human baby. The sugar and oils in baby formula are heavily processed and devitalized, and if the formula is cows' milk-based, any hormones that manage to survive the processing are hormones meant for a baby calf. Would it be less cute if your baby's first sounds were "Moo-moo" instead of "Ma-ma"?

Breast-Feeding Positions

Once at home, the hardest part was getting in a comfortable-enough position. Whenever sitting down to nurse, I'd need to make sure I had an abundant supply of pillows around me with which to prop up my arms at my sides and my baby in front of me on my lap. Not until someone bought me a nursing pillow was I able to get comfortably positioned with less effort. I was then able to try holding the baby in different positions to help alleviate the pain I felt due to using the same nursing position, the cradle hold.

Here's an overview of some effective positions:

THE CRADLE OR CUDDLE HOLD: This is the most frequently used position. Make sure your arm is supported so it doesn't get tired. Place baby across your stomach, tummy to tummy, with her head in the bend of your elbow and her mouth directly in front of the nipple. Baby's body should be in a straight line, with her knees in close and facing your body.

THE FOOTBALL OR CLUTCH HOLD: This one works well for mamas who have had a c-section, mamas with large breasts or flat nipples, mamas experiencing difficulty on one side, and small babies or ones who are having problems latching on. Lie baby beside you on a pillow to support her and your arm. Hold her head in the palm of your hand. Her back will lay on your inner forearm, with her feet tucked slightly behind you.

THE CROSS-CRADLE OR TRANSVERSE HOLD: This is also good when having latching-on trouble or with a small/premature baby. This hold gives you more control over the baby's head and a better view of the latch than the cradle hold does. Holding the baby in the arm opposite the breast from which she will latch onto, position the baby the same as in the cradle hold. Her body is at breast level, turned toward you, and her butt is in the crook of your arm.

THE LYING-DOWN POSITION: This position quickly became my favorite once I got the hang of it; it's perfect for co-sleeping. Get comfy lying on one side and line the baby up tummy to tummy with you so that your nipple is opposite her mouth. If she needs it, use a pillow to keep her from rolling back. You might want one at your back, too. She will nurse on the lower boob. If you need boob support, use your upper hand. To feed from the other boob without having to roll over, just lean further over with your upper arm reaching across, propped up on the pillow that's behind the baby's back.

THE TAILOR POSITION: This one is great for older babies and toddlers. With a pillow on your lap or not, just cradle hold your nursling. Remember your back—

> ## NURSING PILLOWS
>
> I attribute part of my learning to breast-feed to having a nursing pillow. Mine was a firm, semicircular support designed to cover my lap and raise the baby up to breast level. Mine also provided support for my lower back because it went all the way around me, opening and closing on the side with a Velcro tab, but some are crescent shaped without this extra back support. In general, nursing pillows allow you to focus more attention on getting baby latched on correctly and less attention on positioning baby's body. They are also great for tandem-nursing twins, preemies, or babies with low muscle tone.

> ## ALL HAIL COLOSTRUM!
>
> Colostrum is only produced in the first few days, and is small in quantity but big in quality. It provides the baby's first immunization because it contains especially high concentrations of immune factors called immunoglobulins and the protective protein, lactoferrin. Not only does colostrum protect against infection, it also clears meconium (the black, tar-like, sticky poo that is composed of amniotic-fluid debris from the newborn intestines), helps reduce jaundice, and satisfies the baby's thirst and hunger until mama's milk comes in.

don't hunch over to bring the breast to the bigger baby. Baby needs to come to the breast.

For more information, see Latching and Positioning Resources found at www. kellymom.com/bf/start/basics/latch-resources.html.

The Trials of Engorgement

Engorgement was another hard thing to get through. Engorgement is when the new mama's body switches from making colostrum, the liquid gold-like substance produced in the first few days after birth, to transitional milk, and later to mature milk. Engorgement happens about two to six days after birth, and lasts about twenty-four to forty-eight hours, if properly treated. The breasts become larger, heavier, warmer, and uncomfortable. Rock-solid, watermelon-sized uncomfortable. This happens not only because of milk storage, but also because hormone levels shift, the onset of lactation brings an increase in blood flow to the breasts, and lymph fluids accumulate in the building breast tissue.

The only funny part about engorgement was seeing milk squirt forcefully out of my boobs, clear across the room in several directions. It was such an amazing surprise that I called Ernesto to come quick to see for himself. I'd always thought that milk came through just one hole in the nipple. Girl, was I wrong. Those engorged nips are like super-soaker fountain sprayers! Uncontrollable ones, I might add. You just never know when they're going to let down and go off.

The research shows that preventing and treating engorgement quickly is critical. Engorgement can cause problems with breast-feeding. It may be more difficult for baby to latch on to a breast that is so swollen that the nipple and areola are flattened; baby won't be able to get enough breast tissue into its mouth to suck effectively. This leads to frustration for baby, frustration and sore nipples for mama, as well as milk being left in the breast, which can affect milk production.

When milk accumulates in the breast, milk production slows down. If the milk isn't removed from the breasts,

TIPS FOR HEALING SORE NIPPLES

In the beginning, especially if you're having problems with thrush (yeast), correct positioning, or proper latch-on, your nipples can crack. They can bleed. They can blister. And they can hurt like hell. But you still don't have to quit breast-feeding. The quicker you get to the source of the problem and fix it, the better. And the quicker your nipples heal, the better.

It helps to offer the least sore breast first. After your baby finishes nursing, express a little milk and rub this fresh milk onto your nipple. Sit around with your boob hanging out until it dries; fresh air is your boo-boo'd nipple's best friend. This time away from your bra or shirt rubbing on your breasts is good for them, too. Using a medical-grade lanolin ointment like Lansinoh can promote healing and does not need to be washed off before nursing. And speaking of washing, using soap on the nipple area is *not* recommended unless the skin is broken.

For more in-depth information, refer to "Healing Tips for Nipple Cracks or Abrasions" by Kelly Bonyata, BS, IBCLC, found at www.kellymom. com.

mama's body will produce less milk. There is also evidence that unrelieved engorgement may damage the cells that make milk, affecting milk production as baby gets older. Engorgement can also lead to mastitis (breast inflammation), plugged ducts, or a breast infection. Use a breast pump as a tool!

Pumping through engorgement was helpful to me. Not only did pumping (I had a manual, hand-held pump) help relieve the discomfort and help soften the areola so Emma-Joy could latch on easier, but I stockpiled the extra milk in the freezer for future independence. This pumping did not disrupt the exact supply and demand from getting properly balanced because I was not pumping as much milk as Emma-Joy was nursing. (Milk supply is regulated by baby's needs and the regulation itself takes longer than engorgement lasts.)

> **TREATING ENGORGEMENT**
>
> If your boobs get too firm, hard, shiny, or lumpy, take action! Suggestions: Breast-feed frequently, avoiding bottles, pacifiers, or supplements at this time. Be sure baby is latched on well; full breasts with flattened nipples can be softened by expressing milk before baby latches on. Wear breast shells for about thirty minutes prior to a feeding to help the nipple stand out. (A breast shell is a plastic, cup-shaped device that has a hole for the nipple and is worn in the bra.) Apply warm compresses for a few minutes before nursing. Between feedings, apply ice or cabbage leaves to reduce swelling. Wear a supportive bra without underwires (they can contribute to plugged ducts), like a sports bra.
>
> For more information on what engorgement is and how to deal with it, visit www.kellymom.com/bf/concerns/mom/engorgement.html. Written by Kelly Bonyata, BS, IBCLC, it highlights what is normal engorgement, tips for treating it, and lists of additional resources.

In fact, I needed more relief than pumping brought and needed the help of green-cabbage-leaf compresses, a little trick I learned from my midwife. Cabbage is known for decreasing milk supply and swelling. The cold cabbage-leaf compresses brought quicker and more comfortable relief than ice packs did, and since they are so effective in limiting milk supply, I didn't want them to be too effective. I only used them for twenty minutes, no more than three times per day for two days. They really did the trick!

Storing Extra Milk in the Freezer

My prenatal yoga teacher clued me in to this tip. She told me that freezing and storing her extra milk during the engorgement period was the key to her being able to resume teaching yoga a few months after her baby was born. Because pumping on demand can be stressful, and therefore leads to you being able to express less milk right when you need it, having some as backup in the freezer will allow you to still get out the door when you need to, without having to resort to using formula.

The following are guidelines for storing frozen breast milk:

1. Use hard-sided plastic or glass containers with well-fitting tops, or freezer milk bags that are designed for storing human milk.

2. Store in a freezer compartment inside a refrigerator for up to two weeks.

3. Store in a freezer compartment with a separate door for up to three to four months.

4. Store in a separate deep-freeze (0° F) for six months or longer.

5. Storing milk in two- to four-ounce amounts may reduce waste.

For additional information on storing, thawing, and warming pumped milk, go to La Leche League's website: www.lalecheleague.org/FAQ/milkstorage.html.

Thrush: What It Is and How to Treat It

Weeks later, with my milk supply more regulated and more at ease with latching on and positioning, breast-feeding was still painful. At my six-week (and final) postpartum checkup at the birth center, I showed the midwives my sore nipples. Based on the pain I was describing, on my nipples' cracked and whitish appearance, and on their knowledge that I had received antibiotics during labor and that both Emma-Joy and I had received them postpartum, they guessed that I was having a problem with thrush, also known as yeast. Looking into Emma-Joy's mouth, however, they didn't see any obvious signs, patches of white in her cheeks. But they went ahead and told me about some ways to treat thrush, including a prescription for Nystatin and a recommendation for gentian violet.

Thrush is a yeast infection of the nipples caused by a fungus called *Candida albicans*. It can be very difficult to treat. Because it thrives in warm, moist environments, such as your baby's mouth and your nipples, it is important to treat both of you.

Medicated treatments include Nystatin, gentian violet, and Miconazole. Oral medication can be given for resistant cases. In addition to medical treatment, there are other steps you can take:

1. Be careful to wash your hands, especially after diaper changes.

2. Wash all items that come in contact with your nipples in hot wa-

BREAST MILK, NOW! OR... EXCLUSIVE BREAST-FEEDING ON DEMAND

Exclusive breast-feeding refers to the practice of feeding a baby only breast milk—no water, juice, formula supplements, other liquids, or solid foods. Both the American Academy of Pediatrics and the World Health Organization recommend exclusively breast-feeding for the first six months of a baby's life. (See the "Weaning" chapter for more breast-feeding recommendations.)

Instead of feeding on a schedule, nurse on demand, following baby's cues whenever possible. Allow baby to finish the first breast first, watch for baby to signal when finished by self-detaching, and then offer the second breast. Babies need to breast-feed eight to twelve times per day until the milk supply is established, about every two to three hours. Most babies will breast-feed a total of at least 140 minutes per day, averaging ten to thirty minutes per nursing session. Nursing on demand instead of on a schedule will not only help establish and regulate the milk supply, it is good responsive parenting, setting the stage for bonding, attachment, trust, security, and a positive breast-feeding relationship that is as much about comfort as it is nutrition.

ter (some practitioners recommend bleach) and dry in the sun or on hot in the dryer.

3. After every feeding, rinse your nipples with vinegar and water solution. Mix 1 tablespoon of vinegar to 1 cup of water. Use a fresh cotton ball for each application and mix a new solution each day.

4. Add acidophilus supplements, 40 million units per day, to your diet.

5. Reduce yeast and sugar in your diet.

For more information, visit www.lalecheleague.org/FAQ/thrush.html.

Help from La Leche League

A month later, I was still experiencing pain, mostly a real sharp one during latch-on that would ease up a bit while Emma-Joy nursed. Thinking the problem might not be thrush after all, or something in addition to thrush, I went to my first La Leche League meeting. Walking through that door into a room full of other breast-feeding mamas, nursing newborns on up to preschool-aged kids, was an immediate comfort, if not a bit brow-raising. I knew I was finally in the right place to get the help I desperately needed.

After the meeting, a La Leche leader named Joey spent some time with me listening to what my breast-feeding experience had been so far. By listening and watching me nurse Emma-Joy, she thought she knew what the lingering problem was. Before she set to work with me to correct the source of the problem—still incorrect latch-on—she filled me with encouraging words. She said that if I'd hung in there with this much discomfort for this long without giving up, that I should be proud of myself, that I could breast-feed my baby successfully. I was still in too much pain to feel proud, but her words did help me feel more confident. And after she grabbed my breast in her cupped hand and tickled Emma-Joy's bottom lip open wide enough and got her to latch on in a more painless way

BREAST-FEEDING AN ADOPTED BABY

Debbie Marin L.M., my friend and the midwife I worked for between 2004 and 2006, as a single mom, was able to breast-feed her adopted newborn daughter Munirah. For months before Munirah's birth, Debbie pumped her breasts to stimulate milk production. While she was able to produce a good amount of milk for Munirah, she needed to supplement with breast milk from others. To nurse Munirah with the breast milk she got donated from friends, Debbie used a nursing supplementer—a bag that you hang around your neck that carries the milk through a tube for the baby to receive at the breast. Baby gets not only milk but warmth and comfort this way, too.

Adoptive moms can breast-feed even if their babies are a year old when they come home! Their success isn't measured by having a full supply. Rather, success includes the extra chance to bond, and in most cases, some breast milk production with health benefits for baby and mom.

Many women like myself who had the benefit of pregnancy still need help and support to breast-feed successfully, and adoptive moms have even more hurdles. Many adoptive moms give up early on because they expected too much from their particular body and felt they'd failed. But with help and support, it's completely doable.

What's Wrong with Formula?

Plenty of times I've heard from well-meaning people that formula can't be that bad because after all, they were formula-fed and turned out just fine. But don't forget that formula feeding, on the scale that it's been happening since it began being mass-marketed to consumers worldwide, is a relatively new development in human history, and all the consequences may not be known for many more years. Cow's milk is not recommended for children under one year of age, yet cow's milk is the basis of most formula. The list of reasons why cow's milk is not recommended for young human bodies is a long one. Health organizations as well as the federal government have issued warnings that obesity, overweight, and adult-onset diabetes are reaching epidemic proportions in increasingly younger Americans, and it could be years before the role, if any, that cow's milk formula feeding is playing in that epidemic is firmly established. Soy-based formula carries its own health concerns, with high levels of phytoestrogens in the form of soy isoflavones.

And did you know how downright creepy and evil one of the big formula manufacturers is? Nestlé pulled one of the worst global marketing scams of all-time. In a nutshell, they hired a scientist to conduct studies to justify their claim that their Good Start formula could reduce infants' risk of developing allergies. Turns out that their scientist, Dr. Ranjit Chandra, came under intense scrutiny for academic fraud; the *British Medical Journal* even discredited and retracted one of his studies for which the research may have been fraudulently produced. According to *Mothering* magazine's website, "Evidently, the Nestlé Good Start infant formula study was never even conducted and the raw data Chandra cited could not have actually been collected."

Further, "Regular independent monitoring has shown that Nestlé is the single largest and most prolific violator of the World Health Organization's International Code of Marketing Breastmilk Substitutes." There was a clear conflict of interest with Nestlé funding Dr. Chandra's studies. Therefore, it's not a far-reaching claim to say that scientists, when given incentives to do so, can pull research that will favor their funder's marketing interests out of their asses.

Join the boycott, coordinated by the International Nestlé Boycott committee, the secretariat for which is the UK group Baby Milk Action (www.babymilkaction.org). Also, visit Infant Feeding Action Coalition (INFACT) at www.infactcanada.ca/Nestlé_Boycott.htm, and look behind the scenes by visiting boycottnestle.blogspot.com.

with her lips flared out, a wave of relief washed over me. My desperation waned and I felt a hint of relaxation instead of the usual flinching. Though not 100% painless, it was certainly better. She told me now that I knew how to really get a good latch-on, and the correct way to unlatch Emma-Joy when the latch-on was too shallow (she said teaching baby how to latch-on correctly was baby's first lesson in discipline), my nipples would start to heal and that I was on the road to learning how satisfying a breast-feeding relationship could be. (Through all my breast-feeding hurdles, Emma-Joy was always getting enough milk and was perfectly thriving.)

Joey gave me several more tips for successful breast-feeding, recommended a few book titles from the Le Leche League library, and gave me her phone number, telling me I could call her with any question or concern any time. I was so thankful. I wanted to run out and start an I Love Joey fan club, but decided that spending thirty dollars towards La Leche League membership would be a better show of gratitude. By the time the next month's meeting rolled around, breast-feeding had become much more enjoyable. I continued attending the monthly meetings, learning more, helping other new mamas with babies younger than Emma-Joy, and making a few new friends, too.

The Health Benefits of Breast-Feeding

The longer babies are exclusively breast-fed, the more protection they have from diseases. Protection declines in proportion to the amount of supplements, such as formula, they receive. Scientific studies call this effect a "dose response." Some conditions that show a dose response to breast-feeding are childhood leukemia and lymphoma, ear infections, respiratory infections, diarrhea and other gastro-intestinal illnesses, Haemophilus influenzae (HIB), obesity and overweight, and meeting developmental milestones.

The mortality rate for breast-fed babies is lower than the rate found among formula-fed babies. Breast-fed babies have more efficient immune systems. The frequency and severity of colds, asthma, pneumonia, sepsis, gastroenteritis, meningitis, and some forms of childhood cancer are all significantly reduced when children are breast-fed. Breast-feeding has been found to reduce the incidence of allergy and the frequency of certain diseases later in life, including breast cancer, osteoporosis, diabetes, ulcerative colitis, and Crohn's disease.

For mama, breast-feeding provides significant protection against breast and ovarian cancer, and these women experience less osteoporosis later in life. You lose your pregnancy weight while eating more calories than when you're pregnant. Breast-feeding is as much about comforting and bonding with your child as it is about feeding.

In addition to human milk being essentially free, breast-feeding reduces health-care costs for families and governmental assistance programs. Breast-feeding improves public health overall because the longer the duration of breast-feeding, the more physical and emotional health benefits there are for both mother and baby throughout their lives.

Breast-feeding is healthier for the environment, too, as it uses none of the metal, paper, plastic, or energy necessary for manufacturing, packaging, and transporting formula.

Studies show differences of five to ten IQ points between breast-fed and formula-fed babies, with the breast-fed baby's higher IQs lasting into early adulthood. One possible cause for this difference is the natural occurrence of docosahexae-noic acid (DHA), an omega-3 fatty acid, and arachidonic acid (AA) in human milk, both of which play a role in infant brain development.

Breast milk is free and already prepared to the perfect temperature and concentration; there are no bottles to buy, wash, or prepare as with measuring formula and water; your body makes the most perfect, superior, specific food for your specific baby that no formula can even come close to replicating (formula lacks about 400 of the identified components and nutrients of human milk, and the list keeps growing as research continues—the living components of human breast milk will never be able to be reproduced by science); you get to nourish at the same time as nurture your baby; and the special calming hormones can't be beat! (Nursing produces prolactin and oxytocin, the "falling-in-love" hormones that aid bonding.)

Barriers to Breast-Feeding

So if breast-feeding is all that and more, why don't more mamas exclusively breast-feed their babies? For starters, certain hospital practices have been identified as obstacles to initiation and continuation of breast-feeding. (Remember that nurse who essentially just dropped Emma-Joy off, taking my recuperating and exhausted new-mama word for it that I knew what I was doing?) Breast-feeding is seldom seen in popular media as the preferred way to feed your baby. Instead, bottles are the symbol of babyhood. Even with campaigns in place to improve breast-feeding rates, nursing in public can be discouraged, and at the same time, there are hardly ever places provided to nurse discreetly in public settings. It's far from unheard-of that breast-feeding women are asked to stop nursing or leave shopping areas, restaurants, and even airplanes. (Other passengers should be thanking you for breast-feeding on the plane. With your boob stuck in baby's mouth, that mouth ain't crying! Plus, the sucking and swallowing action helps baby's ears at takeoff and landing.) While it is not expressly illegal in all fifty states because it is a basic civil right, only thirty-six states have laws with language specifically allowing women to breast-feed in any public or private location and only twenty states exempt breast-feeding from public indecency laws.

Exclusive breast-feeding takes commitment. A lot of it. And for some, breast-feeding exclusively and on demand may be unrealistic. New motherhood can bring feelings of isolation, and the demands of parenting in a nuclear two-parent family—or more demanding, a single-parent family—in a society that doesn't value caretaking work and leaves it unpaid, thereby forcing new mothers to return to work quickly, can be overwhelming. If exclusively breast-feeding on demand is causing guilt, unmanageable stress, or undue hardship, one solution may be to supplement with formula.

Just as breast-feeding shouldn't physically hurt, if doing it exclusively on demand is a burden more than a joy, then something needs to change. If the problem is that mama is not getting enough sleep, then maybe a solution is to pump so your partner or other caretaker can nurse the baby with a bottle of breast milk so mama can get more sleep. This will help stave off postpartum depression, but should not be done until baby is three or four weeks old.

Some may question breast milk's healthy attributes due to environmental pollutants that may find their way into a mother's body. According to a 2003 statement issued by the world's foremost authority on breast-feeding support, La Leche League, breast-feeding remains the best choice in a polluted world. The statement says that scientific research consistently finds that even in a world exposed to so many chemicals, breast-feeding offers advantages that outweigh the risk of ingesting contaminants. It also states that the high levels of antioxidants found in breast milk may prove to be essential to compensate for and outweigh the risks of toxic effects from the environment. Sounds to me like working to eliminate toxins from the environment makes more sense than eliminating breast-feeding. (To avoid dioxins in tap water, I switched to filtered water, affordably delivered in five-gallon bottles to my house.) In addition, formula may be contaminated both as a product of the same environment and through manufacturing. Coupled with formula's well-documented nutritional inadequacies, choosing it over breast milk citing environmental reasons alone is misguided. Doing so overlooks how formula itself adds to the ecological burden of the planet.

Nursing Bars, by Rahula Janowski

Anyone who likes to bake or is nursing might find this recipe useful. I made a huge batch during the last week of my pregnancy, individually wrapped them, and stored them in the freezer. They kept me nourished during those two-hour-long nursing sessions, and I try to make them as a birthing present for others. Also, older kids love them, and they're a good on-the-go snack or breakfast. The recipe calls for honey but you can substitute rice or barley malt with decent results. They're good for nursing because oats are good for milk production and nerve-soothing, and the flax and raisins are nutritionally dense, and also because they're easy to have at hand. I always had a few in my diaper bag, a couple next to the bed, a bunch in my nursing station, etc. (This recipe is adapted from a book called *Uprisings*, published in 1983.)

1. Lightly toast 4 cups oats and 1 cup sunflower seeds. It's OK not to toast the oats and seed, but toasting them brings out their flavor nicely.

2. Mix together with 2 cups whole-wheat pastry flour, 4 teaspoons baking powder, 4 teaspoons cinnamon, 2 cups raisins. (Sometimes I use 1 cup raisins and 1 to 2 cups other dried fruit, chopped to raisin size. Apricots and dates are particularly good.)

3. Blend 1/4 cup of flaxseeds with 3/4 cup water until goopy.

4. Mix with 1 cup safflower oil (or canola or other light oil), 1 1/2 cup honey (I've used barley malt with OK results—less sweet but vegan!), 1/2 cup water, 1 teaspoon vanilla.

5. Mix the wet stuff into the dry stuff.

6. Drop ½-cup sizes onto a cookie sheet and bake at 350° F for 20 to 25 minutes.

I like the way these come out as cookies. They have crisp edges, which is nice. But if I'm making nursing bars, I usually double or triple the recipe, and then bake them in a cake pan (well, several pans), spreading them about a half-inch thick, and baking for maybe a bit longer (as soon as they start to brown around the edges, take them out), and then cutting them into one-by-two-inch bars. I also like to individually wrap them or pack them one or two to a plastic bag; it's a bit wasteful but it's also perfect for nursing moms. You can tote a few of them around with you at all times, put some in the spots where you nurse, and stash the rest of them in the freezer.

A Breast-Feeding Manifesto

To all those punk mamas-to-be and brand-new rad mamas:

Breast-feed your babies. Breast-feed other people's babies if the need arises. Get help from knowledgeable women—lactation consultants, midwives, breast-feeding mothers.

Do it all the time when your baby is a newborn. It will probably be more physical contact with one person than you have ever had in your whole life, even if you are a sex fiend or one of those people who is constantly hugging everyone. This is good for your baby and good for you.

Make up stupid names for your breasts, for the milk that comes out of them, for the act of nursing, like "ninnies," "milkies," "nippies," "nunus." It will help you on your way to clowndom, and the sillier you act, the more your baby will laugh.

Teach your baby sign language for milk and when annoying people are holding your baby, subtly make the sign. Sweetly say, "My baby needs me now" when your kid lunges at your chest.

Breast-feed in front of all your guy friends, who are surely enlightened feminists anyway. If they're not, then school them. You never know when one of your supposed progressive-thinking punk friends will get all uptight because he sees your uncovered tit being used for what nature intended. Yes, it's happened, so be prepared to squirt them in the eye all the way across the room!

Breast-feed in front of all your girlfriends so they'll get over any timidity they may have. When I was pregnant, one of my closest friends admitted that the sight of women nursing their babies grossed her out. I said, "Better get used to it if you want to hang out with me." Today she doesn't even bat an eye or pause her conversation when I bust out the good stuff for my daughter.

Get lazy; you're lactating after all. Take it easy. Read a book with one hand while your kid is still little and grublike enough not to notice. Listen to records when they are old enough to grab a book out of your hand. Once they are old enough for you to be chasing them around all day, take naps while nursing.

Educate the people you live with about what nursing is like and that you may get severely thirsty while breast-feeding. A true friend is one who brings a glass of water, unasked, at the sight of... (cont'd)

Support for Breast-Feeding Mamas

Through the trials, I learned that exclusive breast-feeding is a commitment, one that cannot succeed without support for the mother-and-baby nursing team. I was fortunate to have had access to an in-hospital lactation consultant, midwives, and La Leche League to help along our success. But it takes even more support than that. The support from those involved in our daily lives is required, too.

Non-breast feeding partners and family members can feel left out of the baby-bonding experience. Even with pumping and caretakers other than mama nursing the baby, exclusive breast-feeding makes it hard for couples to split childcare 50/50. (Pumping takes time and patience, too!) To a large extent, this is a biological reality, and it shouldn't be snubbed just because 50/50 childcare isn't happening the first six months or so. However, there are ways for partners and other caretakers to be an integral part of the team. There are ways to support exclusive breast-feeding that lessen the sexual division of domestic labor when caring for a newborn. Bringing water and nourishing snacks to the breast-feeding mama is one way. Doing anything else that needs doing is another, like getting groceries; washing, folding, and putting away laundry; answering the phone; cleaning the house in general; and the list goes on. If mama is taking care of the baby full-time while papa is away from home at work, papa, don't you dare come home expecting a break. Newborns don't give breaks. There is always something that needs to be done. Also, remain confident that there is still plenty of bonding to be done with baby that's not done through breast-feeding, like changing the baby; holding the baby while mama showers, naps, or goes for a walk; or rocking and singing to the baby.

And never underestimate the power of encouragement. There is a huge difference between being told, "Why are you torturing yourself? Just give the baby some formula. That way you get a break and I get to feed the baby, too." and "I know breast-feeding can be hard. I'm here to help in any way possible. I know how important this is for all of us."

And it *is* important, so important that given what has been discovered about breast milk's superiority in just the last decade alone, it should no longer be viewed as just another lifestyle choice. Clearly, it is an important health choice. There are numerous benefits to both the baby and the breast-feeding mother, benefits that spill over to the family, community, and society. It is worth whatever discomfort or obstacles there are to overcome in the

your baby latching on. If you are having problems take a honeymoon, where you and the baby hang out in bed for a few days sleeping, nursing, and cuddling.

If someone advises you to stop nursing while you are on some medication or taking some herbal formula, call La Leche League and ask them to look it up in Dr. Hale's *Medications and Mother's Milk*. Most medications are less detrimental to your baby diluted in your milk than breaking the nursing relationship would be.

Breast-feed in public. Breast-feed in restaurants. Breast-feed in parks and on college campuses and on the public transit system and in record stores. Do not make a habit of breast-feeding your baby in a toilet stall. While socially acceptable, this is very unsanitary—and who wants their lunch in a toilet stall? If you are asked to leave a place because you are breast-feeding there, show up again tomorrow with a whole posse of breast-feeding mamas and babies and stage a nurse-in.

Take your baby everywhere you can. Take your baby to shows if you want. You might hang out in the parking lot when you realize how loud the music is, but you will still have more fun than staying at home. Take your baby to the movies. You may miss some of the film when your baby stops nursing and starts yelling, but it is still more fun than staying home. Some people act like they expect mamas to stay home until their babies are five years old and well behaved. I say, fuck those people.

Breast-feed with groups of nursing mothers. Think of it as performance art, as role modeling for little girls, as totally natural. Better yet, think of it as subversive, as anti-establishment.

Start a zine about breast-feeding, paint a nursing madonna and child, preface that porno term "jugs" with the "milk-" that it deserves.

Make me proud, mamas.—Kaile "MilkJugs" Adney

Kaile originally wrote this as a contribution to my column in Maximum Rock N Roll, *"My Mother Wears Combat Boots." It was published in issue #214, March 2001. Kaile gave me permission to use it again here, cuz she's cool like that.*

beginning because whether you breast-feed or not, there will still be discomfort and obstacles to overcome as a new parent. Once the breast-feeding relationship is firmly established, parenting through breast-feeding is actually a lot easier.

Though it was painful and difficult in the beginning and took a lot of commitment to keep going even after we got the help and support we needed to learn how
to breast-feed, I'm beyond happy that I was able to breast-feed Emma-Joy successfully. Her excellent health and our bonded nursing relationship are irreplaceable.
I was glad to not spend any money on formula when my body made something
much better and for free. And I really think that breast-feeding wound up being
much easier than formula feeding.

Seeing Emma-Joy's flapping little baby arms and later, as an older baby, her literally applauding hands, hearing her gasps of excitement and the shrieks of happiness come out of her face-wide-smiling and gaping-in-anticipation mouth all told
me that a baby's love of nursing is sheer joy. A warming bonus to the intellectual
knowledge that breast milk is the most perfect food for her and that nursing is the
most perfect way to relate to my baby while learning how to be her mother.

6.

The Family Bed Controversy

We called our king-sized mattress our nest. Resting on its box springs (a frame would have held it too high above the floor), pushed up snuggly into a corner of our bedroom, it provided us with the perfect retreat to slumberland. And snuggle-land.

Never did it cross our minds that by following Ernesto's natural primal instinct to keep Emma-Joy close to us during sleep time, we would land in the middle of such a hot topic of controversy in the baby-care world. After all, according to Jeananda Col in Enchanted Learning (www.EnchantedLearning.com), "Each evening, chimpanzees construct a fresh 'sleeping nest' in the trees where they will curl up and sleep. These bowl-shaped nests are made out of leaves and other plant material. Nests are only shared by mother and her nursing offspring." True, we weren't tree dwelling. And also true that Emma-Joy and I weren't kicking Ernesto out of the nest. But still, if our closest primate relatives were co-sleeping, it didn't seem far off that we would, too. Evelyn B. Thoman writes in *Sleep Medicine Reviews*, "Co-sleeping—infants sharing the mother's sleep space—has prevailed throughout human evolution, and continued over the centuries of western civilization despite controversy and blame of co-sleeping mothers for the deaths of their infants." Plus, we knew that baby cribs didn't appear on the market until around 1750 and that up until then, babies slept with their parents.

But we learned from Emma-Joy's pediatrician that bed sharing between an infant and adult(s) is a highly controversial practice. During the normal round of questions at one of Emma-Joy's well-baby visits, the pediatrician asked us where the baby sleeps. We answered, "In our bed with us." The pediatrician didn't raise her eyebrows at us, said of course it was our choice, but she did let us know that the American Academy of Pediatrics (AAP) recommended against co-sleeping.

We of course asked, "Why?" She answered something about danger of suffocation, another something about SIDS (Sudden Infant Death Syndrome, the sudden death of an infant under one year of age), and gave us a one-page handout on the topic. She added that she'd recently read a new report (published in March 2000) on a large study of over 10,000 mother-infant pairs conducted by experts from the Medical College of Ohio and other pediatric institutions, which found that new moms who breast-feed their babies are three times more likely to share a bed with their infant and that the data did not link the behavior to increased risk of SIDS. She informed us that breast-feeding and co-sleeping rates are going up, SIDS rates are doing down thanks to the Back to Sleep campaign, and taking the AAP's recommendation into account, we should do our own research so we could make a more informed choice. Then she added, "But as your pediatrician, I'm obligated to advise you according to the AAP's current recommendations."

We left that appointment not thinking we were going to immediately change up our sleeping arrangements, but, instead, questioned the actual level of danger co-sleeping posed, how the danger of sleeping separately in a bassinet or crib compared, and how sleeping separately would effect nighttime breast-feeding and how much sleep we got.

So far, our co-sleeping had been done quite comfortably and since we'd apparently been doing so safely, we had no reason to jump into sleeping separately as the AAP Task Force on Infant Sleep Position and Sudden Infant Death Syndrome recommended as part of its March 2000 policy statement, "Changing Concepts of Sudden Infant Death Syndrome: Implications for Infant Sleeping Environment and Sleep Position." "A crib that conforms to the safety standards of the Consumer Product Safety Commission and the ASTM (formerly the American Society for Testing and Materials) is a desirable sleeping environment for infants... Bed sharing or co-sleeping may be hazardous under certain conditions." (To read the AAP's entire 2000 policy statement, visit http://aappolicy.aappublications.org/cgi/content/full/pediatrics;105/3/650.) Plus, we learned that 900 babies die each year in cribs, and in the last twenty-five years there have been thirty-six crib recalls.

With the amount of breast-feeding Emma-Joy was doing at night, I wondered how in the hell parents who slept

> **THE MOTHER–BABY BEHAVIORAL SLEEP LABORATORY**
>
> The Mother-Baby Behavioral Sleep Laboratory at the University of Notre Dame, headed by James Mc Kenna, Ph.D., is a great source of very interesting information! Visit www.nd.edu/~jmckenn1/lab/index.html for FAQs on advantages to co-sleeping, long-term effects of co-sleeping, videos of interviews and lectures, essays, articles, and responses to the AAP's most current policy statement (from 2005).

separate from their babies got any sleep at all. I was short on a full night's sleep already and could not imagine having to actually get up, walk to where the baby was crying, pick her up, nurse her, and hope she would stay asleep when I put her back down before retreating to my own bed. How in the world would that tired-ass ritual promote the breast-feeding relationship? I didn't need any more obstacles in that department; it took great effort to get over the ones we had in the beginning weeks. While co-sleeping, when Emma-Joy wanted to nurse in the night, neither of us had to fully wake up. She'd wiggle and grunt her rooting mouth towards my breast. I'd respond by positioning myself closer to her so she could latch on. For us,

THE SHORT-TERM BENEFITS FOR CO-SLEEPING MOTHERS AND BABIES

According to several researchers and the World Health Organization, there are numerous short-term benefits for both mother and babies who sleep together.

- Short-term benefits for mothers: more sleep; increased sensitization to infant's physiological-social status; increased comfort with and ability to interpret behavioral cues of infant; increased sucking behavior of infant, which maintains milk supply; increased prolactin levels, which leads to longer birth interval (time between pregnancies); increased ability to monitor and physically manage and respond to infant needs; and more time with baby for working parents
- Short-term benefits for babies: increased breast-feeding; increased sleep duration; less crying time; increased sensitivity to mother's communication; more light sleep and less deep sleep appropriate for age; and increased ability to read maternal behavioral cues

learning to nurse while lying down had so far been the easiest nursing position to learn. This allowed us to fall back asleep quickly; she didn't have to wake herself up more to cry in order to wake me up, and I didn't have to wake myself up more to get up out of bed in order to nurse her. More times than not, because co-sleeping aided in synchronizing our sleep cycles, I'd already started to wake a minute before her. This synchronicity gave me added confidence that by having Emma-Joy close to me during sleep, I'd be alerted instantly if she were to stop breathing or if she had somehow gotten covered up—you know, the SIDS alarms. Besides, babies breathe more regularly when in skin contact with the mother. Plus, I could not imagine Emma-Joy tolerating sleeping separately. She had made it perfectly clear that she preferred to sleep with us. She'd screamed bloody murder every time I ever tried to put her down in a bassinet for a nap.

While I researched the controversy surrounding co-sleeping and how it "may be hazardous under certain conditions," we continued to co-sleep. I discovered that the danger of suffocation for a sleeping infant is mostly blamed on waterbeds, sofas, soft mattresses, or other soft surfaces, as well as soft materials and objects in the infant's sleeping environment such as pillows, quilts, comforters, sheepskins, stuffed toys, and loose bedding. Anything that could cover the infant's face accidentally or entrap the baby is considered hazardous. That includes the possibility of overlying; therefore, to lessen this risk, co-sleeping parents should not be intoxicated and other children should not co-sleep with an infant. Safe co-sleeping recommendations, put out by the AAP themselves in its 2000 policy statement, reflect the removal of the above-mentioned suffocation and entrapment hazards, as well as state that baby should be placed in a nonprone sleep position (not on tummy).

SIDS and Co-Sleeping

I discovered that SIDS is a disease of unknown cause and has several individual risk factors. According to the AAP, the following have been consistently identified across studies as independent risk factors for SIDS: prone sleep position, sleeping on a soft surface, maternal smoking during pregnancy, overheating, late or no prenatal care, young maternal age, prematurity and/or low birth weight, and male sex. Consistently higher rates are found in black and American Indian/Alaska Native children—two to three times the national average. Co-sleeping itself was not in that list of independent risk factors, however, the AAP reports, "The risk of SIDS associated with co-sleeping is significantly greater among smokers." This is because whether parents are smoking in the bedroom or not, toxins are respirated out of the smoker's lungs through the night.

I also learned that while there are significant differences in SIDS rates between breast-fed and formula-fed babies, there's no conclusive evidence that breast-feeding itself will reduce the risk of SIDS. That's because the literature on breast-feeding and SIDS is inconsistent. (One thing that experts do agree upon, however, is that no psychological harm comes from co-sleeping.) For example, according to Dr. Linda Folden Palmer, in her book *Baby Matters*, SIDS rates for babies who are exclusively breast-fed and sleep in

OCCURRENCE AND POSSIBLE CAUSES OF SIDS

The occurrence of SIDS is rare during the first month of life, increases to a peak between two and three months old, and then declines. It is generally agreed upon that the risk of SIDS is over by the time the child reaches his or her first birthday. SIDS deaths have decreased by more than 50% since 1992 (down to well below 1 per 1,000 live births), the year the AAP released its recommendation that infants be placed down for sleep in a nonprone position. (Interestingly, according to the National Infant Sleep Position Study led by the National Institutes of Health, the number of adults routinely sharing a bed with an infant more than doubled between 1993 and 2000.) It is generally accepted that SIDS may be a reflection of a variety of causes of death. According to the AAP in its 2005 policy statement, "The predominant hypothesis regarding the etiology of SIDS remains that certain infants, for reasons yet to be determined, may have a maldevelopment or delay in maturation of the brainstem neural network that is responsible for arousal and affects the physiologic responses to life-threatening challenges during sleep. Recent examinations of the brainstems of infants who died of SIDS have revealed unique deficits in serotonin receptors in a network of neurons throughout the ventral medulla." In addition, some behavioral studies have demonstrated that infants have more arousals and less slow-wave sleep during bed sharing. Though no epidemiologic evidence exists that bed-sharing is protective against SIDS, in the near future, it might be discovered that it is indeed when done safely and with already-known individual risk factors removed.

a nonprone position in safe beds with sober, nonsmoking parents, are around one-fifth the rates seen with the standard crib-sleeping, formula-feeding scenario. She says, "The practice of room-sharing or breast-feeding alone cuts SIDS rates considerably. When combined with safe co-sleeping, the infant survival chances are even higher." But an article published in the *British Medical Journal* in 1995, "Bottle Feeding and the Sudden Infant Death Syndrome," concluded that bottle (formula) feeding was not a significant independent risk factor for SIDS. The article is a summary of the results of seventeen case-control and one cohort study that analyzed feeding methods in relation to SIDS. Eleven showed an increased risk of SIDS in bottle-fed babies, and seven showed no relationship. These inconsistent findings between breast-fed and formula-fed babies are related to different ways of measuring feeding

THE AAP REVISED ITS POLICY, AND SO DID FERBER!

Richard Ferber, author of the 1985 best-seller *Solve Your Child's Sleep Problems*, provoked strong reactions with his "Ferberizing" method—training a child to "sleep through the night" with incremental bouts of crying. Proponents of co-sleeping and gentle discipline called him "the sleep Nazi," and criticized him for promoting the idea that the problem is with the child instead of the parent, and for setting up unrealistic expectations since "sleeping through the night" for a child really means a five-hour stretch, not an eight-hour one. In the May 29, 2006, edition of *Newsweek*, Ferber said in the article "The Little One Said 'Roll Over,'" that he wishes he never wrote this one sentence: "Sleeping alone is an important part of [your child's] learning to be able to separate from you without anxiety and to see himself as an independent individual." In the 2006 edition of his book, he omitted the sentence. Joining the rest of his pediatric sleep-expert colleagues, he does not believe there are psychological consequences of co-sleeping. He now writes, "Whatever you want to do, whatever you feel comfortable doing, is the right thing to do, *as long as it works*." The fact that Ferber now accepts, if not embraces, bed sharing is encouraging to those who hope that other experts and mainstream medical organizations will also change their stances as more information on co-sleeping's safety and advantages are discovered.

and of considering potential confounding factors, such as socioeconomic variables.

Interestingly, while the literature on breast-feeding and SIDS is inconsistent, researchers do agree that breast-feeding is the superior feeding method and there are numerous ongoing campaigns to increase breast-feeding rates across the board. Therefore, breast-feeding interventions like sleeping separately, which are promoted through warnings, lack appropriate substantiation. For example, consider the title alone of this Consumer Product Safety Commission (CPSC) report, "CPSC Warns Against Placing Babies in Adult Beds." Hearing the title alone, a parent might become unnecessarily alarmed, as there is no differentiation made between safe and unsafe adult bed-sleeping practices. If reports like these, which are essentially warning against all co-sleeping, are ultimately undermining breast-feeding success, then a great disservice has been committed. More responsible warnings would use their source's statistics to include information on the comparative risks of exclusively breast-fed babies, co-sleeping in a safe family bed with

CO-SLEEPING PROMOTES BREAST-FEEDING!

Co-sleeping means that night nursing will be more comfortable than having to get up and nurse in a chair or sofa. This is probably the reason why co-sleeping mamas tend to breast-feed for longer than those who don't. There is a great UNICEF leaflet in PDF format, ready to print out, titled "Sharing a Bed With Your Baby: A Guide for Breast-feeding Mothers" (revised June 2005), found online at www.babyfriendly.org.uk.

nonsmoking, sober parents, and include a statement acknowledging that co-sleeping has been shown to promote breast-feeding. Additionally, warnings that lack appropriate substantiation could have the opposite effect. A proponent of co-sleeping, Dr. James McKenna, who runs the Mother-Baby Behavioral Sleep Laboratory says, "A sweeping recommendation against bed-sharing could be dangerous. People will go underground and not do it safely."

In November 2005, the AAP revised its March 2000 policy statement, updating its recommendations aimed at reducing SIDS. The 2005 policy reviews and updates its previous recommendations in several areas, including bed sharing. The new recommendation, "A separate but proximate sleeping environment is recommended: The risk of SIDS has been shown to be reduced when the infant sleeps in the same room as the mother," has been a source of controversy among breast-feeding advocates because it discourages the practice of bed-sharing, or co-sleeping. According to a recent editor's note in the *Journal of Human Lactation*, "Lactation advocates fear that the recommendation may discourage mothers from breast-feeding... It has been argued that sleep environments are so widely varied that it is impossible to provide a universal recommendation either for or against bed sharing and that individual resources and circumstances must always

TEACH YOUR BABY HOW TO GET DOWN OFF THE BED SAFELY

Once your baby starts crawling, the beelines made to the edge of the bed get faster and faster. Help your baby not fall on his or her head! (You've already started helping by losing the bed frame that makes your bed too tall, right?) When baby gets close to the edge, gently turn its body around and guide it down, feet first, off the bed. Do this every time it crawls to get off the bed. In a couple months, it'll get it! It's so fun to see baby turn itself around and head down backwards, feet first, gently to the floor without you. And it's great when baby applies this learned skill to other could-fall-on-my-head situations like couches, stairs, and playground equipment. Other parents who haven't taught their babies this handy trick will be impressed when they see your little carefully crawling critter scooting backwards to get down off things without landing on its head, and will want to know how you did it!

be considered." While the AAP's advocating for sleeping in the same room as the infant is viewed as a new and positive step for many care providers, it is possible that future discoveries about the behavioral and biological factors that result in SIDS death will necessitate the AAP's reconsideration of their recommendations once again, for even more positive steps towards promoting breast-feeding through co-sleeping. (To read the AAP's entire 2005 policy statement, visit http://pediatrics.aappublications.org/cgi/content/full/116/5/1245.)

Still, some experts are not waiting around for the next AAP recommendation. They actively encourage bed-sharing as it promotes attachment, listening and responding to your baby's needs, breast-feeding, better night's sleep, babies thriving, and catch-up bonding for those who got a slower start. In *The Baby Book*, Dr. William and Martha Sears write, "Is it all right to let your baby sleep in your bed? Yes! It is not only all right, this is where we believe babies belong." In *Natural Family Living: The Mothering Magazine Guide to Parenting*, Peggy O'Mara writes, "For working mothers especially, sharing sleep with the baby can be a lifesaver. You will get more sleep, and nighttime feedings will boost your milk supply."

> **BUT WHAT ABOUT INTIMACY?**
>
> Co-sleeping parents' sex lives needn't suffer! First of all, babies won't have any idea what all that bumpin' and moanin' are all about. But when they do get old enough to start mimicking behaviors they've seen, it's time to get creative. Who ever said sex is just for the bedroom? Visit other rooms in the house. Set up a "date" futon somewhere. Get it on in the shower. The living room floor. Get cookin' on the stovetop. (But be careful to not turn on a burner by accident—ouch!)

We wound up making an informed decision to continue to co-sleep, sticking with centuries of ancestral wisdom and common practice. We'd been careful to set up a safe family-bed environment and none of the other individual risk factors applied to us. We kept our king-sized mattress on its box springs on the floor without a frame so it wouldn't be too tall. Ernesto and I each used individual sheets or blankets so none would drape over Emma-Joy between us. She didn't like to be covered with a blanket anyway, so we dressed her in pajamas that would keep her comfy, not too hot or cold. She didn't sleep on a pillow. She slept snuggly between us, one arm outstretched to be in contact with Ernesto; the other kept me in close range. I'd roll over to nurse when she needed me to and we continued to get more sleep than if we'd both have to fully wake to nurse elsewhere. Our family bed provided the perfect setting for bringing up a cage-free baby, one who, once able, had the freedom to get up and out when she needed to, one whose needs were responded to quickly and therefore, respectfully. It was perfect for us and remains so. It's monkey-see, monkey-do with us, knowing it's what our species has literally done forever, human babies having the longest period of dependency of any species.

7.

Babywearing

I was first introduced to the idea of carrying my baby on me in a sling by the midwives and birth educator involved in my prenatal care. I really got attached to it when Emma-Joy's needs dictated that she be carried on me that way, instead of lugged around separate from me in the plastic bucket baby carrier that doubled as her infant car seat.

When running a few errands with her, Emma-Joy wouldn't last five minutes before she began to fuss if she were strapped in her car-seat-turned-baby-carrier. When I transitioned to wearing her on me in a sling—when she was about two and a half months old—she tolerated being out and about for much longer periods.

It was immediately obvious that she preferred to be carried on me than separate from me. I should have already known this because her behavior at home had been similar. She did not want to be sitting separate from me in a bouncy seat. She wanted to be in my arms.

The kind of sling I used was a simple one that my Aunt Laurel had sent me, called an Over the Shoulder Baby Holder, a rectangular piece of fabric with a loop sewn around two rings at one end. The other tail end of the fabric was left alone, easily able to be secured around me through the two rings. A small amount of padding had been sewn into the fabric's edges for extra security and comfort.

Still-newborn Emma-Joy was so secure and cuddly in there. As she gently bounced against my chest and belly while I walked, she'd be rocked to sleep. She was close enough to hear my heartbeat and feel my body breathing. It dawned on me that she was feeling the same exact walking, heartbeat, and breathing movements she did while in my womb. These movements were familiar to her, so of course being in the sling comforted her more than being carried in a hard, plastic baby carrier did.

Because she was happier, more soothed, and calmer being carried this way, I became more soothed and calmer, too. I became far less anxious going the grocery store or running other errands because Emma-Joy was less likely to cry to be held. When she did fuss while in the sling, it was amazingly easy to get her attached to my breast so she could nurse while still in there. I could pull one edge of the fabric up for added cover-up if I wanted, and my hands remained free to go about doing whatever it was I needed to get done. I started wearing her in a sling while at home, too. It was suddenly easier to make myself something to eat or dig around in the garden. Because the sling I was using just slipped on and off over my head without any straps or buckles, it was convenient to lift her up and off of me when she fell asleep and I wanted to lay her down.

In addition to the immediate personal benefits I experienced by carrying my baby in a sling, I found out there were other health and psychological benefits for both babies and their caregivers. I learned that carrying helps babies cry less, thrive better, learn more, and develop motor skills. And it helped me exercise—it was like lifting weights and walking at the same time! Slings can be an excellent bonding tool for dads, grandparents, and other caregivers, especially if they are feeling left out because of the exclusive breast-feeding relationship between mama and baby. For older babies and toddlers, slings provide an emotional safety net to retreat to, because exploring on their own—crawling or walking—can easily be overstimulating.

Carry your baby in a sling often enough, and you will hear "Is that safe?" from complete strangers more times than you ever care to. Another frequent question was "Aren't you scared you're going to drop her?" to which I'd reply, "If I were, I wouldn't be carrying her this way." If I were in a good mood, I'd add, "Besides, those plastic bucket-like carriers are much bulkier and heavier, much easier to drop than my baby snug in her sling."

The truth of the matter is that most of the reported babywearing-related accidents are due to the wearer tripping and falling. Therefore, it's important to develop the reflex of holding and protecting your baby when something unexpected like a trip or fall happens. (Don't let the possibility of tripping and falling deter you from babywearing, though. Babywearing does not lead you to more trips and falls, something that you probably don't do a lot of anyway, right? Babywearing is safer than crossing the street! And I don't know about you, but I prefer having my baby attached to me when crossing a street rather than out in front of me, being pushed in a separate stroller.) I will never forget the time I saw a mama out in public miss the last step of the stairs she was walking down. Thanks to her catlike reflexes, she was able to break her fall and roll onto her back, totally saving her baby from a belly-flop squishing. After she was helped up, everyone around her applauded, me included. It was an amazing save.

Another cause of a large subset of baby-carrier accidents is that babies are sometimes left sitting in frame backpacks, which can topple over when bumped or when the baby moves. So if you carry your baby in a frame backpack, when you take baby and pack off together, stay close enough to ensure that both stay upright.

For the mobile set—older babies and toddlers—babywearing may even be safer. Instead of running loose in crowded or dangerous places, a child in a sling is held safe and secure right next to your body. I was downright thankful for my sling many times in airports and on public transportation.

I learned that there are more ways to carry a baby in a sling than the one cradle hold I was using. As she developed some neck-muscle control, which carrying her in a sling actually helped with (as it did with warding off flat-head syndrome like some babies who are in plastic carriers too long develop), I could carry her facing outward with her back against my chest, her little baby legs tucked up in front of her in the pouch-like sling. As an older baby and toddler (most slings accommodate children up to thirty-five or forty pounds), she could ride on my hip or my back with her little butt sitting in the sling, with her legs dangling out.

Carrying Options

In addition to the type of sling I had, I learned about other carrying options. There are front and back carriers, baby frame backpacks, and wraps. When Emma-Joy got a little older, we got a baby backpack from Ernesto's dad's house that had been sitting around for about 10 years just waiting to be used again. (We waited to use it until she could sit up on her own because I'd learned that using a carrier that forces babies into an upright position too soon isn't good for their spines.) It was the one that Ernesto had used to help carry around his sister Elena, who was born when he was eighteen. Lucky us that it had been saved. We got a lot of use out of that thing. It made hiking with a toddler fun. And it more evenly distributed the added weight than the sling did—great for longer periods of carry time that would have killed my shoulder had I used a sling.

By doing a simple Internet search using the keywords "baby wearing" or "baby carriers," you can access lots of information on where to get one and how to choose and use one. These two sites are ones I highly recommend as they are the best babywearing sites I've ever seen:

WEARYOURBABY.COM—THE MAMATOTO PROJECT: Detailed information on a wide variety of carriers, numerous online videos, a page of common sense safety reminders, printables on hands-free breast-feeding and making a wrap, and lots of encouragement. From their site: "The Mamatoto Project was created to educate the general public on the advantages of babywearing, and to promote the use of a simple piece of cloth as a traditional baby sling among those who care for infants and toddlers. We offer how-to guides for babywearing parents and caregivers. We discuss the advantages of babywearing with doctors, doulas, midwives and other health care professionals. We help coordinate babywearing classes and events. We coordinate the efforts of babywearing lovers to get wider coverage of babywearing in books, magazines, and television. "Mamatoto" is Swahili for the mother-baby unit. In that culture, babies are never seen apart from their mothers, so the two are considered one."

THEBABYWEARER.COM: Here you will find chatrooms and forums to discuss and exchange information about babywearing, learn babywearing terms, find information and article links, learn how to choose the right baby carrier for you, read tips on special babywearing situations like twins and babywearing while pregnant, and more. Cool babywearing DIY links, too!

Learning from Babywearing

Of course, we did have to put her down sometimes. In learning to respond to her needs, we were learning how to balance our own. By doing that, we adjusted our thinking, too, about what babies are like. Instead of just picking her up for intervals between "downtime"—those intervals determined by her fussiness—and holding her just long enough to make the fussiness go away, we carried her lots and put her down when we needed to attend to our personal needs—intervals between the "on us" time.

Over time, we noticed that the amount of time we carried her naturally decreased as she increased in age and motor skills. She would use body language to signal her need to get down, just as she would signal her desire to be carried. As in any mutually respectful relationship, we too signaled our need for her to get down or up accordingly. Though the times that she needed to be carried or put down didn't match our needs to carry or not carry 100% of the time (for example, if she signaled to be put down to explore a mud puddle while in the middle of the street, or we needed to put her down because we had to drain the boiling pasta), we got through relatively amicably.

Carrying Emma-Joy, in addition to breast-feeding on demand and co-sleeping, was the third ingredient in the recipe called "attachment parenting." We didn't

WHERE THE TERM "BABYWEARING" COMES FROM

"Babywearing" is a term that was originated in the 1980s by a pediatrician, Dr. William Sears, father of eight children and author of several books on attachment parenting. He came up with the term after observing women in other cultures, from Bali to Zambia, carrying their babies all day in a sling, carrying on centuries of tradition. When he interviewed mothers to find out why they wore their babies most of the time, they answered, " It's good for the baby," and "It makes life easier for the mother."

These sentiments reflect what psychotherapist Jean Liedloff, author of *The Continuum Concept*, observed while spending two and a half years deep in the South American jungle with the Yequana tribe.

According to her, "In order to achieve optimal physical, mental and emotional development, human beings—especially babies—require the kind of experience to which our species adapted during the long process of our evolution." For infants, these experiences include constant physical contact, which includes co-sleeping and being carried in arms; breast-feeding "on cue"; caregivers being immediately responsive to signals "without judgment, displeasure, or invalidation of his needs, yet showing no undue concern nor making him the constant center of attention"; and "sensing (and fulfilling) his elders' expectations that he is innately social and cooperative and has strong self-preservation instincts, and that he is welcome and worthy." For more information on the continuum concept, visit www.continuum-concept.org.

know what it was but we were doing it. I first heard the term used by another mama at a meeting of the Wiggly Baby Society—the weekly potluck lunch gathering for new parents and their babies at the Gainesville Birth Center—when Emma-Joy was about six months old. And when I did hear it, I was happy because that meant here were a group of others to share experiences with and learn more from.

Peggy O'Mara, in her book *Natural Family Living: The Mothering Magazine Guide to Parenting*, writes, "Coined in the early Nineties, the phrase 'attachment parenting' describes what is actually the oldest form of child-rearing, the form practiced by most cultures around the world." It has also been referred to as "responsive" or "in arms" parenting. Attached, responsive, in arms, or whatever else it could be called, we'd joined a global tradition.

We'd been taking this approach because we felt that we were better at responding to Emma-Joy's needs by doing so. And it felt easier and more natural than the mainstream consumer-culture's approaches of using things like plastic baby carriers, bouncy seats, and cribs, which kept us separated. Emma-Joy had let us know consistently and early on that those separating approaches weren't going to work for her. Through more contact, we improved our ability to read her signals, and were therefore able to become more responsive to her needs, helping us to not only meet her basic needs but also to build mutual trust and respect. Our recipe felt like the beginning seeds of practicing what was right and just.

Tips for Safe Babywearing for Both You and Baby

1. Choose the right carrier both for your size and your baby's age.

2. Practice different carrying positions first with a stuffed animal or doll. Back carries are the trickiest to learn.

3. Wear your carrier correctly so it's comfortable. Your body will thank you.

4. Switch positions/swap shoulders. Your body will thank you for this, too, especially if you're wearing your baby for long periods.

5. Work your way up to wearing your baby for long periods. Again, your body will thank you for the gradual build up in endurance.

6. Support your baby with your arm until you've gained confidence in wearing her. Continue to support your baby whenever you bend over.

THE DIY BABY CARRIER: SEW ONE YOURSELF!

1. Don't like to sew? So what!? To make a wrap, all you need is a twelve-foot-long piece of fabric. (And some patience in learning how to use it. For wrap carrier instructions, you can visit www.pookababy.com/101/instructions.html or www.mobywrap.com/instructions.php.) To make a no-sew pouch, all you need is an old T-shirt that's too small for you, with the sleeves and top cut off under the armpits. You can even improvise a sling by using a hoodie or a bed sheet! Check this out for bed-sheet instructions: www.jenrose.com/sling/slingtxt.htm.

2. You're OK with sewing? There are patterns galore, with simple step-by-step instructions available for free at www.wearyourbaby.com (click "Make A Carrier"), www.thebabywearer.com (click "Babywearing DIY links"), or do an Internet search to find more using the keywords "baby sling patterns."

7. Check the seams, buckles, and straps regularly.

8. Don't use a baby carrier while you're in a moving car. Always use a properly installed car seat instead.

9. Don't cook with heat or handle hot liquids while wearing your baby on your front or hip. If your baby is on your back, be careful. Also while cooking, watch out for curious grabbing hands around the knives, glasses, spices, and hot peppers!

10. Above all, use your common sense!

8.

Virtues of Cloth Diapering

A young punk boy once wrote me a letter, not because he was a parent, but because he wanted to know whether I used cloth diapers for my daughter. He said that his mother had used cloth diapers for him and his siblings, except when they were traveling, and that he thought cloth diapers were cool because the disposable ones were a waste of resources.

I told him that like his mom, I also used cloth diapers at home and around town, and sometimes disposables when traveling. When I was about seven months pregnant and getting into "nesting" mode, I started collecting all the essentials for taking care of a newborn and, of course, the question of diapering needed to be answered. I automatically thought of using cloth because the disposables did seem wasteful, no pun intended. During my investigation into the matter of how a cloth diaper even works, I found out more about what's wrong with disposable diapers.

It takes time to get the hang of cloth diapering; I really had no idea what to do with the two packages of birdseye-weave prefold cloth diapers that two of our punk friends, Cave Dave (aka Replay) and Radio Dave, had gifted us at our baby shower. As a sleep-deprived new mama, I really could have done without the cloth-diaper trials and errors, but I'm stubborn and didn't want to give up too soon. Once I got the hang of it, I found that using cloth was just as easy as using disposables and they are definitely easier on the wallet, not to mention on the planet, on baby's bum, and on potty training. (Since cloth diapering leads to more frequent diaper changing, your little one may potty-train early, or at least easier. That's because your child can better feel when they have peed; they are not artificially removed from the consequence, which helps immensely in the potty-training arena.)

With that said, I do understand why a lot of parents choose to use disposables. When you've got to change a baby's diaper twelve to fifteen times a day, on average, during the newborn months, on top of all the other sleepless childcare duties, the last thing you want to do is have to wash them, too. Ariel Gore, in her book *The Hip Mama Survival Guide*, said it perfectly, "Don't you think it's just a wee bit fishy that when we all decided we had to save the world, the first people expected to give up their conveniences were us moms? When it became a question of my sanity or some shit covered in plastic in a landfill forever—call me a polluter—my sanity won out."

So, if you are able to deal with the initial extra work and won't take it out on your sweet little punkin, here's some information I uncovered that helped me commit to using cloth diapers. Plus, if you have a partner, like I do, who recognizes that I did all the physical work to carry the baby for more than nine months, plus the actual birthing and now breast-feeding, you can negotiate for diaper washing to be his or her job. You'll still have to deal now and then with carrying a dirty one in your backpack until you get home and with scraping the shitty ones into the toilet, but at least you won't have to haul that stinky diaper pail to the laundromat twice a week, if you're like us and don't have a washer and dryer at home.

First, most disposables today consist of a "cloth-like" outer layer, an inner layer made of wood pulp, and a water-repellent layer. Many brands have added fragrances and perfumes as well. There have been hundreds of complaints made to the U.S. Consumer Product Safety Commission about rashes and allergic reactions to chemicals, perfumes, and plastics, as well as injury, though rare, due to foreign objects like wood splinters and metal scraps found in diapers themselves.

There is no safe way to dispose of them. You can't just flush them down the toilet. Most people simply toss the pissed-in and shat-in diapers into the garbage. Throwing them in the trash adds more than 4,275,000 tons to landfills each year, the equivalent of over 18 billion diapers and about 84 million pounds of raw poo to the environment each year. I bet you didn't know that putting raw poo in the garbage is an act made illegal by U.S. Code Title 42 Chapter 82!

Viruses from human feces, including live vaccines from routine childhood immunizations—among them live polio—have been recovered from landfills. Approximately one-third of the solid waste of small-town America consists solely of disposable diapers. No long-term studies have been done to evaluate the potential effects that disposables' leachate, liquid that may leak from a landfill, has on our ecosystem. Cloth diapers use less renewable and nonrenewable resources at all levels of production and use than do disposables.

Calling them "disposable" really isn't accurate. They are nonbiodegradable and will be around forever. Some estimates are that 30% of the United States' non-biodegradable garbage is disposable diapers. Of course, you can use the "green-friendly" types of disposables that are biodegradable and chemical-free, but they are more expensive and can be hard to find unless you're shopping in a bigger health food-type store. (The Nature Boy and Girl disposable-diaper brand, based on a Swedish invention, is made of a corn-based material and are compostable/biodegradable in six months. The cheapest place to get them is online with free shipping at http://natureboyandgirl.net.) The regular ones are expensive enough. During the two to three years that your baby will wear them, they will cost, on average, $3,000 more than using cloth diapers.

In the 1950s, diaper services flourished. Now, because of disposable diapers' popularity, the larger cities and their suburbs are usually the only areas with diaper services. Diaper services are more expensive than home or laundromat launder-ing, but still less expensive than disposable diapers. We didn't have a diaper service where we lived and could not have afforded one anyway, so my partner hauled them to the laundromat about twice a week.

And since I'm talking about diapers, I'll mention diaper rash. In a study of one-month-old babies, those in disposables had three times the number of rashes and ten times the severe rashes than the cloth-diapered babies. Another study reports that only 7% of cloth-diapered babies experience diaper rash, compared with 78% of disposable-diapered babies. That's because most rashes are caused by wetness, heat, and/or chemicals on baby's delicate skin. The chemicals used in disposables that make them extra absorbent—often sodium polyacrylate—form a gel that when wet touches your babies delicate skin and can cause irritation. The chemically derived extra absorbency tends to lead to fewer diaper changes, there-by allowing baby to sit in a stew of the three main diaper-rash culprits. Disposables do not allow for the breathability that cloth does, causing a moist and increased-temperature environment in the diaper, a prime breeding ground for bacteria and yeast, two more rash-causing culprits.

But if you do have to deal with diaper rash, the best cure for it is fresh air! If you've got wood or tile floors and can handle a little mop-up action every now and then, allow baby some nudie-kazoodie time each day. Have them naked when outside! And don't use powder with talc! Talc is no good for baby! Since the early 1980s, several thousand babies each year have died or become seriously ill with pneumonia and/or inflammation (swelling) of the airways following accidental in-halation of baby powder. And its connection to cancer remains uncertain; some studies suggest that a specific link to talc exposure and cancer has not been established, while others, like the Cancer Prevention Coalition, assert that talc particles cause tumors in human ovaries and lungs. Instead, arrowroot powder is a good alternative. Though many a mama swears by it, cornstarch may make a yeast rash worse, and babies have lots of chub folds that yeast loves to thrive in. If there's no rash, there's no need to use diaper-rash ointment as a preventative. The best preventative is keeping the diaper area clean, cool, and dry. Unnecessary ointments, while blocking moisture, can also block air circulation. But if you need one to help a rash along, get one that doesn't have any petroleum by-products. We need to have less dependency on nonrenewable resources like oil, don't we? One mama told me that a small amount of freshly expressed breast milk onto her baby's rashy bum, allowed to air dry was helpful. Another reported using olive oil steeped with fresh calendula.

And another money-saving tip: instead of spending extra on disposable baby wipes (save them for traveling), use soft little washcloths with warm water, and launder them along with the diapers (more on this later). And you know to wipe baby girls front to back, right? No one wants potentially infecting poopy bits in their urinary tract!

Until 1961, when Proctor and Gamble introduced Pampers, babies were diapered with reusable cloths. Now, the majority of new parents have never even seen or felt a cloth diaper. Instead, they learn about diapering from magazine and prime-time TV ads. I myself didn't have any idea about using pins, about how to fold a cloth diaper, what kinds of diapers to buy, how I could make them, or how to wash them. So, after some months of trial and much error with different kinds and ways, here's what I learned about the different types and what worked easiest for us.

Types of Cloth Diapers and Covers

PREFOLDS: These are the most economical and are called prefolds because you have to fold the diaper before using it on the baby. They are rectangular pieces of cotton that you can get in different sizes, according to how much your baby weighs. You can keep them on baby with an inexpensive newfangled gadget called a Snappi, a Y-shaped rubber-band sort of thing that grips the diaper in three different spots, instead of diaper pins, so you never have to worry about sticking your wiggly baby with a diaper pin. Prefolds are used with diaper covers, described below.

FITTED/CONTOUR DIAPERS: These are easier to use but cost a bit more than prefolds. These are cut and sewn into a diaper shape so no folding is necessary, unlike the prefolds. Most have Velcro or snap closures. For the ones that don't, use a Snappi. If they have elastic sewn around the leg holes, they'll leak less than prefolds. These too come in different sizes and are used with diaper covers.

ALL-IN-ONES (AIOs): These are the easiest to put on baby because they are a diaper and a cover sewn together all in one piece that usually close with Velcro. They too come in different sizes according to baby's weight and cost about the same as a fitted diaper plus a cover.

POCKET DIAPERS: These are pockets into which you stuff either a prefold or a contoured "stuffer." Most are made with a microfleece "suedecloth" material on the inside that wicks away moisture from baby's bum and with a polyester waterproof outer layer that acts like a diaper cover. Some, like Wonderoos, can be used all the way from newborn to toddler size because of their adjustable snaps. Others come in different sizes, according to baby's weight. Pocket diapers are especially good for overnight soaks because you can stuff them as full as you need to. I recommend hemp cloth stuffers called Wonder-Fulls for overnight use. For daytime use, stuff them lighter for a trimmer fit.

LINERS: Liners are not necessary, but they can help make getting poop into the toilet easier. There are flushable and reusable ones. The flushables do not provide any extra absorbency but act as an extra layer between baby's bum and the diaper for an almost stay-dry effect. The Imse Vimse ones are made of paper pulp and a bit of viscose, a natural polymer made from wood pulp, and are chlorine-free. Some folks wash and reuse these once or twice if they've only been peed in. Reusable ones provide slightly more absorbency but not much because they are thin cotton, silk, or fleece. I made my own by cutting a piece of fleece into nine-by-four-inch rectangles and used them mostly just when I'm out and about to make public restroom poopy-diaper cleanup easier.

DOUBLERS: Doublers add absorbency, making them excellent leak prevention. They are either rectangular or contour shaped, and simply lay into the diaper, though some snap on. Hemp is more absorbent and trimmer than cotton, but 100% cotton terry and fleece or flannel is less expensive and softer. Organic velour offers the absorbency and trimness of hemp, the softness of cotton terry and fleece or flannel, but is the most expensive.

DIAPER COVERS: These are just what they sound like. They cover a cloth diaper, preventing your lap or anything else from getting soggy. You'll also hear them referred to as wraps. Back in the day, you'd hear them called rubber pants. Today's covers allow more breathability, though you can still find the economical, old-school rubber-pants variety. You need fewer of these than you do diapers, as they don't need to be washed every single diaper change. Most covers have Velcro or snap closures, elastic around the leg openings to help prevent leaks, and come in different sizes according to baby's weight. They are commonly made from polyester and urethane laminate. Covers made out of wool, often called wool soakers, are also common, stay cool in summer and warm in winter, and are supremely absorbent.

GREENMOUNTAINDIAPERS.COM AND DIAPERPIN.COM

For further investigation into modern cloth diapering, types and styles available, as well as how to wash and care for them, visit http://greenmountaindiapers.com and http://diaperpin.com. Both of these sites are full of very useful information. GreenMountainDiapers.com even has a downloadable how-to guide.

Quantity and Quality

You will need more newborn-sized diapers than you will any other size, unless you are going with an adjustable one that fits all the way from newborn to toddler-plus size. Generally speaking, two-dozen newborn diapers will do if you wash every other day. From about three to six months, a dozen and a half diapers will do, again if you wash every other day. Starting at around six months, if you're washing every third day, a dozen and a half will do. At no time did we find that we needed more than two dozen when we washed every other day.

As with just about everything, there are different qualities of diapers. There are diaper-service-quality (DSQ) prefolds, made of 100% cotton, which are superior to non-DSQ prefolds. The non-DSQs will *not* stand up to rigorous washing and drying and have less absorbency. Be warned that some of these are not even cotton all the way through; some contain polyester batting in the center strip.

Fitted cloth diapers with elastic stitched around leg openings provide superior leak protection over prefolds, but are more expensive. And another factor that increases cost is material. Cotton is the most economical, while hemp is usually the most expensive. Cotton's absorbency is good, while hemp's is amazing! Finding the balance between quality and expense is key.

How We Did It

At first, we used prefolds because they were the most economical. We simply folded one up into a rectangle shape and then laid it into a diaper cover. We didn't yet know about Snappis or that elastic around the diaper cover's leg openings would help prevent leaks. Let's just say that there were quite a few misfires, the most significant of which involved clueless us at a secondhand store sans a diaper bag, grabbing clearance-rack T-shirts to wipe up the dumpsite.

After learning more about different types of cloth diapers from new mamas I'd met at the Gainesville Birth Center's weekly potluck gathering, and graciously accepting their outgrown hand-me-downs, we found convenience and leak-free diaper days with fitted cotton-terry cloth diapers with snap closures and Bummis covers. Once baby grew into a supreme wiggle monster who hated getting her diaper changed, we switched to Bumkins all-in-ones because, as their name suggests, there are not two separate things to put on, just one that attaches with Velcro with swift ease. Our nights stayed dry by using Wonder-Fulls hemp stuffers stuffed into a Wonderoos pocket diaper. And a word to the wise parents of clever babies who eventually grow into wannabe diaper-free escape artists: put the diapers on backwards so the Velcro or snaps are in the back.

We used a dry diaper pail, kept in the bathroom, with a tight-fitting flip-up lid that opens when you step on a pedal. The peed-in diapers just got tossed in. So did the diaper covers after three to five changes, as needed. The pooped-in diapers got tossed in the toilet to soak a little while. It took us a while to get past the gross-out factor of needing to get our hands in there to wring them out before tossing them into the diaper pail, but we got over it. We just became better hand-washers.

If you just can't get your hands in there for the ol' dunk and swish, there are devices to help you out. One is a Potty Pail and the other is a Diaper Sprayer. The Potty Pail is a prewash system that can also be used as a portable bathroom utility sink. It incorporates a spray hose and a sprayer pail that sit on the toilet. A Diaper Sprayer is just what it sounds like, a small handheld sprayer that you can install yourself in minutes, thereby turning your toilet into a bidet!

In the newborn months, we washed every other day. After that, we washed every third day. You can sprinkle baking soda in your pail with the dirty diapers to control the odors. While the diapers are washing, rinse the pail well and place in the sun with the lid off, not only for a quick dry, but for help with odor and bacteria removal, too.

• To wash, we used half the amount of detergent we normally would for one load. Use detergents that have no phosphates, only minimal additives, and no oils as they will coat your diapers and make them less absorbent. For an extra rinse, we run the diapers a second full cycle sans detergent. Some people prefer to add vinegar to the rinse cycle as it helps get rid of detergent residue. Do not use bleach or fabric softeners as bleach causes premature breaking of the fibers, thereby shortening the life of your dipes, and fabric softener adds a coating to the diapers that make them less absorbent. Plus, bleach is just such a nasty, environmentally unsafe toxic liquid whose residue can cause skin irritation.

• Dry on normal heat for about sixty minutes. To make diapers dry faster, add a dry towel to the dryer. Drying in the dryer helps sterilize the diapers, as does drying in direct sunlight. Direct sunlight also is great at getting out stains!

Where to Get Them

Cloth diapers and diaper covers can be found used for low prices in thrift stores or on Internet auction sites. Believe it or not, cloth diapers are quite popular used items on Internet auction sites, which, if gently used, hold their resale value. Babies, especially newborns, outgrow diapers very quickly, so you won't be using a set of diapers for long. If they are properly taken care of and never bleached, one set of cloth diapers can diaper several babies—another economical reason to use them, especially for people planning on having more than one child. Or you can search for an online store, usually a mama's home business, which sells them new at retail prices.

Buying a few and then using them as a pattern to make more yourself is cheap and relatively easy, too! You can also find premade cloth diaper patterns as well as diaper fabrics for sale in online stores. And wouldn't a few of your punkin's bum covers look darling with a patch from your favorite band sewn on the backside? Create and customize; cloth diapering doesn't have to be boring and shitty!

9.

"Your Life Is About to Change Forever"

I've probably said it more than a thousand times since Emma-Joy's birth and I'll say it again: The oft-written and -spoken words that having a baby changes your life is the understatement of all time.

When I started telling people that I was expecting a baby, they told me this countless times over. For the months that I was pregnant, every time I heard another person tell me this, I'd look at them with the blankest of smiles and nod, thinking to myself, *Yeah, no shit. Of course it's gonna change my life! You don't think I've already thought about that?*

After Emma-Joy was born, I wanted to hunt down every single one of them and shake them like a rag doll and scream, "You said having a baby was going to change my life, but you forgot to tell me what that *really* meant!" I was pissed that I'd been given such short shrift of the truth. I wasn't even given the freaking tip of the iceberg! Was there some secret code of silence among those who knew better so that we expectant parents wouldn't want to bail on our choice to have a baby? If there was, then they all win the tight-lips award because not one of them gave me an ounce of the reality—ahem, change—I was really in for.

If they had, I wouldn't have changed my mind. Not at all. The hormones that had a grip on me were far more powerful than that. I was having a baby on purpose and excited about it, after all! But I would have at least been clued in and the new-mother shock could have been lessened.

Couldn't they have just hinted something along the lines of:

Babies are cute and all, but they're a lot of work and hell on getting anything done. Having one not only changes your life, but life as you know it will be snatched from beneath your feet, ripped from the clutches of your hands, turned around in-

side-out, pulled, twisted, flogged a bit, trampled, shredded, and thrown back at you, landing squarely in your face without being able to recognize anything from your former child-free life, the one you knew so well, the one that you loved, the one that was much, much easier. You are in for the most demanding, exhilarating, and profound experience ever. Babies require all your physical and emotional energy; they are humbling.

At least then I wouldn't have been so freaked out by the sleep deprivation, constant flow of bodily fluids, 24/7 diapering, washing extra clothes, nursing, carrying, rocking, singing, and playing. I would have known I'd have no time for myself. I wouldn't have started a new project just one month before Emma-Joy was born—an oral history book about the Hardback Café in Gainesville that still isn't done—just because I thought I'd need something to keep me busy while she lay around being a newborn.

So I was the moron. I thought I actually knew more than what they were saying, but I didn't have a clue. How could I have even thought that I did? I'm an only child who didn't earn my money growing up by babysitting, and the closest baby in my life was my cousin Alex who was born when I was already an adult and had moved away from home.

So I found out the hard way, by firsthand experience. Now that I think about it, maybe hearing it again and again from random strangers to close family and friends should have been the warning itself. That many people knew what I was in for but didn't have the heart to tell me straight up:

Your self will be put on hold indefinitely. A new self will emerge. And you will be tired. Very, very tired. Oh, you will also have no more social life or if you do still have a little one, it will only be among people who also have a kid. Don't dare pursue the same social life you had with your child-free friends. You will only end up talking about your kid and parenting-related issues and you will feel boring, boring, boring. And more tired. Then you will start to feel jealous and resent that they have free time and you don't. You will long for an occasional uninterrupted, adult conversation. Your wildest dream will be one of a whole entire day to yourself. You will long for just one. You will feel frustration you've never felt before, frustration that the smallest tasks like getting yourself some lunch, taking a shower, or running an errand a block away are now not possible without a lot of juggling. Your heart will feel like it has been ripped out of your chest, wounded with emotional rawness, and pinned to your sleeve, unable to heal, outside your body forever. You will become a new person.

That would have at least given me a clue and an opportunity to say my good-byes to life as I once knew it. But I still would have been unprepared for how it changed me. I'm still figuring that one out. Perhaps the changes will be unrecognizable for years to come. Becoming a new person who's parenting a new person takes time. A lifetime.

One day when Emma-Joy was just a couple months old, I looked long and hard in the mirror and was surprised to see someone I didn't even recognize. Yes, those were my same eyes staring back at me, still green, the same little pug nose, my thin lips. All the parts were there. But the whole picture had changed somehow. The change I'm talking about wasn't just because I had a leaky-boobed, pear-shaped body, either.

Was the difference in how I perceived myself? I wasn't just Jessica anymore. The new me had a new, longer name—Jessica Emma-Joy's Mom. Did I look different to myself because I really was different with all new feelings and hormones and sleep patterns? For a while, I wondered where I was. I didn't quite get it yet that having a baby really did change me in significant ways far beyond the surface-level lifestyle stuff. This was thanks to the crazy new information, thoughts, and hormones more than running around my brain, they were running my brain!

I talked to my midwife about it. She said, "Yes, all these changes are real. When you give birth, you give birth to more than just a baby. Your lifestyle will never be the same. Your body will never be the same; you'll have a different shape, a different cycle. And your outlook, the way you view the world will be different; you've been born into a mother. You see things through a mother's eyes now. From here on out, you're a member of the motherhood club. You know things now that you might not have the words to describe for years. But you know them. You feel them."

Because I didn't quite get it all yet, I was surprised that I felt like she nailed it exactly. She gave me the words to how I'd been feeling. Words that I hadn't learned how to speak yet myself. I was confused, but with her words of wisdom, she helped me a lot. I understood that even if someone had fully forewarned me about the multitude of changes I was in for, I wouldn't have understood what they were saying. It's one of those things that you have to experience for yourself before you can really understand it, and even then it takes a while, even when you're paying close attention.

Before talking to my midwife, it didn't even cross my mind that I had just joined the ranks of scores of women before me. It was all new to me and so I felt my new experiences were unique. She called it the motherhood club. To find out more, I sought out stories written by the club members.

By combing the archives of *Mothering* magazine, hunting my library's shelves for books, and learning about a whole new genre of mama zines, I felt less of an outsider in the club that I'd intentionally signed up for but admittedly knew nothing about.

The stories I read were vast and varied. Countless times I thought to myself, "I could have written that—I know *exactly* what that mama's saying!" I didn't think that because I too had been a poet, playwright, or actress like some of these mamas had been, but because I too was a woman, a mother, a person longing for life beyond nursing, diaper changing, and cooking. I read stories that helped me figure out my new membership. And I read more that showed me that in time, there would be life beyond motherhood.

I wasn't looking for my old life because by then I'd at least learned that it simply did not exist anymore. I was looking for a life that creates new full days, including this new life of the daughter I now have. It was a new challenge because there is no formula for figuring it all out. The one that had been dished out society-wide—the one that says that now that I'm a mother, I'd drop my previous interests and identity, give up my future plans and goals, become a mama martyr else I feel guilty, and settle down for a trip down nuclear-family lane while my male partner brings home the bacon—didn't make sense to me.

Reading other formula-dropping mama's stories showed me that I didn't have to reinvent the wheel; I had to reinvent myself, to take cues from their collective wisdom on how they did it, and have faith that I could find my own way on this journey, too. Even after knowing I wasn't alone, and that what I was feeling was something normal that the majority of new mothers feel, I was overwhelmed that I'd never "find myself" again on this journey of the self. It's a journey you really have to explore with and for yourself, even though time to just yourself, as a mother, is rare. I felt silly feeling lost and alone given the fact that I had advantages of having a partner and a few friends with kids and being part of a community, until I realized that this journey into motherhood is probably the biggest transition I will ever face in my lifetime.

I didn't know where to go from there. Just trying to write was an event itself. When Emma-Joy was four months old, I couldn't get enough hours of uninterrupted time to finish an entire column for *Maximum Rock N Roll*. If I did have a few hours after she went to sleep for the night, I'd have a hard time choosing whether to read, write, get something else done, or go to a show a few blocks from home. I had serious doubts that I'd ever be ready to work again, let alone play music again.

There was never a dull moment during the exhausting daytimes. But, along with the never-ending duties, there was new fun to be had. Imagine getting to spend the early morning lying in bed, playing little baby games, and looking at little baby books. Taking the baby swimming for some exercise. Taking a two-hour nap together. Roller-skating a few miles to and from the downtown farmers' market and Wayward Council, the nonprofit punk-record store, pushing the baby in a red velvet 1950s Italian thrift-shopped pram. Watching Ernesto move the table in the living room so he could playfully circle pit to Naked Aggression with baby swinging in his arms. Watching him rock the baby to sleep so I could start writing.

Time brought confidence and slowly—taking baby steps all the way—the lifestyle shift became more comfortable and less shocking. And I started understanding the person I'd become. Thankfully, the changes felt good and seemed to fit together.

I sleep less and live more. I drink less and feel more. I try harder and communicate more. I'm more fierce and ideal driven, realistic and committed. I listen more and talk less. I give more, share more, and receive more. I cry more and am more careful, yet every day I take chances. I'm more patient, organized, particular, capable, vulnerable, interrupted, and efficient. I'm more honest and learn more and am more creative. I'm more responsible, reliable, and reasonable. I'm pushed to my limits. I got smarter about what really matters, what's true, real, and worthwhile. All of this with less personal time and less sleep and less nightlife.

The Errand-Running Time Warp

Used to be no effort to run a few errands. Send out four or five zine orders, grab a burrito, check a book out from the library. No problem, forty-five minutes.

With a young'un, it takes actual planning to just run those same three little errands around town on my bike: Try to get Emma-Joy dressed without a struggle. Find a snack for her to bring along. Does it look like it's going to rain? Yes? Damn, now I can't do anything because Ernesto's got the car and walking with an umbrella while carrying Emma-Joy is tricky. I can't handle her squirming out of the sling trying to get down into the puddles. And she's not going to stand the rain splashing her little face if we ride the bike. No sign of rain? Good. Now, should I ride the bike and have her in the bike seat, the safest bet, but have to deal with buckling her in and out of the seat over and over and taking her helmet off and on every time to do so? Or should I just ride with her in a sling on my hip to avoid that hassle? That way I'd also have a way to contain her when we get to the very exciting, full-of-things-to-knock-down-and-put-in-her-mouth post office, grocery store, and library. Ugh, at least two hours no matter which way I do it.

I am quicker to organize and get involved with issues that affect my immediate community and less active with every large-scale, far-reaching campaign event under the sun. Surprisingly, I am more comfortable now with behind-the-scenes movement support than being on the front lines organizing, or housing pirate radio, doing food pickups, and tabling.

So I didn't really know what all those people meant when they were saying that having a kid would change my life and I thought I knew how to pare my activities down in order to attentively care for a child. I'm still learning every day how to exchange my former, childless life for a new one, one that has my most unique relationship with a new person-to-date integrated into it, one that doesn't follow a societally scripted for-mula of mom hanging up her spunk.

And yeah, I swore that I wouldn't become one of *those* parents: the ones who constantly talk about their kid and anything else parenting-related, but reality struck me and I quickly learned that becoming a parent leaves you little choice but to be focused on your child. Well, it did for me, anyway, because by talking with others about kid stuff, I learned from their experiences (which is especially helpful when parenting in a unconventional way). Having a parenting relationship with a brand-new person is unique and truly freakin' sweet, fun, and amazing. Therefore, I can (and will, if allowed to) talk forever about all things parenting, and whether that's lame or not is not my concern. And now look at me, writing an entire book about it, sheesh!

Full-On Baby! (4-11 months)

10.

The Baby Gender-Coding Phenomenon

What's the baby supposed to look like? For starters, most people can't just let the baby be a baby; it has to look like a boy or a girl. Gender-coding pressure actually starts before the baby is born. People routinely ask pregnant women if they know yet whether they are having a boy or a girl. When people asked and my response was that I wouldn't know until the baby was born, some would be OK with it, but some, in all seriousness, wanted to know how I would know which color of clothes to buy and how I'd know how to decorate the baby's room. I have to admit that it was kind of fun telling one of my well-meaning, but clueless coworkers that I decorated by selling my drum set.

Of course, after my baby was born a girl, we were gifted with little pink outfits. Lots of them. No big deal; babies grow out of their newborn-sized clothes quickly. And friends who had babies older than ours generously gave us hand-me-downs that were all colors. We dressed Emma-Joy in all the colors we received—pink, blue, and everything in between. But unless she were wearing pink, people—enlightened feminists included—would say, "Hi, you cute little guy!"

At our neighborhood bagel shop, Ernesto and I once overheard three women discussing feminist theory. One, a professor, was explaining to two students how the femme-fatale character always existed outside of the mainstream because the dominant patriarchal paradigm would not allow her existence otherwise. Upon walking past their booth to an empty table, one of them commented on how cute my little boy looked in his baseball cap. Quick on his feet, Ernesto explained that no, our little boy is a little girl and that by dressing her in a light blue shirt and a red and blue hat, we were smashing the dominant gender-coding paradigm and raising a femme fatale of our own. They chuckled.

And, of course, I have mistakenly called a little boy a little girl and vice versa. Feels pretty silly to be guilty of one's own pet peeve, but I realize there's no need to even ask if it's a boy or girl. Just a friendly "Hey there, you cute little baby" will do.

One woman next to me in a grocery checkout line was actually offended when she couldn't tell whether my baby was a boy or a girl. In a huffy tone of voice, she informed the person in line

> ### Sex Versus Gender
>
> Sex is a biological term, used to differentiate between those born with male or female anatomy. Gender is a socially constructed concept of appearance and behavior, powerfully enforced by culture, which delineates between boy and girl. "Gender is a way of making the world secure," says feminist scholar Judith Butler, a rhetoric professor at University of California, Berkeley. Debra Rosenberg writes in "(Rethinking) Gender: What Makes Us Male or Female" (*Newsweek*, May 21, 2007), "Though some scholars like Butler consider gender largely a social construct, others increasingly see it as a complex interplay of biology, genes, hormones and culture."

next to us (loud enough so that I would hear), "Well, when my daughter was a baby, I'd tape a bow to her head so people would know. You just can't tell when the baby's wearing green and purple."

Children's appearance, their clothing and the length of their hair, is only one aspect of gender-coding. Rather, appearance is the catalyst that allows the real gender-coding to occur: how others will interact with your child. In her book *Growing a Girl*, Dr. Barbara Mackoff, a psychologist educated at Harvard University who has worked in various educational and clinical settings, writes that from the moment of birth, the baby's sex is the most important determinant of the way the world responds to him or her.

If people believe they are talking to a baby girl, their voices inevitably shift up an octave, they'll comment on how this or that facial feature is beautiful, call her a heartbreaker, and warn you to get a shotgun come dating age so you can chase the boys away.

If people believe they are talking to a baby boy, their voices stay lowered, they'll predict his future as a linebacker, tell him he's handsome, and if the baby grips their finger, praise his strength.

If you don't believe me, try this little experiment yourself:

1. Dress your baby in all pastel pink. Slip on some extra lace or ruffles for an uber-girly effect. Pay close attention to how people interact with your baby. Note any gender-specific language.

2. The next day, dress your baby in all navy blue. Go for a shirt or hat that has sports equipment or trucks printed on it. Pay close attention to how people interact with your baby. Note any gender-specific language.

3. Compare the two days of interaction. Use what you find from the comparison to help you examine your own gender-biased baby interactions. You

GENDER PREJUDICE DEFINED

Carrie Carmichael, author of *Non-Sexist Childraising*, defines gender prejudice as "actions based on the idea that simply being a girl or boy determines how a child thinks, feels, and acts."

may even become self-conscious or appalled at your own gender-biased baby talk. This is a good thing! Let your discomfort turn into action, and become more aware to interact more gender-neutrally.

Based on the results of experiments like this and several other "Baby X" studies, I clearly see a real case for gender-neutral baby appearance and interaction!

When you dress your baby in more gender-neutral clothing, you may discover that others interacting with your baby will use less gender-biased language, which is, of course, one of the desired outcomes of a gender-neutral appearance. Why's that desirable, you ask? Because gender-biased language and interaction with babies is just the beginning of a childhood full of sexist limitations placed on a child's full potential.

But don't forget that woman next to me in the grocery checkout line. She represents the majority of people who want and *need* to know what sex your baby is, and

FUN WITH GENDER-CODING

If you're up for a little gender-confusing fun, try these:

1. While at the beach or other favorite swimming hole, let baby be naked.

2. When a preschool-aged child approaches and asks if baby is a girl or a boy, respond with, "I don't know. It's so hard to tell when they don't have much hair." (I have Lily St. Regis from the movie *Annie* to thank for that one.)

3. If the preschooler gives you a little head tilt to one side and looks like a puzzled panther, give yourself a point!

4. To celebrate, get your hands on a copy of the *Girls Will Be Boys Will Be Girls* coloring book, wherein you'll find no pictures of girls playing princess or boys hauling dirt with toy dump trucks. Instead, you'll see pictures of kids doing whatever their hearts desire, along with fabulous phrases like "Grandpa, when we finish knitting, can we bake cookies?" and "We'll decide for ourselves what girls can be." (See the Resources section for more information.) Or see if you can sell some of those obnoxious gendered outfits and toys to make some money to buy the out-of-print but fabulously wonderful *X: A Fabulous Child's Story*, by Lois Gould, published in 1972. (See the Resources section for online text information.)

from them, you will undoubtedly hear more questions like "Is your baby a boy or a girl?" (This is an attempt to gather crucial information that tells them know how to interact with the baby.) If you choose to answer, you could go for the straight-up and factual "male" or "female" response. Or, if you're feeling more challenging, saying "I'm not sure yet" or "It doesn't matter—babies are babies" will usually suffice.

Some will skip the questions and just assume. If any of these people refer to your baby as a boy when your baby is a girl and you don't correct their mistake (and you shouldn't), they will apologize to you if they find out later in the conversation that your baby is not a boy. Be prepared. Let them know that not knowing is OK, reinforce that gender neutrality is OK. Respond with something along the lines of, "No apologies. Neither of us minds."

It's true that babies really don't care if they're being called boy or girl. So if the baby doesn't mind, then why should we? Because this early gender-coding socialization sets kids up for not being able to be their true, beautifully individual selves. If we help set a "beyond pink and blue" stage for them to perform on starting at birth, they'll have a better chance later on. When adolescence creeps in, they will forge their own identities, instead of settling for or feeling trapped by culturally imposed limits on their behavior possibilities. They need our help because culture is powerful, it providing females and males with dramatically different social and emotional experiences. They need our help to fight sexism in childhood.

11.

Battling Isolation

I wasn't prepared for the shift in the friends department. Or the feelings of isolation I'd never felt before.

It all started in our birth education class, the meeting-new-friends thing. Here were about eight other people who were expecting right around the same time we were, who had similar ideas and hopes about birth, but who we didn't have a whole lot in common with besides that. And we were spending more time with them weekly than our friends.

As my pregnancy progressed, I spent more time than ever before at home. I was going out less, seeing fewer bands, attending fewer meetings. I was reading more about pregnancy, birth, newborn care, and midwifery, and less about bands in zine interviews, the history of the women's liberation movement, and anarchism.

Once the baby came, our friends trickled in to meet her, visit with us, and bring us food. That was a special and welcoming time, and very much appreciated, but I needed to nap when the baby napped, and I couldn't hang out or chat it up very long.

And after the first few newborn weeks passed, the parade of visitors subsided, our mothers went home, and we were left most days alone. At home with my new baby, with Ernesto off at school and work the majority of the daytime, I started feeling very alone, isolated, and disconnected. The high of the birth over and the visitors gone, this was when I needed the most support.

Rather uncharacteristically, I found myself creating errands as a way to escape these feelings. I really didn't need to go get pushpins or browse baby gadgets I wasn't going to buy anyway. But at least it felt like I was getting out in the world, even if the extent of my conversations were with strangers and the depth of our conversation was puddle-like—they'd all ask the same questions about the sex and age of my baby. Also uncharacteristically, I started paying more attention to whether my appearance was "approachable" or not. I'd later realize that sprucing myself up to resemble what society thought "good moms" should look like reflected my lack of self-confidence as a new mother.

Taking care of a newborn is all consuming, especially for a first-time parent. The majority of my childless friends didn't think to stop by because understandably, they'd never before felt what I was feeling. Friends with kids couldn't stop by because they were all consumed by their own work and kids. And besides, I didn't know how to ask for help anyway, because I wasn't sure what I needed. Everything was new and unknown.

I remembered there was a weekly program for new mamas and babies at the hospital where I'd had Emma-Joy. It was within walking distance from our apartment, so I went. Yes, I was out of the house with baby and happy for it. The little snacks they had for us were nice, too, as was the friendly nurse who offered to hold my baby for me for a few minutes so I could sit for an uninterrupted moment to enjoy my snack. But there, I also felt out of my element. It was a well-intentioned program, one I believe was an attempt to support us new mamas making new mama friends, but I really wasn't interested in hearing a talk from a children's shoe-store employee who had coupons that we could use "before your baby even starts to walk!" Plus, having us come listen to a presentation didn't do much for us in the way of actually interacting with each other.

It was around this time when I received a letter from a mama who'd been reading my column in *Maximum Rock N Roll*. She wrote, "I think there are a lot of people out there who have kids but definitely feel disenfranchised, out of the loop of 'traditional' parenting, for various and assorted reasons."

I definitely felt like one of those "people" who are out of the loop of "traditional" parenting. Choosing a different life and parenting style, in the face of the mainstream pressures and expectations that dictate whether you are a "good" or "bad" mother, itself dictates a need for support and networking with others who have similar, progressive views. She got me thinking that this non-mainstream parenting gig probably brought more feelings of isolation than those following a more mainstream parenting route felt.

I needed to find my tribe.

When Emma-Joy was a couple months old, I began attending a weekly lunchtime potluck called "The Wiggly Baby Society," organized by midwives at the birth center where I received my prenatal care. There, I met fellow new mamas and

GET A POSSE

Find your community. Because a lack of trusted sources of help can add to new parents' stress levels, creating a support network is crucial. Unless you already have a solid group of friends in your chosen community who have babies, you will have to go outside your usual community for what you want to find. If you're going the midwife-model-of-care route, it is standard practice for midwives and freestanding birth centers to offer and/or organize childbirth education classes, breast-feeding support groups, and playgroups. It's never too early in your pregnancy to start going to them! There, although you will have to be cautious to avoid the natural-everything-by-the-book-or-bust-nazis, you have a better chance of finding others who share your non-mainstream core ethics in terms of medical decisions, food choices, politics, and the church of no god, if indeed that is your church of choice. Start a playgroup in your own home or community center! You will learn more from other seasoned mamas who have firsthand experience with pregnancy, birth, and parenting than you will from remaining isolated with only books, magazines, and the Internet.

babies. I kicked myself for not having gone sooner. I mistakenly felt that it wasn't my place anymore since I didn't wind up having my baby there. Here were the others I needed to find, the others who were not just going with the mainstream, status quo parenting flow.

I also started going to La Leche League meetings, for a monthly breast-feeding support group. There, not only did I get much needed help with breast-feeding, but I also met more seasoned mamas with older babies and kids. I could see what developmental changes would be in my near future. It felt uplifting to be in a room full of other breast-feeding women, even if that was all we had in common. The more meetings I attended, the more I discovered that I had more in common with some of them than just breast-feeding.

Eventually, my friend Kaile, who had her first baby just three weeks after I did, started having a "Baby Brunch" at her house for us and other new mamas.

I was getting a posse.

I was finding strength and comfort in numbers. In addition to not physically being home alone with my baby, I felt a sense of relief to know that I was not the only one going through these feelings of isolation and disconnection. I wasn't the only one with nipple pain and sleepless nights, leaking cloth diapers, and not one uninterrupted adult conversation in months. We were trading survival tips and diaper covers, learning from each other instead of reinventing our own individual wheels.

How to Find Allies Against Isolation

Many new families in our society experience isolation when they become parents. Often, there is a lack of extended family close by. New moms or dads are left alone for long periods of time with their kids to conduct the nonstop childcare duties that can often keep them from getting out into the community. New parents who were involved in countercultural communities before having a child, regardless of if they are living as a nuclear family or living in a collective or cooperative housing arrangement, often find that their child-free friends do not know how to be supportive even if they express a desire to do so. Together, proactive new parents and an aware, proactive community can do much to alleviate the experience of isolation.

Here are some tips to help new parents experience fewer feelings of isolation:

1. Feelings need to be recognized and validated by the larger community, not just by the parent feeling the isolation.

2. Help with the physical tasks of childcare. Wash a load of laundry or a sink of dirty dishes. Offer to go grocery shopping. Come over to hold the baby so mom can take a shower.

3. Before the baby is born, help make postpartum plans. Do your new parent friends need help with transportation to the pediatrician appointments? How about help with meals? Arrange for a different person to drop off a healthy, prepared meal every other night for the first six weeks; after that, once a week until the baby is three months old. Drop and go if they're not up for visitors. Stay and chat if they need company.

4. It's important for new parents to know how to get help from you if they need it in a pinch. Make a list for them of several friends' phone numbers as well as an indication of when the best times are for them to help out.

Postpartum Depression

How do you know if what you're feeling is isolation common to new mothers or something more serious, like postpartum depression (PPD)? PPD refers to depression after pregnancy. The exact number of women who suffer some degree of PPD is unknown. There are three different classifications of depression after pregnancy: the baby blues, postpartum depression, and postpartum psychosis. The baby blues can happen in the days right after childbirth and normally go away within a few days to a week. PPD can happen anytime within the first year after delivery. The difference between postpartum depression and the baby blues is that postpartum depression often affects a woman's well-being and keeps her from functioning well for a longer period of time. Postpartum psychosis is rare, occurring in only 1 or 2 out of every 1,000 births, and usually begins in the first six weeks postpartum. Symptoms may include delusions, hallucinations, sleep disturbances, obsessive thoughts about the baby, and rapid mood swings—from depression to irritability to euphoria.

There may be a number of reasons why a woman experiences depression after pregnancy. Pregnancy and/or thyroid hormone-level changes, stress, or fam-

Avoiding the Baby Comparison Game

While you're busy building your baby community, it's easy to fall into playing the baby comparison game. When meeting new baby friends, the usual questions include "What's your baby's name?" and "How old is your baby?" Once you've registered your baby's age into their heads and their babies' ages are registered into yours, you almost can't help comparing. Thoughts might creep in like, *Hmmm, my baby isn't sitting up yet, but that younger baby is. Is my baby slow?* Or, *My baby's a genius! Crawling already at only five months old, while these other lumps of dough can't even get up on all fours, over the hill at eight months old!*

First, make sure your brain-to-mouth filter is turned on so you can keep those thoughts to yourself. Then, go ahead and just toss those thoughts right on out. The more time you spend around babies, the quicker you will learn that the range of normal development is extremely wide and that individual variation among adult humans also applies to infant ones. The most important thing is that the baby's healthy. So what if your baby was an early crawler? That just means you have more chasing and keeping up to do. So what if that other baby sat up before yours did? You have more time left before having to engage in a game of sit-behind-the-baby-with-your-catcher's-mitt-on in case she tumbles backwards.

ily history of depression can all be contributing factors. Other contributing factors can include fatigue, feeling overwhelmed by the demands of caring for a new baby, lack of confidence, loss of personal identity, changes to appearance, less free time, and less control over time.

According to Lori Calkins, in her article "Thoughts on the Isolation of Motherhood," "When isolation contributes to the difficulty of adjusting to motherhood, feelings of depression need to be addressed not only with a label or a medication, but with an evaluation of the circumstances contributing to the difficulty." To address feelings of isolation and depression, an evaluation of self-care skills, relationships, and community support is useful. Simply labeling a mother as having PPD puts all the weight of the problem on the mother without looking at the contributing factors.

12.

Going Back to Work

I had a feeling the baby wouldn't come on or before its due date, so I had no hesitation going to work that very day. Some of the women I worked with, however, were nervous that I was there, teasing me with remarks like, "Hey, what are you doing here? Aren't you supposed to be having this baby today? We really don't want to play midwife here."

At closing time, I bid them all a happy farewell. I drove home from work that night, my last night of work for an undetermined amount of time. I walked in the door with a shit-eating grin plastered across my face and bounced my nine-months pregnant self around the living room, telling Ernesto how happy I was that I didn't have that oh-so-strenuous part-time after-school tutoring job anymore. He quickly laughed at my delusion and told me, "That part-time job was vacation."

Yeah. My bubble burst. I guess it was kind of silly being excited about not having to work part-time just so I could start working around the clock for no paycheck.

So call me silly. Even with my bubble burst, I was excited to be having a baby and not equating baby with job. Yet.

I took advantage of having a few days just to myself until my full-time job appeared on the scene. I cut and dyed my hair and relaxed at my gentle/prenatal yoga class. I went to shows and had fun. At one of them, my friend Cave Dave (aka Replay) danced around atop someone's shoulders with a big pillow stuck up under his shirt, a tribute to my overdue baby.

Although I was enjoying my little vacation—call it the calm before the storm, if you will—I was ready for the baby to come.

THE (UN)COMPENSATED WORK OF CHILDCARE

A recent Harvard/McGill University study compared 177 countries, and found that only five do not have some sort of paid leave for new mothers: the United States, Swaziland, Lesotho, Liberia, and Papua New Guinea. The United States is the only industrialized nation in the world with no paid-leave policy at all, offering only twelve weeks of unpaid leave—and that's only for full-time employees of companies that have more than fifty employees.

In addition to paid leave, several countries give parents a monthly child stipend, regardless of income. For example, Australia gives a $4,000 baby bonus. Finland gives a monthly stipend until the child's fifteenth birthday. France too gives monthly stipends to stay-at-home parents. So does Germany and most other European countries.

Just as women and men are valued differently in U.S. society (women still make only seventy-seven cents to every dollar a man makes; African-American women earn just sixty-nine cents to every dollar earned by white men; Hispanic women, fifty-nine cents per dollar), childcare work in the United States is not valued financially or socially as equal to other work. Being "just a parent" is a social demotion for women and even more so for the men who are "stay-at-home" dads. Paid childcare workers are among the lowest paid in the country.

Fast-forward six months into motherhood. During that time, I gained an entirely new outlook on work, what it is, and how it's (not) compensated. Before I had Emma-Joy, I guessed I'd return to work after three months. But when that time came, I was not ready. I was just beginning to get the hang of things, and to throw something else into the new motherhood mix would have been too much for me to handle well. Working as "just a mom," I felt like I was already working my ass off around the clock.

First, parenting is the best job I've ever had. It's the most demanding, intense, all-consuming, challenging, and fun job ever, but talk about overworked and underpaid! (To those of you who dismiss the exhausting demands of taking care of a kid with "But you get paid with you child's love and affection," please bite your tongues.) The job description includes just about every possible task you can think of (breast-feeder, burper, spit-up wiper-upper, bather, diaper and clothes changer, entertainer, soother, rocking-chair rocker, holder, etc.) and then some more that people without kids surely have never thought of (vaccination researcher, appointment scheduler, parenting-book reader, playdate seeker, household-chores coordinator, outgrown-clothing consignor). The fact that there was no training manual, no scheduled breaks, no calling in sick, and my boss was a little lump of nursing, crying, sometimes smiling, pooping dough was a tough adjustment. I didn't really know what I was doing half the time, winging it as I went, reinventing wheels, getting through hour by hour, day by day, with baby Emma-Joy giving me the necessary on-the-job training. And still, I wanted to keep doing it, staying committed to not farming Emma-Joy out to germy, crowded, and costly daycare.

Both Ernesto and I thought it would be different. We brought this baby into the world ideally planning to share the job equally. It didn't work out that way for a couple reasons. First, exclusively breast-feeding a baby tips the scales. For the first six months of her life, the longest stretch of time I had been away from her was six hours. Second, during this time, Ernesto was a full-time student and a part-time worker. He was away from home for longer stretches of time than the standard eight-hour full-time workday.

We decided that I would not need to work during the newborn months because our rent was only $300 a month, we had no debt, and it would be easy to just scrape by for a while on financial aid, food stamps, and his part-time work-study job. We were not sacrificing by "doing without" things like cable TV, a new car, cell phones, fancy dinners out, new clothes, furniture, or movies because we already didn't spend money on those things.

So my role was cast as the primary caregiver, which means I took on most of the baby-related work. I can honestly say that I had no idea of what I was getting into. It was really hard. Learning how to take care of a baby, how to parent in a way that reflected our ideals, how to meet my own needs at the same time, and how to get anything else done, is too much for any one person to do.

When Emma-Joy was three months old, I wasn't ready to return to work. But six months into it...I couldn't be 24/7 mama anymore. Maybe it was because she was high-needs and high-energy. She nursed constantly and needed constant motion. And she started crawling everywhere too soon: the day she turned five months old. Whatever it was, I needed a break.

It literally just hit me one day that I'd had enough. Before Emma-Joy came along—because I did have free time to myself, even though I was living a busy, active life—I never realized how important or what a privilege it is to have downtime, alone time, time to recharge, to just take a break when needed. With the full-time parenting gig, I needed more of a break than the four hours a week I attended my silversmithing class. Instead of the straw that broke the camel's back, let's call it the shitty diaper that zapped my sanity.

Tipping Point

There I was, trying to get both baby and me dressed and a diaper backpack packed so we could bike to eat some free Hare Krishna lunch. I got her dressed with little resistance. The bag got packed without a hitch. I put her down to play with a toy while I got myself dressed, and I kid you not, less than two minutes later, I returned to see her playing with what at first looked like a little yellow puddle of cat puke.

I was instantly grossed out, but it wasn't until I lifted her up out of it that I really got bummed. It was her own poop. And there wasn't just one puddle of it. Let's hear it for the cloth diapers I used: they leaked. And, of course, since she was already crawling, she had crawled a trail of bright yellow poo all over the floor and all over herself.

I thought, OK, no big deal, this is just part of the having a sweet, smiling baby. I picked her up so I wouldn't get myself shit-slimed and hefted her into the tub. Of course, I had just laced my shoes up and had to somehow manage to get them off so they wouldn't get soaked, all the while hanging the baby over my arm, over the tub so no more day-glow-yellow grossness would smear anywhere else.

I got her rinsed, dried, and dressed and started in on rinsing the poop off the diaper and into the toilet. Speedy-crawler baby snuck up behind me and pulled herself up onto the toilet bowl rim, thinking she'd like a splash in the yellow water. Ugh! I removed her from that situation, but she quickly returned, this time behind me to the diaper pail, full of poo water and soaking dirty diapers. Ugh! That was it! It was too much to handle.

I quit.

I scooped the baby up, shut the door to the shit-infested bathroom, ignored the poo smears all over the living room floor, and just started rocking in the rocking chair, holding baby close to my chest and bawling my eyes out. She was so sweet; she just put her head on my chest and her arms out on my shoulders and let me release all my tired, lonely mama stress.

It took a little while, but the tears stopped and I was able to finally get us both out the door, on the bike, and to the campus to find Ernesto. I was feeling fine when we got there, until I noticed that I still had a yellow splotch of shit on my arm. I lost my mind all over again, handed Emma-Joy off to Ernesto, and then disappeared for a while. I couldn't even talk. I sat on the ground hiding between two garbage cans so no one would talk to me. I tried to read a chapter of the book I'd brought with

PARENTING EQUALLY, THIRD-WAVE FEMINISM'S NEXT FRONTIER

Not only is equal parenting good feminism, it also benefits kids and partnerships in several ways. Kids get quality one-on-one time with both parents. They grow up observing behavior that is not modeled along gender lines. Partnerships are enhanced by communication, cooperation, and raised consciousness.

It's really no fun keeping track of how many hours mom took care of baby or how many hours dad did chores. "Oh! It's five o'clock! Time to switch jobs!" just isn't going to always work out. Tight scheduling, done with the intention to keep things perfectly equal is not more important than uninterrupted time during projects, reading together, and playtime fun. Sometimes one parent winds up doing more child and house work if the other is ill or has something else important going on. It helps to adopt a "from each according to ability, to each according to need" approach. Good communication and awareness about individual needs being (un)met are key to achieving balance. Talk about the kids' needs, what the household needs are, and what your individual preferences are for meeting those needs. Negotiate. If needed, use a "talk book" to record feelings and observations of unbalance and suggestions for achieving better balance. Make the opportunity to discuss them!

A pretty good guide for parents who want balanced and equal lives can be found at http://equallysharedparenting.com.

me, but couldn't concentrate, wallowing too deeply in self-pity.

After a little time alone, I caught up with Ernesto and Emma-Joy. He asked if I was OK. I told him that I would be as long as I didn't have to be 24/7 solo mama anymore.

That night when Ernesto got home from work, he had a brilliant idea. He would quit his job and I would work instead. Bingo! So simple, yet my brain was so drowned in being mama that I hadn't been able to think of it myself. I wracked my brain to come up with job ideas.

Never in a million years did I think I'd ever be looking at getting a paycheck job as a way of having a break! I'd still be a full-time mama, because parenting never really stops, but at least I'd have something additional going on, away from the baby for a few hours.

Would it suck having "breaks" that would essentially be filled up by having to perform some other responsibility and not being able to just do as I pleased, like the pre-kid me did? Yes. But what sucked the most was the realization that it would be this way for a very long time and that this very long time would, fortunately or unfortunately, pass way too quickly and then I'd be, oh my gawd, *old*, with a grownup kid!

The next morning, I got us up and out of bed instead of just lolling about playing baby games. I got two newspapers and scanned the want ads. Not

THE "MOMMY WARS" ARE A MYTH, OR EVERY MOTHER IS A WORKING MOTHER!

Distinguishing "stay-at-home moms" from "working moms" is meaningless. Neither of those terms is accurately named. And besides, they're divisive. Moms should be more appropriately described as "working-for-no-paycheck" or "working-two-jobs-for-one-paycheck."

Instead, mainstream media hypes the two kinds of motherhood, labeling it the "Mommy Wars," a term coined in the late-1980s by *Child* magazine. Supposedly, it describes the fight between working and stay-at-home moms, but perhaps it's just the antifeminist mainstream media's way of pitting women against one another.

It's a false conflict. Masses of women are not giving up the hard-won gains of second-wave feminism by leaving the workforce and retreating to the home. The truth is that the supposed-Mommy Wars focus only on a very narrow slice of the population. Heather Boushey, an economist at the Center for Economic Research and Policy in Washington, reported in December 2005 that the number of thirty-something women who hold advanced degrees and choose full-time parenting over full-time career is a tiny share of all women with children, representing a mere 3.2% of all U.S. mothers. These advantaged women are actually more likely to be in the labor force than their less-educated counterparts of similar ages. The figures show that *all* women between twenty-five and forty-five with children are more likely to be in the labor force than in the past. (According to the Bureau of Labor Statistics, women now make up 46% of the labor force, and nearly 75% of all working women are mothers.) She summarized that women are not increasingly dropping out of the labor force because of their kids. "The main reasons for declining labor force participation rates among women over the last four years appears to be the weakness of the labor market."

The Mommy Wars myth obscures the real issues that all moms and caregivers face. Simply heating up the "war" offers little by way of solving the issues of equal access to benefits in the form of access to health care and social security, or respect and social value. It is a classist, elitist, minority viewpoint that well-educated mothers will be leading lesser lives if they do not work outside of the home. The real-life discussion is the work-family balancing act that most parents face, finding solutions to the challenges that affect us all (cont'd)

The Mommy Wars myth excludes the largest segment of mothers—the ones who do not have a choice, the working poor and/or single parents, the ones who live at or near poverty, forced into a forty-hour-plus work week by a "reformed" welfare system that fails to address their basic needs. Instead of discussing the fake Mommy Wars, fight for these mamas and speak up for change. A better discussion would be about how our society can better support mothers and caregivers so that they can choose to work either outside or inside the home, whether it is part- or full-time, without additional guilt, financial strife, or other barriers. Much worse than having to make a difficult choice between working and not working is not having the choice at all.

In addition, a closer examination of sexism, as well as men's role and responsibility in parenting, is warranted. Doing so will help illuminate the fact that having a child is the single biggest predictor that a woman will go bankrupt. Two reasons for this are what a recent study at Cornell University turned up about evidence of discrimination. First, mothers are 44% less likely to be hired than non-mothers for the same job, even with the exact same qualifications. Second, the mothers who did get hired were offered an average of $11,000 less than the non-mothers for the same job.

surprisingly, nothing attracted me. Actually, there was nothing I thought I could do. Though I had a college degree, I also had a baby. For some crazy reason, potential employers think they can demand commitment and responsibility in exchange for part-time work at minimum wage. My primary commitment and responsibility were in taking care of Emma-Joy, and I just couldn't offer much of either for any part-time job I saw listed.

I started thinking that maybe going back to work would actually take more effort to juggle that it would be worth financially, break-wise, or quality of life-wise. But over Krishna lunch the next day, my friend Kurt tipped me off to a part-time teaching job he had just been hired for at the University of Florida, teaching English as a Second Language at the English Language Institute (ELI). He said they needed more teachers. The ten-hours a week teaching, plus ten hours of paid planning time I could do at home sounded perfect. I finished my lunch, grabbed Emma-Joy, and pedaled off to apply. I hoped no one there would notice that my shirt resembled a spit-up rag.

I had my interview the next day. I was expecting to breeze through it because of my qualifications and experience, but left feeling defeated. As soon as I told them I was only available when my partner was not in class because we had to juggle childcare, they said, "Oh, it doesn't look like you're flexible enough."

I was left wondering how people with babies make it work. How do they save their sanity, earn even a modest income, and care for their children themselves without shuffling them off to daycare centers? I knew that there had to be plenty of partnered and sin-

BREAST-FEEDING AND GOING BACK TO WORK

1. Find out about places at work for expressing and storing your milk.
2. Start working only after your milk supply is well established.
3. Pump or express milk at work.
4. Take milk home for the next day's feedings.
5. Breast-feed frequently when at home.

I also recommend reading *Nursing Mother, Working Mother*, by Gale Pryor. Mothers who have decided to combine breast-feeding with working will find this an immensely helpful and reassuring book.

gle parents who do it every day without expensive daycare, but I didn't know how. Where was the ideal, cooperative childcare among other parents I envisioned? I decided it needed to be organized in the near future, for sure!

Feelings of defeat subsided when I got a call from the ELI two days later. Luckily, because of unexpectedly high enrollment, I got the job.

The bittersweetness settled in quickly. Sanity crept back in during time away from home, while working in the classroom. It got my brain stimulated in ways I'd missed. But bringing paycheck work home when I was already coming home to work as mama was hard. Not being able to sleep when the baby slept, because there were papers to grade and lessons to plan, was just short of torture.

But it was worth it. Separating from Emma-Joy a couple hours a day really helped my parenting for the remaining majority of the day. And it helped Emma-Joy and Ernesto get more attached. Breast-feeding was still going strong—Ernesto would feed Emma-Joy bottles of pumped breast milk while I was away. In time, because Emma-Joy slept a bit better the older she got and because I got into a more streamlined groove with my new teaching job, I got more rest.

Things got even better when Ernesto graduated with his BA in history. He then had the time to dedicate to a more balanced approach to childcare.

EARTHWORMS, TURDS, AND PUKE

On my first day back to work, I was only gone three hours for the orientation, and each of those hours brought a new surprise to the new daddy on duty. Things started out fine. Emma-Joy was crawling around on the porch like she always does while Ernesto kept an eye on her and tried to get something done at the same time. (Mistake #1: It's either impossible or twice as hard to get anything done when on baby duty.) When he looked up to see what had her attention, he noticed something hanging out of her mouth. Reaching into her mouth with the standard finger-hook maneuver, he fished out an earthworm. And it wasn't one of those hard, shriveled earthworms. This one was a live, wiggling one. Where it came from, we still don't know—never saw one on the porch before or since.

Needing a change of scenery, they ventured off to the big patch of grass in front of the apartments a block away. Emma-Joy loved to be outside and was having a grand time playing with twigs and leaves. I guess Ernesto forgot that this was also the big patch of grass where most of the apartment tenants walked their dogs because what else besides twigs and leaves did Emma-Joy find to play with? You guessed it. Dog shit.

Ernesto caught her hand just in the nick of time. Imagine the scene all slow-motion style:

Emma-Joy grabs turd. She wonders what this new toy is. She is happy about discovering something new and wants a more intimate acquaintance with it. She smiles with mouth wide open to greet her new friend. But here comes Dad with an urgent interception like he's sliding into home plate, "Noooooooooooo," grabbing her hand just as the prized fresh turd is about to become a snack.

Safe! But now how to deal with the mess a block away from home?

He scooped her up and hustled back towards the house. Emma-Joy, of course, was persistent in trying to get her shit-smeared hand into her lonely, empty mouth. He said it was a real battle trying to carry her all the way home, wrestling her small but strong arm down away from her face, not to mention finally getting to the front door and struggling to get his key out of his pocket and into the doorknob to unlock it. Somehow he did it without a shit catastrophe and without dropping Emma-Joy.

With her cleaned off, things were relatively calm for a while until Ernesto just happened to look out the window in time to see our car about to get a...(cont'd) ticket. He yelled out the window, "Hey, wait!" as he grabbed the baby and dashed downstairs to negotiate with the parking ticket guy. The guy wasn't a complete dick like most of them around there were, but he insisted that the car needed to be moved pronto.

Move the car. No problem, right? Wrong. As Ernesto went to put Emma-Joy in her car seat, he noticed that it wasn't buckled down. Useless when it's not buckled and impossible to buckle with a baby in your arms, he had to bang on our neighbor Wicks' door and ask him to hold baby for a minute.

Ernesto got the car moved, but for some reason, Emma-Joy needed to throw up that very minute and did so all over Wicks. This wasn't a little baby spit-up, episode either. He said she started coughing, really hacking, and all of a sudden she just projectile puked all down the front of Wicks.

Oops, uh, thanks for baby-holding. She's never puked like that before, I promise.

A minute after Ernesto helped wipe off Wicks' shirt, out comes the neighbor in whose vast, empty yard Ernesto had just parked the car.

"You can't park there without asking! You have to ask first! Blah, blah, blah…"

With the sweet baby in his arms and feeling totally frazzled and worked over, Ernesto humbly apologized, explained and smoothed things over so the car could stay in her yard for a while.

When I returned home after my relatively leisurely meeting and he told me all that had happened during the last three hours, I of course had to laugh and feel a little sorry for him, but in my head I was thinking, *Welcome to my world. I've dealt with this new-parent craziness for six months straight.*

I worked away from home as a part-time teacher in the mornings, he as a part-time house renovator in the afternoons. He took care of Emma-Joy in the mornings and I did in the afternoons. We had to learn how to parent equally in the evenings. Because Ernesto recognized that I'd been doing more childcare and housework, we were very careful to avoid the "second-shift" phenomenon, wherein women wind up doing more domestic and child work than men do, even after both have worked away from home during the day. And we both were able to reintegrate activism into our new lives as parents—Ernesto taking on organizing for the establishment for an independent, community-based review board to oversee the police department, me taking on organizing with Gainesville Area NOW and Gainesville Women's Liberation.

We continued on this childcare, work, and activism path for two years. We felt we'd struck the perfect balance. The older Emma-Joy got, the better we got at meeting our individual needs, too. We were happy, but even with our frugal lifestyle, we realized our work arrangement wasn't sustainable. I offered to go back to work full-time as a public school teacher so Ernesto could be the full-time parent. Ernesto offered to go back to school so he and I would be on more equal ground in the pay department. Not really wanting to teach public school full-time, I took him up on his offer.

Just before Emma-Joy's third birthday, we up and moved 330 miles away to begin our next adventure together. The "Building Community Takes Time" chapter will fill you in on the ensuing craziness.

13.

Thrifty Mama

I'm a fan of free stuff. You know, the kind scored out of college students' apartment dumpsters, hand-me-downs, and unsold yard-sale goodies left out on the curb. Sometimes, I'll set out looking for stuff that I need, like bookshelves or a toilet seat. Usually, if I'm patient, I'll find what I'm looking for without resorting to spending money. It's also incredibly fun to score not-particularly useful stuff, like glasses frames with no lenses or a silverware organizer, just because it's free. OK, so I have packrat tendencies, but still, it's the most fun to laugh about the fact that someone probably paid money—and sometimes a lot of it—for something that might soon end up in a trash can. How many times have I found new clothes, still with the tags on, discarded with a big "thanks, but no thanks" sentiment after the holidays? Too many to count. And at any semester's end, the canned food that students toss out is enough to feed the entire neighborhood for a week. In short, I take pride in being able to live fat off others' wasteful habits. Scavenging, reclaiming, recycling, and refashioning the used into something new just makes good sense.

So when I found out I was pregnant, I didn't hesitate to fill out a few post-age-paid postcards that promised free baby products. I should have known better; free corporate marketing products are not the same as free discarded things. The corporate stuff comes with strings attached. And the longest of those strings is the one to your mailbox. By filling out just a few of those postcards, I did receive some free unnecessary baby things, but I also got myself on a never-ending corporate mailing list. Not a week went by that I didn't receive a sample mainstream parenting magazine or a huge envelope full of coupons and "big savings" offers. The "big savings" offers were irritating because I know people buy into the marketing gimmick—the one where you don't really save money because you bought something you didn't really need, just at a discounted price. Beyond irritating and just plain peevish were the corporate freebies subscriptions to *Baby Talk* magazine (from the publishers of *Parenting* magazine) and the Nestlé corporation's infant-formula marketing magazine, *The Very Best Baby*. It might have been my own stupid fault for filling out those freebie postcards, thus landing them in my own mailbox, but these free magazines are also widely distributed through obstetrician and pediatrician offices, places where parents-to-be and new parents are more vulnerable to corporate marketing. It's well known that folks are more likely to follow, or in this case buy into, advice and information they receive from and/or at their doctors' offices than from another source. Companies rely on *Baby Talk* to conduct marketing surveys and introduce new products and services to consumers. As a "reward" for the feedback you give to these surveys, you are gifted with the free subscription, wherein you are heavily advertised to and encouraged to buy into the baby-as-consumer mentality.

I can't tell you how good I felt about my thrifty ways when I glanced at the special bonus insert titled "Everything You Need for Your New Consumer," included inside an issue of *Baby Talk*. Thumbing through its twenty-odd pages, I honestly saw almost nothing that I had needed to use during my first six months as a parent. Going into a new situation, with no experience, I had been nervous about not having the things I would need to help me care for my baby. In hindsight, I should have known that baby-stuff marketing wouldn't be different from any other type of marketing. And I wish I'd had the advice I'd later hear from an experienced mama named Faith, on the anarchist parenting listserv, "All you need is boobs and a sling!" So rest assured, you don't need the tons of stuff that you probably can't afford anyway! And even if you can afford it, feel good that you won't have to.

I understand fully that needs differ, given the fact that we all have unique circumstances and all make different lifestyle decisions. However, if you are interested in knowing how to accommodate a little one into your life for very little money, you might find the following information useful.

Car Seat

Even if you don't have a car, you will more than likely ride in one with your baby, and for that you need a car seat. This is the one thing that you should not get used because you won't know if it has been in an accident, even a minor one, and if it has, you shouldn't use it. Car seats can be expensive and it's usually the super-duper deluxe-looking ones that are more expensive and are actually the least effective. If the cost of a car seat is prohibitive, call your local department of motor vehicles or ask your healthcare provider. Your state may have a program that provides free or reduced-price car seats to those who

qualify. For example, I attended an hour-long "Safe Kids" information session, paid only $10, and walked away with a new car seat that was the exact size I needed for my baby's age and weight.

Nursery Furniture

I laughed out loud when I saw the pages in *Baby Talk* under the headline, "Your Dream Nursery for an Affordable Couple Grand." Since when is a couple grand affordable? Nursery, schmersery. Baby does not *need* her own room at that age. It's a *lot* less work (and provides a lot more sleep) if baby's in the same room (if not the same bed) as her parents at night. Plus, closer proximity promotes breast-feeding, and room sharing is now encouraged by the American Academy of Pediatrics. Cribs, bassinets, playpens, and changing tables are luxury items, not necessities. And you certainly don't need them to match some pastel, fluffy bunny theme. (Though if you feel you really, really do, just get yourself a can of paint and some stencils and do it yourself.) My aunt Lisa kindly offered us the crib my cousin Alex slept in, but we declined.

Some might raise their eyebrows a bit at the concept of the "family bed," but with a little education along the lines of the fact that more babies die SIDS-style when in cribs alone, than they do when they sleep in bed with you safely, they back off a bit. (For more, see "The Family Bed Controversy.") We were given a bassinet (mine from when I was a baby) and a playpen, both of which went relatively unused; I did try both of them out, but baby Emma-Joy was having none of either. So instead, they held stuffed animals. My mom gave us my old changing table, which I refurbished myself and used during the newborn months, but if you don't get one free, you can easily do without. Changing tables become ineffective once the baby is older and squirming all over the place, about to flip over the side when you change her diaper. Just put a towel down on the bed or floor and change the baby there.

Carrying and Strolling

You absolutely do not need a stroller that looks like a baby Cadillac. Those monstrous strollers that have the snap-in-place carrier/car seat/sleeper on top of the stroller base are not only ridiculously expensive, they're heinously ugly. They are horrible to navigate, especially through crowds and on uneven surfaces, and are a royal pain in the ass to fold and unfold in and out of a car's trunk. Finding an easier way to do things should be a driving force in any parenting style, and simply carrying the baby is really so much easier. Besides, it's just not nice to have your little soft, fleshy bundle strapped down into hard, form-fitted plastic all the time.

Use a sling or another type of baby carrier. (See the "Babywearing" chapter.) These are a lot less expensive and if you don't want to buy one, all you need is a long, rectangular piece of fabric. Tie it over one of your shoulders so it crosses your chest, with the other end hanging like a little hammock under your arm. It's nice for the baby to be snuggled tight and it's also easy to nurse the baby when she is already so close to the milk source. No one will even know what the baby's up to in there. "Wearing" the baby this way in a sling also frees up your hands. It's an ideal solution for getting around together on any public transportation, too. When your back needs a break, get a little "umbrella" stroller for the times when they're too tired to walk. These can usually be found at a thrift shop for under five dollars. Baby backpacks are also very handy and can easily be found used for a cheap price. It's fun to ride a bike with the baby on your back; just make sure to have a helmet on the little head! You can get an XS-sized child's helmet and pad it out well for under fifteen dollars.

Clothes

Infants only get their clothes dirty if they spit up on them or if their diaper leaks. They do not scoot or crawl for several months and they grow out of their newborn clothes very quickly. Therefore, do yourself a favor and do not buy brand-new baby clothes. (And please don't fall for the *Baby Talk* "feature story" on pajamas. Kids do not need pajamas that have a matching stuffed animal and slippers, not to mention the matching hair ribbons.)

For the reasons I just mentioned, thrift and consignment shops are teeming with practically brand-new baby clothes. Babies simply grow out of them before they have a chance to wear them out. Also, since your baby will outgrow these clothes so quickly and with little wear, you can always re-consign them in a few months. Some people are gifted more newborn clothes than their baby can wear even once before outgrowing them, and these brand-new, tags-still-on clothes are also common to find at the thrift and consignment shops. But even better than the thrift and consignment shops are the people with kids older than yours! If you don't know anyone with a kid, just wait, you will definitely meet some. Don't be shy to tell them that you'd be more than happy to take any outgrown clothes off their hands. Seriously, we had to spend almost no money on clothes for our baby (and at every age, including up to now); we have a couple boxes of clothes saved just waiting for her to grow into. People with kids are generally generous to other people with kids. It's a great network to tap into.

Toys

The same goes for toys. Whatever you don't get handed down, you can find loads of at secondhand stores. Leftover yard-sale curb scores are a great source for toys, too, as is witnessed by the little-kid rocking chair and tricycle we got. (As with any other free curb and dumpster scores, it should be obvious that you'd want to give them a good wipe-down before giving them to your babe.) Toys, especially stuffed animals, just seem to come out of the woodwork. Family members, random neighbors, and friends will constantly give you toys for your kid. And when the baby is too young, you will have more fun with the toys than she will! Even when babies get older, they seem to prefer pots, pans, cups, lids, spoons, wooden thread spools on a string, empty boxes both small and large—anything that's not intended as a baby toy but really does make a great one—so no sweat on having few toys anyway.

When you both get bored of a toy, be sure to re-consign it or pass it down to some other kid who you know would love to have something different to play with. Organize a toy swap! Start a "toy library" at a community center or your local info shop where folks can come check out toys for a couple weeks, bring them back when due, and check out new ones to bring home. Looking at the mainstream baby magazines, you will see that they want you to buy all the "right" toys at the "right" time. (Marketing disguised as an article.) Don't believe the hype. Your kid will develop just fine without all the "right" toys at the "right" time. Your kid might even be better off without those age-specific developmental toys because that way she can decide for herself what's interesting without being told what she's "supposed" to be interested in. Plus, baby's primary caretaker is usually the "right" thing at the "right"

No Choking!

Babies love to put things in their mouths! They want to rub things on their teething gums for relief. (For this, offer frozen baby washcloths or frozen watermelon rinds instead.) And putting things in their mouths is a sense stimulator—they learn from this sort of experimentation and exploration. So, until they're older than three years, hide the marbles and any other toy that has a piece to it small enough to fall through a toilet paper roll. If you do need to remove a piece of contraband from the kidlet's mouth, calmly sweep their mouth with a hooked finger. Fishing in a kid's mouth with your frenzied straight finger has more of a chance of sending small objects straight down their throat.

time that baby prefers and is better off playing with anyway.

Diapers

You will save gobs of money by using cloth diapers. (And not send ten miniature garbage bags full of yuck to the landfill every day.) They are not as much trouble as they sound and can always be found used, for cheap. If you can't find them at a secondhand store or get then handed down to you, then you can find them easily, and in abundance, on an Internet auction site. I was surprised to be able to get five used covers for fifteen dollars that usually cost fifteen bucks each brand-new. If you want to use brand-new cloth diapers, you will still save money in the long run over using the one-time-use throwaways. If you know how to sew, cloth diapers and covers are relatively easy to make yourself, too. Think you can't use cloth diapers because you don't have your own washer and dryer? Think again! We didn't have our own washer or dryer and were able to manage the dirty deed with only minor gross-out. (For more on cloth diapers, see "The Virtues of Cloth Diapers.")

Feeding

If you are one of the 95% to 98% of women who are physiologically able, then breast-feed your baby. It's free! Breast-feeding will save you at least $1,000 the first year alone because you won't be buying formula. If you aren't able to breast-feed, then consider obtaining breast milk from a milk bank or getting other lactating friends to nurse your baby and/or donate pumped milk to you. (For more information, see "Breast-Feed Your Baby.")

When your baby starts eating food in addition to breast milk at around six months, you need not only rely on boxes of rice cereal and jars of baby food. Try steaming a sweet potato, mashing it, and then scooping it into an ice cube tray. Freeze it and pop out a sweet-potato cube for babe when you need one. You can either thaw it, remash it and spoon-feed, or pop the frozen cube into a "mesh feeder" that has a handle that babies can hold themselves. (It was invented by a dad whose baby nearly died choking on a biscuit.) It doubles as frozen teething relief, an alternative to frozen plastic teething rings. It'll cost you about three dollars. These mesh feeders are great for fresh fruits and veggies, too.

As baby gets a bit older and moves past single foods, I found it much easier to just grind up a portion of whatever we'd prepared for ourselves. This way, you won't start a habit of preparing different meals for your child; s/he will come to expect to eat what everyone else is eating (barring any unforeseen allergies that is). Using a KidCo Food Mill, made of safe polypropylene with medical-grade stainless steel components, I was able to turn healthy, fresh table food into healthy, fresh baby food. It's operated by hand, no batteries or electricity required. It retails for between eleven and sixteen dollars and is portable, so I take it along in the diaper bag when we're out and about. And at home, grinding up a little extra and freezing into ice cube trays is good for a quick snack later. (For more information, see "First Foods" and "Toddler Chomps.")

Mommy and Me Classes

Skip these types of classes. They are usually expensive. They're mostly for new parents to feel like they're doing something, and babies couldn't care less about them. Is the class you're thinking about focused on movement? You can do movement exercises with your baby at home. Music? That, too. No need for special baby music classes. Make your own shakers out of empty water bottles and dried beans. Spoons are good for banging on pots and pans. Sing songs to your baby that you remember enjoying from your own childhood. Sure, these classes will get you out of the house, but you can do that for free at parks or at potluck-lunch type gatherings at your local birthing center. See the "Battling Isolation" chapter for more ideas.

Washing and Drying and Wiping, Oh My!

You do not need a thousand, or even a dozen, special towels, blankets, burping rags, or bibs. The baby is fine with a regular soft cotton towel after bath time. Stitch a couple of snuggly fleece blankets yourself. Use any piece of cloth for a burp rag/spit-up wiper-upper. Add one of your uber-punk safety pins to a piece of cloth around the baby's neck and voila, you have a bib! The mags and baby stores will have you thinking that you need all kinds of creams, potions, and soaps for bathing and wiping and soothing. A good old wet washcloth is all you really need for general wiping off. If you need soap for washing, any nontoxic, eco-friendly soap will do. Especially nice is the Dr. Bronner's all-in-one baby castile soap that is scent-free. Baby's natural smell is so, so good; don't cover it up with scented "baby" products that have synthetic ingredients that can irritate baby's skin. Instead of using disposable wipes at all, save some money by using little cloth washcloths dampened with warm water. When away from home, simply have some with you in a plastic baggie. After using, drop them into the diaper pail along with the cloth diapers and wash them all together.

Books, Music, and Fun

Going to the library is free! There are loads of pregnancy, birth, and parenting books you can check out. There are board books for babies, and story times for toddlers and preschoolers. It's a nice social time for them, too! Check out music, too! Feel free to totally skip kiddy-type music—go for the stuff you love. Punk will put a babies to sleep just as well as Mozart if they are *used* to falling asleep to punk. Libraries are perfect for escaping yucky weather—they are usually comfortably heated or air-conditioned, carpeted for young feet to pad around on, and have comfy chairs for nursing. As babies get older, take advantage of other children's programming. Be sure to check out the library's bulletin board to see what other free community stuff is going on. Perhaps there is a community center you favor? Low-cost and free programs abound there, too. And don't forget your favorite neighborhood playgrounds.

This is in no way an exhaustive list. Ask other parents you know for their cost-saving ideas. And if anyone criticizes you for not buying "new" things for your "new" baby, tell them that you would rather spend time with your baby than working extra hours to afford those things that the baby doesn't need anyway.

14.

First Foods

Emma-Joy's pediatrician told us that we could start introducing solid foods when she was six-months old, but since she was still exclusively breast-feeding on demand, that it wasn't crucial—there was no rush to suddenly get her eating a certain amount or variety of solid food at this age. She said that even one-year-old breast-fed babies are still getting 80% to 90% of their nutrition from breast milk and that it is best to take it slow, introducing one food at a time as a way to be gentle with her still-maturing digestive system and to observe any potential food intolerances or allergies.

So, starting at around six months old, we offered Emma-Joy a little iron-fortified rice cereal mixed with breast milk, but she really wasn't into it. She didn't want to suck it off our finger or eat it from a spoon. She did, however, like to splash her hand in a spilled puddle of it and smear it all around. We didn't push her to be any different.

The next month, I learned at a La Leche League (LLL) meeting that first foods at this age are more for fun, play, and experimentation and that babies who are not breast-feeding are the ones who need the extra iron from iron-fortified baby cereals. This is because breast-fed babies are rarely anemic, as the iron in human milk is well utilized with an absorption (bioavailability) rate of 50% to 75% (compared to an absorption rate of 4% to 10% of iron from formula). When I asked if it was a big deal that Emma-Joy was seven months old and still not too interested in food, the LLL leaders and other experienced moms there advised me that as long as she's happy, healthy, and growing well, that there was nothing to worry about and that she'd eat solid foods in her own time.

Just as babies have their own personalities and temperaments, so do they have their own timeline of feeding skills, appetites, and interests in food. To help create a healthy feeding attitude and model trust and respect with regards to food, pay more attention to your baby's developmental readiness than to a predetermined timetable.

Babies are ready for solid food when they:
• Are at least six months old
• Can sit up on their own
• Are hungry even after more frequent nursing that's unrelated to illness or teething
• Don't have the tongue-thrust reflex anymore
• Show interest in food, not just banging the spoon
• Can pick up things with one finger and thumb (a very cute thing like built-in baby chopsticks, but it's really called the pincer grasp)

Babies are *really* ready for solid food when they pick up food from your plate, eat it, and want more.

Over the next few months, she did start enjoying mashed avocado, banana, and chunks of ripe cantaloupe, but that was about it. Although she was developmentally ready to eat more solid food by most counts, she lacked two of the most important traits—interest and hunger for it. She stuck with the boobies. Though the information I'd received from the pediatrician and from LLL both told me that it was perfectly OK for a baby her age to consume way more breast milk than solid food (the American Academy of Pediatrics' most current recommendation states, "The optimal primary nutritional source during the first year of life is human milk"), my simple lack of confidence left me wondering if her eating hardly any solid foods at all really was fine.

I asked one of my midwife mama friends about how she'd introduced solid foods to her son who was quite a bit older than Emma-Joy. She could barely keep herself from cracking up as she recounted, "I didn't do anything but nurse him. But the day I saw him eating food out of the garbage, I knew it was time to give him something other than na-nas!"

I decided to follow her lead. Rather, I decided I'd follow Emma-Joy's lead. She still nursed like a fiend and was perfectly happy and healthy doing so. Though she dabbled in the realm of solid food here and there with more frequency, it wasn't until she was eighteen months old that she really started to get an appetite for food other than breast milk. And it was around then that it was hard to keep her out of the cat food all of a sudden.

Whole Foods Make the Best First Foods

Whole foods, left close to their natural state, have more nutritional value than foods that have been processed. For example, chunks of ripe peach have more good stuff in them than the peaches you'll find in a jar of baby food. A crunchy celery and nut-butter snack does a lot more for you than does a Ding-Dong or Twinkie.

Rice cereal, though a very popular first solid-food choice, is processed away from its whole-grain rice state. Peggy O'Mara writes in the March/April 2007 issue of *Mothering* magazine, "It is not a good idea to start with rice cereal... it has a high glycemic index and may raise the baby's levels of blood sugar and insulin. It is not as rich in nutrients or flavor as other foods, such as vegetables and fruits... the cereal became popular decades ago to complement formula feeding because it could be more easily fortified with iron."

For information on making your own baby food, see the "Thrifty Mama" chapter and check out this book: *The Natural Baby Food Cookbook*, by Margaret Kenda and Phyllis Williams.

Here are some good whole foods to feed to babies aged six to twelve months:

FRUITS: Mashed banana, plums, juicy peaches, soft pears, apricots, mashed avocado, frozen blueberries, unsweetened apple sauce, or small apple chunks that have been slightly cooked to soften first.

VEGGIES: Chunks of sweet potatoes or yams, mashed potatoes, carrots, green beans, peas (babies love frozen peas), and squash. Steam these fresh veggies until they're tender instead of using canned that might have too much salt added.

PROTEIN: Babies love to pick up cooked beans of all varieties: black, kidney, pinto, lima, garbanzo, etc. Remove the skins first if you can because they're harder to digest.

GRAINS: Whole-grain cereal Os, breads, and crackers are better than sugary teething biscuits. Babies love to gnaw on hard bagels, bread ends, and rice cakes. Whole-grain pasta and oatmeal, too.

FLUIDS: After your baby's first birthday, offer water, diluted 100% fruit or vegetable juice (50% or more water, 50% or less juice), milk (rice,

---

FOOD ALLERGY AND INTOLERANCE

Wait until your baby is one year old or older to introduce these foods, which can be allergenic: citrus fruits, strawberries, kiwi, corn, tomatoes, egg whites, soy, wheat, peanuts, chocolate, and cow's milk. In addition, cow's milk is too high in protein and minerals for a baby under one year old. Yogurt is OK, though, because of its live bacteria.

Honey should also be avoided for baby's first year as it can contain botulism spores that baby's system can't handle.

CHOKABLE FOODS

Babies and younger toddlers are not yet mature enough with their chewing and swallowing for the following foods (in no way an exhaustive list):
• Chunks or slices of raw apple or carrot (cook them to soft instead)
• Rice cakes
• Whole nuts and seeds
• Whole berries or grapes (quarter them)
• Popcorn kernels
• Potato or corn chips
• Peanut butter
• Meat chunks
• Hot dogs (meat or tofu)
• Hard candy
• Cookies
• Stringy foods (take the "string" out of green beans and celery first)

almond, oat, soy, goat, or cow—kefir is OK, too), or weak, non-caffeinated herbal teas. There are all types of non-spill sippy cups available. Until they're a year old, breast-fed babies can get their thirst (and hydration needs) completely quenched by nursing.

1 Year Old

15.

Toddler Chomps

I remember asking Ernesto, "So what are we going to feed her now?" Until then, it had been a no-brainer. There was the boobie milk, of course. And the short list of "good first foods" we'd posted on the refrigerator. But now that she had most of her teeth with which to chew just about anything, verbal skills with which to communicate, and interest and hunger for more solid foods, I was stumped about taking this next step, even though there had been a slow, gradual buildup leading me there. His answer told me how obvious and silly my question was, "She'll eat what we eat, of course."

A little light bulb went off in my new mama brain, just like it had when he'd answered, "In bed with us," when I asked where the baby would sleep. I mean, had I, who so far hadn't been paying much attention to ads and marketing aimed at new parents, been temporarily stumped and duped into thinking I may need to buy some Kid Cuisine, the prepackaged, overprocessed kiddie grub conveniently located in my grocer's freezer that's loaded with unhealthy fats and oils, too much sodium, sugar, artificial colors, and flavors? The super-sensational fruit-roll squisher splashers? The bite-sized, ready-in-a-jiffy Kiddo's pizza poppers? Did my subconscious believe the marketing that suggested kids only want to eat food specifically packaged, labeled, and branded "kid food"?

In hindsight, it was weird to me that I didn't know what kids ate. On one hand, given that fact that I'd had zero prior kid experience and Ernesto had a lot by comparison, it wasn't 100% strange that I didn't know what kids ate. (I had known to breast-feed because I knew my body automatically and naturally made the milk. But food after primarily depending on breast milk? It's embarrassing, but true: I had to ask.) Given that both Ernesto and I were very food-conscious, including being mindful about healthful quality, source, and distribution, having worked at Phoenix Rising organic vegetable farm, and having also been involved with Food Not Bombs for several years, I really should have known what kids ate.

Of course, Emma-Joy should eat what we eat! Because of our food-consciousness, she'd be eating healthy food. And there would be no getting in the habit of preparing separate, special meals. I just needed to figure out how much she should be eating.

> ## PAVE THE WAY TO BETTER MOODS AND BETTER HEALTH
>
> 1. Expose your child to a healthy variety of foods.
> 2. Encourage trying new tastes, but don't insist.
> 3. Involve your older, toddler in planning and preparing meals.
> 4. Model eating in moderation by grazing.
> 5. Let go of the idea that an appetite will be spoiled before "mealtime." So what if your kid is not hungry at mealtime? If sitting at the table together for a family meal is an important, special time to you, everyone can still be together enjoying each other's company even if not everyone is choosing to eat.

Self-Regulation Theory

Not a believer that kids should be required to clean their plates or else get no dessert, or that they should be forced to eat something that freaks them out, I turned to self-regulation theory. Given that infants can and do regulate their own breast milk intake (breast-feeding helps establish good eating habits right from the start), it should logically follow that they are able, as toddlers, to self-regulate their food intake.

Self-regulation theory, or SRT, states that only with self-regulation will a person appropriately implement advice. Here, advice refers to the modeled behaviors and information about healthy food choices and habits given to a child. SRT consists of several stages; again, the stages are described here specifically in reference to young children's healthy food choices and habits. First, the child is deliberately allowed to be in control of his/her own eating behavior. Next, this allowance fosters in a child the ability to evaluate how his/her eating behavior affects his/her own health. Finally, if the desired effect is not realized (desired effect equals feeling "good" instead of "bad," satisfied with taste/texture, hunger satiated, and not feeling too full, etc.), the child will change his/her eating behavior. If the desired effect is realized, the child reinforces the effect by continuing the behavior. Children as young as three years make the food connection between good food equals feel good, and bad food equals feel bad.

According to a 2005 article published in *Pediatric Nursing,* "Nutrition Education Aimed at Toddlers (NEAT): An Intervention Study," by Mildred A. Horodynski and Manfred Stommel, "Early childhood is a period when self-regulation develops rapidly. Young children come equipped with certain capabilities regarding their eating; they can learn to self-regulate their eating, but often need their parents to support it. Feeding requires a division of responsibility, such that the parent learns how to set appropriate limits and the toddler learns acceptable boundaries. It is the parent's responsibility to choose appropriate foods and offer them to the toddler. The child is primarily responsible for deciding if and how much to eat. Thus, the parent should follow the toddler's lead in regulation of food volume and timing."

Some parents may wonder if SRT allows for unregulated junk-food consumption. Will kids only choose to fill up on Cheetos and M&Ms? Maybe, when out at another's house (like doting grandparents'), a playdate, or a birthday party. And so what? If you don't have a lot of junk food at your own house, then an occasional romp in the junk-food jungle won't kill your kid (though it may be a setup for some wild-ass caffeine- or sugar-rush ride or an artificial color/flavor sensitivity). And maybe your kid will choose differently at another junk-food event on down the road if there's an associated bad feeling or tummy upset. You just may be pleasantly surprised to witness your toddler not overindulging and eating excess amounts of the stuff that s/he's not used to, the stuff that makes for an upset tummy. (I know I was!) If your kid has access to junk food more than occasionally, then set up respectful, legitimate boundaries. Keep the junky treats on hand at home to a minimum without forbidding them. You don't want a struggle that results in your kid wanting such-and-such even more, do you?

Again, don't underestimate the power of modeled behavior. If you or another caretaker is pigging out on crap all the time but you expect different from your toddler, do not be surprised that you'll have consistent food battles. (If you must, hide your personal stash of guilty pleasures.) SRT is not about a food free-for-all. Remember that it is a parent's job to provide nutritious food. The "let them eat what they want as long as they take an all-in-one kids vitamin" mentality doesn't work. That free-for-all mentality doesn't account for excess sodium, sugar, or fat, lack of fiber, or establishing unhealthy eating habits.

Picky Eaters

I've heard several parents exclaim, "But toddlers are notoriously picky eaters! How did you get Emma-Joy to eat kale and lentils?" Yes, toddlers literally are picky, using their little built-in thumb and forefinger-like chopsticks. But before I explain what's inaccurate about that commonly held belief, I need to rewind. Breast-fed babies get exposed to a variety of flavors in mama's breast milk and may be more willing to try new foods as an older baby or toddler. "One of the first ways that babies learn about flavors is through amniotic fluid and breast milk," says Julie Mennella, Ph.D., a taste researcher at Monell Chemical Senses Center, in Philadelphia. "We're finding that foods eaten during pregnancy and lactation can influence a baby's willingness to accept those foods later." Research also suggests that breast-fed babies may be less picky eaters as kids (and into adulthood) than formula-fed infants, especially if their moms eat a balanced diet while nursing.

Also, keep in mind that your toddler isn't growing like a baby anymore. In their first year, babies, on average, triple their birth weight. Therefore, they eat a lot. By comparison, toddlers, between their first and second birthdays, may gain a third or less. For example, a seven-pound baby at birth may weigh twenty-one pounds at her first birthday, but just under twenty-eight pounds on her second birthday. Toddlers typically grow more in height than in weight, and this is a normal slimming down, relying on excess stored baby fat for energy. Toddlers seem to eat less than they did as babies because their growth patterns change.

Consider, too, what toddlers do. They've begun walking and want to be up and about checking everything out all the time. They are too busy to sit still for anything, eating included. Toddlers can be moody little critters, so be prepared for finicky eating. What they like today may be shunned tomorrow. You may swear s/he has a teenager's appetite one day, then one of a bird the next. The erratic behavior, though it may be confusing, is perfectly normal toddler development, so keep the behavior-modification guns holstered.

Embrace the fine art of grazing; it's not just for cows. As with on-demand breast-feeding, throw out scheduled feedings. Nibbling throughout the day is nutritionally better than eating three big meals of breakfast, lunch, and dinner—for children and adults alike. Set up a low, self-serve table with an assortment of

---

POOR PARENTAL BEHAVIORS WITH FOOD

1. BRIBERY: Never use food as a reward or punishment. Don't encourage overeating as a way to get dessert. Don't send your kid to bed hungry for not doing something s/he needed to.

2. RIGID CONTROL: Delete "Clean your plate" from your personal lexicon.

3. STRUGGLES OVER EATING: Also delete "You're not getting up from the table until you've eaten X amount of X."

4. GUILT: Spare the "Do you know how lucky you are? There are millions of kids starving in Africa who would love to eat the dinner you're not touching." (My mom told me that her mom, my Grandmary, used this one on her and her siblings, to which they'd reply, "Oh yeah? Name three." When Grandmary used it on me as a kid, I asked her for an envelope so I could mail them my leftovers.)

5. FORCE: Don't be a jerk by requiring that "You have to eat your leftover dinner from last night before you get new food."

6. DISCOURAGING OR FROWNING ON MESSES: Relaxing about messes will aid your child's budding independence. Don't continue to feed a child who can feed his/herself, regardless of how messy s/he is.

healthy nibbles. Or make snacks available on a low shelf in the fridge. If, after you try teaching your toddler that the self-serve snacks are not for picking up and dumping, your toddler continues trying to do so, then s/he is probably too young for it on his/her own. Also remember that running and playing with food still in his/her mouth is a choking hazard.

When out-and-about, get in the habit of snack-packin'. It was easy for me to get in the habit of never leaving home without at least two snacks and a water bottle because the times in the beginning when I hadn't snack-packed, I could count on Emma-Joy having a hunger-induced meltdown. And it sucks needing to hunt down an affordable healthy quick fix if you're stuck in the middle of fast-food and convenience-store land.

Though Emma-Joy took well to eating the same food we did, including the stereotypically kid-hated foods like spinach, kale, brown rice, tofu, lentils, and lima beans, and was a master grazer, there are plenty of breast-fed babies who really do become picky eaters later on. This pickiness will not necessarily turn you into a short-order cook, preparing separate, special meals.

Focusing on weekly and monthly balanced nutrition instead of daily intake is one key; making available a variety of foods is another. Variety is key to balanced nutrition. Toddlers need an average of 1,000 to 1,300 calories a day for the year between their first and second birthdays. Some days they may consume more than this average, and some days, less. Nutrition balances out over time. Worry not about balanced meals; instead focus on balanced weeks.

In *The Baby Book*, Dr. William and Martha Sears write, "It was our job to buy the right food, prepare it nutritionally, and serve it creatively; then our job was over." That is to say, parents and children play different roles in the food game. Parents can relax with their job done and leave the rest of the responsibility with the child à la SRT (deciding how much, when, and if s/he eats). Trust that your child will not go hungry. Sure, there is a balance to be struck between being negligent and controlling when it comes to feeding a toddler, but getting rid of force, coercion, and pressure and going with the flow of needs and moods helps everyone win. And it sets the stage for healthy eating habits, and fosters goals of parenting a free child by modeling respect, trust, and responsibility.

It's been well established that growing up with poor eating habits as a child—including high caloric intake as well as the consumption of energy-dense fast foods—often leads to continued bad eating habits as an adult. Research suggests that lifelong food preferences are set during the first three years of life and it is generally easier to change knowledge than actual behaviors—eating habits are particularly hard to break. Over time, an unhealthy diet can lead to clogged arteries, weakened bones, and high blood pressure. Healthy eating habits can reduce the risk of several life-threatening health conditions, including obesity, coronary heart disease, type 2 diabetes, stroke, cancer, and osteoporosis.

So do your kid (and yourself!) a favor, and model healthy eating habits and food choices. Toddlers learn about what to eat and why to eat it from their parents and caregivers. Toddlers can self-regulate eating when parents recognize and respond appropriately to their needs. Remember that what and how your kid regularly eats impacts the development of both mind and

> FIVE (NOT SO) FUN FACTS
>
> 1. On average, American preschoolers get about fourteen to seventeen teaspoons of added sugar a day, mostly from fruit-flavored drinks, high-fat desserts, and cola-type soft drinks.
>
> 2. Twenty-five percent of toddlers eat french fries on a daily basis.
>
> 3. Many children do not obtain adequate amounts of calcium, potassium, fiber, magnesium, and vitamins A, C, and E.
>
> 4. Within a twenty-four hour period, an estimated 62% of toddlers aged nineteen to twenty-four months consume a baked dessert; 20% consume candy; and 44% drink a sweetened beverage.
>
> 5. More than 80% of U.S children exceed the recommended daily allowance of total saturated fat, but consume less than adequate amounts of fiber, fruits, and vegetables.

body. Eat small amounts often. Choose more whole foods and fewer processed foods. Learn about nutrition! Find out what the bad, better, and best sugars are. The good, bad, and in-between fats, too. Know the difference between unsaturated and saturated fats. Learn about how vitamin C aids iron absorption but that calcium inhibits it. Brush up on how many fruits and vegetables a person should have each day. Buy seasonal produce from your local farmers' market! Look up recommended protein, carbohydrate, fiber, and cholesterol intakes. Read the label before you toss the box of whatever into your grocery cart. Does it contain partially or fully hydrogenated oils? What about trans fat? Talk to your kid about why you're reading labels. Don't forget the vitamins and minerals. Reduce the amount of salt and sweeteners in your diet. And whenever possible, eat organic.

Eating healthy doesn't have to be hard. As with anything else you're not used to doing but want to do better, it will take practice. Taking one step at a time, you can and will improve your knowledge, and then good habits will follow. Set a healthy food goal that's realistic, not unattainable. Make it a goal to get better, not perfect. What is perfect anyway? To be sure, it's something too rigid and boring. Eating should be neither of those things.

Time is something all parents need more of, whether you're taking care of baby full-time or doing paycheck work... or both! Eating healthy, once you get in the groove, does not have to suck away time that you don't have enough of already.

Though I was food-conscious before I got pregnant, I did have to change my eating habits. It used to be that I thought nothing of skipping breakfast, grabbing a bean burrito for lunch, and then having a plate of whatever was around for dinner. Pregnancy, breast-feeding, and then also keeping up with a very active toddler not only necessitated an increase in my caloric intake, but also that I become more of a grazer so as to maintain a sufficient energy level throughout the day.

Healthy Food and Snack Ideas

Of course, this is in no way an exhaustive list, but here are some healthy food and snack ideas. Both vegetarian and vegan diets can provide all the nutrients a growing child needs. Vitamin B-12 is not readily found in plant foods, so to guarantee your kid gets enough (about 2 micrograms a day), you can supplement with a B-12 tablet.

FOR VEGANS: Graham crackers; steamed vegetable chunks; brown rice; tofu cubes; oatmeal; dried fruit; cut-up nut-butter sandwiches with banana; pita bread with hummus; unsweetened applesauce; vegetable nori rolls; edamame pods; warmed or roasted garbanzo beans w/Spike seasoning; apple slices tossed in cinnamon and peanut-butter dip; Ants on a Log (raisins on nut butter on celery sticks); frozen banana pieces (cut half in rounds with nut butter, dark chocolate, or maple syrup dip); avocado half topped with lemon juice, salt, and pepper (eaten with a spoon); frozen mango (great way to make use of mango that's too ripe to eat fresh); marinated tempeh strips; pesto-garlic toast; black beans cooked with kale; roasted pears; carrot sticks with tahini-molasses dip; popcorn seasoned with nutritional yeast, Spike seasoning, and tamari; chopped, steamed kale squeezed into balls w/Bragg's Liquid Aminos dip; frozen quartered grapes; veggie/tofu/tempeh/bread sticks with nutritional yeast gravy; veggie dog ka-bobs; nut-butter spoons (predipped and tops wrapped with plastic wrap for storage); dark chocolate-covered matzo (premade and frozen), smoothies topped with granola (these smoothies rival ice cream more than juice, consistency-wise: always use frozen bananas as base, then small amount nondairy milk—coconut milk or homemade tahini milk for thicker consistency—and frozen fruit(s) of choice. Never added sweetener or ice); figs and almonds (soaking almonds—walnuts, too!—overnight, then storing sealed in the fridge is a great way to keep happy snacks on hand. Doing so gives them a unique texture, gets rid of bitter-tasting tannins, and makes the proteins easier on the digestive tract).

FOR VEGETARIANS: All of the above, and: yogurt with cut-up fruit pieces; whole-grain blueberry muffin; tortilla rolled with beans and cheese, and mild salsa for dipping; hardboiled eggs; string cheese and cubed cheese; whole-wheat toast with cream cheese; veggie shred pancakes (grated zucchini, carrot, or spinach cooked in); English muffin pizzas made with tomato sauce, cheese, and spinach; plus all the above vegan foods.

FOR OMNIVORES: Pita pockets stuffed with lean meats and lettuce—kids love to stuff the pockets themselves; plus all of the above vegan and vegetarian foods.

NOT-SO-JUNKY TREATS: If treats offer some nutritional value instead of empty calories, then they're not so junky: for example, cookies made with oil and brown rice syrup instead of butter and refined sugar. Added dried fruit, nuts, or oatmeal is good, too. Carrot cakes or fruit pies made

B's FLAX MUFFINS

B, as Emma-Joy renamed her, is my mom. She changed, experimented with, and perfected this recipe over time. These muffins are perfect for a quick grab-and-go breakfast or snack for crumb-munching toddlers!

1. Mix all dry ingredients:

> 1 1/2 cups wheat flour
>
> 3/4 cup ground flax seed
>
> 2 tsp. baking soda sifted with
>
> 1 tsp. baking powder
>
> 1/4 cup unprocessed raw sugar (or less)★
>
> 2 tsp. cinnamon
>
> 1 cup each: chopped walnuts, chopped dates, raisins, other dried fruit chopped into mini bits

2. Mix wet ingredients to equal 2 cups (16 oz.):

> 2 tsp. vanilla
>
> 6 Tbsp. egg whites
>
> equal parts of unsweetened applesauce and unsweetened soy milk

3. Combine wet ingredients to dry and mix well.

4. Add one mashed ripened banana and mix well again.

5. Scoop into a greased mini-muffin pan. (Makes 24 mini muffins plus 3 regular-sized muffins.)

6. Bake at 350° F for 14 minutes or until an inserted toothpick comes out clean.

★ *You can also make these with no sugar but they don't raise up as well. The dates give them a lot of sweetness.*

with oat flour, graham cracker, or whole-wheat crust are better than grocery-store birthday cakes with the gobs of disgusting hydrogenated oil and artificial color and flavor frosting. Kids love cobblers: peach, apple, pear, etc. Added nuts and oats to these are yummy, too. Smoothies always rock (our personal favorite is frozen strawberry, peach, and banana in the blender with rice milk, orange juice, and 1 added tablespoon of cod liver oil), as do homemade frozen fruit and juice popsicles. And oatmeal raisin cookies. And zucchini bread. And...

16.

Discipline Notes: Setting Up a "Yes" Environment for a Free Child

"My baby's twelve months old and I've only told her 'No' maybe five times." When I heard a mama share this with a group of us new mamas at a gathering of the Wiggly Baby Society at the birth center, I at first just took it to mean that her baby was "well behaved." But as the conversation progressed, I gathered clues that her only saying "No" five or so times was owing more to a conscious choice she'd made, rather than to her baby's temperament.

Because Emma-Joy was just a couple months old, I hadn't even begun to think about the practicalities of child behavior, issues of discipline, or as the conversation eventually led, baby-proofing the house to create a "Yes" environment. Up until then, Ernesto and I had formed our general theories about what we thought raising a free child meant, but had only put theory into practice with caring for newborn Emma-Joy. Past that, we'd only casually wondered how we'd handle inevitable parent-child conflicts without relying on tired-out models of "discipline" based on children being treated as parental property, as things to be controlled, oppressed, disrespected, and punished, instead of as equal human beings with their own thoughts, desires, and interests.

When Emma-Joy started crawling the day she turned five months old, the baby-proofing was thrust upon us much sooner than I'd expected. Initially, just trying for safety and damage control, we ran out to get outlet covers, swept really well to get rid of in-the-baby's mouth contraband like dustbunnies and paper clips, and relocated Boneless (the cat)'s food and water dishes, as well as the breakable pieces of my handmade pottery, to higher shelves. That was fine for a while. Until she really started getting into things. You know, like everything.

"No, no, no, don't throw the cassette tapes everywhere. No, no, no, don't pull the tape out of the cassette! No, no, no, don't pull on that cord. No, no, no hands on my first-pressing colored vinyl records! Ohmigod, take that stapler out of your mouth!"

Baby-Proofing Your Home

That kind of constant interference with her natural, curious exploration had to change. We needed to get smarter about sharing our space with a child. There was no balance in our environment; it was adult-centered and adult-controlled. We had to create a more amicable arrangement where Emma-Joy would be as free to move about as we were and where we weren't expending our parenting energy on safekeeping certain material possessions. I got down on the floor and took a look around each room from baby's-eye level. Seeing things from this point of view helped me see what needed to change.

We cleared the low, built-in shelves of my 7-inch record collection and instead stocked them with board books and toys. I fashioned tie-down curtains out of scrap fabric to enclose the bottom of the two-by-four-foot constructed stereo stand where the cassettes were. We carefully wrapped and secured electric cords to make them less tempting. Office supplies were moved above the computer monitor. We bought a five-by-six foot carpet remnant and placed short baskets of stuffed animals and baby-friendly musical and playthings here and there. In short, we turned our apartment into a "Yes" environment where we not only freed ourselves from constant worry about safety and saying "No, no, no," but also freed her to live more comfortably and welcome in what had been anything but a kid-friendly space.

Baby-Proofing Yourself

An early crawler, Emma-Joy continued on a fast path. She was hard to keep up with. At seven months old, she literally walked everywhere by getting up on her knees. Not one person told us they'd ever seen anything like it. She took to her feet before she turned eleven months old. She didn't take a first step; she took a first walk

"NO, NO, NO" HAS GOT TO GO, GO, GO!

How many times a day are you saying "No" to your child? If you actually try to count, you may be surprised. Are you saying "No, no, no" instead of one firm "No"? Saying "no" repeatedly and too much makes it lose its effectiveness. Your kids will tune your "Nos" out. And they will say it a lot back to you because you say it a lot to them. Support your toddler's autonomy by restricting your use of the word "No" to issues of safety. Safety is the main reason for wanting our kids to respond to our "Nos"; it's much more important than a well-mannered toddler.

Instead of "No", use the word "Stop" as an emergency brake. If your kid is headed full speed ahead towards the street, "Stop!" is much more effective than, "No, don't run into the street!" Chances are if they are hearing the more common word "No" first, they may tune it out and then only hear the last words you said—"run into the street." In situations like these, the fewer words the better.

In the kitchen, be sure to stock all the unbreakable, not sharp, and nontoxic things in the bottom cabinets—metal pots and pans, plastic bowls and cups, reusable water bottles, dish towels, and cloth napkins. Relocate the breakable, sharp, and toxic (I recommend getting rid of toxic things all together—you really don't need that gallon of bleach anyway) things to out-of-baby's-reach cabinets and shelves. Do this in the bathroom, too. Babies love to be where you are—having them play on the floor in their own cabinets is fun for them, and you will better be able to get done what you're trying to. When they need to be on you, sling the baby and keep about your business.

Set the house up in stations. Have a music crate, a book nook, a general play area for toys, and baskets of fun, interesting things strategically placed. Have something to explore in every area of the house.

Do you need nice furniture? If not, get used futons and cover them with a protective layer and then a soft sheet over that; go frame-free, folding the futons in half to make a floor couch. Have low chairs at a low table, and floor pillows strewn about, too. With furniture not too tall to access or too tall to fall off, living "on the ground" is a big help to crawling babies and toddlers. Plus, toddlers love to roughhouse, bounce, bonk around, and go nuts. With the sparkly, breakable things up and out of reach and old cushions stacked in a corner, a rowdy kid can burn energy and you'll save energy not having to corral them away with "Nos."

With cupboards full of safe, fun stations to explore, and furniture rearranged and reconfigured, you've created a capital Y-E-S environment that encourages freedom and independence.

clear across her Abuela's living room in Montana. Back in Florida a week later, she started running. Her physical abilities far exceeded her emotional, social, and intellectual development. This made for some frustrating times for all of us. Looking back to the day she was born, remembering how she picked her head up off my chest to look at me with that furled brow of hers. I joke that she was born frustrated.

On the go, yet very much still attached, she wanted me everywhere she wanted me to be. She wanted to do everything all at once. She was curious about everything; nothing escaped her. I didn't yet understand toddler behavior the way I do now, so I didn't know how to deal with her; after all, she was still supposed to be a baby. I remembered that our childbirth educator had said that until eighteen months old, babies aren't capable of manipulation or other purposely "bad" behavior. That's the premise on which I'd been operating, and by the time Emma-Joy turned eighteen months old, my misinterpretation was obvious. I'd took it to mean, along with my intention to parent a free child, that everything was permissible. I'd made myself completely available to her, unable to differentiate her temporal desires from her genuine needs. My total focus was on her. And she was in control.

She was running me ragged physically, emotionally, and creatively, but I didn't know why. Though very verbal at just eighteen months old, it was constant guesswork to figure out if she really wanted my help or not, if I could walk away for a moment or not, if I was doing things exactly the way she wanted me to or not. I felt like a steamrolled doormat and sometimes, like I was being bullied into placating her every desire. There were no boundaries. I wasn't consistent. I felt stuck because I knew the path we were on wasn't a good, sustainable one, but I lacked confidence and tools to fix it while remaining committed to gentle, patient, respectful, free-child parenting.

Things came to a head the first time we tried the timeout technique. I'd read in a book that for every year your child is old, that's how many minutes the timeout should last. One evening she kept hitting me, even after I'd modeled gentle touches by taking her hand in mine while calmly repeating "gentle touches" and after firmly telling her "No hitting; hitting hurts me." Running out of patience, I hauled her to the bedroom, told her she was having a timeout because she hit me, and closed the door on her. I left her there for a minute and a half.

I stood outside the door the whole time. I didn't hear a peep. When I opened the door to let her out, she stood there smiling and said, "Hi, Mommy!" I reminded her why she'd gotten a time out and we went back into the living room together. There, she promptly smacked me in the face again, hard.

Instead of me repeating the time out, she gave herself one. "I go timeout," she said excitedly as she ran to the bedroom and closed the door on herself.

What the f...?

Ernesto and I stared at each other in disbelief. At eighteen months old, she'd made a complete mockery of what was supposed to be a punishment. Toddlers were supposed to be scared of being in a room alone. Terrified. Devastated, even. That's what the book had said anyway.

But not Emma-Joy. No, our eighteen-month-old freely mingled with self-imposed exile. Made a fun game out of it, even. Unfortunately, I was too upset at having been repeatedly hit to find it humorous.

At a complete loss for how to proceed or get to the root of her full-throttle behavior, I promptly started asking other parents what they'd do if they were me. Because none of them, not even Emma-Joy's pediatrician, had ever heard of an eighteen-month-old making a mockery of timeout, they had no advice to offer. "Wow, sounds like you have your hands full with this one" was the best they could do.

I didn't want to know how to break her spirit or anything. Quite the opposite. I just wanted the magic recipe that would keep her spirit intact but at the same time calm her ass down a bit so that our days would be more predictable and enjoyable.

I started reading everything I could, trying this tip, modifying that suggestion to fit our situation. Though I was learning a lot quickly, things were getting worse before they were getting better. There was no magic recipe. There were times when I'd be stuck in the middle of the street with a screaming child who wasn't willing to be either in the umbrella stroller or on my hip in the sling, and I was sure that

Ten Toddler Tips

1. **Redirection, not Restriction:** First, redirecting cuts down on the amount of "Nos." For example, "You can pour water in the tub or outside, but not in the middle of the floor." Redirect without touch, as touch can get you defensiveness and anger. If you must touch, do so gently without jerking or muscling your kid away from the "No" but towards the "Yes." A child's individual temperament (easy-going/low-maintenance kid versus feisty/higher-maintenance kid) plays a role with redirection. So does parental patience.

2. **Transitions:** Too many transitions in a day might be too much for a kid to handle sometimes. Just as adults need to take "mental health days," so do kids. Cancel what you had planned on doing; back off the multitasking if it's not working for your kid. Research suggests that kids who feel listened to in this way will demonstrate more cooperation and positive interaction for days afterwards. Also, giving language cue warnings on time to transition is good, "Ten minutes until we have to leave. Five minutes until we have to leave." If rushing around isn't avoidable, bringing snacks and comfort items and staying realistic about what you can get done with a kid in tow will help stave off meltdowns.

3. **Toddler Tantrums:** Toddler tantrums are signs of growth and are about autonomy, not making parents feel miserable. They are about what the child thinks s/he needs right then to feel good. In the first three years, kids are learning about managing the intensity of their needs. They learn that it's sad to not get what you want, but that you'll live. They will also learn that it's no fun to have a meltdown, and learn what will help them bounce back after having one. Don't panic, and try to reshape the world to fit your kid's immediate demands. They move on quickly and so should you; don't make a big deal out of it and don't get stuck there, because your toddler won't!

4. **Toddler Aggression:** Tips from Rahula Janowski and Tracey Kenyon-Milarsky, from the anarchist parenting listserv: Reflecting their feelings helps, "You're upset that we had to leave the park" or "I know you're frustrated because you couldn't do that by yourself." (This also helps teach emotional intelligence.)...(cont'd)

I'd made the wrong choice having a kid, that being a parent was something I just wasn't cut out for.

I'd been so diligent in my care for her as a newborn; so mindful of being responsive and respectful. I'd gone out of my way to create a mutually amicable living space. But now with her budding independence upon us, it seemed as if everything had backfired. There was no cooperation; "respect" and "trust" were words from a foreign language; she had all the freedom and I had none; and to top it off, when we'd resorted to punitive discipline, we couldn't even get that thing right!

One of the biggest pieces of the puzzle that I'd been lacking was that I'd become completely child-centered. Allowing her to be in charge because I was a reluctant authoritarian, I'd unfairly put too much responsibility on her. In learning how to meet her needs, I relied on her to lead the way and teach me how to be a parent. I hadn't yet learned that babies come hard-wired needing someone to lead them, not just take care of them. I was depriving her the opportunity to watch and learn from me; I was, after all, the grown up with more life experience, but because I lacked parenting experience, I acted as a child in need, also.

In her essay *Who's In Control, the Unhappy Consequences of Being Child-Centered*, Jean Liedloff writes, "Being played with, talked to, or admired all day deprives the babe of [the] in-arms spectator phase that would feel right to him. Unable to say what he needs, he will act out his discontentment. He is trying to get his caretaker's attention, yet—and here is the cause of the understandable confusion—his purpose is to get the caretaker to change his unsatisfactory experience, to go about her own business with confidence and without seeming to ask his permission. Once the situation is corrected, the attention-getting behavior we mistake for a permanent impulse can subside. The same principle applies in the stages following the in-arms phase."

I had been so concerned about not being adult-centered that I'd gone overboard in the other direction. With the new piece to my puzzle, I worked hard to figure out how to put everything together—parenting with the intent to distinguish between legitimate and illegitimate parenting authority, how to be in control without being controlling, and the desire to parent a free child while avoiding both adult-centered and child-centered practices.

I stopped asking her permission, "Can Mommy do this and you do that?" I stopped asking her question after question to try to figure out what she wanted, "Do you want to go outside or play with this toy? Do you want to take a bath or go to bed now?" Instead of just trying to nurture her thoughts, desires, and interests, I started paying attention to my own. I made conscious decisions to stop being a doormat, to

Redirecting helps toddler aggression, too. Have drums and pillows for hitting. Lightweight, soft balls for throwing indoors. Crunchy, tooth-sinking foods for biting. For example, if you have a rule that only soft things can be thrown but your child throws a hard thing, give a verbal reminder of the rule and physically give your child something soft that is OK to throw. Even invite your child to play a throwing game with the soft things. Also, explain why, too: that is, throwing hard things can hurt people or break things inside.

5. SELF-SOOTHING BEHAVIORS: Most kids have some. Keep your eyes open to them. They will show you what works. Though what works might be silly to you, they hold value for your toddler.

6. LESS TALK: Though it's never too early to explain why to kids, too many words to a toddler can be overwhelming and grating. Keep explanations to toddlers brief when they can't have what they want right then. But don't "talk down;" stop the baby talk. Does your two-year-old ever ask you to stop talking? Emma-Joy, though a very verbal kid, sure did.

7. MORE MUSIC: Use music as a nonverbal tool for diversion, calming, and reassurance. Music can interrupt distress and help with redirection. Rhythm soothes kids. It can also help a parent stop their frustration from escalating. Let your child pick out the music. Rock together in a rocking chair. Singing and dancing is an easy and fun activity to redirect to.

8. BUDDING LANGUAGE SKILLS: A toddler's language acquisition is amazing, understanding/comprehending up to twelve new words a day (not always spoken). If you can get a toddler to express what is upsetting them, it's like having the key to a treasure chest. It will help you meet their genuine needs.

9. INDEPENDENCE AND SELF-RELIANCE: Toddlers are optimistic creatures, thinking the impossible can be achieved, but they are still very much dependent on you being there for them. "I do it myself!" was Emma-Joy's mantra, though if I dared leave her alone to do it herself, she'd become overwhelmed. Don't burst their autonomy-emerging bubbles; let them try to do things themselves. When they succeed, celebrate with them; when they fail, recognize they've learned something. ...(cont'd)

10. Toddlers as Scientists: Rahula Janowski writes, "When [my child] was a toddler, I tried to keep in mind the idea that toddlers are scientists, conducting experiments such as *Hmmm, if I stand up in the chair, what happens? OK, daddy speaks sternly. What if I stand in the chair NOW? What if I stand in the chair with mommy? What about NOW?* Or *Yesterday when I pulled the cat's tail, this happened, I wonder what will happen today?* I think they are trying to find things out, but they aren't doing it in a 'test my limits' kind of way, more of a test reality kind of way. So our job is to be the constant in the experiment. As in, *No matter how many times or under what circumstances I stand in the chair, daddy/mommy/other adults will always gently sit me down and tell me 'We sit on our bottom in the high chair.'* As for the cat, when [my child] was not gentle with the cat, we would remind her with words, show her physically (i.e., take her hand in mine and pet the cat together), and also, remove the cat from danger. The cats definitely got some rough pulls and stuff, but at four years old, she is unfailingly gentle and respectful with them. If I threw food at another adult and you said 'don't' and I did it again, obviously I'm being an asshole. But we have to have a completely different set of expectations for toddlers; they're in another world entirely. That is, we expect them to behave appropriately, but we have to be ready for it to take two million reminders before it becomes normal behavior. The thing I found most useful about the 'scientist' approach was that it didn't trigger me the way the idea that she was 'testing me' did. And I was able to have longer patience and take a little more joy in her exploration of the world."

model self-respect by setting boundaries, and to be consistent. And I reestablished my commitment to parent positively without punitive discipline or punishment.

On my journey to figure out this hard, ideal-driven way to parent, I came across lots of similar ideas and theories: positive discipline, gentle discipline, attachment parenting-based discipline, nonpunitive discipline, and Taking Children Seriously (a libertarian parenting philosophy for discipline and education). I read about all resources I could, taking and leaving bits and pieces of each (see the "10 Toddler Tips" sidebar, as well as the other two "Discipline Notes" chapters). None of them, however, revealed a single, linear way of thinking nor provided a simple checklist to follow. I read about nonviolent communication, how different personalities and temperaments can work together, and traits of healthy families. I did my own research into how the developing human brain works from infancy well into childhood.

Radically rethinking parenting, I discovered that discipline is not separate from parenting and that parenting is not separate from teaching. I embraced the idea that parenting a free child requires a fundamental paradigm shift, one that demands radical honesty and self-examination in order to shift from authoritarian parenting to cooperative parenting. Viewing my desire to parent in a way rooted in cooperation greatly helped me to move from avoiding any authority in my parenting and, consequently, being ruled by my child, to discovering the difference between legitimate and illegitimate authority.

17.

Cutting the Cord

When my baby was about ten months old, I was finally able to be away from her for about twelve hours. Afterward, I often wondered when I'd ever be able to be away overnight or even for a few days. When Emma-Joy was almost seventeen months old, I asked several other nursing moms when they were first able to spend the night away from the baby. Their answers varied, but one thing was consistent: they all said to just go for it, that the baby would be fine.

They told me that the baby would still want to nurse when I got back and, if for some reason she didn't, I'd have gotten off easy in the weaning department. They also said that my biggest inconvenience while away would be that my breasts would get engorged with milk and hurt.

Truth is, even before I asked for my friends' advice, I had already made up my mind and booked a flight to California. I had a plane ticket, but I didn't have a mind at ease despite my friends' encouragement and support. Although I knew I was going no matter what, for weeks I was nervous about leaving Emma-Joy. I found out firsthand that separation anxiety doesn't only affect children, and that it starts even before you leave.

I kept thinking about the first time that I had I left her—for just three hours, my first day at paycheck work since her birth. She had gobbled a live earthworm, picked up a fresh dog turd off the grass, and puked all over the next-door neighbor. I thought that somehow none of those things would have happened if she had been with me. I thought about our first twelve-hour separation and how bad my boobs had hurt, even though I had pumped a little, because she hadn't nursed all day and my milk just kept building up. I thought about how much I had missed her after only twelve hours. I thought about being more than 3,000 miles away from her and got really scared because I wouldn't be able to immediately come to her rescue if she needed me. I was very uneasy, all the way up to my moment of departure. I just had to convince myself that she and Ernesto would be totally fine without me for four days, because really, they would be.

Ernesto was very supportive, even encouraging. He knew he was in for a lot of work, and that there might be episodes during which he'd have a difficult time soothing Emma-Joy because he didn't have "the boobies." Yet he was also looking forward to the bonding experience, and looking at the four days as an exercise in building his own confidence as a new parent.

When they dropped me off at the airport, I hugged, kissed, and waved them goodbye. The butterflies in my stomach mounted but didn't escape. Emma-Joy didn't cry when I walked away; she just waved and yelled cheerily, "Bye, Mama!"

Excellent. I could at least have a guilt-free flight.

And guilt-free it was. I swear that as soon as I started flying away, my anxious butterflies flew back to where they had come from. I was at ease because I had resolved that I couldn't turn around now, even if I wanted to.

Eight hours later, I landed in San Francisco and was happy to just be there, ready to have my first baby-free fun since I got pregnant over two years earlier.

I met up with my dear ol' former bandmate Becky, and we ate at my favorite Thai place. Afterward, I had to find somewhere that would let me use the restroom for about ten minutes so I could express breast milk and give my engorged breasts some relief. After nursing a baby on demand for seventeen months and then going a whole day without nursing at all, ouch, I hurt. My tits were hard, leaking rocks.

Later, we ate another round of kick-ass food and then went to the show at Kimo's. It was really dark in there, really, really loud, and I was really, really, really happy. I surprised myself and didn't drink. As much as I wanted to let loose, I also didn't want to feel like shit for the rest of my three days off. It felt good to be in a place where I hardly knew anyone and where no one knew I was a mom, where my name could be Jessica instead of Emma-Joy's Mommy, a place where I could just relax to some super-loud music.

The next day was just as exciting. I slept my first full night in a year and a half! No baby woke me up three times in the middle of the night to nurse!

We found our way to the early show at Mission Records. Ironically, I had to leave the early show early to get to Bottom of the Hill to play with Citizen Fish, the main reason I took a few days off in the first place. Although I was only going to play four songs per night with them, I seriously doubted that I'd be able to pull it off. I had only practiced for twenty minutes the night before I flew out.

The anxiety butterflies were back swirling in my stomach, but after the sound check, my stomach calmed down and I experienced a huge surge of energy that I hadn't felt since I was pregnant. I had just reclaimed a part of my life that had been ignored for two whole years!

After the show, I was still so excited that I decided to do something with that breast milk that kept building up with no baby to nurse. I marched up to the bar and got a White Russian minus the milk, with an inch left at the top of the glass. The bartender quickly corrected me and told me that what I had just ordered was called a Black Russian. Yeah, whatever it was called, I just wanted it to have an inch left from the top.

I then marched into the women's restroom with my drink, aimed my boobs (one at a time) toward the glass, and *voilà*, I finished the homemade touch to the now-White Russian. Next,

TIPS FOR TAKING TIME OFF

Primary caretakers, here is my advice about taking time off for yourselves.

1. Get over the guilt. You deserve this!

2. Recognize that time to yourself is not only important, it's necessary. A happy, recharged mama or papa is not only a better mama or papa, but you'll be doing something for your own individual needs and desires, hence doing away with parental martyrdom.

3. If you are a still-nursing mama, don't forget to pack an empty bottle. You'll need to relieve the engorgement by manually expressing milk from each breast every four hours, more or less as needed. And don't cry over spilled milk. You don't have any way of storing it while on the go. Just flush it or rinse it down the sink if there are no White Russians to be made.

4. Pack clothes that will allow you to dress differently than how you usually do. This will make you feel like a new person!

5. Bring pictures. You'll get a dose of sweetness and rid yourself of separation anxiety.

6. Don't call home too often. If you have a cell phone, wait to be called. This way, you'll have more fun time and less phone time. And your partner or other caretaker will feel more confident and trusted.

7. For fun, bring home little treats for the happy reunion.

I had to find innocent—but hopefully already drunk—bystanders to partake in the most DIY beverages of them all.

Of the six or seven who guzzled the signature drink, all of them agreed that it was a damn good one. One guy even exclaimed, "Yugh, there's a lot of booze in there." I agreed, "Yeah, there are a lot of boobs in there." Becky videotaped the entire episode and it's still pretty damn funny to watch.

The next day we played at an early show at 924 Gilman Street in Berkeley. Again, I had a great time playing. So great in fact that when I called Ernesto for the tenth time to see how things were going, I also asked how things would be if I stayed another few days to play a couple more shows.

He responded, "Ugh, I have a lot to get done and I haven't been able to do anything until baby goes to sleep."

I thought to myself, *Oh, really? Not able to get anything done? You had to wait until after baby went to bed to get anything done? Yes, I know exactly what you're saying.*

I also knew that I should go home as scheduled and not push our first successful separation. He had finally experienced what I had experienced many, many times. I had proved to myself that I could both still be myself and be a good mom. And I felt grateful that I would be able to reclaim even more of myself for an even longer period of time in the near future.

I flew home the next day. As soon as my baby saw me, she wanted to nurse. I was glad, but I really don't think I would have been too bummed if she hadn't wanted to anymore. Only four days apart and she looked like she had grown. She had definitely started saying more words. She had changed and so had I. She—living things for the first time. Me—re-living. And I was ready to go again—ready to get back to my old routine as a mom and also ready for another opportunity to leave.

18.

Organizing Cooperative Childcare

When I was pregnant, a handful of acquaintances and friends were also expecting or already had a child. I thought it would be exciting to share information and childcare with them. Early on, I connected with a few of the more experienced parents and picked their brains about how to deal with things I had no idea about, like sane ways to deal with cloth diapers and getting sleep. But it took me about a year and a half until I was ready to trade childcare with others. Rather, that's the time when I felt Emma-Joy was verbal enough to be able to effectively communicate her needs to other caregivers.

Around that time, two mama friends of mine started organizing a childcare co-op as an alternative to for-profit babysitting services.

The basic idea was that after getting to know each other and their kids through playdates and potlucks, a core group of parents would trade childcare services. The organizers researched the Internet to learn about other childcare co-ops, and then called a meeting through word-of-mouth for any interested parents in our community to attend. At that first meeting, they shared their findings with all of us, and we looked at the details of the other co-ops and discussed what we thought would work for our individual and collective needs. We then came up with a game plan.

It was wonderful to think that I'd soon be able to have about ten hours a week free from any childcare duties in exchange for about ten hours a week of watching someone else's kid. After all, it is often easier to take care of two kids who play with each other, than just have your own who needs you to provide all the entertainment.

Our initial game plan, in very simplified terms, went like this:

1. We gathered for monthly potluck-style meetings where all the parents would come together and hash out any problems that arose the preceding month.

2. Weekly playdates were held so that the parents and kids continued to get to know each other and our parenting styles and to hopefully build friendships and community.

3. "Friday night sits" were organized, where rotations of two to four parents would care for four to eight kids (two children per parent), so that parents could go out three Fridays a month in exchange for giving care on one Friday a month. For example, we'd have three kids come to our house one Friday night and then the next three Friday nights, our daughter would go to each of those other three kids' houses.

4. Smaller "pods" of consistent care would be shared between two or three other families. Our "pod" worked like this: On Monday, our daughter went to one family's house for five hours. On Tuesday, we had that family's kid and a second kid come to our house for five hours. And on Wednesday, our daughter went to that second kid's house for five hours. In short, our three girls played together three nights in a row, but we had two of those nights off (Monday and Wednesday) in exchange for doing the care for all three of them on Tuesday.

5. A phone tree would be available for unscheduled and emergency childcare. Along with our phone numbers and directions to our houses, we all wrote down times that we'd most likely be available to help someone else with childcare if they needed it in a pinch.

6. Each parent would have to fill out a medical release form and a getting-to-know-you/general information form. Each family received these papers for each child involved in the co-op, and was expected to keep them collected together in a folder for easy access. (See sample documents in the Resources section.)

7. We developed a mission statement: "To develop friendships with the parents and little ones in our community and participate in a shared childcare experience without monetary exchanges or institution-like facilities and to have friends who want to take part in our children's development. We are families who want to know other families with similar parenting philosophies and desire a radical approach to caring for children."

Changing with Our Needs

In the first year of the co-op functioning, we had a few families come and go, but it remained mostly stable, with about fifteen families involved. The families were not a homogeneous bunch. There were single-parent and two-parent families, and some parents who were not interested in receiving care but who just enjoyed watching another child so their own kid had a playmate. We had working moms and dads and stay-at-home moms and dads, and some who were students, too. We had non-parent members as well, "politically active parent allies" we called them, who believed that it takes a community to raise a child, that children learn and benefit from being around different people, and who in turn benefited from the kids' creative energy. The kids themselves ranged in age from eighteen months to five years.

I'd be sugar-coating if I said our co-op was without any tensions. We indeed had some, mostly having to do with the structure of our co-op. The highly organized structure we started with turned out to be too formal and outside of the needs of most of the members. Our co-op went through a few logistical changes during the first year, which demonstrated that our co-op was flexible enough to absorb our different needs at different times. And it changed both according to what worked best for us as individuals and as a collective.

For instance, we discarded a "points" system and implemented a "give as much as you can, take as much as you need" self-governing principle. Initially, families would receive points when they acted as caregivers, and have points taken away when their children were cared for. The idea was to have zero points at the end of the month. But certain people had more of a need. One single mom in the co-op felt that she was giving as much care as she could, like she was watching kids all the time, but she still ended up needing more care than most and would end up with negative points at the end of the month. This made her feel guilty. On the other hand, some two-parent families didn't mind if they were caring for children more often than their own children received care. From this, our co-op borrowed the motto, "To each according to his/her need, from each according to his/her ability." This worked best for everyone involved.

We also got rid of the role of a rotating secretary who was responsible for coordinating everything for a month. Instead, individual jobs were doled out to individual parents who could keep the job for as long as they wanted to keep doing it, or until they found someone to take it over or trade jobs. There were seven jobs:

1. Membership: Invited potential new members to playdates and/or regularly scheduled sits, put together formal welcome package of information, and maintained waiting list;

2. Treasurer: Collected donations at monthly meetings for copy and postage expenses (two-dollar monthly suggested donation per family);

> **A CHILDCARE CO-OP PRIMER**
>
> 1. Make a short list of other parent-friends with whom you share a similar parenting philosophy.
> 2. Make a short list of trusted, non-parent friends whom you think would be perfect parent allies.
> 3. Assess your needs for childcare in terms of hours per week.
> 4. Assess whether you think your kid is ready for outside care. Can your child communicate his or her needs verbally or nonverbally?
> 5. Brainstorm a simple proposal for starting a co-op that you could see getting off the ground with relative ease.
> 6. Call an organizational meeting—and make it inviting. For example, have a dessert potluck or fun activity for the kids to do together.
> 7. Start small and slow.
> 8. Be open to growth as you work out any kinks.
> 9. Let the kids take their time getting used to care-swap. The monthly meetings and weekly playdates help the more hesitant and anxious kids immensely!
> 10. Have fun and get your needs met at the same time!

3. Sunday Playdate Coordinator: For a month at a time, planned playdates at different parks and free outdoor events;

4. Monthly Meeting Secretary: Organized monthly potluck meetings, created meeting agenda after soliciting agenda items from members, recruited facilitator for meeting, typed and distributed meeting minutes to members;

5. General Secretary: Helped families to find care; maintained phone and address list; maintained co-op procedures, rules, and forms;

6. E-mail Listserv Moderator: Maintained e-mail listserv for the co-op;

7. Webmaster: Created and maintained website for the co-op.

The easiest and most sensible change was allowing a family to call others from the phone list when they needed unscheduled childcare. Previously, co-op participants had to go through the secretary. And it became even easier when we started an e-mail list. If a family knew they were going to need extra childcare for a week or two, they would post their needs to the list and then individuals responded to let them know which of the times they could cover. It also worked in the reverse: if parents knew they were going to have some extra time available to give care, they posted the offer and waited for whomever to take them up on it. Since not everyone involved had e-mail, it was one person's job to call those without e-mail and give them the information posted on the e-mail list.

Once we ditched a lot of the formality, we enjoyed the simplicity of caring for each other's kids and spending time together. The hyper-organization had been too time-consuming, and was counterproductive to our care needs being met.

I don't know what I would have done without our childcare co-op. I loved it so much. My To Do list became less overwhelming. When I had scarce time to myself before the co-op started, I would not be able to choose just one of the things on my list, so I'd choose none and just go for a shower, nap, or beer instead. After the co-op started, I was able to take on big things that had been put on hold. I was even able to reach a longtime goal: I set up my own silversmithing studio at a collective artists' warehouse space, The Art Store.

And I think the other parents involved loved it, too, which is exactly why it just kept evolving. Our individual goals were met; our kids didn't have to be farmed out to strangers at for-profit daycare centers; we received regular, dependable childcare when we needed it for free; and our kids had a lot of fun together and built lasting relationships.

19.

Never Join the "MOPS"

Never in a million years join a group of mothers who call themselves the "MOPS." Seriously, don't do it. Although it might be a convenient acronym for "Mothers Of Pre-Schoolers," it's hard to get past the obvious, encouraged, and sexist stereotype of a mother in this society.

A sign in front of a church advertising a MOPS' meeting time made me do a double take. *What the...? A mothers' group called the MOPS?* I thought of showing up to ask a mop or two, "Who were you before you became a mop? Who will you be when you are done mopping?" But I feared being in a room of mama mops trading tips on how to clean the house, instead of trading tips on how to negotiate with their partners for shared chore duties. I couldn't bring myself to attend a meeting, so for all I know, that's exactly what they were doing. But with a name like MOPS, I doubt it.

Seemingly, such a name is encouraged by mainstream, sexist society.

Open any mainstream parenting or women's magazine and there you'll see advertisement after advertisement hawking wares to make mom's life easier for juggling baby and housework. There, mom will be center page with her arms thrown up in exasperation, the baby covered in a mess of food, the dog wrapped in the phone cord, dirty dishes on the floor, and a caption, "Oh no! I haven't even started dinner!"

Of course, what the advertisement is trying to sell doesn't even matter. Could be anything from paper towels to TV dinners to Mop N Glo. And of course, this gross marketing isn't limited to magazines. TV and radio are big venues, too.

TV commercials show mom, not dad, sneaking up on dirt with a newfangled vacuum cleaner attachment. And wait, there's mom getting high fives from dad and dad's friends for preparing and serving them Super Bowl snacks. Radio commercials tell me—not Ernesto—that I can have dinner prepared in under ten minutes with a little help from Mrs. Paul or some other frozen-meal company. (And what's up with those Hungry Man commercials that feature a single man, not a father, who apparently cannot cook for himself?)

Do any of these things being advertised to mamas have any helpful value? Maybe. Take the paper towels, for example. They aren't the most ecological or economical choice over reusable fabric towels and cloths, but sure, they can make cleanup and disposal a little easier, if you need something to be easier right then. A better example might be the frozen food. Definitely not what you want to be eating most of the time in terms of healthy and low-cost choices, but now and then they are the easy way out from the added stress that preparing a good meal every night can add. After all, sometimes you just wanna hang out with kiddo in the garden all afternoon!

But come on, do we really need to be advertised to for those moments when we need a little easier or quicker? No, people usually don't need too much help figuring out when they need a paper towel or which frozen meal to grab. And are these household things being advertised to mama instead of papa? For sure. And that's just the point.

Moms are expected to raise happy, healthy, clean children and keep her home and her man happy, healthy, and clean, too. And let's not forget that she's supposed to look perky and lovely the whole while doing it all. (That's the conveyed image in the advertisements anyway.) Weren't the 1950s shot down by the '60s and '70s for ideas like that? Why then are these marketing-driven images still used? Oh yeah, mainstreamed sexism is more profitable than feminism, equality, or images of how real-life moms look.

The second wave of feminism scored us some hard-fought wins with regards to gains in the labor force. But third-wave feminism finds us still fighting for, among other things, more equality in the home. Women *can* have both work and family without the family part of the equation meaning taking total care of the kids and the home. Today, mainstream media calls men superdads for working full-time and participating in their children's lives. There's rarely any mention of the household demands; they are assumed to be taken care of by mom. What will mainstream media call it when domestic life is more equalized? As men do more of their fair share of domestic chores, will the superdads be superduperdads? Or will the "super" prefixes cancel each other out, having the effect of normalizing the division of domestic labor so parents can feel good about just being called mom or dad?

DECONSTRUCTING THE SUPERMOM MYTH

Mamas, protect yourself from the supermom stereotype by learning how to recognize it. If you are passing the time in the grocery checkout line by casually flipping through women's magazines, be cognizant of the fact that you are subjecting yourself to advertising and images geared specifically towards women. Start counting how many ads show a woman with a cleaning product for sale. Pick up a men's magazine instead. (You may have to go out of your way to do this since the majority of magazines at grocery checkout stands are ones marketed to women—after all, that's who's doing the majority of the grocery shopping for the family, right?) Count how many ads show a man with a cleaning product for sale. You actually don't even need to look at these types of magazines to see the supermom stereotype—look all around you; its imagery is pervasive.

After you're better able to recognize the supermom stereotype, vow to avoid those types of magazines. Proceed to envision that you are surrounded by an invisible, impenetrable protective bubble so as to repel the other insidious mama-needs-to-clean-the-house advertising and supermom imagery, especially if you are prone to wanting to do it all, if doing it all means to you doing more than your fair share of work, housework, and care of children.

Next, talk about your discoveries with other mamas, and talk about where and how you are exposed to the supermom myth in other arenas and ways than just advertising.

Now, take action! Hold a consciousness-raising session where you and other mamas take turns truthfully answering the following questions: *How is the constant work of home life (cooking, cleaning, laundry, etc.) divided? How are the occasional tasks (school conferences, bill paying, car maintenance, taking out the garbage and recycling, etc.) divided? How is the mental accountability (making the grocery list, reading parenting books, scheduling doctor appointments, arranging carpools for kid activities, etc.) divided? Give examples of what has happened when you/your partner hasn't done their expected jobs.* After each has taken her turn, analyze your personal experiences. Dig out the common truths among the group. Strategize how you can take individual and collective action that will bring change. Make the personal political. And, above all, demand "back pay." Go on chore strike if need be. For however long you've been doing more than your fair share, insist that your partner do the same. After the penance is paid, negotiate for fairly shared domestic work.

Mamas, supermom is a super myth, and if you haven't already, throw her lurking ass out! Though your body may have come equipped with a uterus with which to grow a baby, neither your body nor mind is hardwired to be a superior cleaning being, a laundry expert, or an award-winning, coupon-clipping grocery shopper. It's easy to feel the pressure to meet the supermom expectations of work plus family plus household, especially when you hear common but insulting questions like, "What are you doing besides being a mom? Are you back at work yet?" Questions like that or loaded comments like, "Wow, you must be so busy keeping house and taking care of the baby, too!" imply that choosing to raise kids full-time instead of earning a paycheck is a less-respected choice, that it's somehow not "real" work because there is no paycheck or social status attached to it—and if you don't have an outside job, you should be prepared to do all the child- and house-related work. The majority of mothers in mainstream society are damned if they do and damned if they don't; that is, no matter if they have paying jobs or not, whether they are single or partnered, they are still doing more than their fair share of the household work and childcare.

Consider for a moment the antiquated image of dad being the one who brings home the bacon. Is he really bringing it home, or is he instead bringing home the paycheck with which mom then has to go out and buy it, cook it (along with all the other food), serve it, then clean up the mess and the kids, too? If both parents worked hard all day—dad away from home and mom at home with young kids—the remaining work to be done should be shared, instead of dad coming home expecting that his work is done. Chances are that he already had more scheduled breaks in the day than mama did. Rewind to the beginning of the day to see that the morning routine is slanted, too. Let's suppose dad's shift starts at 8 a.m. What time did mom's start? As early as 6 a.m., taking care of kids, preparing breakfast, and packing lunches? Meanwhile, dad is getting ready for work uninterrupted. (After an uninterrupted night's sleep, while mom was woken a few times to nurse a young'un.) When does mom get to attend to her personal needs uninterrupted? After dinner and she's bathed and readied the kidlets for bed? After dinner, did dad get to watch TV or have an enjoyable moment with a kid on his lap reading a story?

Sounds terribly Cleaverish in Mayberry, doesn't it? Now consider a family with both parents working outside the home—for the majority of these families, it's mom who comes home to work an unpaid second shift with the kids and household duties. With the publication of *The Second Shift* in the late-1980s, sociologist and U.C. Berkeley professor Arlie Russell Hochschild became one of the first to talk about the domestic inequalities in households with both parents working. She told *Mother Jones* magazine, in a 1997 interview: "Women are spending more and more time at work, but men are not spending much more time taking care of needs at home (the second shift). We're still stuck in this stalled revolution, and we've come to think of that stall as 'normal.'" Nearly twenty years after its first publication, *The Second Shift* remains just as important and relevant today as it did then because women are still doing the majority of childcare and housework, even though they also work outside the home. Current studies continue to show that the dads in these families have more leisure time than the moms and are whiling it away by watching television, playing sports, and getting more sleep per night.

In 2002, *Sex Roles: A Journal of Research* published a study on women and their roles in the family. The study found that "seven out of ten married parents believe child care should be shared equally, but two-thirds of the moms said they mainly cared for children." A study in a 2000 edition of *Social Forces* concluded that "women continue to spend about three to seven times as many hours as men on cleaning and laundry tasks." In September 2004, the *New York Times* reported, "The average working woman gets about an hour's less sleep each night than the average stay-at-home mom. Women still do 80 percent of the food-related work at home. And men spend more time than women both at their jobs and on leisure and sports." The U.S. Bureau of Labor Statistics confirmed this domestic inequality with their "American Time Use Survey Summary" for 2004, which found an average working woman spends about twice as much time as an average working man on household chores and care of children.

Women do more than their fair share, whether they work outside of the home or not. But what about when dad is the stay-at-home parent? Do these working moms feel they can come home and not do anything because they've been at work all day? Family therapist Robert Frank researched stay-at-home dads and found that the moms walked in and helped with dinner, baths, and bedtime. The big question is, then, *Why do women do more, no matter what the work/at-home arrangements are?*

Though it's tempting to blame all the inequality on advertising, society's pervasive imagery of motherhood, and sexist benefactors of male privilege and patriarchy, it's more complicated than that. Some social scientists argue that women themselves collude in the inequality out of feelings of guilt or inadequacy. These feelings may come from internalized societal messages about what good mothers do or they may be out of comparison to other mothers, their own included. "Sacrificial mothers feel almost noble about the inequitable nature of their household duties," writes Carin Rubenstein, Ph.D., a social psychologist and author of *The Sacrificial Mother: Escaping the Trap of Self-Denial.* "They take…pride in how much more they do, believing it makes them better mothers and wives and superior women. But they're wrong."

This tendency is referred to by many as "the inner mother martyr." Modeling this sacrificial, martyr-supermom behavior to kids shows them that mothers do not value themselves enough to take care of themselves, and kids are more likely to grow up perpetuating domestic labor being divided along gender lines. The advantages of a more balanced, equal domestic arrangement are numerous compared to a continued, unequal division of domestic labor that relies on myths that bring heavy costs to emotional well-being and healthy partnership. In addition to stronger partnerships, happier individuals, and kids growing up witnessing domestic equality and cooperation, closer bonds between dads and children are formed, kids learn that dads can be as nurturing as moms, and moms will have more opportunities for quality time with kids.

Mamas, pop the unattainable ideals-of-motherhood bubbles and put down your mops! Your identities need not start and stop at being a mother and domestic goddess.

2 Years Old

20.

The Great TV Debate

Television. TV. The telly, boob tube, and idiot box. The plug-in drug. The electronic babysitter. The brain drain.

In the 1940s, television was hailed as one of the greatest twentieth-century inventions for its far-reaching informational and educational potential; it therefore held great potential for increased participation in democracy. However, it didn't take long for network TV to become a major avenue for passive recreation, advertising, propaganda, values transmission, and misinformation. Though a fraction of television programming remains high quality, even commercial-free PBS programming ain't what it used to be—needing to raise money, PBS allows its corporate underwriters to turn their credits into something more closely resembling regular advertising trappings. (Since March 2004, loosened PBS guidelines allow sponsors to speak on camera, display a product, play jingles, and mention corporate slogans.)

Regardless of income level, 99% of US households have color televisions; even in the lowest-income-bracket households (less than $15,000 a year), 64% have cable or satellite TV and 25% have large-screen TVs. In 2006, the FCC estimated that there were more than 65 million cable television subscribers in the United States, with most subscribers receiving more than fifty-four channels; and more than 26 million satellite-TV subscribers. For now, TV rules as the media of choice. It's only a matter of how and when streaming media, thanks to high-speed Internet connections, surpasses television as the media of choice for teens and adults in the United States. However, due to its ready accessibility, television will likely remain the media of choice for the pint-sized crowd for a longer time than that.

I have my own parents to thank for my cable-free life. I remember my dad bootlegging cable from a neighbor when I was a kid and at first, being excited to see movies on HBO like my friends had. But it didn't stay hooked up for very long. After that, the sole reason I wished we had cable was so that I could watch MTV like I had seen on a family visit to my Uncle Andy's house in New Jersey in 1984. When I moved out of my parents' house in 1988, I didn't have a TV to bring with me and didn't wind up missing having one.

Through a decade of roommates and collective house living, I never did get my own TV. Sometimes a roommate would bring one with them into the house, but for the most part—aside from seeking a place to watch the *Simpsons* on Sunday night—I lived TV-free, and none of the houses I lived in had cable. I really liked it that way.

When I was a high school English teacher, I brought the First Annual National TV Turnoff Week (April 24–30, 1994) into my classroom. I had written on the board:

The average American watches more than four hours of TV each day. At this rate, by age 65, that person will have spent 9 years of their life watching television. Upon graduation from high school, the average American child will have spent more time watching TV than in school.

My students' first reactions varied from thinking what I'd written wasn't true to not caring if it was true. After I challenged them to turn their TVs off for just one day, they struggled with the idea. "But there's nothing else to do between 8:00 and 10:00, when I have to go to bed," blurted my usual first-period charmer. He continued, "When my family watches TV together, it's the only time we're not fighting." I continued on, sharing a couple studies on attention spans and the correlation between the length of family conversations and commercial breaks. I gave them a list of ideas for what they could do instead of watch TV: talk, bike ride, read a book, draw, write, play games. Countless times, I heard, "Read a book? Yeah, right." None of what I said bothered them; they were unfazed. But you should have seen their faces when I told them that I didn't even own a TV. They didn't get it. Confused, one kid asked, "You mean they really do pay teachers that bad?"

A few months before Emma-Joy was born, my parents gifted us a video camera and a thirteen-inch TV/VCR combo unit. They insisted we make homemade baby movies to share. Upon Emma-Joy's arrival, I enthusiastically obliged. The combo unit was handy for watching the countless hours of newborn footage that only parents and grandparents could bear to see.

TOO MUCH TV

Plenty of research demonstrates the negative effects of television viewing by children. Some effects of excessive TV watching include:

1. INFLUENCE: TV can be as much as an influence on kids as families are.

2. HEALTH: TV is a passive activity. It's easy to lounge back with a snack and watch. In a study of preschoolers (ages one to four), a child's risk of being overweight increased by 6% for every hour of television watched per day. If that child had a TV in his or her bedroom, the odds of being overweight jumped an additional 31% for every hour watched. TV is saturated with advertisements targeted at kids for junk food—what a cycle of snacking while watching and then wanting to snack more because of watching! TV time takes away from active, healthy playtime.

3. LITERACY: According to the "Zero to Six: Electronic Media in the Lives of Infants, Toddlers and Preschoolers" report by Kaiser Family Foundation and the Children's Digital Media Centers, "Children in households where the TV is on 'always' or 'most of the time' are less likely to read than are children in other homes." The average American home has the television on for well over eight hours every day.

4. VIOLENCE: "If your child watches three to four hours of noneducational TV per day, he will have seen about 8,000 murders on TV by the time he finishes grade school," reports the American Academy of Pediatrics. This has a numbing, desensitizing effect. And teaches that if the good guys use violence, then it must be OK to use force to solve problems. According to pediatric researchers, this can lead to hostility, fear, anxiety, depression, nightmares, sleep disturbances, and post traumatic stress disorder.

5. SEX: Prudishness and individual values of morality aside, implied sexual activity on TV does not show the risks associated with and results of sexual activity. It portrays sex as only fun and exciting, but without potential consequences.

Without cable, the TV received no channels. We kept it that way. At around eighteen months old, Emma-Joy started patting the unilluminated box that sat alone on a living room shelf, urging us to "turn it on." She'd become aware of the moving pictures and sounds that came from it from having been at childcare co-op friend's and grandparent's houses and just out with us at places like restaurants or the credit union.

I taught her how to turn it on. With no videotape in it, all the screen showed was static. I broke out the home movies of Baby Emma-Joy, much to her delight.

We started checking out videos for her at the public library with the intention to limit her viewing time to one video once a day (thirty to forty minutes). Her first favorite was a video that just showed different animals from around the world, without narration and set only to music. She'd ask to watch it over and over again. It usually wasn't hard to stick to our limit and get her interested in something else. There were times, though, when it was just easier to let her keep watching the video.

From the animal video, she moved on to become interested in Sesame Street, Bob the Builder, and Caillou videos. Later, Uncle Jason brought over *Mary Poppins* and *Bedknobs and Broomsticks*. Ernesto and I stood on a slippery slope. Whereas we'd previously strongly dissed the electronic babysitter, we were tempted to go there. While videos were only slightly different than television programming because commercials did not interrupt the story every few minutes, we knew it was not only best to limit Emma-Joy's video time but also best to watch the videos together. However, when dinner could be prepared quicker than when Emma-Joy was helping or when we could get something else quickly done, it was hard not to take advantage of her sitting passively, consumed by the characters and stories, even if she'd already maxed out the day's limit.

After we moved from Gainesville to Hollywood (see "Moving from Home: Building Community Takes Time"), the viewing limits really became an issue. When friends would call asking how things were going. I'd answer, "Well, Emma-Joy's watching too many videos every day and I'm not proud that it's how I'm getting breaks." Transitioning to our new environment and parenting arrangement was tough. In his first semester of law school, Ernesto was virtually absent seven days a week.

Between the videos she checked out from our neighborhood branch of the public library and the batch of videos that had been handed down to her from Ernesto's little sister, her beloved Aunt Elena, Emma-Joy was well stocked with choices. *The Little Mermaid* quickly became her favorite, followed by *Peter Pan*, *The Lion King*, and *Cinderella*. Increasingly, I became more willing for her to spend more time watching videos. I hated the idea that precious childhood time was being wasted in front of a video monitor, but I took advantage of the downtime her viewing provided.

I quickly saw there was a price to pay for the downtime. Even Ernesto noticed the changes in Emma-Joy's behavior, and he was hardly spending any time with her. Even though she was watching videos and not television dosed with advertising aimed at kids, she started begging for the character crap she saw at stores and that other kids had—the characters she recognized from the videos she'd been watching. Her imaginative play became not very imaginative, as she instead focused on re-creating scripted scenes from the videos rather than act out scenes according to her own musings. And she uttered new phrases that reflected new attitude, like she was an evil stepsister and I was her downtrodden Cinderella.

It was weird to me that all of her favorite movies were Disney titles. It was even weirder that although she couldn't yet read, the majority, if not all, of the videos she wanted to check out from the library were Disney titles, too. I suspected Disney had their own color palette and video-case design formula to attract the pre-reading crowd. Trying to dissuade more Disney selections, I offered up other choices during library trips. Most of my suggestions were cast aside.

CRITICAL MEDIA EDUCATION SKILLS

Media education begins when children are very young. Children should be able to learn to be critical of all media, not just TV. By teaching media education skills, children can learn to understand both the obvious and hidden messages in all media. Once children learn these critical skills, they will begin to ask questions and think about the media messages they watch, read, and hear. And they usually will enjoy doing it.

3 BASIC MEDIA EDUCATION POINTS FOR TELEVISION:

1. Shows are created by people. To give their message a purpose, they write the story, decide who is going to act in it, and what to leave out.

2. Music used in TV and movies makes you feel a range of emotions. Help kids understand how a message is delivered depending on what sounds accompany it.

3. Messages in TV, movies, and commercials have their own values and points of view. Teach children how to compare their own values against the promoted values. It is important for kids to learn that they have a choice in taking or leaving the promoted values. An example of a promoted value is on how you look. Examples of your own values may be "We value friendship, feeling good, and feeling strong".

3 TIPS TO TEACH THESE 3 BASICS:

1. Play "spot the commercials" to help your kid tell the difference between a show and a commercial. This is tricky during kid shows especially because many ads are for toys based on TV characters.

2. Talk about whether what happens in the show would happen in "real" life.

3. While watching together, ask your kid how a certain message is created. Ask why they think it is created. Offer your own thoughts.

I was familiar with other parent's criticisms about Disney productions—the deliberate dominant cultural indoctrination and social values being promoted, as well as the rampant marketing associated with the characters. I now witnessed these complaints firsthand and they became my own. The shift in Emma-Joy's imaginative play could have been influenced by any of the videos she watched, not just the Disney ones, though she did tend to act out scenes from Disney movies more than any others.

I needed to quit being lazy about her video consumption and get my pre-Disney daughter back. First, I started watching them with her instead of doing something else while she watched. She preferred that we watch them together anyway. We got in the habit of talking about why things were funny or scary, rude or considerate, and the difference between real and make-believe. I started asking questions that would challenge some of the sexist social messages, like, "Why is Tinkerbell pulling Wendy's hair instead of wanting to be friends and cooperating?" and "Why are there only Lost Boys? Where are the Lost Girls?"

Second, I made her perfectly aware of where her new habit of begging for character crap came from. "You only want those things all of a sudden because you saw them in a movie you like. You did not want those things before you saw the movie." I was planting seeds of media awareness so that over time, she'd be able to understand how desires are manipulated by marketing.

Third, when Emma-Joy initiated imaginative play together and suggested that "You be Peter and I be Wendy," I'd oblige, but only if we made up our own things to say and not just copy the movie. Not only did this approach help stimulate creative imagination, but it was also another fun way to subvert Disney's cultural and social messages.

In addition to these three approaches, I introduced the idea of "jelly brain." "Jelly brain," I explained, "is something that happens when you watch movies too much; your brain only sees and hears the ideas from the screen and it interrupts your own 'getting smarter' thoughts." I also reintroduced quantitative limits—one long movie and one short one a day. (Giving her a choice of one short movie meant that it would be something other than a Disney production.) At first, Emma-Joy tested this limit by watching a movie almost to its end, then telling me something like, "I changed my mind. I don't want to watch this one. This one doesn't count because I didn't watch all of it." Her testing was tricky, but without too much effort spent on negotiating the daily limits, the time spent on movies was lessened when we'd started meeting more folks and getting out more.

When our lease was up, we needed to move. The new place we rented down the block came with free cable; several neighbors had quite an elaborate bootlegged operation going on. Though he'd never think of being a paid subscriber, Ernesto was happy to screw the cable into the back of our TV/VCR combo unit.

He was even happier to watch baseball games, episodes of *Frontline* on PBS, and Jon Stewart and Dave Chappelle on Comedy Central. Now nearly four years old, Emma-Joy was equally thrilled to discover Nickelodeon, the Cartoon Network, and the Disney Channel. Though I must admit really enjoying the family time watching *Spongebob Squarepants* at 7 p.m. every weeknight and could deal with PBS Kids and Animal Planet, the rest of it became unbearable.

I flashed back to a radical parenting workshop that I'd co-facilitated at the Third Annual Southern Girls Convention in July 2001. I'd taken then-sixteen-month-old Emma-Joy—still so new and TV-free—with me.

We had a standing-room-only discussion on several topics, including kids and media. One comment during this part of the discussion came from a guy who said that one reason he was scared of having a kid is because he was really anti-TV and anti-consumerism. He asked us if we thought that having no TV in the home would really be fair to a kid and wondered if a kid would just totally rebel against something so radical as not watching TV.

I told him that we didn't plan on having TV in our house, just a VCR and monitor for watching videos. I told him I didn't think for a second that it would be unfair to my child. If anything, we'd be creating just one TV-free refuge for her because almost everywhere else she goes would have TV. Just because there wasn't

ESTABLISH MEDIA HABITS EARLY

1. Set time limits on total screen time. Screen time means TV, videos, DVDs, video and computer games, and Internet. The American Academy of Pediatrics currently recommends no more than one to two hours of high-quality TV and videos a day for older children, and no screen time for children under the age of two. A recent study found that 90% of two-year-old children are watching television, and 50% of U.S. kids younger than one year old are watching TV. Children in the United States average four hours of screen time a day, excluding computer games and Internet.

2. Help choose shows that are appropriate for their ages and interests. Be clear and consistent with what you consider appropriate. Explain why.

3. Keep TVs, VCRs, DVD players, video games, and computers out of kids' bedrooms. According to "Zero to Six: Electronic Media in the Lives of Infants, Toddlers and Preschoolers" by Kaiser Family Foundation and the Children's Digital Media Centers, in 2003, "One in four children under the age of two years has a TV in his or her bedroom." Preschool children with TVs in their bedroom watched an additional 4.8 hours of TV or videos every week. Instead, make media a family activity when possible. Watch together and discuss. Help kids analyze, question, and challenge the meaning of the messages for themselves.

4. Help them "talk back" or question what they see, especially during an act of violence, or with an image or message that is misleading or unhealthy. This kind of questioning builds lifelong skills for being a critical media consumer.

5. Look for media "side effects." Be aware of the impact that TV and movie content could be having on your kid. Look for increased aggression, nightmares, eating unhealthy foods, less physical activity, and changes in cooperation, moods, and overall attitude. Make changes in media use, if needed.

going to be TV in our house certainly didn't mean that she would never see it. She would not become some socially depraved, TV-deprived freak.

I explained how I'd learned this when I became a high school teacher in 1994. I had been out of the TV-culture loop for several years, but after just a few months of being a teacher, I could tell you all about any popular college or professional sports team or popular TV show star. Really. I didn't even have to watch the damn thing myself to still be smacked with TV's crap propulsion. I even heard all about the "cool commercials" that were replaced by cooler, newer ones every week or so.

I told him that it's easy to avoid the TV issue when kids are little—just don't have one. But what about after the age of two, when their awareness is more keen and the potential to want what they see outside of the home creeps in? I only had one idea to share with the guy: to help avoid potential conflicting interests, kids should be given freedom to explore things that will probably be different from your own interests. One reason why kids rebel is when beliefs are dictated to them and when they are forced to participate in things they don't want to, or in this case, forced not to participate in having TV at home.

Remembering this conversation helped me put into perspective my grievances with now having cable TV in our home. Being a strong believer in guiding, not dictating, really talking to kids about everything openly and honestly, with conviction and without your ideologies hidden from them, I revisited the actions I'd taken when Emma-Joy was getting too sucked into Disney movie world a year before. And I told myself to be patient, that we wouldn't be living with cable forever, just while we rented this place.

I started watching some of the shows with her, deconstructing them as I watched so I could offer my peanut-gallery banter. While some of the more whacked-out Nickelodeon cartoons were fun jelly-brainers, the shows on the Disney Channel aimed at kids older than her were downright painful jelly-brainers. I let her know why I thought so. We learned from each other by having open dialogue between us, debating

TELEVISION STATISTICS, COMPILED BY TV-FREE AMERICA

1. Number of minutes per week that parents spend in meaningful conversation with their children: 38.5 minutes.

2. Number of minutes per week that the average child watches television: 1,680 minutes.

3. Hours per year the average American youth spends in school: 900 hours.

4. Hours per year the average American youth watches television: 1,500 hours.

5. Percentage of parents who would like to limit their children's TV watching: 73%.

6. Percentage of American children have a television set in their bedrooms: 54%.

7. Percentage of Americans who can name the Three Stooges: 59%.

8. Percentage of Americans who can name at least three justices of the U.S. Supreme Court: 17%.

our differing opinions, about my general and specific criticisms of TV, the difference between quality programming on say, Animal Planet, and the utter trash on, say, the Cartoon Network, about what she learned from and liked about certain shows and why.

When begging for the things she saw advertised on TV, became an issue, I taught her more about advertising specifically aimed towards kids than I had a year ago. When Ernesto and I noticed her emulating the beyond-her-years "tween" behavior from some of the shows we'd been letting her watch, we brought it to her attention, pointing out the specific behaviors and letting her know that if she couldn't keep herself from the TV copy-cat acting, then we'd have to help her "be her real self, not the fake TV kids" by not letting her watch them any more.

The daily time limits were negotiated as we went, depending on the day. If a friend was over to play, there was a no-TV rule: "Time with friends is better without TV." I was aware of the balancing act between watching TV shows with her for "teachable moments" and using TV or video time as a kid occupier when I needed to get something done solo. In the short term, I might be able to get whatever accomplished, but then there might be the "deprogramming" price to pay later. And then there were the times that she got bored watching and I couldn't believe it was me asking her from my backyard silversmithing-studio shed, "Do you think you can just watch for just fifteen more minutes so I can finish soldering this bezel, turn off my tanks, and bleed the torch lines?"

I well knew that TV and videos weren't the be-all source of dominant culture and negative social values information, but that they are biggies with young kids. Children of all ages are sentient beings and absorb information from countless sources outside the realm of parental influence at home. They soak it all up from the barrage of advertising, gender coding, magazine covers, overheard conversations on busses, and from family gatherings and friends, too.

Just like there are no hard and fast rules for any other parenting topic, the TV debate must be handled according to the individuals involved. TV can really suck some kids (and their adults!) in, while others can better self-regulate. TV advertising can be a great source of conversation and guidance and aid in developing critical-thinking skills, or it can be something that's just accepted as part of a "that's life" sentiment.

I knew all this, but still, after living with cable for two years, I cheered instead of cried the day the cable man came to clip away all the rigged-up cable wires.

21.

Weaning

Weaning is the process by which a child becomes accustomed to take food other than by nursing. Nursing, of course, refers to breast-feeding. Until she turned one year old, Emma-Joy didn't eat much other than breast milk. She just wasn't that interested. Mashed banana and ripe avocado or pieces of cantaloupe were pretty much the only other things on the menu. We offered her other foods, too, like sweet potato, and red and black beans, but she really loved bananas, avocados, and cantaloupe best of all. (The "First Foods" chapter has a discussion of introducing first foods and the reasons behind whole, fresh foods versus jarred baby food and infant cereals.) Although her appetite for solid food increased after her first birthday, she would only eat a lot of it if I weren't around.

Simply put, if her first food source were around, she'd suckle up. She preferred the liquid gold that kept her free from illness and infection; provided her body the perfect nutrition that changed in composition according to her growth needs; and the security, trust, and comfort that the nursing relationship provides. She was a healthy baby whose only visits to the pediatrician up until fifteen months old were for the recommended schedule of well-child checkups. She never had an ear infection, and the few colds or congestion she did have usually related to teething, as teething is known to suppress a child's immune system.

The American Academy of Pediatrics (AAP) recommends that babies be exclusively breast-fed until six months and that breast-feeding should continue with mixed feedings of iron-rich foods until their first birthday and longer, if the nursing relationship remains mutually agreeable. The World Health Organization (WHO) recommends nursing until age two or longer, if it's mutually agreeable. The worldwide average age of weaning is four years, three months.

If the worldwide average is over four years, why do the AAP and WHO feel it's necessary to promote breast-feeding durations? Because, according to the AAP, while 70% of moms in the United States initiate breast-feeding (only 46% do so exclusively), by six months, only one-third of those moms are still nursing (and only 17% exclusively). At one year, the number drops to 18%. These statistics indicate that the rates of initiation and duration of breast-feeding in the United States are well below the Healthy People 2010 goals, which are 75% initiation, 50% at six months, and 25% at one year.

Certain hospital practices have been identified as obstacles to initiation and continuation of breast-feeding, including disruptive hospital policies and practices, inappropriate interruption of breast-feeding, early hospital discharge in some populations, commercial promotion of infant formula through distribution in hospital discharge packs, and misinformation and lack of guidance and encouragement from healthcare professionals.

My initial plan, not based on anything tangible, was to nurse her for her first year. When her first birthday rolled around and there were no signs of her about to give up the boob, I started thinking of another timeline and went with what felt natural and right for us; I kept nursing her "on demand."

Soon after her second birthday, I started wondering how much longer I would want to nurse her. She still loved her "boobies," as she called them, but I needed more of myself back. I started reading firsthand accounts of how other mothers weaned their nursing toddlers, what worked for them and what didn't. The accounts of "child-led weaning"—following your child's cues and your own common sense to set the pace of weaning, also known as the "don't offer, don't refuse" method—spoke to me the loudest as being the model for how I'd like to wean my girl. That was the one that was most closely in line with my parenting style. The other methods, such as quitting cold turkey and weaning by abandonment (when mama leaves town for a week or two), seemed like a glaring contradiction to my whole approach to parenting thus far. We were a team, and I felt like the mutual trust we'd built up to that point would have been delivered a surprising blow. My gut told me that she needed it more than just for nutrition; I'd seen its calming power work its wonders and magic on her spirited intensity, and to strip it away via cold turkey or abandonment would have really been pulling the proverbial rug from beneath her feet.

Our nursing relationship had taught me empathy. Through it, I was more easily able to see things from her point of view, to put myself in her shoes, so to speak. I feared that after she weaned completely, she wouldn't have a need for me anymore, I wouldn't be as empathetic or patient, and that our relationship would suffer.

However, I wasn't convinced I could nurse her all the way to kindergarten, if that's what she'd be leading me towards.

I had those fears about stopping nursing her, but I decided to seize a

> **EXPERT RECOMMENDATIONS ABOUT BREAST-FEEDING**
>
> Check out these websites to find out what three important policy-making groups have to say about breast-feeding.
>
> 1. American Academy of Pediatrics' policy on breast-feeding, updated 2/1/05: http://aappolicy.aappublications.org/cgi/content/full/pediatrics;115/2/496
>
> 2. World Health Organization recommendations: www.who.int/topics/breastfeeding/en/; www.who.int/child-adolescent-health/NUTRITION/infant_exclusive.htm
>
> 3. WHO and UNICEF launched the Baby-friendly Hospital Initiative (BFHI) in 1992 to strengthen maternity practices to support breast-feeding. The foundation for the BFHI are the Ten Steps to Successful Breast-Feeding described in "Protecting, Promoting and Supporting Breast-Feeding: A Joint WHO/UNICEF Statement": www.babyfriendlyusa.org

window of opportunity. She and Ernesto had plans to go to her Abuela's (grandma's) house without me for ten days. They were abandoning me instead!

For a few weeks before they left, I talked to my daughter about the trip and made sure she knew that I'd be staying home. And I put the bug in her ear that mommy's milk was going to be gone soon. I talked about it in terms she understood, like, "Did you know you've drunk almost all my milk? It's almost gone. The boobies might be empty soon." And she asked, "Mommy have no milk? Me drink it all?" I replied, "I still have a little bit, but not a lot."

Still, I wasn't convinced that I would be able to deny her the beloved boobies if she returned after ten days and requested them. I had absolutely no idea if this was going to be her time of weaning or not. However, I didn't pump any breast milk while she was gone. By doing so, I would have kept up my milk supply, and I didn't want to do that. I wanted to help it be gone.

The first few days, I was engorged and in slight pain. My boobs were as hard as rocks and a cup-size or two bigger than usual. But by day four or five, they were back to normal.

When my girl and I spoke on the phone, she point-blank asked me, "Mommy have little bit milk left for me?" I told her the truth, "Yes, a little bit." I did still have milk for her if she wanted it when she returned, but only enough for a single nursing on each side. If she wanted more than that, I'd be in trouble.

I'd later regret not following the advice of some seasoned mamas who had recommended that I make up a name for my breasts and the act of breast-feeding. I have to admit to total red-hot-ears embarrassment whenever my too-tall-for-her-age two year old (on her second birthday, she was already three foot, two inches) blurted in public, "I want booooobies!" So if it's not too late for you to adopt a code name for the milk delivery girls, then here are some winners: nunus, nanas, ninnies, nippies, beebees, babas, milkies, gagas, mamas, mimis, lulus, yummy-yums. My personal favorite is how my friend Carrie's youngest requested to nurse, "I want juice!"

I also regretted not nipping in the bud two rather irritating toddler nursing behaviors: nipple twiddling while nursing, and the ol' if-I-can't-nurse-right-now-then-I'll-just-stick-my-hand-down-your-shirt-and-hold-the-boobie-for-comfort trick. So unless you're fond of playing Tune In Tokyo or don't mind the risk of your toddler engaging in a little self-serve action out the top of your tank top, say, while out at a restaurant, then believe me when I say: Stop them before it becomes an unbreakable habit!

I was nervous when I went to pick her and Ernesto up at the airport because I still wasn't committed to nursing or not nursing. I was totally on the fence. I just brought a little bag of toy surprises with me and was happy that we'd all be together again.

When I spotted them walking down the corridor, I couldn't believe that Emma-Joy looked so different to me! She looked like she had grown up so much in ten days! She was a big girl all of a sudden, a big girl who did not ask for milk, boobies, or nursing.

There was the decision, made by her. I was relieved to know that she was going to be OK without it anymore and so was I.

She went to sleep that night without needing or wanting to nurse. She was still in the groove of Daddy putting her to bed. But the next night was a struggle.

By that time, however, I had become committed to not nursing anymore. I had seen that she was fine without it and I wasn't going back. I had really enjoyed that full night of sleep. Ordinarily, she'd wake up wanting boobie milk for comfort two or three times during the night, every night. It took an hour and a half that second night of rocking-chair comfort and verbal explanation and negotiation to remind her that Mommy's milk was all gone. She calmed as I held her, sang to her, and let her "hold the boobies." She slept through the night at my side, and it was smooth sailing thereafter.

A lot of people have told me that I got off easy, that completely weaning a toddler is usually more of a struggle or it's drawn out over months. But I really think that the ease with which I weaned her lies with the individuals involved. She was able to comprehend the concept of Mommy's milk being gone because she drank it all. Through our nursing relationship, we had built a solid foundation of trust and security. So, cognitively and emotionally, she was able to deal with such a huge change in her life, and the change had not come about by cold-turkey denial or my abandoning her.

And I was OK, too. My fears of her not needing me anymore or of me not empathizing with her as much were alleviated. She still needed me, and more importantly, wanted me to·interact with her. And I was still patient and empathetic. If anything, our relationship got better. Nature took its course, even if her weaning was not the 100% natural, child-led way. (Since nursing is a relationship involving two individual people, it rarely is 100% child-led.) She's on her own naturally timed course of growing up and, therefore, becoming more independent and confident that she doesn't need me, or even want me, for everything. I believe that our trust-filled nursing relationship has a lot to do with how independent and confident she was at the time of weaning. And I was more willing to hold, cuddle, bathe with, and lie next to her than I had been during the last few months before she weaned.

If you are facing the issue of weaning, go with what you feel is best for the both of you and your family. I know that sounds over-simplified, or perhaps painfully obvious, but it worked for us.

Life After Weaning

From the time my girl was born until she weaned, a lot of my wishes and needs had been put on hold. I realize that a lot of myself would have been put on hold regardless of my choice to breast-feed or bottle feed, but I know that my choice to breast-feed for as long as I did kept me more physically attached to parenting and more detached from the activities that make me feel like myself.

So after two and a half years of parenting, I finally felt like I was able to reclaim parts of my life that make me more than "Mommy." I was able to start playing in a band again, and I really didn't realize how much I missed it until I started playing again. I can't say I was unhappy during the first two and a half years of Emma-Joy's life, but I became so much happier on a daily basis by having regular practices and shows again!

And I was able to bring my girl to shows. Before weaning, I was reluctant to bring her with me because she was clingy and I couldn't just enjoy the show; I'd be tending to her needs, including her demands to nurse. But once she wasn't demanding the boob anymore, it became really fun to bring her along.

She'd get her kicks out of entertaining everyone before the show, on the microphone saying her ABCs and singing "Twinkle, Twinkle Little Star." She'd dance while we played, periodically coming up to give me leg hugs, and clap after every song with a big "Yeah, Mommy!" to boot. And if she needed something while I was playing, she'd get Ernesto or a friend she was comfortable with—she was never unattended. When she was still nursing, it was definitely harder for someone else to meet her needs if I were around; I had the milk-filled boobs and they didn't.

Weaning not only allowed me to reclaim more of my life, but it also brought about a big hormonal shift. The positive-feedback loop of lactation is almost entirely hormonal. The demand stopped, so the supply stopped. The downside of the hormonal shift was that a big, bad yeast infection thought it had been invited to my body, which is a side effect of ending lactation. Another weird thing that happens is that you shed more hair than normal and you get teenage-sized zits for a while. But there's a positive that far outweighs those three negatives combined—your prebirth sex drive returns immediately! (The same hormones that induce lactation suppress ovulation and desire for sex.)

Yes, horny in spite of the yeasty beast, geriatric-style hair loss, and a pimply face is a much, much better way to feel. I figured that the time I had been spending on nursing could now be spent on getting it on. Just like playing in a band again made me happier, so did sexual prowess. And when I'm happy, I'm a better mom.

22.

The Gender-Coding War Continues

Gender identity, coding, and socialization remain at the forefront of my consciousness, especially because I have a daughter. The data about the nose-dive in our daughter's self-esteem during adolescence, teachers short-changing them in the classroom, widespread sexual harassment and violence against females, and the links between stereotyping and a disturbing loss of competence and confidence as girls approach adolescence are no strangers in the headline news. And because adolescence is something that creeps up, sneaking in with its unpredictable makeover, the poor things can barely get a grip on why they're left feeling the way they do. I know I couldn't when it happened to me. The hormones are raging uncontrollably and unfairly, while society and culture are busy stereotyping you—girls and boys alike—telling you how you should be looking and acting and marketing these looks and behaviors to you in every form of media.

Still a decade away from Emma-Joy's adolescence, I felt obligated to continue the on-my-toes vigilance to fight back against sexist gender coding. Emma-Joy had grown from a baby into a toddler, and the gender-coding was far from over. And I knew from experience that it gets worse with age.

One time while at the credit union, she asked the teller, "Excuse me, please I have a sticker?" The teller replied, "Oh, I'm sorry. We only have stickers for boys. I'm all out of the girl stickers." I spoke up, "Oh, what a coincidence. She's Michael today." (It was true. My daughter had recently become captivated by the movie *Peter Pan* and had, for that portion of the day anyway, renamed herself "Baby Michael Darling.") Confused and reluctant, the teller slowly handed my daughter a sticker with a picture of a truck on it. My daughter was happy, but I was still peeved. Peeved at the teller for pushing that gender-coding crap on my kid and mad that I had to fight gender-coding daily. If I hadn't spoken up, she would have been denied access to something solely because of her sex. At two years old, denied a sticker. What would she be denied at age twelve? In the thick of adolescent Middle-School-Cool, she probably wouldn't want me at her side to stick up for her then. Will she stick up for herself? Will she at twenty-two?

After that incident, whenever we were lucky enough to land ourselves at that teller's counter space after that incident, the teller snidely asked, "Who are you today?" The teller looked as if she were constipated when Emma-Joy once proudly replied, "I Bob the Builder!" She handed Emma-Joy a "girl" sticker, a pink one with a My Little Pony on it.

The Formation of Gender Identity

Psychologists suggest that gender identity emerges by the age of two or three, is fully formed by age five or six, and is later reinforced at puberty. It is influenced by a combination of biological and sociological factors. Gender identity refers to a person's deep, internal self-awareness of being masculine or feminine, boy or girl, something in-between, or an entirely new self-identified "other."

That gives parents and other trusted caregivers just a few years to be on their toes, recognizing, examining, and taking action against the societal coding of such identity formation so that the kids they love will have better chances of growing up being able to truly look and act like whomever they wish to become. I know from my own life experience that even though gender identity may be formed by age five or six, it's strictly enforced by society through gender roles for years thereafter, complete with rewards and consequences for playing by its gender-role rules.

Ernesto and I earnestly tried to reinforce our simplified-so-a-toddler-can-begin-to-understand, healthy gender-education mantra, "You're female, but you can be a boy or a girl." We didn't encourage one type of play over another. Instead, we followed her lead. We played with dolls and dug in the dirt with the same frequency. Same with toy, book, and clothes selection. She chose. (We had a mantra that applies to books, clothes, and toys, too, "All things are for all people." We explained that there's no such thing as a toy that is only for boys, just like there is no such thing as a toy that is only for girls.) If while playing with other kids, I'd overhear one of them say, "You can't play with that. That's for boys" (or vice versa), I'd playfully interrupt to offer a contrary idea.

Once, one of Emma-Joy's male playmates took a football from her, telling her that she couldn't play with it because it was for boys. They just happened to also be playing dress-up and he was wearing a long, flowing wedding gown. I told him that if she couldn't play with a football, then he couldn't wear a gown. He stopped what he was doing for a second and then gave a little chuckle before giving her the football back.

I know that particular situation could have gone either way, he could have ripped the gown off and ran away with the football, touchdown-style, but I just did my best and felt lucky that it worked that time.

Nature or Nurture?

There are, of course, plenty of parents who have sworn that they didn't try to push their kids into gender-specific roles, but are nevertheless surprised that their daughters like princesses and dolls and their boys turn everything into guns and swords. I sympathize, because eventually, Emma-Joy, too, loved loved loved her princess play more than she gravitated towards playing with trucks. I cursed the gender-coding outside world all around her. Believing that gender differences were more socially created and learned than innate biological differences in cognitive abilities or hormones, testosterone (male) and estrogen (female), I was stumped and set off to find out if there really was any scientific claim on the idea of predetermined sex and gender differences.

It was a frustrating search. I wasn't able to find the smoking gun of a definitive answer about whether differences were innate or learned, because even the scientists can't agree about sex and gender difference in the research literature. There are hundreds of sex and gender difference studies wherein the only point that most scientists could agree upon was about the strength of socialization in regards to kids learning gender lessons. But I found two reports that were particularly interesting. They suggested that there are innate differences existing along a continuum, therefore a gray area and not black-and-white differences in male and female behaviors. They also argued for individual freedom to explore preferences.

Ann Campbell writes in her 2003 *New Scientist* article, "I Had to Smack Him One," that scientists, after looking at a huge meta-analysis that included 172 studies worldwide on how parents treated sons and daughters, found virtually no differences whatsoever. She says, "The only real difference was in the toys they were given," but goes on to discuss her own research that suggests the children really might be the ones doing the choosing: "We carried out studies that showed sex differences in toy preference in children as young as one... boys preferred objects like blocks, construction vehicles and guns, and the girls things like dustpans and brushes."

Campbell asserts that the ways boys and girls are treated cannot account for early sex differences, that evolutionary approaches to sex difference are groundless, and goes on to address the question of how babies who are too young to know

WAYS YOU CAN FIGHT GENDER-CODING

1. At home, model behavior that's not along gender-role lines. Males do dishes, laundry, and windows. Females pay the bills, take care of the car, and hammer nails. Both mom and dad cook, give baths, and read nighttime stories.

2. Subvert, don't censor or forbid. Forbid toy guns and swords, and watch your kid make one out of a stick. Deny Barbie, and your kid may want to play with one even more. Instead, offer subversive commentary. "Hey, shoot me with magic potion so I can change into a wizard!" "Hey, Barbie, you want to help me fix my bike's flat tire?" Subversive commentary can go a long way with playing any non-toy game, too. Play house, school, alien capture, or firefighters with a new, gender-mix-up script!

3. When giving clothes, go for more neutral hues and images. There's nothing wrong with a purple T-shirt with a green sunshine printed on it. For toys, consider books, art supplies, and kites over the toys found segregated along gender lines on different aisles at some stores.

4. Be more mindful of the way you speak to kids. Maintain the same pitch whether talking to a girl or boy. Adopt more gender-neutral vocabulary. Replace coded words such as "beautiful" and "handsome" with "adorable" and "cute." Stop asking people whether their babies are girls or boys. Erase these phrases from your personal lexicon: "Boys don't cry." "Boy, you throw/hit like a girl." "Girls should look pretty and not get dirty." "Girl, you'll get hurt if you play rough with the boys."

5. Encourage all kids to be respectful, assertive, and kind. Assume intelligence and competence equally along gender lines.

6. Support kids who have more non-gender-specific tendencies and those who make non-gender-specific choices, instead of criticize them. Kids who are supported feel more secure and confident to stick up for themselves if/when they need to.

7. Converse with kids given any gender-related opportunity! When Emma-Joy observed, "Men have hairy legs and women shave their hair off," I offered, "I'm a woman and I don't shave." She asked me why. I answered truthfully that it hurt, took too much time, and itches too much when it starts to grow back. Thousands of other opportunities await you!... (cont'd)

which sex they are (information they would need to understand in order to know who they should be learning from or imitating) could possibly be modeling themselves on their own sex—boys after boys and girls after girls. She says, "Different sex babies start behaving differently long before they can recognize themselves in a mirror, let alone know what sex they are," and that the entire debate over innate versus learned should be reduced to simply saying that a kid is born enjoying some things and not liking others.

She concludes, "We should give people the maximum freedom to be whatever they want. With that freedom, nature can take its own course."

Sheri Berenbaum, Ph.D., professor of psychology at Pennsylvania State University, is the director of the longest-running behavioral study on children with congenital adrenal hyperplasia (CAH), a relatively rare enzyme deficiency that begins in gestation and causes the adrenal glands to overproduce the masculinizing sex hormones, androgens. Melissa Beattie-Moss, reporting on Berenbaum's research, writes, "Berenbaum's data on girls born with CAH point to the power of sex hormones, particularly those we're exposed to prenatally, in shaping our choices and aptitudes as children." However, Berenbaum herself cautions against making a direct equation that hormones cause a person to like trucks. And she jokes, "There's no dishwashing gene!" But Berenbaum does assert that biology indeed influences behavior that shows sex differences. To that assertion she adds, "It's also true that, for all behaviors studied, the distributions for males and females overlap on a continuum."

She warns against ruling out the impact of socialization on gender identity. "What happens to most people is

"Mom, why does that woman have a moustache?" "Is that a man or a woman?" "Why do some men wear skirts?" "That woman has short hair and rides a motorcycle!" "That man has long hair and rides a bicycle!" Explain your heart out, avoiding stereotyping as you do.

8. Teachers, there are at least 101 different ways to line a class up or choose teams other than along sex lines. Segregating your class into boy versus girl for playing academic games is a bad idea. It's a bad idea for P.E. games, too. Co-ed games are great for building cooperation skills.

that we start out with small biological differences which send us off on different environmental trajectories. Socialization then magnifies the differences until they become bigger over time." For example, say you're a male and you express an interest in tools. As a male, you may have a slightly increased predisposition to be interested in active, visual-spatial things like tools. So you play around with them, use them to build things, tear things down. You get good at using them. You are rewarded through praise and perhaps paid an allowance to fix small things around the house. After a while, your slight preference becomes a strong interest as a result of your experiences having magnified it as such.

Berenbaum is quick to point out that genes—like anatomy—are not necessarily destiny. (This, of course, doesn't allow Sigmund Freud's 1924 writing, "Anatomy is destiny," to hold up any longer, if it ever did at all.) She contends that it is incorrect to think that behaviors cannot be changed or learned because they are influenced by genes. She says, "I would argue that if we know the genes that influence a certain behavior, it might be easier to change them with an environmental intervention because we know what we'd be targeting. With training and support, we can strengthen cognitive and behavioral skills across the gender divide." She goes on to say that while she believes the gender differences are real and do matter because society values males and females differently, "what we should work on is saying it's okay to be whatever you are."

So how about it, parents, grandparents, aunts and uncles, cousins, sisters, brothers, co-workers, neighbors, pediatricians, counselors, teachers, and bank tellers, too? How about presenting more gender-neutral options in how we all speak to young children, in how we offer them toys, and in how you bank tellers offer them stickers? All of us together can influence our society's kids during their gender-formative years without controlling it for them, to aid them in the formation of their identities by letting them choose for themselves. We can help them see, recognize, and rise above the cultural limits of females behaving and looking like girls and males like boys.

We owe it to our kids to nurture their unique strengths and spirits because each child deserves to be treated as an individual, not as a gender-assigned member of one group or the other, especially because in our society, those two groups are valued very differently, in very limiting ways. We owe it to our kids to not shortchange their growing sense of self, or their destinies.

23.

Moving from Home:
Building Community Takes Time

These days, I can joke that I had to be practically dragged, kicking and screaming, down to South Florida from where we'd been living in Gainesville. But at the
time, it wasn't so funny. I did not want to leave a place that was inexpensive to live,
where I had a decent part-time teaching job, where we'd gotten a well-function-
ing childcare co-op going and were plugged into the activist community, where I
had been playing in a new band (Molotonic), where I'd finally been able to set up
my silversmithing studio at a warehouse space, and where we were surrounded by
friends and nearby family. Disrupting the perfectly happy balance we'd achieved
with regards to work, activism, individual needs, and childcare was scary.

But with no opportunity in Gainesville for Ernesto to continue his education
like we'd agreed upon, we had to go somewhere. It just happened that the somewhere he was being offered a substantial scholarship was one of the last places
either of us really wanted to go—Miami.

Moving to South Florida tripled our cost of living. The drunk of a realtor who
showed us the first apartment we looked at laughed when we asked her where the
$300-per-month places were. "That monster doesn't exist here. Six hundred dol-
lars a month will get you an efficiency." So for $850, we got a two-bedroom "doll
house" that was smaller than our $300-place in Gainesville. The scholarship was
nice and all, but we still had to take out a Stafford federal student loan, causing us
to go into debt for the first time ever. Was I going to try to avoid that debt situation by attempting to get a full-time teaching job and stick an almost three-year-
old Emma-Joy in full-time daycare? Hell, no. The highest-paying job I could have
gotten would have been as a public school teacher; considering the demands of
the job and of parenting weighed against the pay, it wouldn't have been worth it.

The part-time, after-hours, adult-ed teaching jobs were only open to the full-time daytime classroom teachers. Was living in a new city with no friends, family, band, childcare co-op, or activist community while reassuming the role of full-time parent any easier? Hell, no, again.

Right off the bat, everything sucked. The landlord was a psychopath, threatening to evict us as we were still carrying boxes in from the U-Haul because we refused to sign a different lease than the one we originally signed a month prior. It wasn't as easy to get around—biking and walking did not get us everywhere we needed to go, and the public transportation system was ridiculously inefficient. And being a first-year law student had Ernesto away from home nearly all of the daytime hours. I felt like an isolated single parent without a support system or any community.

Nothing felt lonelier than the increased time I spent on the Internet trying to inject myself into "online community." Looking for electronic mama friendship had me feeling depressed. So did Emma-Joy's increased time watching kid videos. We needed more than each other. We were starting to drive each other crazy. I combed the local playgrounds and parks with Emma-Joy, looking for new peeps, but we weren't finding who we were looking for.

In Lake Worth, I had a small crew of old friends working on a really exciting community garden that both Emma-Joy and I loved helping out at (the Lake Worth crew was also organizing lots of other radical projects at the time where I could participate with Emma-Joy, like the Free Carnival Area of the Americas warehouse space and Free Kids Dance classes every Monday afternoon). But the distance between where we were living in Hollywood and Lake Worth kept us from going there as much as I would have liked; by car it took us forty-five minutes if there wasn't traffic congestion (using that much gas was to be considered, too), and by Tri-Rail and bicycle took over an hour and a half each way.

Through the anarchist parenting listserv, I met Mona, a work-from-home crafty mama to then two-year-old Gabriel and pregnant with Daphne. We met in person for the first time at a North Miami Beach playground. She was my first South Florida friend, but we didn't get together as much as we wanted because it was a thirty-minute drive between our houses and traffic congestion was unpredictable. Mona told me about a seemingly cool playgroup closer to where I lived that had been formed out of a La Leche League toddler group, and encouraged me to check it out.

I did so eagerly and found the group very welcoming to us newcomers. The once-a-week playgroup was something I started looking forward to, at first, because it was a welcome way to get us out of the house for some social interaction, but as weeks passed, because we were really clicking with a good handful of the other mamas and kids. Although Emma-Joy was getting important playtime with other kids her age, the playgroups were really more for the mamas. What we mamas had in common was stronger than the differences in our liberal or radical politics or lifestyle choices. We were all passengers on the Goodship Mama who shared similar-enough parenting styles.

After a couple months, I called everyone together at a playgroup at my house to try and organize a childcare co-op like we had in Gainesville. I handed out photocopied packets of information that included notes on how the co-op was organized, copies of local press articles that had been written about the co-op, and the forms we used. After a brief discussion of the particulars, my attempt failed. I learned that aside from living in a car-culture landscape that kept many of us inconveniently separated and spread out across the county, it takes time to build community. I was too new in town for enough of the playgroup mamas to be comfortable jumping into the childcare co-op idea.

I was disappointed and without an immediate solution to ease my pangs for building more community than a once-a-week playgroup allowed. I needed to be patient, but patience was something I was short on. As it was, I'd been increasingly running out of patience with Emma-Joy. While lying down to sleep for the night, I started saying positive affirmations to myself: *Tomorrow will be a better day. I will be more patient. My tone of voice will be respectful. I will not yell. Emma-Joy will be able to play by herself for just fifteen minutes without needing or wanting me. She will not have a tantrum.* I had to keep doing them. I wasn't getting the daytime or nighttime breaks I needed.

After Emma-Joy went to sleep for the night, I found myself picking up my old nightly habits, once again. I'd sit outside smoking with a beer in hand, this time my mommy's little helpers, replaying the day, trying to unwind. On one of these nights, I tried to explain to Ernesto what I'd been feeling. I told him that I wasn't feeling myself, that I wasn't as patient as I needed to be with Emma-Joy these days, that I didn't know what was wrong with me, that I wondered if there were any statistics on mental wellness with regards to the effects of mama/kid isolation after moving to a new place. After listening carefully to me filling in the details, he told me that it sounded like I was depressed. I remember feeling relieved that he could once again see something so clearly that I could barely recognize.

He also apologized, thanked me, and assured me that what I was feeling was not because of some personal shortcoming, that it was our situation that was what was wrong, not me. He apologized for not being available due to the demands of being a first-year law student. He thanked me for sticking it out with him and mov-

PARENTING A SPIRITED CHILD

I'd thought I was just a terrible parent who was just not cut out for the job. I'd thought Emma-Joy was just an out-of-control wild ass who loved running me in circles. Neither was true. After reading Kurcinka's book, digging up other resources, and talking with other parents, I learned some effective tools and saw that we were not a hopeless cause of a team.

Kurcinka based her book on personality development research, as well testing it with parents in workshops in a practical, sensible style. Her motto immediately resonated with me: "Progress not Perfection." And the way she presented the temperamental traits of kids like mine who are just "more" of everything, turning labels like "difficult" into "spirited," was consistent with my desire for a positive, happy, healthy relationship.

The most important key I learned about parenting a spirited child is to understand why she is doing what she is doing and that her "extra" traits are ones that, while harder to parent, are ones that will serve her well as an adult.

ing down to South Florida; we promised that next time, we'd be much more careful to move to a place that was more mutually acceptable. He communicated that he was well aware of the demands of being not only the full-time parent, but also the playmate and manager of all things house and family related. We talked about how, ideally, things are not supposed to be this way, how just a handful of generations ago, the isolated nuclear family model was not how people brought up children. (For more ideas on finding community, needing allies, and recognizing depression, see the "Battling Isolation" chapter.)

And we talked about Emma-Joy's intensity. When I needed to do anything that she couldn't help with, she couldn't just play for five minutes by herself. I was always on call. When we did things together that she said she wanted to help with, she'd need for us to be doing something else instead. If we were outside gardening, she wanted to go to the library. If we were inside reading, she wanted to go to the beach. If I dared stand or sit still for a moment, she was like a swarm of flies. Her energy moved her faster than I could keep up with. She was high needs and high maintenance. I wondered if her intensity might be because of some food sensitivity, and tried to weed out potential trigger foods, like anything with artificial colors or flavors. But she was the same intense three-year-old with or without alterations to her diet. She was, I'd later learn, a spirited child. One of the mamas in our playgroup suggested I read *Raising Your Spirited Child: A Guide for Parents Whose Child Is More Intense, Sensitive, Perceptive, Persistent, Energetic*, by Mary Sheedy Kurcinka. I checked it out from the library right away and it did give me some helpful insight and tips. But I still felt like I needed to take a crash course in child psychology. Tantrums were coming with more frequency. Some of them left me bruised; all of them left me emotionally drained. We wondered if the tantrums were purely developmental of if she was having a transitional crisis, too.

We turned to My Morning Out (MMO), a new three-day-a-week morning program for children aged nine months to three years, located a couple miles east of us near Young Circle, just a ten-min-ute bike ride from our house. Emma-Joy had just turned three, but they had a space for her. After checking it out with her, I got an overall good feeling about it. There was a small "teacher"-to-child ratio and all who worked there seemed very gentle and loving with the kids. In exchange for her be-ing there nine hours a week, we paid $160 a month. After paying rent, this was nearly a third of our $600 monthly budget from our student loan income, but it was worth it. Our first venture into paying for childcare bought me some sanity in the form of time alone to get my silversmithing studio on my tiny front porch up and running so I could make jewelry, which I sold at art shows and for individual commissions.

Emma-Joy had an easy time adjust-ing to MMO. I credit her experience with our childcare co-op in Gaines-ville for this. There were only a few mornings when she didn't want me to leave, but when I did and returned three hours later to bike her home, her teacher reported that she'd had a fine

Tantrums

Though Emma-Joy had adopted "no" as her favorite word like clockwork on her second birthday, her tantrums then were relatively few and mild. The first few months after moving to South Florida, however, they became more frequent and harder to deal with.

Everything I read suggested that tantrums in toddlers were inevitable fits of frustration that were part of normal, healthy development and that tantrums in preschoolers, though still fits of frustration, could be also due to combinations of fatigue, hunger, trying to have more control in unfamiliar situations, and stressed-out parental behavior. I learned that kids don't throw tantrums just to be difficult and uncooperative. Often, it's scary for a kid to have such huge, frustrated feelings and feel that out of control emotionally.

Wanting to help lessen the tantrums, I became more aware of how my new stress was a contributing factor, and paid better attention to cues of hunger, fatigue, and other triggers. But when one would still come, I learned to deal with them this way:

1. Neither ignore nor over-respond. Stay close and use only minimal intervention to prevent injury to self or others.

2. Let the tantrum run its course instead of attempting to stop it with punishment, coercion, or giving in to it with bribery.

3. Remain loving and patient. Likely you are frustrated, too, but you have the advantage of a more mature command of language and impulse control—so don't also have a tantrum!

4. Later, talk with your preschooler about what happened as a way to get to the root of what caused the tantrum.

time without me. This was something really important to me—finding the balance between honoring Emma-Joy's needs for me to be close and my own needs to be separate for a mama recharge. Just as I'd found the time away from home refresh-ing and an asset to the rest of my day spent being mama when I returned to part-time teaching work, and I also found these nine hours per week away from each other a definite help to my being able to be a patient, gentle parent.

During these first months transitioning to a new city, it might have also helped my own community-building efforts had I been able to just stay there. Even with the once-a-week playgroup and gaining a bit of respite by having Emma-Joy enrolled in MMO, I felt like I had to escape back to Gainesville and hang on to keeping the band going for as long as possible. With birthday money from my Grandmary, I bought an Amtrak Florida Rail Pass. For $249, I got unlimited rides in Florida for a year. Emma-Joy rode free. We'd make the round trip to and from Gainesville on average once a month, staying anywhere from four days to a week and a half. By doing so, I was giving up weekly playgroup and my weekly nine hours away from Emma-Joy, but I was getting to visit with my best friends in Gainesville and still practice, play shows, record, and do a short tour with Molotonic.

But it wasn't sustainable. After seven months of commuting, I played with Molotonic at our last show.

Weaned off Gainesville, I got more locked into a routine in Hollywood. Monday, Wednesday, and Friday were MMO days that eventually grew into a Monday-to-Friday morning preschool schedule (fifteen hours a week for $240 a month). Tuesday afternoon was playgroup. Thursday evening was bedtime story time at the Hollywood Branch of the Broward County Library with our friendly neighborhood librarian, Angel. On the weekends, Ernesto still studied, so to get out of the house, Emma-Joy and I would find free outdoor cultural festivals or music events, go to the beach, or luck out with a visit from my parents who'd drive down from Daytona about once a month.

In September 2003, nine months after we moved there, Mona discovered another playgroup for us to infiltrate. This one met on Wednesday afternoons, was practically in my neighborhood, and had been started by Adriana—a local home-birth midwife and single mama of two boys—as a way to build community among her clients. Not having to drive all over the county to meet people for once was great—and finally meeting some similarly minded mamas in my immediate area was exactly what I needed.

Both playgroups became my community. As the months wore on, easing into new friendships, the isolation-induced depression disappeared. I still felt disconnected from any music and activist community, but daily life with my girl improved greatly. She still kept me on my toes, of course, and there were still days that sent me to bed with beer in my blood and a need to utter positive affirmations, but overall, we weren't driving each other crazy. She was happy with her new friends, too.

At the end of Ernesto's first year of law school, though he still had to stay shackled to his books, he was at least able to take the cuffs off earlier in the evenings to hang out with us more. He and I were both finding our individual grooves, getting over the shock of being transplanted from an ideal, balanced life to a drastically different one. He fully acknowledged that because I'd been doing all of the childcare and house-related work, he'd been able to succeed as a top student, bumping his scholarship up from half to full, something that benefited both of us. Sticking together, supporting each other, made our partnership even stronger. I was proud of us being able to pull through something so hard. With my little family, and with my mama-kid community, I was at peace, feeling less isolated and more settled.

24.

Touring with Tots

I needed to figure out how include my girl in touring. Leaving her behind was not an option. Touring was a big part of my life that had been put on hold as a result of becoming a parent, and after three years, I was eager to reclaim it.

Luckily, I had been tipped off that Submission Hold had toured with a kid who was a bit younger than mine. I immediately felt hopeful and wanted to hear all about how they did it. The first thing I learned sounded like an advantage that I wouldn't have: both parents were in the band together. And they brilliantly thought to take a nanny as a roadie because someone's got to be with babe while mom and dad rock!

Soon after, I found out about another mom who brought her baby girl on tour with J Church. Another advantage emerged: she wasn't actually in the band, just dad was, so no nanny was needed.

After mulling over the possibility of touring with my tot, I decided to go for it. I did have anxieties about it. I rationalized that, at worst, we'd have to cancel the rest of the tour if it started to suck and that, at best, it would just be doable.

I'm glad to say that the experience was way better than I ever imagined it could have been. It was more than merely doable; it was nothing short of amazing and I can't believe it took me nearly three years to attempt it. My band at the time, Molotonic, was based in Gainesville, Florida. We did our own tour, booking the shows ourselves, a 100% DIY tour all the way.

And I'm also glad to say that the experiences of the Submission Hold and J Church parents were so good that all of us are going to tour again, or have already done so.

I held a roundtable discussion with Andy from Submission Hold and Rosa-Maria, whose husband David is in J Church, to hopefully shed some light on touring with a kid in tow. We hope that our experiences will inspire other parents to tour with their tots, too.

It's so much extra work and worry to tour with a child, why even bother? Why not just leave your child with a trusted friend or family member?

Andy: Touring is great and my kid is even better, so the two together could only be the best. In fact, this was one of the things we'd planned on doing when Jen was still pregnant. If we were going to have a kid, he was going to be part of our whole lives, not just our lives as "parents." I think it's important for our children to see that we still do things that are important to us, see us take chances and fulfill our dreams, see us fail and fall on our faces, too. I'd hate to stop doing this and resent my kid for it. I'd hate my kid to feel that he was the reason I abandoned my dreams.

Rosa-Maria: Since Eva is very much still attached to my breast, if I wanted to go, she had to go with me. Instead of us dropping out of the scene to be parents, we try to incorporate her into our lives, making adjustments as necessary. Also, Eva thrives among people. In groups, she likes to stay up late and entertain. We have family and friends speckled across the country that want to see her and meet her.

Jessica: It was a little different for me than for Andy and Rosa-Maria. They had an advantage that I didn't, and that was having both parents touring together with child. I bothered to finally take the plunge to tour with my girl because if I didn't bring her with me, then there couldn't have been a tour and I was just not going to accept that reality. That would lead to resentment, I think, like Andy mentioned. I actually considered leaving her with a friend for a few days, who would then have to drive her a hundred miles to my parents for a few days, who would then drive her back to another friend. They would have had to juggle her around because they all have work or other commitments. I didn't think juggling her around like that would be very good for her. She and I are a pretty attached team.

Where did you go and for how long? How old was kiddo?

A: When Sam was nine or ten months old, we went for three weeks through the western U.S. Then a couple months later we went to Europe. Sam had his first birthday on tour in Germany.

RM: When Eva was four months old, we did a two-week tour through the East Coast with David's "band" DFI. It's just him and a drum machine, so it was just us three on the road. We wound our way from Austin [Texas] to Connecticut, where she met her grandmother and great-grandmothers for the first time [details of this tour are in *Placenta* #2, Rosa-Maria's zine]. We just got back from a monthlong tour of the U.S., plus one date in Canada with J Church, Storm the Tower, and DFI, all in one van. She turned fifteen months the day before we got back.

J: We did a week-long tour around the southeast U.S. Gainesville, Pensacola [Florida], New Orleans, Athens [Georgia], Asheville [North Carolina], Valdosta [Georgia], St. Augustine [Florida]. We could only go for a week because all of my bandmates were in school at the time and that week was their spring break. The last show of the tour was just two days before Emma-Joy's third birthday.

Before tour, what special preparations did you have to make before hitting the road in terms of food?

A: Lots of dried fruit and stuff like that in the van. We've always been pretty food-minded on tour, stocking up at health-food stores and stuff, so that didn't change much.

RM: On the first tour, I didn't have to worry about bringing her any snacks or anything because she was exclusively breast-fed. This last tour was a bit more difficult, since she's a toddler and eats a lot of real food. I had delusions of grandeur when it came to snacking. She was going to have all the healthy stuff she has at home. I brought her a cooler and was going to keep it stocked with perfectly balanced meals, blah blah blah. Yeah, right. I kept forgetting to get ice for the cooler and the soymilk kept going bad. She ate Taco Bell more regularly than I would ever care to admit. And she got cheap cookies to keep her occupied.

J: I brought a whole crate of food for the road. Canned soup. Little cereal boxes and little individual boxes of soy milk. Juice boxes. Peanut butter, jelly, and bread. Granola bars. Fruit leather. Basically anything healthy, nonperishable, and that she would eat. My mama preparation was a big hit with my hungry bandmates.

What things did you pack that were never packed for tour before?

A: A stroller and a little bed thing for Europe. We'd never brought diapers on tour before. Actually, the first tour forced us to stop using cloth diapers for obvious reasons. We brought some toys and lots of books, but we also stopped at thrift stores along the way and replenished the stocks.

RM: We used cloth diapers on that first tour, so it was funny packing the amp and guitar and such in the trunk with the nylon bag for dirty diapers on top of it. I didn't bring a stroller on the first tour. I just brought the sling. On this last tour, because she's older, she needed more activities to keep her occupied. We also brought the stroller the second time around, which turned out to be a lifesaver.

J: Actually, I packed mostly the same stuff, just doubled. Clothes for me, clothes for her. My books, her books. But more art supplies and toys than usual. I could have used a stroller, though. A thirty-seven-pound child gets a bit heavy using only a sling. After Athens, we had to pack in an inflatable Hello Kitty chair that someone at that show dumpstered for Emma-Joy.

Did you have a nanny?

A: On the first tour, we had our friend Hollie come along to hang out with Sam while we played and give us some time away if we needed it. Hollie had been our roommate for years and hangs out with Sam when we practice, so he was super comfortable with her. In Europe, since we couldn't afford to fly Hollie over with us, we asked our friend Caley, from London, to come along.

J: We brought our friend Friedel as a nanny-roadie. We couldn't have done the tour without her! She really planned ahead and thought to bring daily surprises and crafts to do. She gifted Emma-Joy with books that were hers when she was a little girl, a present a day leading up to Emma-Joy's third birthday. She brought socks and yarn and needles for making sock puppets.

Did you prearrange kid-friendly/kid-safe spaces to stay?

A: When we booked shows, we told folks that our kid would be coming along and we'd need a semi-quiet, smoke-free room at or near the venue. Most places bent over backwards to accommodate us, and me and Jen and Sam ended up with some pretty plush digs at times. A couple venues didn't have anything for us though, which was a bit of a drag. For us, kid-friendly/kid-safe meant pretty much a place where his ears wouldn't get damaged and he wouldn't have to breathe secondhand smoke.

RM: On the DFI tour, the clubs were not smoke-free. It was also cold out, so that sucked having to be outside. For this last tour, most of the shows until the East Coast were smoke-free. But the venues that weren't smoke-free usually had some sort of room that they would offer us to chill in, or, since the weather was nice, we could take turns taking Eva for strolls while someone else watched the merch/played.

J: If we didn't know where we were staying ahead of time, it would be arranged while at the show. In asking for a kid-safe place to stay, I'd explain that meant a smoke-free room, relatively quiet, and no forgotten/misplaced drugs on the floor or some other place that'd be within a toddler's reach. Like Andy mentioned, people more often than not went out of their way to help Emma-Joy and me have a comfy, suitable spot. We scored two walk-in closets, an apartment whose tenant was out of town, a basement bedroom, a friend's floor, and one hotel room.

Was special attention given to routing so as to minimize really long stretches of driving?

A: Both tours were way more compact than previous tours. Our times in Europe before Sam was born, we'd play from Sweden to Portugal to Bosnia and anywhere in between. Likewise, a U.S. tour could mean traveling twelve or more hours in a stretch. But now we just pick a small area and really concentrate where we book the shows.

RM: I didn't really have any say in booking them. But this last tour, the drives... Ouch.

J: I was really involved in the routing because I knew that too much in-the-van time wouldn't be fair to Emma-Joy, and I knew that a drive that usually takes six hours would take more like eight hours with a toddler.

About life in the van: how was it dealing with a child who might have a tough time being stuck in a car safety seat during long drives?

A: Lots of books and toys and rest stops. We tried to coordinate naptime with drive time. The U.S. tour was easier for that because we had two vehicles—me, Jen, and Sam in a little car, and two bands and assorted others in the van—so we didn't have to rely on everyone being ready to go when Sam was ready, or vice versa. Europe was a bit more frustrating in that regard because we only had one vehicle and not everyone realized the value of a good nap.

RM: It was rough on all of us, although Eva did pretty well most of the time. There were times that were really frustrating to me when decisions were made about driving that pretty much meant she would wake up in the van, take a nap in the van, wake up in the van, and only really get out of the van when it was time for her to go to sleep again. It's hard for people who don't have kids to understand how maybe driving at night in these instances might be less stressful. It was hard on David and me to try and keep her occupied for such long stretches. Also, if I was next to her, she wanted to nurse, which is really uncomfortable to do while they're in their seat, but if David was next to her and she caught a glimpse of me, she'd get pissed off. Things that kept her occupied: snacks, those amazing mess-free markers that only draw on certain paper, bubbles, books, some sort of shape-sorting toy, and a bounty of boys willing to make goofy faces at her or scream when she screamed.

J: There is no such thing as coordinating naptime for Emma-Joy, ever, so that was not on my side like it was for Andy. Emma-Joy handled the six- to eight-hour drives a lot better than her past history of car travel suggested that she would. Everyone in the van is to thank for that, I think, for taking shifts with her. The twelve-hour drive was uncomfortable and difficult for her, although something unusual got her through it. She weaned at two and a half years old, so at tour time, she had been off the boob for six months. She was really trying to hang in there towards the end of that long drive, but was too uncomfortable in her car seat to fall asleep soundly. After a lot of squirming, irritation, and whimpering, she asked if she could nurse. I obliged her request, though it was tricky maneuvering on my part because of her car seat, and she nursed herself to sleep for the first time in six months. It was so sweet and I was really proud of her, actually, knowing exactly what she needed and asking for it.

How did the other non-parent band members fit into the picture?

A: All our bandmates are crazy about Sam and Sam loves them like the family that they are. There was never any problem with anyone in the band.

RM: Everyone in the bands was great. I felt like she was riding with seven or eight uncles, which was an awesome feeling. It was also nice to see them interact with her without thinking twice about it. I didn't really expect any help, since it was our decision to bring her on tour with us, not theirs. But they would watch her occasionally while I watched the merch table, and I felt really good about building Eva's community. At the end of tour, though, a few of them did state that they would never be having kids.

J: The only special request that was made was no smoking in the van. Suddenly, grown boys were having to take as many out-of-the-van breaks as Emma-Joy needed. Lars took a shift one night to be the one to go to bed early instead of staying up late partying. That way, I could stay up and enjoy myself after the show for a while instead of hurrying to bed to get enough sleep to be refreshed enough to wake up early with Emma-Joy. He woke up with her, dressed her, took her out for breakfast, and played with her at a playground until the rest of us woke up. He was also great when I needed to take Emma-Joy to the emergency room for a pulled elbow. While I comforted her, he was on the phone getting directions to the closest hospital. He drove and waited with us, too, making paper dolls and coloring.

What was the typical scenario while you were at the venue?

A: Typically, there was a room we could use to hang out in, or if not, we went for walks around whatever town we were in or kicked it in the van. Nine times out of ten, Sam would fall asleep with Hollie or Caley as soon as we started to play. We must be his lullaby music. He'd stay sleeping until the show was over, wake up for a while afterwards, and then sleep until nine the next morning like clockwork. It was uncanny, you could set your watch by him, and he didn't even get jetlagged.

RM: Get to show, I sling her while loading in merch, and David loads in equipment with everyone else. I or someone else watch her while D sets up, then D or somebody watches her while I set up merch. I plug up her ears and tape the plugs in. Bands play, Eva dances and claps at the end of the songs and plays drums in between sets. Load up, that's it. Sometimes Eva would get cranky and someone would take her for a stroll. It was predominantly D and I watching her, but sometimes others would take her. Sometimes we would get lucky and she'd nap during a set, and we could just sit back and breathe a little.

J: If we were lucky enough to know before the show where we would be staying that night, we'd go there before going to the venue. I'd get Emma-Joy settled in with some dinner and a bath, and Friedel would stay with her and put her to bed while the rest of us would go to the show. But typically, Emma-Joy would hang outside the show with me because she didn't like how loud it was inside, even with earplugs. When I'd go in to play, Friedel would stay with her outside or in the van. She was always asleep in the loft by the time I finished playing. We got a smooth routine down where we'd do all the loading out before opening the doors to reload the van. Then, I'd carry Emma-Joy from the loft to the front seat and hold here there until everything was in place and we were ready to pull out. I'd then get her into the car seat. This would wake her up and she'd usually stay awake for the whole drive to the place where we were staying, but she'd fall right asleep as soon as I got her inside and snuggled her.

Did anyone before or during the tour have criticisms of your parenting or reservations about your decisions to tour with your child? If so, did you bother defending or explaining yourself?

A: We've never gotten anything but support for the choices we've made regarding Sam. It's been great, sort of unbelievable, really. The most we'd hear is from people who thought it would be crazy to take a baby on tour, but after talking with us and meeting Sam, they understood.

RM: Just, "You brought your baby on tour??" accompanied by a disgusted look, or, "Do you have earplugs for her?" both of which were answered with an eye roll and "Yes." More often than not, though, people would be stoked that she was there and everyone was really into her. So, we got more positive stuff than negative stuff.

J: Only one person said something about how I shouldn't be taking her around "that" environment, how she's just an impressionable young girl. My mom was very supportive and even offered to help with the care juggle if I chose not to take Emma-Joy on tour with me. To echo both Andy and Rosa-Maria, overall, people were supportive and tended to give more props and admiration than negativity.

Compared to tours without a child along, what was the same and what was different? Can you judge whether you prefer one way over the other? Are you planning on touring with child again?

A: The U.S. tour with Sam was the best time Jen and I ever had on tour. Europe was slightly more tiring because the shows ran so much later and I'd get up with Sam every morning. But that was OK, too, because we were able to get some time together to hit the cobblestones and search out the local café before everyone else got up. I love touring with Sam.

RM: Life is different when you have a kid. Parts of it are easier and parts of it are harder. It's the same with tour.

J: The two biggest differences for me are eating healthier and sleeping more at night after shows and less during the day while in the van. It was also pretty different having to evacuate everyone from the van so somebody could take a shit in the van. Emma-Joy was potty trained for peeing but she still demanded a diaper for pooping. So when she felt one coming, she'd let us know and we'd pull over. I'd get a diaper on her and she'd demand that we all get out and leave her alone. It was pretty funny when she'd be waving at us from inside and yelling out the window, "It's not done coming out of my body yet!" Now that I do have a kid, it's a pretty silly question really whether I prefer to tour with her or without her, because even if she were not physically on the tour, I still consider myself with her in some way. She's a part of me and I carry that wherever I go. I will jump at the chance to tour with her again.

All of us have only children. What do you think about touring with two or more kids?

A: Before we went on the first tour, we tried to contact a band called Gunspiking who apparently toured with two kids, but we couldn't get a hold of them.

RM: With two kids, it would have to be less than a month long because a month felt too long sometimes. And we would have to have a separate car, not all be in the van.

J: I think two older kids on tour would in some ways actually be easier than just one. They want to have another kid to play with more when they are four and older than when they are younger than three years old. I think they wouldn't get as bored as when they're the only kid, as well as not feel awkward being around just adults.

Anything else?

A: People think it's a big deal to go on tour with your kid, but really, how many punk tours have you heard of that didn't involve crying jags, temper tantrums, and inappropriate bodily functions?

25.

Weaning Epilogue:
Confessions of an Unweaner

Weaning happened in October 2002. In March 2003, just days before her third birthday, Emma-Joy needed to nurse again. It was an unusual circumstance; we were on a very long drive, twelve hours to be exact, and we couldn't stop for comfortable sleep. To her credit, Emma-Joy had been an amazing traveler all day and when it came time to sleep for the night, still upright and strapped in her car seat, she tried to get comfortable enough for sleep using every trick she knew, but just couldn't do it on her own. She needed the boobies and given the circumstances, I obliged.

I maneuvered enough to get one in her mouth, was surprised that she hadn't forgotten how to properly latch on, and in less than five minutes, she'd suckled herself to sleep. I was impressed. And proud of both of us.

A couple weeks later, while out of town again—but spending the night at Uncle Jason's instead of in the tour van—she asked to nurse to sleep. At first, I resisted. It didn't appear that she really needed it like she did when uncomfortably stuck in her car seat. But when the usual attempts to get her to sleep for the night were turning into a forty-five-minute effort, I gave in. Again, she latched on like a pro. If she were a cat, she would have purred. And again, she was fast asleep in under five minutes.

The following week, her requests for "suckle boobies to sleep" started coming with more frequency—like every third day. I saw where this was going and I thought hard, weighing the benefits against the potential downers. The boobies were her magic sleeping pill. Some kids like music boxes, security blankies, or sucking their thumbs or pacifiers to help them ease into sleep. My girl needed, for whatever reason at this point in her life, to suckle the real deal.

I promised myself I'd only allow her to nurse to sleep at night and for only as long as her suckling wasn't irritating; that was as far as I was willing to unwean. Anything more than that, no way. I was not interested in relactation.

That limit worked for the both of us; we were nursing again with a mutually agreeable arrangement. She got a new sleep routine down: She would suckle for a while—five to ten minutes seemed to be the average before either she stopped on her own or I told her, "OK, that's it, boobies are asleep now." She'd say, "Goodnight boobies, I love you, see you in the morning," and turn over to sleep.

It was like she had her own relationship with the boobies that was completely separate from me. She would talk to them, asking them things like, "Boobies, are you really asleep?" I'd adopted a boobie voice to reply, "Yes, we're asleep. Goodnight."

She suckled to sleep for nearly a year before I introduced the bedtime rhyme, "When you're three, they're free. When you're four, no more." I thought this would gear her up for saying goodbye to nursing once again. She seemed to go along with the idea, saying the rhyme with me every night. But when her fourth birthday grew near, she undid the rhyme. "When you're three, they're free. When you're four, they're free!"

The World Health Organization's "as long as it's mutually agreeable" recommendation rang in my ears. Though Emma-Joy's nightly nursing wasn't outright irritating, I did begin to wonder how old she was going to be before she wouldn't feel a need for it anymore. I was looking forward to the night when I could just tuck her in and kiss her goodnight instead of have to lie down with her, sometimes falling asleep myself.

Another year passed. Then out of the blue, without any forewarning from her or another the-end-is-near rhyme from me, she nursed to sleep for the last time. It was the night before her fifth birthday. Just nine months longer than the worldwide average, or only three months longer if you consider that she didn't nurse for six months between ages two and a half and three; either way, a beyond-average age for my anything-but-average daughter.

I lied down with her, she curled up next to me and suckled like usual. But instead of saying goodnight to the boobies, she said goodbye. Just like that. She'd decided on her own that five was time, "Bye, boobies, I'm gonna be five tomorrow. Thanks for letting me nurse you."

The boobie voice replied, "OK, bye. You're welcome. We love you."

3 Years Old

26.

A Typical Day with My Preschooler

At three and a half years old, my girl was a full-blown three-foot-four-inch, thirty-seven-pound, fully conversational, fierce, and sensitive (Dr. Jekyll/Mr. Hyde-type) preschooler with a Pee Wee Herman-esque sense of humor.

Her favorite laugh-getting technique was to go up to friends and their grown-ups and politely ask, "Excuse me, guess what?" They'd answer earnestly, "What?" She'd then blurt, "Chicken butt!" crack up, and run to the next unsuspecting grown-up, asking, "Hey, who ordered the poo-poo platter?"

Sure, the other grown-ups looked at me with a questioning eye, but I just shrugged as if I had no idea where she had learned it. They'd tell me she's very mature for her age, but I knew better. I knew she was really still my innocent baby, who simply remained sweetly oblivious to silly social expectations.

A typical day for us involved a ritual snail hunt before pedaling to preschool. It took a while for her to make the connection that if she squishes them, they die, and what that meant, even though I pleaded with her to treat them gently. She was a natural brute, but once she developed emotional attachments to certain individual snails, she learned how to limit her natural strength. She called them her pets and would actually kiss and talk to them, "I love you, Snailey."

Each morning, I'd bike Emma-Joy to preschool at nine o'clock. I'd then bask in the quiet solitude that my tiny front-porch jewelry studio provided and work there diligently, careful to avoid wasting alone-time on chores or grocery shopping. Three hours later, I'd bike back to pick her up.

It's hot in the tropics at high noon, so we'd seek refuge inside where the window-unit air conditioner was, and grab a quick snack. Afterwards, my girl would get the idea to dress us up "for the ball." She'd hunt for the only mom-sized poofy thrift-store dress in her closet, find it, and require me to wear it. She'd select her own thrifted dress-ups and within minutes, we'd be in another world, twirling around the living room to her then-favorites, The Strokes, Joan Jett (either with the Blackhearts or the Runaways), Molotonic, or Devo. Ernesto said she was the most natural mosh-pitter ever, and I think he was right. I'd have more bruises after dancing around with her in one afternoon than I'd gotten over the previous three years at shows.

We'd wind up in a tumbled heap of crinoline and slightly tattered rayon on our bed. She'd grab some dolls and make them dance at the ball, too. Suddenly, she'd rip an unexpected fart. Quite amused by these easily audible explosions, she'd jump ass first onto her dolls' heads and squeal with delight, "Smell my stinky butt!" I'd vacate the premises.

In a few minutes, she'd find me drawing in the living room. She'd grab a marker, too. Preferring to draw on skin instead of paper, she'd give herself tattoos with markers, then ballpoint pen, then watercolors. She didn't just prefer to draw on skin, she demanded it—and not just her own. Soon I'd be covered. When I'd suggest it was time to clean up, feigning actual cooperation, she'd impishly insist on drinking the murky watercolor water. A natural-born contrarian if ever there was one.

I'd have to remind myself that kids her age didn't understand sarcasm (though Ernesto took on the task to make sure she does by age five), so I decided not to tell her that was a smart way to clean up the watercolors. Instead, I'd remind her that drinking dirty water could make her sick, but of course, that was why she drank it in the first place. She'd heard it before and didn't heed my advice. My more experienced mom friends' comments would ring in my ears, "She's only three? Just wait until she's twelve! You're really in for it with this one." It was the same incessant "testing" she'd do with matters of mining and eating boogies and Tourette's-style blurting out, "God damn it, damn it, damn it!" in the grocery-store checkout line. To get around my requests to not do either, she'd taken to the secrecy of hiding under a blanket.

Boogies were a two-way street. She ignored my requests for her to quit digging knuckle-deep. I ignored hers for me to stop wiping her nose. When I saw a boogie smeared across her cheek and couldn't control my mama primate preening habits and picked it off, she promptly opened her mouth, "I want it!" I tried to dissuade her, "But it's slimy dirt." Instead of hiding under a blanket so I couldn't see, she retreated to a corner so I couldn't reach. She taunted me by repeatedly thrusting her index finger up her nose and into her mouth no less than ten times. I finally tell her I really don't care, but that her Grandma Bee would hate it and that other kids might tease her. Chances are she doesn't understand social pressure yet. Chances are she does understand, but doesn't care. Later, she tells me she gets mad at me for "wiping one away because it's mine!" I remind myself that boogies are an unnecessary battle; she's right, the boogies are hers. And the mama primate preening habits are mine.

Lunchtime

After fixing our lunch, I'd decide I need a break. Instead of sitting with her and reading a book aloud while she ate, I'd turn on her *Annie* video from the library. Aahhh, that'd usually buy me a little time, but not even videos could hold her attention totally if she didn't want them to. She'd want me by her side, teaching her the words to the songs and acting out not just Annie's part, but all the characters. I'd attempt negotiation so that I could just sit and relax with a zine for a few moments, but it'd disintegrate into bribery with a lollipop. Partially defeated, I'd delve into the world of self-reflexivity while reading *Miranda* zine, wherein the author Kate confesses to putting her kid in front of the TV with his lunch so she can read.

I'd feel better knowing I was not alone, but would feel a whole lot better if there was an easier way to get together a true parenting cooperative like we had the last place we lived. Such zines as *Miranda, The Future Generation, Mama Sez No War, Olympia Mamazine, Placenta,* and *Edgy Catin' Mama,* all of them written by moms and parenting-related, had become my version of the full-time mom's favorite daytime TV drama. Reading them while living in relative isolation from community had brought me a sense of camaraderie and filled me with wild ideas and fantasies of building a real alternative and challenge to the mainstream, traditional, isolated-nuclear family model.

Video lunchtime would just be about all the time I'd be rationed for organizing a parenting revolution in my brain before I'd be called back to the front lines of daily mom and kid duty. Lunch dishes corralled to the kitchen sink to be cleaned up much, much later, video off, we'd be set to tackle the afternoon. Those days, I'd wind up expending more energy trying to get Emma-Joy to take a nap than it was worth in potential benefits. So, I'd have to think up something to keep us busy before she did, because I really didn't want to play dolls or paint nails for the gazillionth time.

What usually would wind up keeping us busy were things that needed to get done like composting, tending to our vegetable garden, laundry, grocery getting, preparing the next meal, etc. Not the things that I wanted to be doing every day at all! And then doing them together with a three-year-old took a hell of a lot longer.

Well-practiced patience was required here, but the older my girl got, I'd be pleasantly surprised. It used to be she couldn't be away from my side for anything. Now if she didn't want to do (or "help" with) what I needed to do, she was more apt to go off and do something on her own, for a little while at least.

The most pleasant of these surprises was her "reading" books to herself on the couch, doing her own toddler/preschool CD-ROMs on her computer, getting out the hammer and some nails and banging away on her "practice" wood scraps outside, and strumming my guitar, singing songs she made up herself. I really blew it with this last one, one day, though. Instead of just getting done what I needed to, I broke out the tape recorder. I should have known that she'd stop, but I couldn't help myself. I'm her proud, geeky mom, and her songs were the most heart-filling I'd ever heard and I wanted to remember all of them.

I was also willing to put aside what I was doing one afternoon when she came to me asking for me to dye her hair pink. When it came down to doing it, she just wanted a streak of color, chose purple over pink, and planned on going red next time. Other preschool parents and grandparents gave me sideways glances, but I assured them that it was all her idea; I really had no influential persuasion going on, in spite of her dad's and my dye-job repertoire.

Nighttime

As the sole full-time parent, getting the basics covered day in and day out could be a tiring drag—dinner, shower, teeth brushing, potty time, bedtime reading, then the fight for sleep. And because Emma-Joy was an ever-changing, learning, inquisitive creature, caring for her was not just about getting the basics covered. There were constant negotiations, conversations, and questions getting fielded along the way.

After her shower one night, she bounded into my bedroom to tell me that when she grows up, she can touch her daddy's penis. Quick on her heels, Ernesto responded, "No, you can never touch my penis." Defeated, she sighed, "That's OK. I'll have my own to touch when I growed up." Sometimes there just wasn't anything I could think of fast enough to continue the conversation that would help her understand the way things are. This time, it was all I could do to keep from cracking up in front of her.

Keeping momentum with the goal of getting her off to sleep (and it was such a goal, because after she goes to sleep was usually the only time in the day I truly got to myself), we'd read a story of her choosing. One night, instead of her latest library pick, she wanted me to read the zine that came in the mail that day. It was done by a mama-zinester's son and titled *Aubrey's Lego Club*. She really liked see-

KEEP AGE-APPROPRIATE EXPECTATIONS FOR BEHAVIORS

This is harder than it sounds. There's general agreement on *how* children develop; it's the *when* they develop that's tricky. The pace at which normal intellectual, emotional, physical, and social behaviors develop varies greatly according to each individual. All development exists across a continuum. Some changes seem to come out of nowhere; a child can just wake up one morning demonstrating new knowledge or a new skill. Other changes are more obviously gradual; children progress from scooting to crawling to walking to running.

It took me years to figure out that most toddler and preschooler behaviors are more directly linked to a developmental stage than they are to the child making a conscious choice to behave a certain way. For example, I could explain a million times why it's not a gentle, kind, respectful choice to squish snails, but not until Emma-Joy was actually able to begin accessing her own internal empathy would my explanations begin to mean anything to her. Sure, most three-year-olds know what they should and shouldn't do, but sometimes they aren't developmentally ready to act accordingly. Punishing a kid for not acting how you think they should act is like punishing a blind person because they cannot see. Get to know developmentally appropriate behavior and work with it rather than against it; this is hard, so patience with yourself as well as with your child is key.

Toddlers especially will do things 50 million times no matter how many times or different ways you try to ask them not to. They are not necessarily pushing to see what the consequences of their actions will be. Mainstream approaches to parenting and discipline teach us to perceive all kids this way, regardless of their stage of development, that they're looking for limits or trying to see what they can get away with. This idea ascribes too much to toddlers; they are just doing what they do and attributing motives to their behavior leads parents to reactions that may not be useful.

ing the drawings and photos and hearing the kid-voice narrative. She wanted me to read it again and again, and I had to indulge her out of sheer giddiness that she just might have been well on her way to loving zines they way I do.

Eventually, sleep took her over and I was free to do whatever during the whopping two or four hours before my own sleep took over. But the mom thing was hard to turn off, just as it was hard not to break out the tape recorder that interrupted both her and me. Instead of doing what I had been planning on doing, I started digging through my recently delivered last boxes of stuff that were left behind at my parents' house all these years and eventually found exactly what I was looking for—the first fanzine I ever did, when I was eight years old, *All About Shaun Cassidy*.

I went to sleep not frustrated that there weren't enough hours in the day for being mom and being myself, too. It felt good that I hadn't wasted time doing something that I could have done while she was awake. So often, I'd feel like the mom-thing and the me-thing were diametrically opposed, and it was a struggle to satisfactorily mesh them together—the real me would on hold until Emma-Joy fell asleep, or worse, until she was an adult! Finding that fanzine was not only exciting because she had been so into the Lego zine we had read and now I could share mine with her, but also because it represented a creative way of blending self and motherhood.

Before I crashed for the night, I wrote myself a note in my journal: *Common interests with E-J will not only connected us on a different level, but will also satisfy my need to merge motherhood with self. If I can find more shared interests with E-J, something that I find fulfilling and that she does, too, I will be aiding her development as well as helping my own development as a mother—my self will never be separate from being a mother—I am developing by reinventing the essence of who I am now, who I am becoming. More music! More art! More Do-It-Yourself projects we can do side by side and together!*

27.

Organizing Childcare for the FTAA Protests

I knew the FTAA (Free Trade Area of the Americas) ministerial meetings were coming to a city near me, so I went to an anti-FTAA organizational event three months prior. The proposed FTAA agreement, an extension of NAFTA (North America Free Trade Agreement), would eliminate or reduce the trade barriers among all countries in the Caribbean and South, Central, and North Americas, Cuba excluded. The agreement was based on free-market fundamentalism instead of principles of fair trade. The reasons for opposing it are numerous; a global race-to-the-bottom threatens the environment, families' livelihoods, human rights, and democracy.

While at the event, another mom and I talked about was the need for organized childcare during the anti-FTAA actions. Since becoming mothers, there had several protests and other political demonstrations that we had not been able to get involved with or participate in due to the lack of childcare. And others felt like we did—that because of the demands of caring for kids, they were forced out being active in ways beyond actively parenting.

Childcare at large-scale events is not organized the way the medic, convergence space, media, and legal help spaces are. And we were all too familiar with attending meetings that felt disrupted because our kids were there, or with not feeling like our kids were in a safe space with us demonstrating in the streets because overzealous cops were there.

I had experience organizing cooperative childcare and had been in touch with the ABC (Anti-Authoritarian Baby-sitting Club), a collective organization made up of non-parent allies who provided radical childcare for political events in the Washington, D.C. area. So I committed to organizing childcare in Miami during the November 2003 anti-FTAA events. Driving home from that initial organizational event, my mind snapped into organizer mode, and as soon as I got home, I got in touch with the ABC to find out if they were planning on attending the protest.

I soon found out from one of the ABC collective members that the project was on indefinite hold due to various reasons. Though disappointed, I wasn't discouraged that I could not facilitate a similar childcare model, especially since one of the ABC collective members promised to be a resource for my efforts.

Help from the ABC

The following is a list of my questions and the ABC's answers that helped my organizing efforts:

How many kids did you provide care for at the A20 event in Washington, D.C.? What was the adult-to-kid ratio?

It was our first time offering care, and I think we had only like five to seven [kids] at the height. We tried to limit the number of adults for two reasons: 1) to not overwhelm the kids, and 2) so it didn't become a hangout for folks. We wanted people who were there to be kicking it with the kids. So we had two [adults], I think, on each shift, but when you get infants or special-needs kids, I feel like that increases the need. Like at this recent conference we've done childcare for, we had like maybe four or five kids, but they were all super young, and in that case having three "caretakers" was a help.

To try to get an approximate head count (so I can have enough caregiver volunteers) I am hoping to "preregister" kids. Did you do this? How did you handle drop-ins who hadn't preregistered?

Yes, we did preregister, and some did. This was most effective at conferences, but some at the demos. We handled drop-ins by having them fill out the info, and tried to have some folks "on call" in case we got swamped.

I am going to ask that parents supply us with dipes and wipes (if needed). Also snacks and juice. What other stuff (besides art supplies) would you recommend I get collected? Did you need blankets and pillows?

Although we did ask parents to supply some stuff for their charges, especially if they had unique food needs or allergies, we also made an attempt to get food, toys, etc., on our own to be prepared and to make it easier for them. We felt it was completely reasonable to ask organizers of the events to give us some money for this. Pillows are definitely good to have, and extra clothes, in case there's an accident, as there was once!

What about parents who get arrested? Did that happen? Did you care for their kids 24/7 until their release?

I don't remember that happening. We did have emergency contact info for folks, so that if that did happen, there would be someone to take care of the young ones. Most parents, it seemed, weren't interested in putting themselves in that situation, though of course we don't always choose when to get arrested, as I well know. Asking them that might be somewhat helpful—i.e. both if they plan to, or [if they] engage in activities that might put them at higher risk (recognizing the volatility of the state's violence), and also who they'd want to have contacted if they are held. Also, that's important to know for medicines, I think, and other things that might be like that, which could be necessary if they even just get delayed, or arrested.

Any security issues? I like the ABC's idea of photographing the kid with the parents upon drop off, to be sure of who's picking the kid up.

As someone who's worked with kids in a lot of settings and seen the many precautions that are taken, I always got really nervous about this part. I want to believe that everyone in our communities is beautiful and pure of heart, but no doubt there are people who would take advantage of being alone with a child or being able to isolate one from the group. I think we found it key to avoid having kids alone with caretakers as much as possible, and to always keep everyone in a big group. Working with volunteers, we couldn't really do much beyond that. Yes, the Polaroid was good, because usually it wasn't the same volunteer person at the end of the day as at the start. Maybe also ask parents if there's another parent/family member who might try to get access to the child who shouldn't.

What were the hours of care? Early morning to late? Do you think providing care all five days of the protest is necessary, or just on the main days of action? What was your schedule like for A20 in D.C.?

This is a hard call to make. At different times we did different things. I would try to get a sense of when the most likely important things are and aim for those. If for some reason you have a huge number of people willing to work childcare, then do more days. Hours, the same. We did start very early in the morning at most demos, and usually went until about 7 p.m.

I'm trying to get use of a nursery/preschool room. That way, we won't have to haul kid toys and games with us, just the consumables that we wouldn't expect to be there already. Am I on the right track here expecting that I won't need to gather a bunch of toys and kid stuff besides the obvious consumables discussed earlier?

Yes, that's the best way to do it. On several occasions we were able to use a nursery, and that was fantastic because they had toys, books, all that; child-safe spaces; and bathrooms with easy access and for small folks. Put pressure here on the organizers again to help with securing a childcare space. They should be making this a priority.

About forms for important information that the parent fills out: Do you still have the ones the ABC used so I don't have to reinvent the wheel?

Yes. [See "Resources" section for the registration and medical-information form.]

What about first-aid training? Did accidents happen? What stuff do you recommend that I gather? Do you have any info sheets about first aid?

I don't remember any accidents. But we did have a talk with a medic beforehand, but that was mostly us who were in the collective (i.e. I think four of us at that time), and so that knowledge wasn't available to all volunteers. He did bring up some important things, like what we need in a first-aid kit, having the poison control number handy, that if an accident did happen and we call 911, tell them it's a child and they get there faster, etc. I also obviously have the number for the medics of the action. I would suggest having a training at least for some folks with a medic.

How did you spread the word so parents knew childcare was available? Whose kids did you end up caring for at A20, anyone and everyone's (like at the AFL-CIO union family kids)? Or were they mostly kids of the anticapitalist, antiauthoritarian, autonomous activists?

I'd say mostly the latter. We put it up on websites, tried to spread the word, but you know, like with anything, it only goes so far.

Getting Organized

At the next big organizational meeting, I announced my intentions of organizing childcare. I let all in attendance know that every one of them could help by spreading the word that childcare would be available because parents automatically assume that there will be no childcare and therefore do not even plan on attending such events. I also let the paid organizers know that they could help in finding a childcare space.

After that, I set to work to get the word out myself by asking several key informational and organizational websites to post that childcare was being organized and that interested persons should contact me to preregister their kids and/or to volunteer to do a shift at the childcare space. Word did get out and kids were getting signed up, though slowly at first. I expected that though, and not until the week before the events did the majority of parents get in touch with me.

One of the aforementioned paid organizers did come through with a potential childcare space, a nursery room at a local church. Jackpot! This was exactly what I was hoping for—a room already set up for kids so that I wouldn't have to create one from scratch. The only problem was that it was a fifteen-minute drive from where the actions would be. I ran the potential problem by all the parents who had been in touch with me up to that point, and all of them said pretty much the same thing, that they'd take what we could get and deal with it. I set to work to create the liability waiver that the church wanted all the parents and volunteers to sign, along with a medical release form and a general information/registration form.

Change in Plans

Things were looking pretty tight and I was feeling excited instead of overwhelmed. There were volunteers coming out of the woodwork, I had all the forms faxed to my contact at the church and was just awaiting final confirmation on the times we could have the nursery room. The only two big tasks I still had to do were put together the required training for all non-parent volunteers, and create a schedule so that all the volunteers could sign up for shifts.

I was calling my church contact every day to find out the exact times we could have the nursery room, but after a week, I started getting nervous. My contact was out of town, back in town but sick and would call me back, and never called back, so I'd call again only to find out that he still hadn't confirmed the times himself with his board of directors. I started making desperate calls to paid protest organizers for leads about any other local churches opening their doors to the demonstrators. When I finally got my answer from my church contact, I guess the frenzied local media hype about the potentially violent demonstrations had informed the church's final decision—that it sounded like too much trouble to have at the church. Instead he offered to clean out his garage and put down a piece of carpet for us.

It was a mere three days before the childcare effort was to begin that he gave me this news, and at first, probably because of shock, I actually considered taking him up on his garage. But after a couple hours and several phone calls to the others involved in organizing the childcare, I called him back to say thanks but no thanks, and was left scrambling to pull this effort off in spite of having no space secured after all.

I'll spare you the details of the overanxious and uber-stressed hours I spent on the phone desperately trying to find another space, because the next thing that happened was also unforeseen and halted me in my tracks. I got word from two different parties, each of which that had been planning on bringing a group of four or five kids for childcare, that they decided to not bring the kids after all. I had to stop to put it all into perspective. Was I going to continue busting my ass to get a space for a now relatively small number of kids that I could easily accommodate at my own house located twenty-five minutes away from the actions? Would ten more minutes between the childcare space and the actions be an issue for the parents and volunteers? If people had been deciding at the last minute to not bring their kids, then I could for sure count on others deciding at the last minute to bring their kids. In that case, would there be enough space at my house?

Attempting to process all this in a relatively short amount of time made me feel like a failure. There were too many unknown variables to account for. All this hard work had crumbled too easily. Still burning with desire to make something, anything, work out, I called or emailed each parent, volunteer, and co-organizer to explain the latest developments. After talking to several of them, I stopped busting my ass and we turned to cooperative childcare. After talking to one more, I took her idea to march with her kid in the big legal, permitted march and ran with it. I contacted everyone again to tell them that we should all march together as the Mom and Baby Bloc. Even though I was no longer going to be on duty at the childcare space for three straight days, I was not just going to sit at home feeling like I had been dumped.

What wound up transpiring was inspiring and empowering, even though the ideal, organized childcare space had not come through as planned.

We held a Mom and Baby Bloc meeting at the convergence space. There, we voiced our safety concerns about bringing our kids into a potentially unsafe environment although we were only planning on participating in the permitted marches, and came up with a safety plan:

1. The Mom and Baby Bloc and Power U Center for Social Change, a nonprofit community organization in Miami, would march in solidarity with each other; we would all feel safer in a larger group.

2. A street medic and a legal observer would march with us.

3. In case of tear-gas or pepper-spray exposure, we'd be prepared with wet hand towels/bandanas soaked in apple cider vinegar and sealed in plastic bags, and have a clean, thin layer to go between the nose/mouth and soaked towel. We would dress the kids in long sleeves and pants, socks, and closed-toe shoes and bring the kids extra changes of clothes in doubled Ziploc bags. For eyes, we'd bring a 1:1 mixture of water and plain, unflavored liquid antacid like Maalox, Mylanta, or a generic equivalent premixed in a squirt bottle.

4. We'd carry plenty of bottled water and nutritious snacks, and also bring Rescue Remedy and throat lozenges.

5. In case of emergency, we would walk with intent, not run, as running incites trample, something more dangerous than tear-gas or pepper-spray exposure.

Our "Childcare, the FTAA, and the Baby Bloc" Statement

As parents, it is important for us to be part of these protests. The decisions being made in the Intercontinental Hotel this week will affect our children's futures. We must make our voices heard to protect our children from the negative affects of free trade, and to act in solidarity with the millions of families around the world that are not able to be here.

We bring our children to these demonstrations to teach them about resistance. We want them to learn that when they see injustice, they need to stand up and speak out. Because it is not always safe to bring children to these events, and many of us cannot afford to pay for childcare, we believe it is necessary to arrange collective childcare for these events. Having a safe space for children provides parents with an opportunity to make their voices heard without putting their children at risk.

Childcare is also an issue in our everyday lives, not just as activists. Our ability to make a living and find adequate, affordable childcare will be affected by the FTAA and free trade. By organizing collective childcare, not just at marches and demonstrations, but in our communities, we build self-reliance and reduce our dependence on the system that exploits us.

Unfortunately, childcare arrangements are rarely made at large-scale events. Organizers automatically plan a space for medics, legal help, and media, but not for childcare. Activists and organizations that plan these events need to make childcare part of the planning. As parents, our time is limited so we should not be expected to do all the planning.

The FTAA specifically affects us as parents:

Privatization: One of the cornerstones of free trade is privatization of education, welfare, healthcare, and other services that affect parents. For example, welfare-to-work programs force women out of their homes and away from their children, without providing necessary services like childcare. The jobs they are given don't pay enough for them to afford adequate childcare, so mothers/families are put in a horrible situation.

Breast-feeding: Formula and baby food companies like Nestlé will use free trade agreements like the FTAA to squash opposition to their immoral marketing techniques. These companies go into developing nations, launch ad campaigns that show healthy, pudgy babies drinking formula, and then hand out free samples of formula telling...(cont'd)

After we solidified our safety plan, we drafted a statement titled "Childcare, the FTAA, and the Baby Bloc" (see sidebar) to be distributed to fellow protesters and the press. Later that day, some of us marched together with our kids on the last leg of the Root Cause march (a three-day, thirty-four-mile march), all the way to the barricade that surrounded the hotel where the FTAA ministerial meetings were being held and all the while flanked on both sides by bike cops, Robo cops, riot cops, cops on horses, cops in cars, and from above by cops in helicopters. Up until now, things had remained safe all three days of the march, so we felt good about doing the last leg of it with our kids. It was very festive with chants, drum and flag corps, and huge, colorful street puppets. Heading back to our car, away from the large group still assembled at the barricade, Emma-Joy and I and one other mama and her child were detained by the cops and questioned as to where we thought we were going. It was more irritating than scary as Emma-Joy was tired and ready for dinner. They tried to tell us we weren't allowed back in the area where our car was parked. There was lots of radioing back and forth between the cops and who was supposedly in charge. They put us on a wild goose chase, walking to this cop or that cop to determine if we'd be allowed to get to our car. Eventually, we were able to duck into the lobby of the hotel that my mama friend was staying at. Luckily, the clerk at the front desk told the cops that I was just a hotel guest who needed to go get my car. The cops then escorted Emma-Joy and me and watched us drive away.

The next day, we all met at noon at Power U to make signs and organize ourselves. Even more mamas and kids marched together as the Mom and Baby Bloc in the big legal, permitted (AFL-CIO sponsored) march, with spontaneous chants and signs like "FTAA needs a spanking," "FTAA is full of poopy," and "Something stinks and it's not my diaper." With Power U, we were a sizable group that was able to stick together well. Though at butt level because she was in a stroller, Emma-Joy snapped pictures of colorful costumes

women that it is better for their babies. Before they know it, nursing mothers have lost their milk supply, the free samples have run out, and they are forced to spend the little money they have on formula. This trend has been a major cause of infant death in developing nations, because the formula is mixed with too much water as a way to make the formula last longer; babies then do not receive adequate nutrition, leading to starvation. The formula is also mixed with contaminated water, leading to diarrhea and other disease. Without proper medical care, death can follow. The FTAA will consider any efforts by developing nations to stop these tactics as illegal by using the premise that limiting the business of formula companies will be a barrier to free trade and therefore illegal under the FTAA. The WTO [World Trade Organization] has already made this claim to stop anti-formula legislation in Guatemala. Since many of us are breast-feeding mothers, this issue is very deeply rooted in our hearts.

The FTAA affects us on many more issues from privatization to job security to the environment. We are here to say **PUT OUR FAMILIES FIRST— STOP THE FTAA!**

and protest signs with the camera I'd given her expressly for that purpose. Later, we'd be able to use the pictures she took as a great way to talk more about the costumes, the messages on the signs, why all the people there had gotten together to march, and why all the cops were there. Nearly the entire march route had been flanked by cops on both sides—they were on bikes, foot, horses, and even sitting atop two tanks—and above us in the air in helicopters. At the end of the march route, the kids enjoyed watching radical cheerleaders and drumming and joined in the dancing in the streets. The moment we noticed a shift in the gathering heading toward the barricade, we knew it was time to get the kids out of there. As the Mom and Baby Bloc and Power U retreated together, we heard the signs that told us we'd gotten out of there exactly when we needed to. The tear-gas canisters and rubber bullets were flying.

The day after that, we took kids to the really free, free market where they got to take whacks at a *papier-maché* dollar-sign *piñata*, eat yummy free food à la Food Not Bombs, learn how to fold origami cranes, paint, make music, run, play, and listen to stories by a guy with his old-timey paper spindle "TV." This was really fun for the kids and us, too. Imagine a storyteller with a wooden, four-sided box with a scroll-like paper screen stretched across the front of it. The scroll was hand-wound across the front to create an effect of the illustrated pictures moving as the story progressed. Though there were some cops hanging around the perimeter of the really free, free market, we felt much safer there than we had the day before. When parents wanted to be involved in more direct action than those events were, and needed care for their kids, it was done cooperatively either at my house or one of their hotel rooms.

The downside was that there were several folks who wanted or needed care for their kids who wound up not participating with us because the initial childcare space fell through. It really bothered me that, in spite of my efforts, I couldn't make it happen. Once again, there were parents who could not get involved who wanted to, or who could not participate in ways they wanted to

What happened due to the space being canceled on us was, as I said before, exciting, inspirational and empowering. When things fell through, we were able to group together collectively and quickly, even though many of us had never even met before, to strategically get ourselves off the sidelines with our kids. But as I said before, too, there is a big need for childcare to be a given, just like the convergence, medic, food, housing, media, and legal spaces are. If parents had the big issue of childcare removed from the forefront of our brains, then we could actually think about something else and participate in more ways!

So the work I cut out for myself didn't have the closure I thought it would have. I thought I'd close up the childcare space after the week's last event and be moving on to see what work I could do next. Not so. This job isn't done until we demand that event organizers make childcare something to be expected. After all, we're fighting for a better world here. Shouldn't part of the fight reflect what that better world would look like?

28.

Who Gives a Shit About Kids and Cursing?

The thought never crossed our minds to change how we spoke now that we were parents. Our normal, casual language was peppered with the more colorful, though not always socially acceptable-for-kids, words. Once Emma-Joy became old enough to pick up on the extra emotive quality of the f-word and use it in her own expressive language, I wasn't taken aback in the least. It was a normal part of our vocabulary, so it was normal for Emma-Joy, too. After all, is there really any difference between saying "fudge" instead of "fuck?" It's the intent and context of words that matters, not the actual words.

At first, there were two specific instances in which she'd use it consistently and correctly. When she'd stub her toe, it was always met with a hearty, "Fuck!" And when traffic was bad and the other drivers were worse, she'd astutely observe, "Fucking hell!"

How could I possibly be taken aback when she sounded exactly like me when I stub my toe or when traffic sucks? I am well aware that there are other ways to deal with frustration and anger—for instance, being more patient in traffic, or taking a deep breath when I stub my toe—but sometimes those tactics just don't fit the occasion or mood. I don't have a degree in language acquisition, but I do know that kids learn their formative language skills by copying. So, was I proud to hear that my girl was mastering a language skill of using words correctly in their appropriate context? Yes. And did I also find humor in it? Of course I did, although I will admit to stifling my giggles because I didn't want to give away the f-word's taboo status.

When Emma-Joy began picking up on the f-word's power to raise eyebrows at age three, we tried to explain simply that in our house the only "bad" words are the ones used to hurt someone's feelings (for example, unprovoked name-calling and insults or racist, homophobic, or sexist language). And we told her that some people don't like to hear kids say "curse" words at all (for example, shit, fuck, damn, piss, hell, ass). We then gave her two simple examples of the people who don't want to hear kids use "curse" words at all, not even when she stubs her toe: her grandparents and her preschool teacher. We were relying on her sensitivity to censor herself around grandparents and at school, even though she really didn't understand why she should.

In doing so, we created a dilemma. My girl is smart and sensitive enough to use the words correctly, and by age four, used them around us like we do, as adjectives and expletives rather than insults. But her preschool-innocent self just didn't get why certain people got all riled up when they heard them come out of her little girl mouth. To kids, words are just words. Taboos are thrust upon words by adults and enforced to preserve the status quo and power structure, forces that kids don't seem to acknowledge naturally. If this was reason enough not to allow her to curse, that is, not allowing her to curse until she was old enough to understand how and why some language is regarded as taboo, then we'd blown it by not changing before she was born how we casually spoke.

We relied on our limited knowledge of language acquisition. In not hearing us insult others, she'd learn that insulting others is not something someone should do. She'd learn effective communication skills by picking up on how we'd tailor our language and tone outside of the safety of our home when with different audiences. For example, she wouldn't be hearing us use "curse" words around grandparents or at her school, either.

There were, however, a few awkward situations for which we felt awful and responsible for her ensuing hurt feelings and confusion.

Once, at a family gathering, we were all hanging out in the living room when my girl heard a cousin say, "What's this fuckin' thing?" She blurted, "Hey! Fuckin's not nice to say in front of grandparents!" But a grandparent scolded her for having said the f-word. She defended herself, explaining that she was only copying what someone had said so she could tell them it wasn't nice to do in front of grandparents. She was told sternly that she is not allowed to say that word at all. I attempted to come to her defense, to take responsibility, making it clear to my family how we've explained "bad" words to her and how we do not even make special note of her mimicry, but I was cut off and treated like a child also. The voice of authority spoke and again my girl was told she's "not allowed to say that." She burst into tears and I carried her away from the situation.

As I walked into the next room, I heard Ernesto step up to the heroic plate and explain that he'd rather our girl hear and mimic meaningless cursing than the sexist bullshit that's often present at the dinner table at family gatherings, how just the night before our girl had heard, though it hadn't been said directly to her, what one of her "joking" loved ones would "like to do" to her favorite character, The Little Mermaid. With his explanation, our whole philosophy about the power of language had been laid out. Language—in the form of sexist and degrading talk or mean-spirited criticism—really has the potential to do a lot of harm on young children, much more than any four-letter word could. We believe that words do have the power to hurt, in spite of the old "sticks and stones" adage saying otherwise. Many a racist slur and sexist put-down has had the effect at making the target of such language feel "lesser than" and dehumanized. We were going to stick by our idea that it is more important to challenge and fight against racist and sexist language than it is to be polite.

I've heard a few other parents reason that cursing is a reflection of poor values. I've then asked, "Exactly what poor values are reflected?" On two occasions, I was met with a blank stare that asked back, "You don't *know*?" Perhaps I am overlooking something they value: authority. The authority that commands, "Do as I say, not as I do." The authority that reinforces a child's position in society, "Because I am the adult and you are the child." But perhaps they are overlooking more important antiracist, antihomophobic, and antisexist family values.

So if it is simply an issue of values, how in the hell are we going to explain that to our girl? Values are a concept that will likely escape her youthful comprehension for years to come. More important than figuring out the question of whose values, I needed to think harder about how to avoid setting Emma-Joy up for any more situations that could lead to more of the confusion that causes hurt feelings.

We hadn't made any headway in figuring this all out when it happened again. At a pizza counter, a woman came in with some choice words slipping out of her mouth. Upon seeing my girl, she apologized and said she wouldn't have cursed if she had seen my daughter. My partner told the woman that it was OK, that our girl says those words, too. The woman was aghast and reprimanded him with a snarly voice, "Little girls should *not* say those dirty words." Whatever, lady; you just did.

As a reaction, to help our girl avoid more incidents with uptight hypocrites, we came up with a resolution: Since kids saying "curse" words really upsets some people, let's all try not to say them. All three of us agreed to it. To Ernesto and me, that resolution sounded simple enough for our preschooler, even if it is was a lame kowtow for us.

The results were nothing short of annoying. Nothing changed and it became a silly game. Even if Emma-Joy heard the word "stupid," she'd programmed herself to correct the perpetrator, "Stupid's not nice!" Argh! We were stuck in that rerun of a not-so-funny sitcom episode for an entire year!

It seemed as if she had lost the ability to differentiate "curse" words from more acceptable adjectives. This is one way I think the status quo's cursing taboo has a negative effect on children's grasp and understanding of language, because it is arbitrary which words are profane and which are acceptable. This is, of course, in direct contrast to the belief held by some that cursing itself hinders language development because people rely on expletives rather than expanding their vocabulary—for example, just saying "Damn it!" when mad, instead of articulating the degrees of anger, from "upset" to "infuriated." What that belief overlooks is the numerous other ways language development is hindered, and that by teaching your kid all of the possible ways to articulate degrees of anger and other feelings, expletives included, your kid will actually gain a more nuanced ability with word choice as they grow older.

It also seemed that Emma-Joy began thinking that if any word had the potential to hurt someone's feelings, they were "bad" and "curse" words. Whereas she'd previously understood context and intent, it now no longer mattered. On one hand, it's good to develop sensitivity to the power of all words, not just a handful of so-called bad words, but on the other, the mixed messages make it difficult for children to navigate through the language minefield.

Would it be years before Emma-Joy truly mastered when not to "curse" at all in order to avoid valueless, illegitimate-authority reprimand? I wonder now how old she will be when she feels free enough to expletively express herself with conviction to the uptight authoritarian hypocrites?

If she's anything like our good friend Scott's daughter, it will be when she's about ten. Scott's daughter was still in elementary school when she called her teacher an asshole. When Scott was called to come to school for a conference about the incident, he started the conference himself by asking what had happened. When the principal finished recounting the events, all Scott said was, "At our house, there are no bad words if they are used appropriately. Sounds to me like the teacher was being an asshole."

29.

Discipline Notes: Relationship Is Everything

Either fortunately or unfortunately, there is no rule book for parenting a free child. If there were, it would likely recommend keeping an open, holistic view that equates parenting with discipline and teaching, instead of thinking of them as separate features. It would also, as Emma Goldman suggested, encourage parents to aim to develop a well-rounded individual. And it would mention that Mikhail Bakunin wrote, in an essay in *The Political Philosophy of Bakunin*, that parents loving their children and exercising authority "does not run counter to their morality, their mental development, or their future freedom" and have suggestions for "ways of raising children that will not psychologically cripple them but instead enable them to accept freedom and responsibility while developing natural self-regulation." A rule book would also include something along the lines of: *The great irony of parenting a free child is that you have to be willing to give up some of your freedom while nurturing freedom in your child.*

Linear thinking or checklists do not work, no matter what parenting style you subscribe to. However, the following are some principles upon which parenting a free child is based. While reading, keep in mind that any included suggestions are fluid; they are not absolutes, so change them up as to fit your needs. Also, keep in mind that many of these principles and ideas overlap each other; some cannot exist without another. They are meant to be explored with your child, not just giving them a try once or twice. Take what resonates with your family and leave what doesn't.

If you are an expectant parent, a good place to start thinking about how you want to parent is by asking yourself: *How was I parented? What did I like? What did I dislike? How is my relationship now with my own parents? What do I see as positive and negative parenting behaviors?*

This is a loose guide of ideas and notes that I've been assembling over the years by reading books, essays, articles, and journals (all of which are listed in the "Resources" section); participating in discussion groups both in person and online; and sharing and trading thoughts and personal experiences with other parents over the years. I will continue adding to and subtracting from it for many more parenting years to come.

1. RELATIONSHIP IS EVERYTHING. Love your child unconditionally. A parent-child relationship is a rare, intimate, and precious one. Base your developing relationship with your child in mutual respect instead of fear. A relationship of love and mutual respect ensures socialized behavior; fear doesn't. One trait of a healthy family is when no one family member is dominant: kids aren't ruled by parents, parents aren't ruled by kids. You and your children are on the same team; remove the idea of being adversaries. Every action increases team unity—or decreases it. You all win or you all lose; no one wins over another. Withholding affection as a way to show parental disapproval towards a child's behavior damages the relationship long-term. Preserving a healthy, intimate relationship with your child into adulthood is the goal, while guiding them through childhood and teaching life skills. Engaging cooperation rather than by coercion or punishment is a good way to do this. Relationship is more important than outcome; the act of "growing up" will take care of most "outcome," but relationship can't be invented later. If you have to choose between relationship and outcome, choose relationship—your child will grow up regardless.

2. BE AWARE OF PARENTAL INTENT. Parental intentions are key! Make a conscious decision to not act oppressively towards your child. If we parents oppress our children, we are setting them up to be oppressed, compliant societal cogs. We are training them to be oppressed as adults. Instead, train children to be free, to use their voices as powerful weapons, to stand up, to get together, to call out injustice. Allow your children to call you out. Allow yourself to be called out and to admit if you've made a mistake and to say you're sorry. This builds trust. And respect. In the adult-centered world, be your child's ally. If they speak up but are still silenced or ignored, stick up for them. This models solidarity. Cynthia Peters says in an interview in *Parenting for Youth Liberation*, by Tim Allen, "We are behaving non-oppressively when we support them to understand, absorb information, analyze, think hard, pursue their curiosity, test their conclusions, be wrong, be right, be confused, be empowered, and show agency in the world." When praising your child, make it honest praise;

manipulative praise makes the child responsible for the parent's emotions and that's a big burden for a child: "It makes Mommy very happy when you take your plate to the kitchen without being asked like that." Praise that's rooted in good intention is descriptive and/or celebrates a child's accomplishment with him or her: "I can tell you've really been practicing. Your cartwheels are awesome!" or "Wow, you sure do make a good peanut butter and jelly sandwich all by yourself!" Root your good intentions in empathy; put yourself in your child's shoes and see things from their perspective. Not to sound cheesy, but it's helpful to literally get down on the ground and take a good look around at their physical perspective of the environment you're in together. Model good intentions out in the world and your kid will trust your intentions are good with them, too; let your child see you making a difference to be just and in co-operation with others. (Plus, when kids learn what is just by example, they will later be able to distinguish justice from injustice in social situations.)

3. BE AWARE OF CHILD INTENT. Assume positive intent. If your intentions are positive (for example, you are trying to do what's best for your kid), then assume they are doing the same, trying to do their best. Trust kids to become their best. Compassionate understanding goes a long way; children (and adults) have good—even if sometimes mistaken—reasons for their behavior. For example, if your child has been out of your care for a while and once back at home together again, your kid's falling to pieces, that's because it takes a lot of work for kids to keep it together. S/he feels safest with you, so you get the worst. Parents should not feel responsible for their child's behavior or unique psychology. As Peggy O'Mara writes in "Instead of Hitting" (*Mothering* magazine, issue 127), this "requires a huge leap of faith to trust our children to their own destinies." Children are inherently social and want to fit into the social unit. Only unmet needs make them do otherwise, so meet those needs. Spend the time to figure out *why* your child is acting a certain way; absolutely no action arises out of a vacuum—getting to the *root* of their actions and addressing it at that level is literally being a proactive, radical parent. Don't forget, there are developmental drives behind exhibited behaviors that the child herself knows is not desired, and it takes time for kids to learn the difference between accidents and on-purpose.

4. KNOW THE DIFFERENCE BETWEEN LEGITIMATE AND ILLEGITIMATE AUTHORITY. Because children lack perspective and experience, parents do have some legitimate authority over their child. Part of the story of human evolution is that children come preprogrammed to respond to authority; they look to parents to be confident, competent, and reliable, and to keep them safe. Trust your legitimate authority and use it for mutual benefit; it's easier

to do this when done with good intentions. Root your legitimate authority in honest, good intentions, trying to do what's best for your child. Modeling responsibility earns legitimate authority. Harsh discipline does not make a child respect your authority; it needs to be learned and earned. I respect that Emma-Joy will question my authority. Her questioning will make me stop to check myself. Is what I'm doing legitimate (for example, if I'm looking out for her safety or health—"You may not ride your bike without your helmet," or "You need to stay where I can see you")? Or is it illegitimate (if I'm trying to control, dominate, or rule over her—"Because I said so," or "Because I'm the adult and you are the child")? If, in checking myself, I find that my good intentions are legitimate, I can stand my ground. If I find that my good intentions weren't so good after all, I can make amends and offer up something better. Parents should want their children to be able to correct their errors without fear, guilt, or the weight of parental disapproval if they try. Parenting in cooperation with your child does not require that you give up legitimate authority or that you be permissive in a negative way; it models human fallibility, responsibility, mutual aid, and respect.

5. PRACTICE MUTUAL RESPECT AND TRUST. Expressing genuine concern demonstrates respect: "You really need to get to bed early tonight to help your body fight that sore throat," or "I know how much you love that present from your cousins, but if you bring it with you to playgroup, it could get ruined." An example of expressing trust is "I know you didn't break that on purpose. I'll help you clean it up and next time, be more careful or ask for help." Forbidding or punishing based on a command like "because I said so" does not show mutual respect. That reason exercises illegitimate authority. If the parent is a source of discomfort (yelling, timeouts, losing temper, using force) for the child, the bond of trust is sabotaged and the relationship suffers. Being consistently fair, flexible, and firm, and establishing a track record of wise decisions earns respect. Having established mutual respect and trust will give reassurance to your child when their needs do not match yours: "I know you don't want me to go, but I have to. Remember, Mommy always comes back soon." Having established mutual respect and trust will also teach children about consensual boundaries. For example, stopping tickling or wrestling as soon as they say stop demonstrates that you respect their boundaries; disallowing them to continue jumping on your back when you say stop makes them aware of respecting yours. Show respect for your child's development in relation to the age-appropriateness of a task; if they can't do something themselves, the simple act of engagement becomes more important than the task itself—do it together!

6. STOP PUNISHING. Punishment is not necessary and is worse that worthless. (Rewards and bribes aren't necessary, either—though they're sometimes the easy way out, as I've been guilty of more times than I care to admit.) Punishment is a relationship ruiner; parents lose something special with their child when they spank and punish. Just as damaging is parental language that shames or makes a child fearful or loathe his/her sex/gender, age (past, present or future), or ability: "I can't wait until you can act more grownup," "Stop acting like a baby," "How old are you? You don't know how to do that yet?" and "You're too sensitive. Stop being such a little girl." Punishment is usually superfluous, arbitrary, and unrelated to the action being punished for. Corporal punishment may produce short-term obedience based on fear, but it has long-term negative consequences on character and behavior. Short-term, fear-based compliance is much weaker than voluntary cooperation based on affection, and it's nonintrinsic; children need an intact internal voice to guide them into adulthood, not a dependence on an external voice of harsh disciplinary authority. Control by means of punitive punishment is an illusion; it teaches kids to hide bad behavior. Instead, help them have control of their own lives. It's a parent's responsibility to help children learn about limits and boundaries; punishment interrupts that learning. Instead of using timeouts as punishments, use them as "breaks"—a safe place and time to relax and decompress. Parents "taking a break" is a great model for children; eventually, children will recognize when they need one, and do it on their own. Another idea is to have a "time-in"—a small comfortable, cozy area with for all involved in the family tension to decompress together.

7. LEARN THE DIFFERENCE BETWEEN PERMISSIVE AND NONPUNITIVE PARENTING. Conventionally defined permissive parenting carries a negative connotation. It implies a neglectful free-for-all that lacks respect and responsibility. Neglectful permissiveness actually debilitates freedom. Instead, turn permissiveness into a positive. A permissive parent can be one who is intensely interested in interacting with their kids and helping their kids make sense of the world—helping their kids pursue their own (their kids' own) dreams—instead of "allowing" or "permitting" them to do so. Likewise, a nonpunitive parent is one who uses this type of interaction instead of relying on the less time-consuming, relationship-damaging, short-sighted practices of punitive punishment.

8. REFRAIN FROM COERCION. Parenting a free child calls for critically examining every interaction that you have with your child for inexplicit, explicit, subtle, and blatant coercion. Coercion represses a child's instincts. Kids can make decisions for themselves without being coerced; they have the capacity

THE DOS AND DON'TS OF LEGITIMATE AUTHORITY

Here is a mini cheat sheet for modeling noncoercive, nonpunitive behavior based on legitimate authority, mutual respect, and trust.

Don't make promises you can't keep.

Don't lie.

Don't withhold information.

Don't say you're sorry when you shouldn't.

Don't be a doormat.

Don't give manipulative praise.

Don't draw lines in the sand.

Don't command.

Don't criticize, belittle, or insult.

Don't focus on blame or fear.

Don't put your child in a position where lying is the safest option or will work to their advantage.

Don't parent from your armchair. Less talk, more action.

Don't negotiate safety (car seats, lifejackets, crossing the street).

Don't wait too long to set a boundary. You will feel bullied.

Do say you are sorry when you should.

Do tell the truth.

Do explain.

Do teach.

Do negotiate.

Do give choices.

Do give "wait time" (the time your kid needs to respond).

Do be consistent—it's worth all the effort you put into it.

Do get your shit together.

Do emphasize positives

Do respect your child's individuality, no matter how different his/her personality or temperament is from your own... (cont'd)

for age-appropriate, rational thought. Instead of coercing them into your own, give them opportunity to make up their own minds about religion, sexuality, and political beliefs. Striving to live a lifestyle of noncoercion, you'll make mistakes, but you will get better together with your child. It's a long process of trial and error. A "noncoercive" parenting decision that is actually a sneaky new way to control the kid's behavior is merely manipulative. And modeling manipulative behavior will come back to bite you on the ass.

9. TEACH NATURAL VERSUS LOGICAL CONSEQUENCES. Consequences are usually enough for learning from a having made a poor (or as the case may be, wise) choice; consequences can be natural, logical, cultural, social, negative, and positive. A neglectful, permissive parent's version of "natural consequences" is to stand back and allow the crap to fall as it may. An extreme example of this is if you do nothing when your child runs in the street; the natural consequence could be severe injury. Obviously, you need to block that and limit the child's freedom in order to protect them. An interactive, permissive parent's version of "natural consequences" gives the child a lot of information, is nonpunitive or co-ercive, considers if the child's actions are adversely affecting others, explains how to lessen potential risk of a negative natural consequence, helps interpret things in positive ways, and makes your kid aware that certain actions are frowned upon at some places. An example of this is after talking to your kid all

about his/her choice to go barefoot, the "natural consequence" could be a painful splinter, a joyful, comfortable romp around the grass, or her not being allowed into the place she wanted to get a bite to eat for lunch. "Logical consequences" can be used judiciously with an older child when the "natural consequence" of bad judgment is beyond that child's ability to handle it. For example, if your five-year-old

Do give logical, descriptive, genuine praise.

Do celebrate successes with child.

Do teach by example, like cooperation.

Do model respect and responsibility.

Do get to know your child's temperament—how much stimulation, food, rest, and quiet s/he needs.

Do tailor environments to the ability of the child—you know, don't take your four-year-old to the opera.

Do be unshockable and be able to one-up them.

throws a ball through a window, it's unreasonable to expect a five-year-old, or even a nine-year-old, to fix that entirely on their own. However, helping the child feel some of the impact of the mistake, like chipping in on and helping with the repair, then setting limits on where and where not to throw the ball are logical consequences. Logical consequences are also arranged in advance as a contingency should an environment, event, or object inspire out-of-control behavior. For example, "Sure you can play with that stick in the house, but I know sticks make it really tempting to hit things. So if the stick becomes a weapon, it will have to go back outside." When doing this, always follow the three Rs: Reasonable, Related, and Revealed in Advance.

10. MODEL COOPERATION. Don't only wait for the stressful times to enlist your child's cooperation to help you do something. Model all the time that we help each other, that we are a team, that we cooperate. Starting when Emma-Joy was very young, I sang, "Co-op-er-a-tion, we-work-to-ge-ther," in a simple melodic rhythm like an annoying habit when we were doing anything together cooperatively. She quickly understood the word as well as the concept. It also didn't take her long to ask me to please stop singing it.

30.

Slave to Fashion, Part 1

I gave my kid free reign over her clothes choices and this is what I got: a wannabe-beautiful-princess slave to fashion. Regardless of whether I allowed Emma-Joy to choose her own clothes or not, I'm sure I would have still had to go through this girly-girl phase with her. By now, I believed it was part of her healthy preschooler sense of self emerging.

As soon as Emma-Joy was able to dress herself and voice an opinion about what she wanted to wear, I went with it. I could discern no valid reasons why I wouldn't. Just like you should stop feeding a child who can feed herself, it seemed logical that I should stop dressing a child who could and wanted to dress herself. Who really cares if stripes and plaid don't match? In addition to fostering her independence, I thought the decision to make her own clothes choices held potential for building self-esteem and decision-making skills.

Emma-Joy's relationship with clothes didn't start out so bad. I mean, at first, how could it? Babes in warm-weather climates need little more than their diaper and a onesie. And it was actually easier than that because she spent lots of time nudie-kazoodie.

The I-wanna-pull-my-hair-out clothes craziness didn't start until three years down the road, when it became apparent that my girl and I have the exact opposite taste in clothes. I remember gagging during a thrift-shopping day when she was old enough to contribute to the selection process. That trip, I resorted to lying. I had to. Even though I knew I needed to get over whatever it was that was making me act contrary to my idea that it benefits kids to be in control of their own appearance, there was just no way I could buy that light blue gingham frock with lace around its hem and at its neck, a floppy bow bigger than her head. So I lied and said it wasn't her size. I lied and said all the other poofy-frillies weren't her size either. Conveniently, she also liked a shiny black vinyl mini skirt that was her size, so I bought that. I came up with an on-the-spot criterion: "We have to both like it if I'm going to buy it." Yes, yes, yes, I do realize that me imposing my style on my child is no different than the sports fans who dress their children in their favorite team jerseys and cheerleading outfits. Just like she's sure to outgrow her uber-girly taste in clothes, I'm sure to get over imposing my taste on her. I did not see her taste for frilly clothing as a rejection of my values or of myself; I just needed time to get over my genuine distaste for her usual thrift-store selections. Trust me on this one—they were laughably beyond-heinous in an early-1980s polyester *Little House on the Prairie* sort of way.

On subsequent thrift trips, my lying ways carried on with the same mantra, "Darn, it's not your size." It was only a few months before she had some replies of her own. She'd say, "That's OK. I can grow into it." Or, if I suggested something that she didn't like, "I will *never* wear it. I only wear things that sparkle." Over the months, her taste changed slightly as she moved from glittery sparkles to things with bows to things with "diamonds," but it was all the same girly gag-o-rama to me.

At home, things weren't any kind of a big deal for a long time. She'd just sort through her clothes and choose something. It wasn't until she hit three and a half that getting dressed became the day's major drama. She became much more selective.

Maybe it started after a weekend with her cousin who changed outfits ten times a day. Or maybe it was the influence of a new friend who only wore the same overalls every single day. (I promise you, those overalls were crustier and stankier than the filthiest of the punks you know.) Perhaps a natural selectivity would have emerged on its own, but it seemed that Emma-Joy's sense of beauty was completely molded by other sources besides Ernesto and me. She had learned lots about what beautiful princesses look like while at preschool and from movies and library books, too.

I may never clearly understand what, during the course of her development, spurned her state of clothing hyperconsciousness. I do know that the issue came to the point of me half just resigning to it and half exerting great patience to negotiate through it.

It started out that she all of a sudden had to change outfits several times a day. It didn't really bother me, but it was driving Ernesto crazy. That lasted maybe a month, until she swung the other way. That's when she stood on a chair gazing into her closet, unable to choose a thing to wear. She'd enlist our help. But whatever we suggested was met with a resounding "No!" The entire closet, end to end, would be gone through and not a thing agreed upon. Nothing in her dresser would do, either. It became a drudging game, an extreme test of patience, sometimes ending in bribery, sometimes in tears if we were in a hurry, and depending on my level of patience, sometimes in ultimatums. It was tough to find the balance between the importance of honoring her autonomy and the frustration it caused.

That changed, though, when she found a "green dress like I've always wanted." She wore the dress at some point during every day for a week. Right around the time her interest in wearing the dress every day was waning, she found a polyester-lined purple, pink, and blue flowered lacy midriff top at our friend Adriana's garage sale. It wasn't immediate that she wanted to wear it every day. She fluctuated between the "I can't choose, you choose, but I'm not going to like anything you choose" game and wanting to wear that purple flowered shirt for days in a row. But finally, the purple flowered shirt won. It came to that she never wanted to take it off, not even for a bath, not even for it to be washed.

On a visit, my mom finally convinced Emma-Joy to let her hand wash it and she could wear it again when it was dry. Those few hours of drying time on the clothesline were long ones filled with, "Is it dry yet? Can I wear it now?"

I was starting to really hate that shirt. Not because she wore it every day, but because of why she was wearing it every day. She'd go up to random people and ask, "Do you like my shirt?" And she'd of course receive the props she was digging for. When we kindly asked her to stop asking people if they like her clothes, to just be patient for an unsolicited compliment to come her way, she obliged, kind of. She instead approached people, silently striking a pose, usually one with her chest puffed out, until they said something approving of her get-up.

That was it. I was locked in frustration just like she'd stuck herself to the purple flowered shirt. I could not convince myself that she'd stop wearing it, soliciting admiration, in her own time. Totally irritated, I told her she couldn't wear the shirt every day anymore. She protested, "But it's my favorite! I want to look beautiful!" I told her that no matter what she wears, she's beautiful. "But my other clothes aren't my favorite. They're not beautiful." And on and on until we were, over the course of a few days, at a standstill in our negotiating and ability to hear what each other was really saying. There were a couple of days that were totally debilitated by the impasse. And that had to change. *Time to choose your battle, mama,* I told myself.

I budged. I took her to a thrift shop as part of this deal: You can pick out a few things you think are beautiful if you promise to wear them and not your purple flowered shirt every day. She agreed. But the shopping was utter hell. An hour and a half in one store and she couldn't pick out a damn thing. Even more hours in three other thrift stores yielded three skirts, a shirt, and a dress. I was completely exhausted and worn down after those hours and hours of indecisive yet uber-selective beautiful clothes hunting. In spite of my gender-coding awareness, I was not going to forbid the skirts and dresses any more than I was going to mandate androgynous or more "masculine" clothing. Damn, this conscious parenting felt a lot more demanding than what I imagined the more authoritarian, controlling model to be.

I realized that this first step toward us recovering from the crippling effects of the purple flowered shirt did not do anything to get a grip on what was the root of my irritation and her intense need to "be fancy." But it was better than a standstill.

Along with the new clothes came a couple new guidelines:

1. You can wear whatever you want as long as it's not filthy in the basket waiting to be washed.

2. If you want to wear it bad enough, hand wash it yourself like Grandma Bee taught you.

3. Stick to your promise to not wear your purple flowered shirt every day.

I thought they were fair and simple enough because I'd drawn them directly from the issue at hand and would hold her accountable to the deal we'd made. But because I try my best to be conscious of illegitimate authority and coercion in my parenting, I've thought about them in a couple different ways. On one hand, I think these rules might be an actual benefit to her because it gives her some boundaries to operate within; without boundaries, there's constant growth-stunting exploration of where the limits are. But on the other hand, these guidelines are definitely somewhat coercive because I'm limiting her absolute freedom of clothing choice in favor of my own agenda: that by not allowing her to wear certain things under certain circumstances, she will stop digging for compliments so often and will learn that being "beautiful" is not necessary for positive attention.

Two weeks into their implementation, things had improved a bit. I thought the guidelines had been helpful to both of us. The three thrifted skirts, shirt, and dress were to thank, too. But the issues were far from resolved. I started to wonder if they ever would be. She had been easy about wearing a different outfit every day, but don't think for a second that she was not parading herself in front of various people every morning until she heard a compliment like, "Oh, you're stylin'." (To which she'd joyfully exclaim, "You're the best!")

Rivaling her slaving to brightly colored, sparkly, ruffly beauty, she's a natural contrarian. She'd wear what the guidelines allowed, but she started to deliberately put her shoes on the wrong feet, wear her underwear inside out *and* backwards, and wear no socks so her feet would stink more than if she had worn socks. And if I dared let on that I liked her choice of outfit, she would change. For the record, more often than not, starting the day she turned two years old, she automatically said "No" to just about everything I'd say or ask, even if I asked her if she wanted to go to the beach and get ice cream, something she lives for. She has to say "No" first, and then an enthusiastic "Yes!" follows a few seconds later.

Also, after I put the three clothing rules in place, she started changing her underwear twice, three times, up to four times a day. I'd ask her why and she'd say because they were giving her a wedgy or that she got a little pee in them. When I'd help her gather them into the dirty-clothes basket, I would notice that they were dry and the larger-sized no-wedgy briefs. I donned my Encyclopedia Brown hat and came up with this—she'd figured out that underwear was the time-to-do-laundry gauge. When there were no more clean pairs in the drawer, it's off to the laundromat we go. And she knew what that meant: she could then wear her *favorite* beautiful shirt! (See guideline 1.)

I felt like Emma-Joy's clothes behavior that had prevented us from getting on with our days had been behavior that essentially was begging for boundaries. When I set them and they seemed to be working (as evidenced by the fact that there has been a lot less struggle between us), it was confusing that she seemed to then work hard to finagle around them. She'd beg every day, "Let's go do laundry!" I would stop her in her tracks to let her know I knew what she was up to. Of course, the champion contrarian denied my theory. However, the begging to go do laundry would then usually cease...until the next day. I couldn't help but wonder if this was her preschool brain's way of expressing that she needed more boundaries with regards to clothing. I strived to find the balance between setting boundaries or not. When I saw signs of behavior that suggested to me that she was wondering where the boundaries were, I set some realistic ones like I think I did with the three guidelines above: for example, "Only change your unders when they're not clean or they're uncomfortable." And when I saw that I'd set a boundary that might not have been necessary or needed modification, again based on clues from her behavior, I removed or modified them. For example, I told her she needed to wear socks with closed shoes so she wouldn't get blisters like she had in the past without socks. She insisted every morning for a week that the socks bothered her, and I realized that maybe she hadn't stopped wearing them just to have stinkier feet after all. Getting larger-sized socks solved the problem: the boundary hadn't, so it was done away with. I'd apparently misinterpreted her new, anti-sock behavior when she'd told me, "When I don't wear socks, my feet are stinkier. Smell my stinky feet!"

Her need for beauty went beyond just clothes. Even with the books I'd check out at the library, if they were not colorful enough or if there were not enough beautiful girl characters whose dresses were also beautiful, forget it. Forget the *Woody Guthrie, Poet of the People*, a beautifully illustrated children's book. Forget the *Players in Pigtails* book about how one determined girl followed a dream and became a player in the first-ever All-American Girls Professional Baseball League.

So I would remind myself to be patient and that it was rather unrealistic to expect an almost four-year-old to latch onto every new idea I introduce her to, that she's going to have her own ideas, and that she's going to be influenced by other forces, too. I reasoned that I could try my best to guide her, but that she is her own person and it's OK for us to be different in a lot of ways and have different tastes. Even when she'd look at what I'm wearing and say, "Yuck, mommy. Change please. Your clothes are not beautiful," I'd respond, "That's OK. I'm comfortable wearing this. You don't have to like what I wear just like I don't have to like what you wear." (Contrary to my implementing the "If I'm going to buy it, we both have to like it" rule, since the majority of her clothes were handed down to us, there were plenty of things she wore that I didn't particularly care for.) With that, I hoped to model mutual respect and tolerance. I reminded myself that for both of us, learning anything well takes time, and wondered just how long it would be before I really could stomach the freaky frilly frocks.

31.

Growing Up Punk:
Interview with Angelina Drake

At a Roach Motel reunion show, it struck me that the voice of a kid who has grown up in the punk music scene needed to be heard. That's where I met up with Angelina Drake, the merch girl who was going on fifteen, whom I'd seen grow up since she was about three years old.

I wondered what it was like for her to be in the midst of her mom and dad's drunk punk party friends and acquaintances all night long. I wanted to know what she had to say about being brought up in and around a local punk music scene.

So I decided to ask her all about it.

Jessica Mills: *Were you required by your parents or by the club to stay at the merch table all night in order to be allowed into the show?*

Angelina Drake: I came not sure whether I could get in, or if I would be sent home. We figured doing merch would be a good excuse if I needed one, plus it gave me something to do. I felt more like I belonged to something. We arrived early and there were no problems getting in. I wasn't restricted to the table, but I liked the spot—good for people-watching.

You told me that you thought the show was good. What made it so?

All my life, Roach Motel has been a legendary name in my house. So it was exciting to finally see what all the fuss was about. I'd only known Bob Fetz [the lead singer of Roach Motel] as this sort of quiet, nice guy who wore Dockers and was a friend of my mom. Then, there he is, seated onstage over a pitcher of beer bellowing how hard it is being the singer for the Roach Motel! That transition was incredible. And the fact that my dad had only moments before been installing Bob's dentures in the parking lot really added to the irony. It was also cool to witness something that means a lot to my parents, experience it, and maybe understand them better. There they were: dad in a freshly buzzed mohawk and mom right up front pogoing. They were living in the moment, just like I've done at shows. It was thrilling and comical at the same time.

Has your enjoyment of shows increased? I ask this because I remember one Fugazi show in particular when I was eight months pregnant and you stood in the back with me most of the time, practically falling asleep by my side.

Yeah, I definitely appreciate them more now. At that time you mentioned, in 2000, I was used to less-populated local shows, big arena concerts, or outdoor events. I wasn't quite ready for the sweaty, smoky, loud interior of a sold-out Brick City [in Gainesville, Florida]. Gradually though, I got more and more into the music. I could go to venues with a parent and enjoy it. Around twelve or thirteen, I was able to attend all-ages shows without them. Now, especially within the past year, I try to see as much local music as I can.

When I was younger, I knew of plenty of bands from listening to my parents. My mom would mention a Radon gig, and I knew that they were a band, but it didn't mean to me what it does now. Not that I'm just discovering it because they were always there, but now I see for myself and can create what the music means to me. What makes local stuff great is the ability to speak to the band—to really touch the music, and know people without viewing them in such a "rock star" light. This is so unlike most music targeting my age group; you might only see a band on TV or at a huge concert, and then they're celebrities.

So, you actually really like punk rock and don't hate it just as a way to rebel against your parents?

Yeah, I'm into it now, but I've certainly gone through my phases. I don't think I considered it rebellion, but it's hard to be young and not susceptible to what the media throws at you. What's cool about my upbringing is that I was always at least aware of good music. It was never unattainable. In third grade, I remember drawing pictures of my hero at the time, Joey Ramone, wearing my pink sunglasses. That was my first time getting into the "Ramnoes" as I used to spell it. Then, in fourth and fifth grade, I liked Hanson and more radio-friendly stuff. Punk was always around, just not as rampant as MTV ear candy. My parents let me get through my Spice Girl phase and enjoyed it with me. We had so much fun! No, I never thought of it as defiance. Luckily, the support I received gives me a greater appreciation for good music now.

I think that's how more parents should be, supporting and guiding their kids through whatever the kids' interests are, not just dictating what is permissible and acceptable and what isn't, according only to the parental agendas. People keep warning me that my daughter will rebel no matter what, because that's what all kids do. They say whether it's kids turning to punk because their parents are super conservative or kids playing a super-conservative role because their parents are rockers, I should expect it. But I don't think that's necessarily true and I think that how your parents have supported you proves that.

Absolutely. I've had my phases, but I think that maybe some inherited "rock awareness" kept me from being too absorbed by them. I've had a blast enjoying my parents' music. Punk rock sing-alongs were (and still are) prevalent in my dad's car, and when I was around eight, my mom and I had tailor-made dresses and painted our faces for two KISS concerts. How many kids get these kinds of memories?

Do you have a first memory specific to your folks being involved in something subcultural?

Well, early on, it didn't seem out of the ordinary. My best childhood friend's mom worked at the Hardback [a legendary punk club in Gainesville in the 1990s], and most of my other friends had parents connected within the scene. It wasn't until I got a little older with suburban kids at school that I realized we weren't exactly the typical American family. I was like, "What? Your mom's not a rock star?"

In initial memories, my pals and I spent a lot of time running around the daytime, usually an empty Hardback Cafe. Being so little, I couldn't fathom why the bathrooms were so grody or what the graffiti meant, but I knew it was an important place for bands to play. My friend would tell me that she heard [that] people peed in the courtyard and we just thought that was wild.

I remember not understanding why I couldn't wear my Ovarydose [my mom's band at the time] shirt to school. I got really excited when they were interviewed on the radio station and I could hear my mom over the radio. I called in and asked her what a boob job was. They all laughed and she answered, "Something I never want to get."

What is it exactly that sets your parents apart from your other friends' parents who are not in the scene?

I think that the parent-child relationships are very different. I'm close with my family because I know a lot about them: what they're passionate about and that they didn't stop being themselves when I came along. Many kids don't know much of their parents' lives pre-family, or can understand their love of music. My folks have been very open about things with me. They're able to maintain the balance between rock and roll and responsibility. As a result, I haven't gotten into much trouble because it doesn't seem exciting or rebellious. By allowing me to make my own decisions, I think that I've made the right ones.

Do other kids tell you how lucky you are or how cool your parents are?

Yes! Though only a few of my friends realize how involved in the scene my parents are, I get it from them a lot. But I try not to let my mom catch on to how cool she is.

Is there anything that you haven't liked about your parents being involved in the scene?

Well, it's been tough sometimes when they're out partying or at band practice. [When I was] two and a half, my mom went on tour with Mutley Chix for two weeks. That was my weaning process. From what I hear, I was quite the terror for my dad, still wanting to nurse and not dealing well with the separation. As I got older, I could understand band duties, and my mom tried not to schedule practice when I was with her.

Other things like crashing at party houses or feeling uncomfortable amongst all older people came into play as well. But the independence skills I've gained from talking with a lot of adults are valuable. It's easy to feel insecure when you're the youngest one in the room, but as soon as you actually talk to someone and have a good conversation, they can usually get over the age thing and you meet some really interesting people.

It took a while to adjust to drunk people, too. I've rarely been around my parents drunk, but it was scary at first. Now it's actually kind of amusing.

Every year for the past few years, I've been to your super-cool birthday dance party where your folks have decorated up a local music venue and your friends come for the afternoon. I remember the first one I went to, I walked in and the first song I heard was a Ramones song and all you junior high kids were having so much fun. I thought it was so awesome. Do you bring your own records to play?

It was all stuff I picked out. Unfortunately, not many of the fifty or sixty kids there from school shared my music tastes, but I guess that's junior high for ya. So, I compromised and had to play a good amount of rap and techno so people would dance. I don't like rap, but I chose the stuff I could tolerate, nothing violent or degrading. I snuck some good sounds in there, too. If I only played my music, the parties wouldn't have gone over as well.

Are you interested in playing music?

Yes. I took drum lessons for a year, but didn't have my own set, so I've taught myself as much on guitar as I can. I'd really like to improve on either, but varsity softball eats up most of my weekday time. I'm at a point where, as soon as I can, I want to get more lessons.

Are you interested in anything else that you think is an element of the punk scene? I saw you at an antiwar demo a couple weeks ago and noticed that you were there on your own—no parents. Just you, a friend, and your bikes.

I consider myself very socially aware and am interested in sociopolitical issues. I'm in the Student Activist Coalition at my school. We attend and support antiwar efforts to promote peaceful solutions. My parents are split on the issue, so I've mostly come to this conclusion alone. I've been to many political events with my parents, but now I also attend things on my own.

I know that you've been raised primarily vegan. Can you talk a little bit about that?

Being raised vegetarian/vegan is something I'm very thankful to my parents for. As a baby, I ate what they ate and grew to love good food. I've always been given the option of trying meat if I ever wanted, but I've had no desire or need. I've found this is the case with many kids raised veggie. Personally, I enjoy eating healthy, and have tried not to impose it on my peers. Elementary school came with a lot of questions from other kids, but I was always confident and informed enough to answer them. Young people now eat so poorly in general, without understanding what it does to them. I'm happy to stand out from this crowd.

So all in all, what does being raised in this crazy scene mean to you? How does it all fit together for you—the music, the politics, the food choices?

I guess that it's all come together to greatly influence who I am. The scene has raised me as aware of music, issues, people, and of myself. I've had experiences very different from most people my age, and it's been fabulous. I think they've made me more mature than a lot of my classmates. I get along well with my parents and at the least can say that things have never been dull. Growing up in such interesting environments, and things turning out the way they have, I couldn't imagine it any other way.

4 Years Old

32.

Setting Up an Art Center

Setting up an art center in what had been intended as the dining area of the second place we rented in Hollywood proved to have several benefits. My motivation to set one up was a reaction to the "art projects" Emma-Joy had been learning to do at preschool—the projects where everyone makes the same thing, step by step. She loved coloring, painting, cutting, gluing, and doing projects, and I wanted to do more to help foster creativity, knowing that creativity is something that needs to be cultivated, otherwise it gets killed.

According to the authors of *The Creative Spirit*, to cultivate creativity you need to allow "open-ended time for the child to savor and explore a particular activity or material to make it her own." Creativity is killed by commonplace practices in schools and homes. Two of the world's experts on creativity, Beth A. Hennessy and Teresa M. Amabile, have identified common "creativity killers" as surveillance, evaluation, rewards, competition, over-control, restriction of choice, and pressure.

In the early-1990s, my art history professor said to us on the last day of class, "To those of you who already have children and to those of you who may have children in the future, do not give coloring books to your children. Instead, give them blank paper." Still nearly a decade away from even having any desire to have a child, I immediately sensed his wisdom. And I remembered his sage advice right when I needed to.

I also remembered what one mama in the Gainesville childcare co-op had once shared with me with regards to her unschooled son's art experience, "Don't leap. After his grandma leaped on him for spilling paint and not doing a neater job, he stopped wanting to do art. It took a long time for him to get back to feeling free enough to even want to do art again." The book that had helped her to get her son making art again was *Don't Move the Muffin Tins: A Hands-Off Guide to Art for the Young Child*, by Bev Bos.

After getting my hands on a copy, I made a list compiling which of Bev Bos' ten rules I thought would be an asset to our home art center, and adapted them slightly:

1. Don't interfere with the basic use of art materials. Forget whatever my intended use for a particular material would be.

2. Avoid models that show her something to copy. Models can be insulting and intimidating.

3. Recognize that her name written or painted on anything she makes can be part of the art itself. Don't "correct" by saying, "You should write your name smaller or neater on the back."

4. Don't interrupt by telling her that she should not be making twenty versions of the same thing or by saying something like "Stop wasting; you already made one!"

5. Don't insult her development or creativity by being adult centered. Realize that she may not yet be perfectly able (or even intend) to cut out perfect circles, color in the lines, or draw a complete person.

6. Gently guide and suggest, don't leap.

7. Discourage her from wearing clothes she cares about. Suggest that she should instead wear something she does not care about getting stained. Don't encourage her to be careful or to not get messy. Never coerce her into wearing an apron if she doesn't want to.

Then I got busy setting everything up. To store the art supplies, I carefully assembled scavenged cinderblock and wood-plank shelves that wouldn't be too tall for her to reach things on easily or that could tip over. I also used a dumpster-scored cupboard of shelves that had once been a TV stand.

I stocked the shelves with the following supplies, stored in plastic baggies, small reusable food containers with lids, shoeboxes, and coffee cans:

• markers• crayons• colored pencils • glue and glue sticks• erasers• buttons • felt• old picture frames• beads • shoelaces• yarn• stamps and stamp pads • stencils• curling ribbon• cloth ribbon • shoeboxes• rulers• empty toilet paper and paper towel tubes • feathers• google eyes• empty cardboard oatmeal canisters • index cards• envelopes• stickers • tissue paper• pipe cleaners• wooden popsicle sticks • old socks• fabric scraps• colored embroidery floss • colored foam sheets• blank books• hole punch • foam stick-ons• safety scissors• shape-cutting craft scissors • glitter and glitter glue• safety pins• wooden

clothespins • modeling clay• found objects• a variety of dried beans • empty
soda bottles• paper plates• egg cartons • straws• string• old magazines
• shells• small stones• twigs • tape: regular, masking, packaging, and duct •
paper of all kinds: colored construction, foil, recycled 8.5" x 11"
cardboard, card stock, stickers, and a roll of butcher paper.

On one of the shelves, I also placed two books: *The Ultimate Book of Kid Concoctions*, by John E. Thomas and Danita Pagel, and *The Beginner Book of Things to Make: Fun Stuff You Can Do All By Yourself*, by Robert Lopshire.

A separate "painting crate" included watercolors, tempera paint, paintbrushes, chalk, sponges, plastic food trays and empty yogurt containers, old shirts, and an apron. Since the art center was adjacent to the back door, leading to a semi-covered porch area, painting (and glittering) was to be done outside. This arrangement aided me adhering in to Rule 6, above. Outside, we already had a two-sided easel handed down to us from a friend; one side was a chalkboard, the other had clips at the top to hold paper or cardboard for painting. Next to the easel stood an outside art table that I bought for ten dollars at a yard sale, used as another painting surface or drying area. Also outside was my studio shed, scrappily assembled out of plywood, the outside of which was fair game for mural painting.

Some of the supplies came free or I already had on hand, some I'd purchased from dollar stores or the flea market, and the remaining things came from the local arts and crafts supply store. In total, I spent eighty-five dollars to set it up.

Purposely, I had no table in the art center for her to sit at. This was for two reasons. First, we didn't have a suitable one. Second, I thought it could possibly be space-restrictive; that is, it might have encouraged Emma-Joy to only make art that would have fit on the table, and also it would have taken up too much of the center's space, disallowing free movement around the table to gather supplies. Our house had no carpeting throughout, so the wood floor was a perfect work surface. The only art supply that was off-limits when unsupervised were the permanent markers. Any messes from glue, crayon, water-based marker, or other supplies were met with a weekly scrubbing, done in cooperation with each other. Maintaining the art center by replenishing exhausted supplies, or adding new ones was done with minimal cost; I was diligent about adding recycled, reusable materials and found objects.

Emma-Joy dove in. Having an art center gave her quite a creative boost. I often heard her refer to herself as an "artist" or "project girl." Every wall and windowsill in the house was fair game for her to display what she chose. One corner near the front door even became "Emma-Joy's tattoo parlor," where anyone who wanted one could get an original temporary tattoo, hand-drawn with water-based marker.

Besides the benefit of boosting her creativity and own personal enjoyment, I was thrilled that as soon as there was downtime, Emma-Joy didn't immediately ask, "Can I watch TV?" In the past, I'd had to be patient and repetitive with our house TV limits. Now, whenever Emma-Joy did ask to watch TV, the art center provided an easy, alternate choice.

It felt good to be able to provide such a free, active space for Emma-Joy to develop her art interests and creativity. It was an activity that did not need surveillance, which would have stifled the risk-taking, creative urge. The only rewards for her best efforts came from her own intrinsic satisfaction. The only time evaluation played a part is when she asked us for it. There was no competition with others to see who could make the best thingamajig, even when friends were over and they were making art together; there was enough choice in materials to dissuade them from wanting to make the same things. I needed only to exert minimal control over how the art center operated (painting and glittering outside, no unsupervised use of permanent markers), thereby encouraging originality and exploration. She had unrestricted choice in how to use the materials that aided experimentation, and there was no pressure to meet prescribed quantity or quality expectations that might have been beyond her developmental capabilities. The seven rules I'd set up for myself to follow in implementing the art center were easy to follow, too.

In setting up a home art center, I had not only created a free space for Emma-Joy to explore her creativity—it turned out to be so much more. It became a place for her to exert her independence. She used decision-making and problem-solving skills. She learned about color. She experimented with cause and effect and how different materials could or couldn't work together. She became a designer. She gained more self-confidence and esteem. She loved it! And she watched a lot less TV!

The art center became a space from which we all got enjoyment. We all grew to depend on it, and I don't imagine our house will ever be without one.

33.

Punk Rock Kids Spring Break

I sat for a full hour talking to my friend Jason about how lame I was for coming all this way and feeling too tired to go to the punk show that just a day before I had been excitedly losing sleep over. I had been up since 7 a.m.; volunteered at my girl's preschool, stuffing colorful plastic Easter eggs with temporary "He Is Risen" tattoos (really! It was too, too weird); grocery shopped; made lunch; packed our suitcases; and driven for six hours. I wanted so badly to go, but after getting my girl to sleep for the night, I just couldn't pull myself up off the couch. I droned on and on about how I should really just quit whining and go.

Jason helped me feel less lame and less old by reminding me that most of the other show-going people had most likely slept until noon that day and either attended one or two classes or worked a relatively slack part-time shift. Somehow I convinced myself that yes, I did put in a long day with my four-year-old at my side every waking moment, and that my body deserved some sleep.

I could have actually handled the show well even as tired as I was. It was the morning I was scared of. We were to leave at 10 a.m. for the long-awaited Punk Rock Kids Spring Break Weekend Vacation.

I'm glad I chose to go to bed because as it was, we still got on the road two and a half hours late. I guess that's expected, given our cast of characters: three kids (Emma-Joy, aged four; Sofia, aged five; and Captain, aged six); one sixteen-year-old big sister, Angelina; one mama, Karen; one non-parent, "Uncle" Jason; and me.

Not your average nuclear-family vacation—more like the Brady Bunch meets the Addams family, I guess, except we were heading to a hippie haven called Hostel in the Forest, and our three kids were nonstop chanting in unison from the back of the extended family van, instead of the extended cab truck often found in these parts, "Barbies are stupid! Barbies are idiots! Barbies are fuckers!" Meanwhile the nondriving others were reading a collection of essays by Noam Chomsky, and *From Beirut to Jerusalem*, by Thomas L. Friedman.

Arriving, I was happy to be greeted by someone who did not call me "sister," tell me "Welcome Home!" or hug me. All the folks at the hostel wanted in exchange for a night's stay in a two-story tree house and a meal was fifteen dollars per person over the age of twelve, and a chore of our choosing done.

Our tree house, named The Peacock Hut, was adorned with random hanging beaded thingies, dream catchers, and trippy hippie murals and was furnished only with DIY bunk beds that the kids immediately fell in love with. My four-year-old was so excited by the bunks that she snuggled in for a nap, something she never does, even if she's genuinely tired. Before dozing off, she told me that the crystal hanging in the middle of our room's dream catcher really was her dream, "a red monster who's nice."

A few of our crew, including the other two kids, started in on their chores. They gathered sticks for the fire, helped prepare dinner in the kitchen, folded laundry, and washed dishes. Even though my girl was snoozing and the two other kids were happy on their own playing with sticks and imitating the few dozen resident chickens, my self-delegated chore was childcare. When I overheard another visitor who had volunteered for compost-toilet duty receiving her instructions, I knew I had chosen wisely!

Keeping an eye on and an open ear to the kids was much more comical than any adventure with sawdust-covered shit could have been. For example, when Captain saw one of the hostel residents wearing feathers poking out of his braid, he exclaimed, "Look! An Indian!" to which Jason quickly replied under his breath without moving his lips, "No, not an Indian, a Native American." Captain heard him and continued, "Native American, go kill some cowboys!" The feathered resident answered, "I like cowboys. They're the other white meat." Young Captain was left confused; he'd never eaten a bite of meat, white or any other color, in his entire life. And we later learned that the guy actually was a bona fide Native American. Captain, however, did not believe this, "Those aren't Indian pants he's wearing." Ah, never a dull educational moment with these kids. My chore was a constant one!

The communal meal of salad, lentil-veggie burgers, salty baked beans, cornbread, and ketchup-coated meat-dogs snuggled in white-bread buns was immediately preceded by hold-hands-in-a-circle-around-the-fire time when all thirty or so of us visitors and residents were asked to introduce ourselves and say what we were thankful for. Emma-Joy had me tell everyone that she was thankful for snails and stingrays.

During this circle time, while we were taking in names like Dirt, Steamboat, Zach Monster, and One Love, we were being serenaded by a forgotten CD left playing in the kitchen—Fiona Apple and Johnny Cash's rendition of "Happy Birthday"—and also by some rebel who was ditching out on circle time and instead playing a White Stripes song on a tuba. Not your typical equivalent to the nuclear family's version of saying "grace" before dinner at all.

After dinner, Angelina and the kids hit the bunks and Karen, Jason, and I wanted to hit the wine. But the only two places where we could really hang out away from the mosquito swarms were the hot tub that was packed with peacefully quiet, naked people who continually invited us to not be shy and join them, and the fire which was ringed by "open-mic night" participants, one of whom was singing about all the different vegetables she likes. Given those choices, I decided that I'd rather be asleep even though I had gotten plenty of sleep the night before. Karen and Jason decided to get brave in the hot tub.

Once again, I'm glad I chose sleep. Those roosters began their cock-a-doodle-do-ing well before the sun came up. And I didn't know this about roosters, but they don't stop. One of them was still sounding off well past noon.

The chickens were cool, though. They let us hand-gather their freshly laid eggs from under their tails without pecking the kids' hands. Even the 110% vegan Jason was OK with this. My girl and I rushed to the kitchen to scramble ours up, and were surprised to see how bright orange a minutes-fresh egg yolk was.

The rest of the morning was perfect. The kids explored freely and had a grand ol' time splashing in their undies around the spring-fed pool and jumping in off the rope swing. They cruised around the "labyrinth," a rather creatively and well-planned-out ground maze of rocks, branches, logs, bricks, altars, and sculptures of all sizes and mixed-media materials. We canoed around the lake and my girl wanted to know, "Why they nudie?" about the people sunbathing in the middle of the lake on a floating dock. We lazed about, reading in hammocks. We followed trails to the glass house, where the morning yoga was done, and to the sweathouse, which was used on full moons.

Eventually, it was time to go, but not before a trip to the outhouse. (All peeing was to be done outdoors, but like I already mentioned, there were compost toilets for the poop.) My girl was reluctant to enter due to the smell, but the beautiful decor drew her in. These outhouses were elaborate, complete with sparkling stained-glass windows and detailed mural paintings. In addition to it being a sensory experience, it was also educational as I did my best to explain how it is healthier for the earth to compost the poop instead of flushing it away with water. And for those who take some time to make their deposit, there's a log—no pun intended—provided for writing, doodling, or reading what the previous poopers have written. It was full of clever rhymes about—you guessed it—crap.

On the road, the kids were up to their usual anti-Barbie chants, but this time with lots more bickering among them. We got a slight reprieve from it only when we stopped for gas and the girls asked, "Can we get out of our seatbelts and punk rock?" And so they proceeded to climb over the seats, bounce up and down, all the while squealing with their air guitars and fists pumping the air. Captain explained to them that when he's punk rock, "I'm gonna stay up late drinking lots of soda and beer and playing rock 'n' roll!"

NONTRADITIONAL FAMILY VALUES

Even though Ernesto, Emma-Joy, and I comprise a relatively traditional nuclear family, we don't limit our familial experiences to just the three of us. Extended families—grandparents, other relatives, and non-relatives, too—are important. And non-nuclear family models are prevalent: single-parent families, co-parenting arrangements between divorced/separated parents, families with gay/lesbian parents, families with more than two partners parenting. Despite the hatred shown by the right-wing extremists on the issue of "traditional family values," studies and experience show that children who are given lots of love and support fare well in whichever kind of family they grow up in.

Just as there is no script to follow for how your family is arranged, so too is there no recipe to follow when it comes to spending quality time and having fun together. Family time together does not have to be spent at theme parks or doing other planned activities that promote consumerism and discourage independent exploration. Some nontraditional ideas include hiking and camping at state and national parks; volunteering together at food distribution, house building, or animal rescue organizations; outdoor music festivals, community garden and art projects; and go-with-the-flow unplanned road trips that lead you to discover uncharted campsites, new playgrounds, and streams to follow.

Not taking more time for more explanations (we had just figured out that daylight savings time had happened the day before and made us later than we thought we were), we got the kids in their seatbelts and cruised the rest of the way home, quite content with our extended family's a-bit-out-of-the-ordinary vacation.

34.

Three Generations March for Choice

For weeks, my mom had been asking me what I wanted for my birthday. I honestly could not think of a single thing I wanted. But when she asked me again what I wanted on my actual birthday, I had finally come up with an answer, "The best present would be for you to march with us in April."

For months, I had been telling her all about what was shaping up to look like the biggest pro-choice march in the history of the United States. She listened in earnest but remained uncommitted, hesitant to take part in something she had never engaged in before, even though she considers herself a lifelong pro-choicer.

So I was surprised when she called me back two days after my birthday with her exciting news, "I'm going to march with you!" She said yes out of a combination of a birthday present for me, her sense of urgency about protecting reproductive rights, and learning that her good friend Holly was making the trip to march, too. I was ecstatic. Since I had first heard of the March For Women's Lives, to be held in Washington, D.C., on April 25, 2004, there was no doubt that I'd be taking my daughter. Now that my mom would be joining us, I really had to start cracking on the logistics.

Luckily, the pieces fell into place easily. My daughter and I would fly to Philadelphia a few days early and stay with my friend Alanna and her new housemates. We'd pick my mom up at the Philly airport a few days later and drive to Alanna's aunt's house just outside of D.C. (My mom felt more comfortable with this part knowing that Alanna's mom and aunt were also going to be marching.) We'd take the Metro into and out of the city on the day of the march. Then, we'd drive back to Philly and crash for the night at the Danger! Danger! House—the name of Alanna's collective house. And then the three of us would fly out together in the morning.

I'm glad to say that all went as planned. Mishaps and missed connections really don't faze me much, but for my mom's sake, I'm relieved there were none. She rolled with the stink and chaos of the Danger! Danger! House, and even went without showering for days. Like daughter, like mother.

After we picked my mom up at the airport, but before we started driving to D.C., we engaged in a bit of sign-making creativity. Well, my daughter did anyway... The housemates were getting the house ready for a birthday party that we'd be missing that evening, and they had a bunch of art supply-type stuff strewn about.

At four-years-old, my daughter had enough large-scale demonstration experience under her umbrella-stroller wheels to know what a march was and that we were headed to a big one the next day. Though the politics and mechanisms of "a woman's right to choose" escaped her, I explained, "I know having choices is important to you. For example, you like to make your own choices about your clothes and what books and movies you check out at the library. This march is about how important it is for all women to be able to choose when or if they have a baby." She definitely understood the concept of having choices, but given that war is more a daily topic of conversation in the media and among the adults she overhears, she knows that war is bad for kids. I didn't set out for her to know the yuckiness of war at such a young age, but it was inevitable given the current wars in Iraq and Afghanistan. Children are sentient beings who take in all that surrounds them, including words and images from the media.

So when she grabbed a dove-shaped cardboard cutout from the party decoration pile and asked me, "How do I spell 'No War'?" I smiled and spelled it out for her as she carefully wrote each letter. She sought out masking tape with which to attach a short stick and finished making her sign. I was honestly impressed that making the sign had been entirely her own idea and that she had done it all on her own, *sans* the spelling help, with her own message. My little DIY diva! We packed her sign and ourselves into Alanna's car and hit the road.

The night before the march, we arrived in D.C. and gathered snack supplies for our backpacks in preparation for the long day ahead of us. That night, my daughter could hardly settle down to sleep as her excitement over the new surroundings and anticipation of the march engulfed her. My mom was anxious, too. Their enthusiasm got me wound up as well, so much so that I didn't sleep well.

Stepping out of the Metro and onto the streets of D.C., I was instantly in awe of the masses. I had never seen so many people gathered in the same place for the same reason. My eyes were overwhelmed with tears. The closer we walked to the assembly place, the more crowded the streets got. By the time we reached the lawn, I began to wonder if we'd ever find our delegation, the Mamas For Choice (MFC), a group of eighty-plus mothers from all over the country who'd organized the delegation via the Internet.

Before searching for the MFC delegation among a million people, I was able to find the mini rally I wanted to participate in, a speak-out and civil-disobedience action, organized by the Morning-After Pill Conspiracy (see http://mapconspiracy.org), promoting wider access to the morning-after pill. We helped hold banners and hailed people to step up and receive a prescription good for twelve refills of morning-after pills, written by feminist doctors from the Access Project NYC. There was also an illegal pill toss, where women threw out morning-after pills to a crowd of women who did not have prescriptions for such pills (some packets contained a message instead of pills, "I'm sorry, you tried to get the morning-after pill but your doctor wouldn't prescribe it," symbolizing the luck and randomness of whether women can get them when they need them). Since I considered myself unarrestable because my daughter was with me, I didn't throw out any of the pills myself. But just being there watching women break the law as an act of civil disobedience, the goal being to put pressure on the FDA to move the morning-after pill from prescription status to over the counter, I felt inspired. By signing the MAP conspiracy pledge, I vowed to practice my civil disobedience in private; back at home, I'd get my twelve-refill prescription filled in order to have the pills on hand to give to anyone who needed them. My mom said she was most impressed by the age range of the women involved in this action, some of whom were older than her and for whom getting pregnant was no longer an issue. She said, "I'm so impressed! It's so awesome to see women of my generation who've never stopped fighting even if they won't need these pills for themselves now."

With the march about to start, we frantically looked for our Mamas For Choice delegation and found them with not even five minutes to spare. Luck was definitely with us as searching for a small group of people among a million is even harder than finding a needle in a haystack. At least when searching for that proverbial needle, you can move the hay around a little. And we didn't know what our needle looked like; most of us had never met face to face before.

With the march having officially stepped off, it seemed like forever until we were moving at a snail's pace off the lawn and onto the street. It was actually incredible how slow the entire march was! Rumor has it that there were so many people (the official number at 1.15 million, making it the largest demonstration in U.S. history), that the people at the head of the march had completed the entire march route before the last of the marchers had even stepped off! Over a million people had the National Mall completely surrounded! And the old, young, and disabled all stuck it out in spite of the heat.

My favorite part of the march was when the procession was at a standstill and I looked at my mom, who was literally marching in place, throwing her fist in the air, chanting along with all the people around us.

My daughter also made me swell with pride. The crowd around us had just been chanting, "What do we want? Choice! When do we want it? Now!" As it died down, she started her own, "Kids need choices! Kids need choices!" She liked the reaction it drew, so she continued, "Kids don't have to do what they don't wanna do! Kids don't have to do what they don't wanna do!" This one raised a few granny eyebrows, so she sheepishly amended with, "Except sometimes when they have to! Except sometimes when they have to!" Again, she liked the favorable reaction, so she started in on a new one, "Kids shouldn't smoke! Kids shouldn't smoke!" as she jumped up and down, shaking her pompoms in anyone's face who would let her.

Whenever our MFC delegation was about to pass a small pocket of antichoice counter-protesters, groups marching in front of us would let us know so we'd have enough time to shield our kids from seeing their awful "baby killer" posters. I was glad Emma-Joy did not see any of them. I'd like to think our "I know I'm wanted because my mom had a choice" and "Pro-woman, Pro-child, Pro-choice" signs had a more positive effect over the antichoicers and their distorted propaganda.

Later, my daughter told me that her favorite part of the march were the radical cheerleaders, some of whom she'd met before. And my mom's favorite part was reading all the different signs and being among such a diverse group of million-plus people. She cracked up at a middle-aged man who had a pillow stuffed up under his shirt, holding a sign that read, "If men could get pregnant, abortion would be a sacrament." And she snapped pictures of signs like "Lick Bush in 2004!" and "Between Dick and Bush, we got screwed!"

Overall, marching with my mom and my daughter was an amazing experience. I felt empowered because we were able to demonstrate safely for something we feel passionately about. And more importantly, my mom and I got to do something together that we never had before. There are many personal things this experience taught me about my mom, and I know she learned things about me as well. And she shared some family history with me that taught me that we are just the newest generations of a legacy of women who believe in a woman's right to choose.

Unfortunately, it takes a severely shit-infested administration like George W. Bush's to draw out folks like my mom, a schoolteacher in her fifties, into action. But fortunately, now that she's gotten a taste of what democracy looks like, she'll stay active in whatever ways she feels inspired and impassioned to do so. Now that she's participated and experienced firsthand something brand new to her that was intimidating to her before, she'll remain confident and empowered.

As for my daughter, I feel confident that her early exposure to people getting together to fight against injustice will serve her well.

And as for me, I will always remember these feelings and hopes for my daughter's future and the ones who come after her when I look at the framed snapshot of my mom, my daughter, and me together holding a sign that reads, "Three Generations for Choice!"

35.

Dad Is Not the Babysitter!

Ernesto and I needed to change things up again. After a year and a half of more than full-time parenting and no paycheck work for me, and more than full-time school and a scholarship as paycheck for him, we were both burnt out. So we switched roles. I went out and got a job to support the three of us, while Ernesto took a break from school. He'd be the full-time parent and I'd be the full-time worker away from home. We both eagerly looked forward to the shift.

It was summertime and that meant Emma-Joy and Ernesto making their own routine together. Because Ernesto's school load was so demanding, there'd been too many days when he and Emma-Joy had gotten no time together. So the both of them tackled the hot tropical climate and spent much of their time away from home—of course, after the chores at home were taken care of.

They were having full days swimming in the ocean, reading and attending events at the library, playing at the park, going to the occasional birthday party, or catching the bus or Tri-Rail for outings and events all around town. He mostly stayed away from the playgroups that had become routine for Emma-Joy and me, not because they were mostly mamas and kids minus the dads, but because he and Emma-Joy wanted to do their own thing instead hanging with a group closer to home all the time. (He felt very welcomed at the playgroups he did go to with Emma-Joy—the mamas loved his super high-energy playtime attention with all the kids.) In fact, if anything, the opposite was true for Ernesto as far as the mamas-minus-the-dads dynamic goes; he was fine with being the lone dad at the mama party. He was not only embracing the opportunity to make up for lost time with Emma-Joy, but also to set an example by breaking what society had prescribed for its parenting mold. (He'd recently been appalled by one friend's husband, who, when our friend told him she wanted to take a few classes so she could finish her AA degree, said, "Well how are you going to do that? I'm not babysitting.")

Eventually, as the summer wore on, he became frustrated by the almost daily comments, usually from strangers, but sometimes from acquaintances, along the lines of, "Oh, is it a Daddy day, today?" The clueless commenters did not see him as the full-time parent, even though he was. He'd matter of factly reply, "Every day is a Daddy day," and leave it at that, saving any frustration to vocalize for when I got home from work, "Argh, it happened again! And this time from one of your girl-friends! I almost expect it now from random jackasses, but to hear it from someone who knows better?!"

He did not see his involvement and contributions to the parenting work at hand as a novelty, but felt he was seen as such. He takes his parenting commitment seri-ously, as he should. Though his short-term frustration was with the ones making comments to him, his long-term frustration was actually with the benefactors and reinforcers of a patriarchal society, one that benefited him as a male, but one he wanted to help change.

To help both of us make sense of how fathers are regarded by both mainstream society and radical thinkers, I asked Tomas Moniz, creator of Rad Dad *zine, to share his insights about fatherhood.*

I Feed My Kids!

By Tomas Moniz

Way back in the day, before Chris Rock starred in a whole bunch of bad movies, he put out a couple standup comedy films that were painfully funny, especially when he talked about parenting. In fact, there's a skit in one of them that has become a running joke in my community. Basically, he ridicules a father for bragging that, "I take care of my kid... I feed my kid!" and Rock's retort is, "Well, you supposed to!"

I often find myself stating similar declarations about my deeds of daddy-dom to my own children and can do nothing but chuckle at my own ridiculousness. I hear myself arguing with them as they're pushing me to buy that $6.99 pint of blue-berries and I start getting all huffy with them because, after I say no, my daughter says, "OK, fine. But can I get this bag of Cheetos instead?" like that's a perfectly valid connection.

And then it comes. It might've been one of those long days or I haven't had my afternoon caffeine fix, but regardless, I can only sit back as I hear myself say some-thing incredulous like, "Hey stop asking for things! Don't I buy enough already? Don't I feed you dinner? Don't I work to put food on the table?" They kinda look at each other and then back at me like I'm crazy because, well, I'm supposed to! What else would I do?

To me fathering, indeed parenting, is predicated on everything I believe in and embodies the qualities I aspire to possess all the time: love, respect, patience, trust, kindness; you know, the things that help you take care of your people, your community.

It seems obvious enough, but let me say it: Fathering is lifelong; it's not a life-style. It is one of those things that continually challenges and rewards. It's hard, painful, and you can't rest on you laurels, "Well, I did a damn fine job today, so it's all gravy for the rest of the week." Once you think you kinda got it down—bam!—a new issue hits, a new twist forcing you to reconsider things once again. Parenting forces you to constantly reevaluate yourself, your politics, and pushes you to stay in communication with your partner(s) or your child. Parenting is never static; change is the one constant you can count on. As a result, I find that when I recognize how fallible I am, how much I have to learn from my children, and how fathering is in reality collaboration, not something I can do on my own, I feel my most powerful, my most grounded.

I think both men and women are at fault for how our society genders parenting and silences parents. And it begins immediately: from who holds the crying newborn, to who changes diapers, and who runs the midnight errands. Men and women play into these stereotypes of who is best with the baby and who is best supporting the baby. And as time goes on the gender polarization continues: who is best with the sick child and who best should teach them sports or to ride a bike. As parents, we need to be aware of these decisions we make. Of course, it might feel easier to just let women take over the role of nurturer, but why? Of course, the kids listen to the man when he lays down the law, but why? Who has taught us these things?

This is one area that both my partner and I were adamant that we paid attention to, and that we created as close to an equitable agreement as possible. I wanted to struggle with a crying baby, I wanted to find my ways of soothing the sleepless infant, but that doesn't mean we didn't realize what our strengths and weaknesses as people were. For example, my partner was not only an amazing cook, but she enjoyed it. I was glad to have the time to play with the baby, alone in our room or in the bath while she cooked. It allowed me to bond on my own, in my own way. However, she hated to clean (and was perhaps the messiest chef I've ever met), so it seemed fair that I would clean. We tried to similarly handle as many of those parenting choices as possible. I would take our children to the store: it was one way to claim my fathering publicly and it also allowed my partner time alone. Consciously looking at what roles we're playing, I think, is a key to radical parenting because it forces us to own our choices. It forces us to see our socially ingrained gender expectations and hopefully rectify them—or at least reconsider them. And ultimately, if we're all doing the work and having the conversations we should be having to create radical parenting, it doesn't matter which gender or who is doing the parenting.

Silence and Disempowerment

There is reluctance among men to publicly talk about fathering. I've experienced this when talking one-on-one with them about how they want to parent; they are excited yet scared, nervous about making mistakes, most are dying to parent in ways that we were not parented. And there are very few good or radical role models. Our society disempowers men who break from the prescribed role of the "male" parent, the role that supports patriarchy, which is based on hierarchy and authoritarianism.

I have experienced external disempowerment as I've prioritized time with my children in relation to work schedules, and also at times with political and so- cial engagements. That is the most infuriating part. I expect it from a work situ- ation—the skepticism and the judgments about not being as committed as other colleagues. (I've been left out of the loop in work decisions: hiring committees form and I don't even know we're hiring. I'm never offered leadership roles be- cause, well, I just am not that dependable in the eyes of my employers.) But when activist friends tend to scoff at why I can't join them for a meeting because I feel like my youngest daughter just kinda needs to be at home, I realize how ingrained notions of parenting roles are. Even with supposedly politically aware friends, I am somehow seen as less committed, less dependable, when ironically the decisions to engage closely with parenting, I think, demonstrate the exact kinds of political points we are working to make.

Of course, this plays into all kinds of notions about the male gender and how "manly" we feel based on how we are seen by others. Supposedly, being manly is not staying home with your sick child when the boys are out. Supposedly, being manly is not refusing to stay late at work because you have to make it to your kids' open house at school. It seems those components of parenting aren't in the realm of men. When I tell a fellow colleague that I am not able to serve on a particu- lar committee this semester because my son is having trouble in high school, he chastises me, "How then are you going to make a difference in the world?" "Par- enting," I say, "is that difference." My answer does not mean that parents should not be committed to work or political organizing. It means that there has to be an understanding of how to balance those commitments. We as parents can support each other when we choose to scale back our involvement and when we demand that our involvement be recognized and supported.

Fathers speak easily of being proud, being happy and supportive. Worse, they speak to issues of discipline. Unfortunately, some women collude in this process and reinforce these assumptions about gender. This collusion is difficult to recognize and address because it plays into so many areas where women have in fact been dismissed by patriarchy. That's why it is imperative

> ### THINGS FATHERS CAN DO TO SLAP THE FACE OF PATRIARCHY
>
> 1. Wear your baby in a sling.
> 2. Take your kids with you everywhere you can—grocery stores, errands, to your place of work.
> 3. Vocalize your support of breast-feeding moms and women's equality in general.
> 4. Take advantage of the Family and Medical Leave Act and fight to strengthen it. Stay home with your new baby! Dads need bonding time, too.
> 5. Take an infant massage class and any other child-parent classes you are interested in.
> 6. Start a new dad's group, one where you take the baby with you.
> 7. Make a point to ask if there are changing tables in the men's restrooms everywhere you go.

for men to work just as hard at challenging the paradigm that puts women in limited roles outside the home as it is for them to work to find a place inside the home. Traditionally, men are not encouraged to soothe a child or not expected to hold a baby for too long before the mother takes control. I've been shocked at how seemingly self-aware couples fall into ridged socially defined, gender-based parenting once the baby comes. The mom does all the babying, the cleaning, and grocery shopping; the father, the working, the providing, and the fixing of things. And the excuse is always, "Well, that's what mothers do, right?" There has to be a way where men can fit in without usurping or taking over. We need to ask ourselves why we don't trust men to be competent at parenting, to be trusted to handle a newborn without being watched over by the mother or the grandmother. A good place to start would be to question the images of bumbling fathers we're inundated with. It is the butt of our parenting jokes: men fucking up, dressing kids, trying to feed kids, trying to be both macho and cool, because parenting in our society equals mothering. This collusion has a lot to do with patriarchy itself. Therefore, to raise up parenting from the diminutive realms of "women's work," it is essential that men work just as hard at creating a space for women in all other areas of society.

Parenting along gender lines is the result of patriarchy—how it has historically devalued parenting and women's work. So men and women are taught to believe and are encouraged to perpetuate the notion that women "naturally" have the ability to speak about parenting because somehow they are better with kids and more

HOW TO INTEGRATE DADS INTO OUR "MAMA-CENTRIC" CULTURE

1. Dads, believe in your ability to parent. You don't need permission to be a dad.
2. Know that parenting does not equal mothering.
3. Believe in other men's ability to parent. Talk to other men about fathering.
4. Combat images of bumbling fathers in the media. Talk to your kids as you encounter these stereotypes à la *Daddy Day Care*, *Mr. Mom*, *The Pacifier*, *Big Daddy*.
5. Reclaim Father's Day. Don't give your dad a tie—find a way to cultivate a celebration of the aspects of fathering that aren't related to work.
6. And, of course, contribute writing to *Rad Dad*! (See the Resources section for contact info.) Create your own fathering creative projects. And invite others to participate.

sensitive and nurturing. Because they are women. These assumptions about gender must change.

The diversity of fathering is multitude while the prescribed role is singular: what can we learn from a gay father about discussing sexuality with his daughters? I want to hear it. What can a working-class father share with us about fighting patriarchy in the household and at work? We need to hear it. How does a white father discuss race with his white son or his biracial daughter? Every single one of us can benefit from hearing that story.

For the last few months I have been talking with numerous parents—fathers, in particular—about what radical parenting looks like. In extending an invitation for them to contribute something to *Rad Dad*, I am always puzzled by the responses I get. When I say it's a zine about fathering and how men impact the world and the children around them, most smile and nod their heads. Already I can tell that they don't know what to think and say. And if we start talking immediately, it is about how little they actually talk about parenting with others. There really is no forum for men sharing concerns, sharing ways they struggle or places to be honest. Part of the pathology of male privilege is always having to see yourself as self-reliant and confident. Men don't need help, right?

If there is one thing radical parenting does, it makes you feel completely unsure and makes you continually question what you are doing and why. As radical fathers, as men who want to slap the face of patriarchy, we need to create even more spaces and places where we can share, support, encourage, and critique who we are and what we are doing, because how we relate to and connect with our own children is analogous to how we envision a better world—a more compassionate, loving, and creative world.

Things are changing. If we look, we can see that there is such hope and possibility around us. I see it every day as I make the breakfast for my kids—breakfast I know they'll only eat half of before we walk to school with the other parents and kids. I see it in libraries and parks where fathers and mothers are spending time with their kids. I see it in line at the grocery store as I smile at a man with his newborn son, while I stand with my daughters. We just smile in acknowledgement. Normally, that is enough for that moment. But not now. It's time to talk.

Because despite the horrible, patriarchal, misogynistic things many fathers have passed on to their kids, there are also fathers struggling daily in so many areas to create a culture of love and nurturing and patience and trust that's at the core of radical parenting. And we need to pass this on, because as Chris Rock would say, "We're supposed to!"

36.

Cofounding the Village Cooperative Skool

After about six months of attending the nine-hour-a-week My Morning Out program (see the "Building Community Takes Time" chapter), Emma-Joy was ready for another preschool, and began going five days a week, three hours a morning. She was three and a half. These fifteen hours a week gave her a stable, social structure, and it gave me a chance to get some work done without interruption. Though I'm not one who subscribes to the idea that preschool is necessary for kids who are already growing up in stimulating, nurturing environments, Emma-Joy and I both benefited from having this time away from each other. If I didn't have to be mama all day, chances were the majority of the time that I did need to be mama would be much better quality. If she got to have fun with other kids instead of getting frustrated trying her best to convince me that I really did want to play animal-princess dress-up make-believe for the bazillionth time instead of work on jewelry orders, she was happier.

It was one of those situations where we had to weigh the benefits against how much of a compromise it was to our ideals. At $240 a month, it was one of the more affordable preschools, was bike-riding distance from home, and had a good reputation among local families for sweet teachers and a safe environment. But its structure was more traditional, it had discipline techniques inconsistent with those we used at home, and since it was attached to a church, the kids were taught a before-snack prayer and went to "chapel" once a week for a half-hour. It didn't matter that the few alternative/more progressive preschool options were too far away, because they were also too expensive.

The traditional curriculum and structure offered little freedom for the kids to choose what they wanted to learn and how they spent their time. And most of the art projects lacked chances for imagination and creativity—you know, the "here's what we're making today" projects where everyone makes the same thing, step by step. Instead of being taught conflict-resolution skills, the kids were told to bring problems to the teachers to be solved for them, usually by means of someone getting a time-out or the generic command, "Say you're sorry." Though we knew about the chapel visits (I'd take her in late that day to miss it), I learned about the prayer one afternoon while Emma-Joy and I sat down together for lunch at home, and she starting saying grace: "God is good, God is great…" I didn't interrupt, and waited for the "Amen" before I asked her about it. She said it was just something that they say at school after they wash their hands, but before they eat. I left it at that.

Emma-Joy really enjoyed preschool. She loved her teacher, Ms. Rae, and had fun with the other kids she made friends with. At home, she constantly sang the songs she learned with her class. She told me about games she and her friends made up and played on the playground. She asked me to get her some workbooks to do at home like the ones she did at school. She never said she didn't want to go.

At the end of the school year, it was Ernesto and I who'd had enough of it. It was just too…well, mainstream. We'd noticed that Emma-Joy was now well aware of what we called kid culture—the junk food, the corporate characters, the girls-versus-boys gender roles. We realized that the older she got, whether she went to preschool or not, she'd be exposed to these things that we didn't have at home. It's not like we wanted to raise her in cage like baby veal or anything. We did intend to explain things, rather than ban them or pretend like they didn't exist. We just found it irritating to constantly contend with these issues at home with a preschooler.

So that summer, while Ernesto was the full-time parent and I was the full-time worker, it was time to engage in a little alternative-institution building and try to organize a co-op school. With families recruited from both of the playgroups we'd been hanging out with, we started having weekly meetings to brainstorm the possibilities.

We started meeting in June 2004, with an average of seven families attending. We began by discussing our goals and determining a collective structure for the group, membership requirements, kids' age ranges, ideal kid-to-adult ratios, days and hours of operation, parent participation, ideal locations and space requirements, daily schedule, snacks and lunch, and costs. We agreed that we were not interested in merely replicating any already-established preschool. We kept notes for every meeting, and we made them available via e-mail and archived them in a notebook for anyone to read who missed a meeting.

UNSCHOOLING, FREE SCHOOLING, WALDORF, AND MONTESSORI DEFINED

Unschooling: A term coined by John Holt, author of ten books on education, including *How Children Learn*, and founder of the unschooling magazine, *Growing Without Schooling*. Unschooling is based on the student's interests, needs, and goals and fosters natural curiosity. Students are in control of their own education, choosing how, when, why, and what they want to learn with assistance from facilitators instead of teachers or curriculum. Facilitators provide a wide range of resources, helping students access and navigate the various resources.

Free Schooling: Also known as democratic schools, free schools provide a setting in which students are independent, trusted, and treated as responsible people. As part of a school community, students develop interpersonal skills and are exposed to the complexities of life in the framework of a participatory democracy. Like the unschooling philosophy, free schools recognize that all people are curious by nature and that freedom to develop their unique talents is essential. A.S. Neill created Summerhill School in 1921 in Germany (which continues today in England) as an experiment in free learning, and in 1960 authored *Summerhill: A Radical Approach to Child Rearing*. Summerhill, a model for progressive, self-governing, democratic education, greatly influenced and inspired the free school movement of the 1960s and '70s. Approximately 300 of the free schools from this era still exist, among them the Sudbury Valley School in Framingham, Massachusetts; Spring Valley School in Palm Harbor, Florida; and Albany Free School in Albany, New York; along with a few public alternatives such as the High School in the Community in New Haven, Connecticut; Alternative School #1 in Seattle, Washington; and Freedom High School in Albuquerque, New Mexico. Other influential writers on free schools include Ivan Illich and Jonathan Kozol.

Waldorf: Begun in 1919, Waldorf education is based on founder Rudolf Steiner's philosophy of anthroposophy, his spiritual-scientific knowledge of humans. The heart of Waldorf education was Steiner's belief in the three major developmental stages of a child's life: up to seven years old, the will is developed through imitation and movement; up to fourteen years old, the stage of feeling is developed through imagination and artistic expression; at fourteen, the thinking stage is developed through abstract concepts and intellectual thought...(cont'd)

We wrote a mission statement:

"Because we share a vision for our children's development and education that none of us feel can be met through already-established institutions and traditional models of education, we will strive to provide an engaging environment as to facilitate a community of learners whose exploratory learning needs and desires will be met.

"We will achieve this by drawing from various contemporary, progressive, child-centered educational philosophies such as unschooling, free schooling, Waldorf, and Montessori."

In August, we wrote a proposal (see the Resources section) and made a presentation to the board of directors at the space we wanted to rent—two classrooms at the Unitarian Universalist Church of Fort Lauderdale. After successfully answering all of the board members' enthusiastic questions, we got a good feeling that our proposal would be accepted. The main things they were concerned about were licensing and liability. I explained that all of us would have our children registered as homeschoolers, which the State of Florida didn't require until the children were age six or older. In essence, we were just homeschooling collectively instead of individually. The only remaining question was if their liability insurance would cover us or if they would require us to carry our own liability insurance.

Ernesto was about to begin a new semester as a second-year law student, so he couldn't be the full-time parent anymore. We decided that I'd resume the full-time parenting and cut back my hours at the birth center. We also decided to let Emma-Joy go back to the same preschool she'd attended the year before, until we were able to get the co-op school started. I'd leave work at noon to pick her up and bring her back to work with me for the rest of my shift. The midwife I worked for, Debbie, then hired a high school student to babysit her daughter Munirah and Emma-Joy during the after-school hours while we worked.

While waiting for the UU Church to accept our proposal, we continued to meet weekly. We began looking for alternate locations in the event the UU Church denied our proposal. Other meeting agenda items during this time included specifying jobs, organizing fundraisers, defining the role of facilitators, establishing our educational/discipline philosophy, securing our nonprofit status, gathering materials and donations, creating a list of what every child needed to keep at school (cup, plate, change of clothes, milk crate to use as a cubby, small pillow and blanket, and an old shirt to be used as a paint smock), and setting up centers.

By then word was spreading, attracting more than just playgroup families to our weekly meetings. Seventeen families attended our largest meeting. I was afraid that some of these families were only passively interested—there was too much of a "what they could get from it, not what they could contribute" attitude. These families wanted to wait to see what the school was like before deciding to join, after the core group would have done all the hard work to get the school going. I wanted

Waldorf education is teacher centered and structured. One criticism of Waldorf education is that reading, writing, and arithmetic are not introduced before age seven and is therefore discouraged, even if a child expresses desire to be taught these disciplines.

Montessori: Respect for the child is at the core of the Montessori philosophy. Founded by Maria Montessori in the early 1900s in Europe, Montessori schools have flourished worldwide. The child is placed on a self-directed learning path, and child's play is viewed as the child's work. Children set their own pace, freely choosing their own hands-on materials and working with them for as long as they need to. Montessori teachers are facilitators and observers. Montessori classrooms are carefully designed into four areas: practical life, sensorial, mathematics, and language. Grouped together within a three-year age span, children also learn responsibility and mutual respect. One criticism of Montessori's philosophy is that is does not include creative arts or opportunity for fantasy play.

For more information about these educational philosophies, see the Resources section.

SCHOOL JOBS

1. Treasurer: Collect monthly tuition, pay rent, and coordinate fundraisers.

2. Supply Buyer/Donation Collector: Buy supplies or secure donations for the arts and crafts, outdoor environment, and main indoor environment centers.

3. Information Secretary: Maintain notebook archive, produce brochure and flyer (see appendix), create forms (see the Resources section), keep operating guidelines up-to-date, and maintain list of member contact information.

4. Liaison: Interact with UU Church.

them instead to join immediately and to take part in the hard organizational work. The collective decided to make one list of members who were committed (there were seven), and another list of those who were actively interested (there were five). We then agreed to place a twelve-family cap for starting out, and ruled that decisions at meetings could not be made without a minimum of two-thirds of the collective membership present. We wait-listed the others.

The idea of a paid facilitator was brought up at one of our meetings in mid-September. We spent many hours discussing whether it would be an asset to have the same person on-site every day, with one other rotating facilitator, to provide a measure of consistency for the children, as well as reducing the on-site requirements of all the other collective members. More time was spent on defining the position and its compensation. For example, would the paid facilitator manage the group's funds as well as the day-to-day activities of the school? Depending on their responsibilities, would this person be paid, or at minimum, would they receive free tuition for their child(ren)?

After several meetings, the collective decided to pay one of the members to be the consistent facilitator. We agreed on paying a living wage of eleven dollars an hour. This particular woman, an experienced early-childhood educator, would be with the kids every school day, along with one other collective member (a rotating facilitator). The main reason the group agreed to have a paid facilitator was so that developmental leaps, issues, and events with the kids could be more consistently observed; new, rotating daily facilitators could not monitor that information as easily. This arrangement increased the tuition cost per month (from $75 up to $165) but reduced the on-site requirements of all other collective members as rotating facilitators. So, instead of each family acting as a rotating facilitator once per week, each family now only needed to facilitate one day every other week. The collective agreed to work on more fundraising to help alleviate the strain of the added cost for some families. The collective also agreed that monthly tuition would be assessed per family, not per child.

It took a while for the UU Church to get back to us, and when they did, we celebrated. We'd be covered by their insurance and the rent was only $500 a month (utilities included), with a $200 deposit for damages. We held two yard sales with donated items from all the families in the collective and raised more than $200 for the deposit. We held on to the remainder to use for art supplies. It was now November. We set a date of December 1, for our school to start, and upped our meeting times to include work days in the classrooms to get the centers organized and set up.

Last, we needed to hash our educational/discipline philosophy. Up until this time, we had a general sense that we were all similar enough in our philosophies. In one meeting's time, we agreed that our collective's philosophy included the following:

1. Child interest-based learning through facilitation not instruction (a child-directed classroom learning environment), by following the children's lead with no play interruption or direction; facilitator(s) join in play only if invited by child(ren), thus allowing child(ren) to unfold into their own being(s).

2. Minimally coercive learning environment (i.e. activities, opportunities, and projects would be offered, not required).

3. An environment that fostered a community of learners through mutual respect, positive reinforcement, natural consequences, and conflict resolution rather than punitive punishment, timeouts, shaming, insults, belittling, or focusing on socially scripted "manners."

4. Gently established boundaries and, as needed, appropriate redirection; school rules established as needed by the community of learners and facilitators together.

5. All learners treated as creative, intelligent individuals.

We got the skool (by this point, we'd quit calling it a "school") up and running on schedule with seven committed families (eight kids). The Village Cooperative Skool started with great enthusiasm, and we were all full of hope and energy to make our experiment work. Most of the kids already knew each other well, the age range was perfect (three to five years old), and our location on five acres was a dream.

However, in addition to some minor logistical kinks, we faced some immediate problems. First, it just wasn't working for a couple of the kids. There were issues of bullying and jealousy that were very hard to navigate.

This caused two families to drop out after the first month. One of them was our paid facilitator. The skool wasn't working for her son, who had gone from being

---

SCHOOL CENTERS

Main Indoor Environment
1. Math and manipulatives table
2. Computer (educational CD-ROMs only, no Internet)
3. Arts/crafts/painting station
4. Writing/reading table
5. Water/sand/rice play table
6. Library

Imagination Station (smaller classroom)
1. Puppets
2. Dress-up
3. Building/blocks
4. Other toys
5. Play kitchen set

Outside Environment
1. Playground
2. Garden
3. Labyrinth
4. Nature exploration

bullied to being the bully. She also felt like she was in an unwinnable situation because of the young ages of the kids and her position both as the paid facilitator and as a mama. She never felt like her role as the paid facilitator was defined enough, or recognized and respected enough. For example, a rotating facilitator would try to force an "I'm sorry" out of her own kid or give a teary-eyed time-out, instead of facilitating according to our collectively agreed-upon philosophy. The times when the paid facilitator took on the role of "experienced early-childhood educator" and explained the reasons "why we do not coerce apologies" (not being able to legislate empathy, working instead on helping the child see the other child as hurting, helping the child help the other child stop hurting, etc.), she was definitely challenged by some of the other mamas.

In addition to the paid and rotating facilitators, there was usually another mama or two hanging around during the first month the skool was in operation. It made the classroom dynamic weird. The kids would go to their own parent or to a longtime friend's parent in search for "authority," and it was difficult to be the paid facilitator when that kid's parent would then act in a way that she considered coercive, counter to the skool's philosophy, or just plain inappropriate for the stage of development the kids were in. Dealing with these parents' demonstrated inability to facilitate according to the skool's philosophy by aiding them to "walk the walk, not just talk the talk" was a detriment to the skool for two reasons. First, we expended a lot of weekly meeting time and energy on these sorts of grievances. Second, we could not get other families to join the skool when they observed facilitator behavior that was inconsistent with the skool's philosophy.

The other family who dropped out cited the most important reason was that not all the parents were on the same page philosophically. The mama in that family said that, at times, it felt as if some were more worried about the snacks being organic than the children being supported in free play and their personal development. She also noted that the paid facilitator's role lacked support: the kids never got the message from their parents that the paid facilitator was the one in charge. Also, her child wasn't ready. She'd started crying almost every day, begging to *not* go to the skool, because she'd been bullied and did not want mama to leave her there. Quite reasonably, the mama didn't feel like she wanted to voluntarily subject her three-year-old to that.

We were down to five families (six kids). Although we were committed to making a go of it and we continued moving forward, we constantly felt like we were operating in crisis mode. When the paid facilitator quit, we'd lost the easiest way to have consistency for the kids and for our own observations; as a solution, we created "The Daily Log," in which that day's facilitators would make note of what facilitators and kids were present; that day's activities, successes, problems, and observations; making special note of dynamics between the kids and issues that needed to be worked on. Though the monthly cost dropped to $100 a month with no longer having a paid facilitator, the skool itself was a lot for such a small group to maintain. To keep with the goal of having two parents facilitating every skool day meant every family needed to facilitate one day a week, with three of the five families facilitating two days a week. Where before we felt a need to cap the number of families involved, now we felt we needed more—and quick—if we were to be able to sustain the skool. As it was, due to skool and work schedules, it was not sustainable for some families to be facilitating two days a week. And if either a kid or facilitator had to be out sick, it was hard to manage. The wait-listed families did not want to board what they saw as a sinking ship.

After five more months, with summer approaching and no new families joining, we decided to take a break from operating the skool, but to continue meeting in order to regroup, recruit, and start anew in the fall.

For all involved during the six months the skool operated, some skool days had been magical, fun, and invigorating, while others had been annoying, tense, and unbearable. Though getting all the remaining rotating facilitators on the same page when putting the skool's philosophy into practice remained a constant task, some of the more trying moments had to do with kid dynamics and conflict resolution. This led us to implementing three things: the "Peace Rose"—a ritual mission we'd adapted from the Montessori model in which we provided a long-stemmed plastic rose that a child could bring to another to help share feelings, take turns, and resolve conflicts; a "caring corner"—a place to transfer out-of-control energy into something nurturing and positive; and firm limits for using the computer—no more than two kids at a time, and if anyone is waiting, limit your turn to ten minutes.

Some of the most enjoyable moments happened outdoors. At lunchtime, we'd gather the basket that held the plates, cups, napkins, utensils, and haul out the composting and recycling bins. We'd all eat together at round tables on a covered patio and afterwards, the kids would wash their own dishes and recycle or compost what they needed to. We strived to be a "zero-waste" skool. After eating, we facilitators would get to watch as the kids developed their own routines and follow-the-leader-type games in the labyrinth and go on "jungle" tree-climbing expeditions. Sometimes we'd pick lemons and make lemonade.

We got to witness our skool philosophy in action indoors, too. A great morning circle time routine evolved; we'd sing, dance, and play games, and the kids would list the different things they wanted to do during their day/week and we'd write it on the chalkboard. During closing time, we'd have conflict-resolution discussion as a group for any issues that came up throughout the day. We had structured days that the kids were actively involved in shaping. Art was happening; we'd simply set out five or six different supply offerings and then sit back to witness creativity. Plays were performed, sometimes with costumes from the imagination station, sometimes with puppets from the makeshift stage. When the kids asked to make movies, we brought a video camera and made movies. When two kids requested to learn more reading and writing, we came up with letter-and-number-of-the-week activities using workbooks, printouts, and hands-on activities. Most kids were consistently interested in these offerings; a few consistently weren't. A few took it a step further and taught each other how to spell words up at the chalkboard. Most kids enjoyed their quiet time after lunch listening to a story, while a few played quietly in the imagination station. Because we'd decorated the walls with big maps, kids asked to learn about different places. We adopted a different place to learn about each month, according to where each facilitator was from (Israel, Argentina, Cuba, Florida, California, New York). On some Fridays, we'd take a field trip to where the kids wanted to go—the zoo, the beach, the park, the fire station. When a kid brought something from home to work on, we'd help out at skool. We built outdoor forts out of palm fronds and twine; indoor forts out of pillows, chairs, and blankets.

In hindsight, although the vision we had of a free school/unschool-y place for kids to hang out together wasn't off mark, we learned that we didn't have the necessary collective experience and knowledge to successfully implement our skool's goals, mission, and philosophy. We needed to learn more about how to help children resolve conflicts peacefully, when to step in during conflicts, and how to protect kids from bullying. We needed to be better about not directing play, understanding the value of children's unhindered play, and realizing the detriment of pushing academics on kids who were not into it. Most of us knew how to do these things with our own kids, but not with a group of children. In this vein, there are several things the collective could have done better:

1. The skool's philosophy and paid-facilitator decisions should have been made first, before we started work on the logistical planning.

2. It was a mistake to leave our skool's philosophy so vague. We should have done workshops on why we were choosing which pedagogy/discipline philosophy. We could have watched videos on Summerhill, done more research on the Albany Free School, or sent a contingent out to workshops conducted by Bev Boss, a preschool director, early childhood development writer, and author of several books including *Don't Move the Muffin Tins: A Hands-Off Guide to Art*

for the Young Child. Even a week-long internship up at the swank, totally developmentally awesome Seedlings alternative preschool in Boca Raton, Florida, would have benefited us.

3. We should have done more fundraising to help pay for the paid facilitator instead of letting cost be a detracting factor for some interested families.

4. We should have held parent-as-facilitator trainings that would have included antibias education, antibul-

> "THE OPENING CIRCLE SONG,"
> WRITTEN BY EMMA-JOY AND ME
>
> Good morning, good morning, welcome to the Village Skool.
> Good morning, good morning, this skool's for me and you.
> We play, we learn, we eat, we grow, we learn to get along.
> We read, we write, we build, we plant, will you sing our song?
> Good morning, good morning, welcome to the Village Skool.
> Good morning, good morning, this skool's for me and you.

lying skills, conflict-resolution skills, and guidelines on facilitating our educational philosophy. We should have made a collective decision to not allow parents who acted contrary to the skool's philosophy to continue as rotating facilitators until more philosophy-based training could take place. Not all of us were able to recognize the tricky balance between getting out of the kids' way and supervising them. We did not foresee how difficult it would be for all of us to facilitate once or twice a week in a way that would be consistent with our philosophy and with each other. Some people were naturals, while some operated as if the skool's philosophy had been discussed in a language they didn't understand.

5. We should have drafted an "Unacceptable Parental Behavior" policy early on. This would have helped alleviate the grievances that arose between the paid facilitator and rotating facilitators/other parents present. Even after the paid facilitator left the collective, a policy would have been helpful in reining in some off-mark parental behaviors.

6. We should have done more active outreach into our communities, instead of just flyering and dropping off brochures here and there (see the Resources section).

Due to various reasons, we never did regroup in the fall as originally planned. (See the "Mom, I Wanna Go to Real School!" chapter for our family's reason.) However, half of the founding families eventually reorganized themselves into a home-based alternative to preschool and kindergarten. Engaging in alternative-institution-building of any kind is no easy task. In spite of our trials, our best efforts were rewarded by all of us—parents and kids—learning about collective process, group dynamics, putting theory into practice, patience, tolerance, and commitment. Our experiential learning gave us a lot more than we realized, in the form of lessons learned that will serve our future organizing well.

37.

Mommy-Daughter Weekend Road Trip

My well-seasoned traveler, now four-and-a-half years old, and I were headed to Orlando for some fun. The Subhumans were playing, and I didn't want to miss the show. Ernesto wasn't able to watch Emma-Joy due to his study schedule, so I decided to bring Emma-Joy with me to the show.

I had excited butterflies in my stomach on the drive up. Maybe they were slightly anxious-mama ones, but I was feeling like some giddy high schooler on her way to see her favorite band in mom and dad's borrowed car. Ahh, some things never change. But other things obviously had. Instead of smoking and drinking beer with my high school friends, I was doling out healthy snacks and singing along with my girl to her favorite preschool pop tape.

When I eventually switched the tape to the Subhumans, she demanded a swift end to it. Uh-oh, the first sign that things weren't going to go so well.

I reminded her that once we got to the show, if she didn't want to be inside where the music was going to be playing, we could hang out outside, no problem. She said she was sure she wanted to stay inside, even if it was loud and smoky.

Wh-wh-what? Smoky?

Damn! I had completely forgotten to ask if there was smoking allowed inside these venues, but my girl sure hadn't forgotten the "it's going to be too loud and smoky" mantra-excuse I give her if/when she can't go to a show with me. Enter the unspoken mama-rationalization factor #1: It's too late to turn back now; two nights of being around some smoke aren't going to ruin her lungs.

We arrived before the bands started playing and when they did, she cooperatively kept her earplugs in. She did ask a few times if she could take them out, so I

ADVICE ON TAKING YOUR KID TO SHOWS

1. Check beforehand if the show is all ages. Some venues are not cool with underage kids coming in with their parents.

2. Remind your kid that wearing earplugs is not an option—it's mandatory.

3. Prepare your kid for what the show will be like: probably no other kids to play with, maybe crowded with sweaty people.

4. Accept that your kid very well may change his/her mind about wanting to be there—the environment may overwhelm a kid who didn't know s/he wasn't ready for the experience.

5. If you and you kid need to leave before the show's over, don't make your kid feel like you're disappointed because of them needing to leave.

reminded her that if she wanted to stay inside, that she'd have to keep them in, but if she wanted to take them out and go hang out outside with me instead, that'd be fine. She always chose to leave them in and stay inside.

At the end of that night's show, she let the band know what she thought of their music, "Boring!" But the kid had a great time! The only young kid in the place, she had a captive adult audience who doted on her. She did not miss having a playmate her age at all.

A bartender hooked her up with Shirley Temples, Sprite loaded with cherries and cherry juice. Our pal Elaine, who my girl hadn't seen in months, brought her leftover Halloween candy. Another friend, Wicks, took her out for pizza. Karoline fed her vegan strawberry cake and gifted her a George W. Bush coloring book that she dove into while sitting atop the piles of shirts behind the merch table. She made new mama and papa punk friends. After the show, she hugged the Subhumans' singer Dick and asked him how he got so sweaty. Enter the unspoken mama-rationalization factor #2: She's having a great time; the sugary Sprite, candy, and cake won't ruin her health or teeth in one night.

With the band heading to a bar and an undecided-upon hotel an indeterminable number of hours after that, I thought I'd have to get going to find a cheap, nearby hotel room of my own. High fives for the punks who overhead me say I needed to go get a room for my kid and me, and told me, "I know we just met, but if you're cool with it, you could crash at our place."

Hell, yeah! With their spare key and their drunkenly backwards-drawn map to their place, my girl and I made our way there on our own. Just in time, too. My overtired yet still excited and sugared-up girl had entered meltdown mode. To say she was really disappointed we weren't going to be staying in a hotel is an absolute understatement.

I should have remembered from the week-long tour with my band that she really took to staying in new-to-her environments, hotel or otherwise. As soon as we got in the door, she was happy again, poking around the collectible toys and petting the kitty. We gathered a blanket and pillows and snuggled tight on the couch.

My girl woke up at a painfully early hour, so we left before anyone else woke up. I had heard our hosts stumble in pretty late, so I didn't think it would be courteous to stick around and wake them with cartoons and my girl's demands for breakfast. We left a thank-you note and drove the four hours home to where the Subhumans would be playing that night. On the ride she asked me all sorts of questions about the band, like why Bruce doesn't bring his kids on tour; where they slept; "Why they talk like that?"; and "Mommy, you pretend to talk like Jasper, OK?"

Back at home, we prepared for the show with a two-hour nap.

The show again was helluva lotta fun and this time, Ernesto got to come. My girl loosened up more than she had the previous night, venturing from behind the merch table, spastically dancing around the empty spaces, feeling more comfortable around old and new "grown-up friends" who gave her more treats and attention. We did the "You copy me, then I copy you" dance she loves. Daddy bounced her around on his shoulders and played circle pit chase with her back behind the soundboard, far away from the real circle pit in front of the stage.

By the end of the night, she had her shoes off and was asking me if she could go "run around in the big circle" by herself. I told her, "No, I don't want you to get squished." She innocently protested, "But tonight I want to get sweaty dancing like Dick. Pleeeaasseee, I'm not sweaty yet, feel me!"

Though she didn't get to enter circle-pit world unaccompanied, she was pretty thrilled by the big sleepover at our place after the show. I couldn't believe she was still awake when she was! Enter the unspoken mama-rationalization factor #3: So what if she's still up at 1 a.m. on a school night? It's a special occasion and she'll have to play hooky tomorrow which means I get to sleep in, too!

There was only one way to end this weekend even more perfectly than it had been already; Karoline and I headed out on foot to the closest bar and left Ernesto and the Subhumans crew at home in charge of getting Emma-Joy into bed.

38.

Slave to Fashion, Part 2

Remember the chapter where I ranted something along the lines of *I gave my daughter free reign over her clothes choices and I wound up with a wannabe beautiful-all-the-time princess* (see "Slave to Fashion, Part 1")? Reducing the saga down to a sentence takes away all the background and particulars, rounded out with philosophical and psychological musings. And that's my intent this time. My kid is just flat-out obsessed with clothes!

It took me a year to realize that what it all comes down to is this: her absolute love of clothes went hand in hand with her desire to be looking sharp, stylin' fancy, and now, stain-free all the freakin' time.

What? This isn't supposed to happen for years!

When preparing for a weekend trip to Grandma Bee and Grandpa Bobby's, she'd pack at least a week's worth of changes. When going to the park for the afternoon, she'd bring along a change of clothes. This kid of mine would beg to go to the laundromat so her favorite shirts could get washed, and only a week after we last did laundry! She'd ask her friends if she could "borrow forever" certain items of their clothing that suited her fancy. Her wish list of presents for the holiday season was all clothes! I couldn't take it. I thought a four-year-old was supposed to want toys, damn it, and the toys she wanted were not supposed to be Barbie fashion dolls!

Her holiday wish list read like a page straight outta *Fashion Victim Quarterly*: Rainbow shirts and butterfly shorts, pink tight pants and velvet party dresses, zipper calf boots and beaded purses. And don't forget the rainbow-colored lipstick.

Yeah, it was all my fault, because instead of laying down the anti-makeup and Barbie law, I allowed her to play with those beauty-standard-imposing things, which she got as presents starting at age two. Instead of censoring, I allowed her to look at library books that had pages full of princesses. Instead of choosing for her, I allowed her to check out movies like *Cinderella* and *The Little Mermaid*. Emma-Joy's fashion-forward drive had nothing to do with the constant barrage of societally enforced gender-coding rules, corporations' deliberate and incessant marketing to children, or the peer and self-policing effects these two phenomena bring to the preschool-aged playground.

When she was almost four, her mantra to me was, "Mom, your clothes are not beautiful. Change, please." At almost five, she had lightened up a bit. When she liked something I was wearing, she would ask me to save it for her for when it would fit her. I'd promise to do so. I am, after all, a queen of hand-me-downs. Plus, I secretly liked that she wanted to cop my style now and then, instead of the flavor-of-the-season style that was being bought and sold all around her.

But I didn't dig that she'd been asking to "do her makeup" as part of her "getting ready" routine. During one of these episodes, I said no, that she didn't need it. She protested, "But I want to look beautiful!" I told her that she was already beautiful without it, that it was not how you look that makes you beautiful, it was the things you say and do that make you beautiful. She pled, "Mom, pleeeease?" I said no again, that I was not wearing it either, and felt confident in this parenting decision because I wasn't doing something myself that I was disallowing her to do. I asked her if she remembered telling me I looked great just a minute ago. She said, "Yes, you do look great, but I just really want to wear makeup. You don't have to wear it if you don't want to, but I want to. Pleeeeease!"

Not opening the floor for negotiations, I whisked her out of the bathroom after a quick swipe of lipgloss, and said, "More makeup is not a choice right now. The choice is staying home or coming with me." She chose to come and she was bummed at me for a little while, but recovered quickly once in the car and her favorite tape began to play.

I didn't understand how a teenager had gotten trapped in a preschooler's body. My gotta-look-good-girl consciousness didn't kick in until age ten, and lasted until I was about seventeen. Did that mean she'd be over it by the time she was ten? Or could it be with her until she's seventeen, too? Longer than that, even?

I hope for the best. I hope that she'll figure out on her own time that the whole appearance package is a bunch of bunk, that corporations profit off of the insecurity they sell, and that it eats away at her time that could be better spent on learning something new or doing something more fun than thinking about how she looks. She'll discover that her desire for things that make her beautiful and to be beautiful can be created and realized by any number of ways other than glitz and glam. Right?

But wait, there was more. She started asking for ballet and tap-dancing classes. She had done two eight-week sessions of acting classes, at her request. Price was right (I scored her a 90% need-based scholarship due to our student loan "income"), the playhouse was bike-riding distance from our house, and she genuinely seemed into it. But at the end of that second session, that was it and she said she wanted to do ballet instead.

I'd been dragging my feet, hoping her requests to learn ballet would fade. I cringed. Ballet was absolutely the only activity I swore she'd never do. But after eight months, I gave in to the requests that never did let up. I'd never seen her so excited, proud, disciplined, and yes, wanting to look beautiful, too.

See, it was my fault again. Not only did I have a preschool-aged fashionista on my hands, but a ballerina on top of it all. Moms like me were supposed to absolutely forbid this girly gag-a-rama, weren't we? I had only myself to thank for allowing it, for patronizing it even, right?

If only I had read the nonexistent *Perfect Parenting for All Occasions* handbook. Then I would have known that kids are gonna choose what they want for themselves, no matter if you forbid it or not. I would have known better how not to facilitate her embrace of gender-coded girlhood.

I realized that I'd rather have a girly-girl by choice, for whatever reasons and for however long she's choosing it, than a girly-girl who is one out of some need to rebel against what she perceives as my being a lame ass. I still wondered, though, how much of it really was purely her choice; the influence of mainstream media and societal expectations are powerful.

I managed to live with ballet; it could have its merits as long as I continued guiding her toward healthy ideas of body image and nutrition. The clothes thing seriously irritated me, but it's not like we really shopped anywhere but the thrift stores and yard sales anyway. And the makeup, well, I kept being a thorn in her side to ward off her sure-to-be future embarrassment over having traipsed around looking like a badly painted clown. She hated clowns.

Hopefully, when she does get to her real teenage years and her hormone-induced world will turn upside down without her understanding why, we'll have built a relationship based on mutual respect and we'll get through it with our sweet mama-daughter bond intact.

5 Years Old

39.

Guiding My Kid Through the Marketing Madness

Walking down the street, my five-year-old daughter and her six-year-old friend got smacked with a huge billboard of a scantily clad woman in front of their faces.

"Whoa, look at her! What's she doing there?" asked one of them.

"She's got her butt sticking out and part of her boobies showing," said the other.

"Well, what's she doing?" I asked back, hoping to start a dialogue.

"Resting," said one.

"Kind of laying down," said the other.

"Yeah, but why?" I asked further.

"Is it advertising?" asked my girl.

"Yes," I said, "Good. Now do you remember what advertising is?"

"They want you to buy something," answered one.

"They are trying to sell you something," answered the other.

"Yes and yes. Do you know what this billboard is selling?" I asked.

"It can't be the woman," said one.

"I have no idea," said the other.

"This billboard is advertising a website for betting on poker, horse races, baseball, basketball, and football," I tell them.

"Huh? I don't get it," said one.

"Yeah, it's weird to have a picture of a woman up there when they're advertising betting, huh?" I asked.

"It doesn't make any sense. And look at the nails they hammered in her legs to hang it up," observed the other. "Good thing she's not real cuz that would hurt!"

I started having conversations like this with Emma-Joy as soon as it became apparent that kid-aimed marketing was getting her attention. When she first saw commercial TV while at someone else's house, I had to teach her the difference between the commercials and the TV show; she was confused at first, frustrated by the commercial interruption of the story.

At home watching videos, not commercial TV, she was almost three-years-old when she started begging for flip flops, beach towels, kiddie cups and plates, markers, toys, and clothing that brandished the images of her favorite characters from her favorite movies. Why? Because characters have personality, and as the marketing cliché goes, "Personality promotes loyalty." Characters, outside of the context of their movies, become products themselves. It is easier to sell kids character personality than it is to sell anything else, because with characters, there are no logos, brand names, or product attributes to learn. In his book *Out of the Garden: Toys and Children's Culture in the Age of TV Marketing*, Canadian scholar Stephen Kline discusses in depth how the rise of character marketing affects how children play; along with the purchased character, children are getting specific social roles, rules, and rituals associated with the character. And if a creative, rebellious kid ever breaks the rules of play for specific character, a playmate would be sure to correct, "My Little Pony can't fly; she's a pony." Further discussing how children's play is affected by marketing, he says that the marketers, by targeting boys and girls separately, have created a divisive play world, and kids recognize it as such.

So I started to plant critical-question seeds, which with careful cultivation, would grow to help make her aware of why she all of a sudden wanted those character things: "Why will that skirt with Ariel on it make you happier than the one with the butterfly? Do you even need the skirt or just want it?" If she was old enough to be duped by marketing, she was old enough to start learning how to repel it.

I'm glad that at five and six years young, the girls couldn't make any conscious sense of the "sex sells" concept. In their subconscious, though, I knew the pervasive, objectifying images had to be making their mark.

Thankfully, both girls had been exposed to Basic Media Awareness 101 at home. Though at ages five and six, they may not understand the actual marketing concepts behind the advertising and commercials they are exposed to and that are targeted at them, the effects are hard at work on them. Therefore, calling it out and breaking it down for kids will help them become ad savvy and critical of the ways marketers are trying to lure children into a consumer lifestyle. Kids need to know that the overwhelming majority of ads try to convince them to buy things they do not need.

Pester Power

Advertising dollars spent on marketing to kids are at an all-time high—$15 billion spent on marketing products to children in 2004, about 2.5 times more than what it was in 1992. Kids today are advertised to twice as much than when I was as a child. Today, the average child in the United States sees more than 40,000 television commercials each year; between 1975 and 1980, that number was estimated to be between 20,000 and 22,000 a year. Corporations want to reach children early to create brand-loyal, lifelong consumers. An additional, more immediate goal is to influence the economic power kids have with their parents (an estimated $670 billion in 2004, up from $500 billion in 2000, according to kids marketing expert James McNeal); the industry calls it "pester power" when kids lobby parents to buy certain products. An average estimate for how much kids under eight spend independently is $30 billion a year; kids twelve to nineteen spent a record $155 billion of their own money in 2001, up from $63 billion just four years earlier. Of course, the same corporations are competing for their pieces of those substantial kiddie pies, too.

The quick, fast-paced, and entertaining television commercials make it easy for kids to remember a song, slogan, or catchy phrase. In addition to knowing that kids watch TV more than they read or listen to the radio, this explains why advertisers spend more money on television commercials than any other form of advertising, for example, print media or radio. And they're not just aiming the commercials at kids for products like fast food and toys. Increasingly, advertisers are relying on "pester power" for kids to influence their parents for adult products like cars and luxury vacations. A 2006 article in the *Minneapolis Star Tribune* reported, "Honda is about to launch an advertising campaign on

PESTER POWER STATS

Perhaps easier to just blame parents and say it's their responsibility to "just say No," it's not that simple. The dynamics of kid culture are changing; consumerism is an increasingly powerful force in kids' socialization. It's no coincidence that a common theme in kid-aimed advertising is antiparent while promoting the authority of commerce; the parental "no" in response to kid's begging for new products doesn't carry as much weight as the parental "no" regarding a safety issue. According to a national survey conducted in 2002 commissioned by the Center for a New American Dream:

1. The average young person says they have to ask their parents for products they have seen advertised an average of nine times until the parents finally give in.

2. Seventy-one percent of children aged twelve to thirteen are most likely to pursue this aggressive "nag factor" strategy. Eleven percent of twelve- to thirteen-year-olds admitted to asking their parents more than fifty times for products they have seen advertised.

3. Fifty-five percent of kids surveyed said they are usually successful in getting their parents to give in.

4. Forty percent say they have asked their parents for an advertised product they thought their parents would not approve of.

5. Among these youth who have asked to buy products their parents disapprove of, fifty-nine percent say they do not give up—they keep asking in the hopes their parents will finally say yes.

Disney's ABC Kids channel. The Cayman Islands' department of tourism buys ads on Nickelodeon, a children's cable channel, promoting expensive holidays. And Beaches Resorts, a hotel chain, has teamed up with *Sesame Street* to make its resorts more appealing to children."

Close behind the advertising dollars spent on television commercials, kid-aimed marketing is prevalent on the Internet. Take a look at www.hummerkids.com for example, one of the kid websites children are directed to from the McDonald's website. On this website, kids can color pictures of the Hummer H3 and check out other Hummer games, downloads, and activities. It's never too early for kids to enjoy learning about keeping the gas-guzzling traditions in the United States alive, after, of course, they've gobbled their McCrap-attack Happy Meals!

Exploiting the Tweens

Corporations are cashing in on our kid's vulnerability. The reasons kids cite for wanting more and more consumer products is to fit in, that their friends have them, that these things boost self-esteem, making kids feel better about themselves. And the marketing experts know it: "Advertising at its best is making people feel that without their product you're a loser. Kids are very sensitive to that. If you tell them to buy something, they are resistant. But if you tell them they'll be a dork if they don't, you've got their attention," says Nancy Shalek, former president of Grey Advertising. In her book *Born to Buy*, Boston College sociology professor Juliet Schor finds links between immersion in consumer culture and depression, anxiety, low self-esteem, and conflicts with parents.

The most vulnerable group to feel pressure to fit in is twelve- and thirteen-year-olds. This is already an awkward time of transition from child to adolescent, and the marketing aimed at this age demographic makes it even more so. Inventing the profitable tween, and now pre-tween, identities that have nothing to do with childhood developmental stages that actually exist along a continuum, marketers mislead these young children into false, manufactured, artificial identities. Kids are bombarded with images that sell them a how-to-get-older-younger bunk parcel of goods. The great irony is that marketers put forth the idea that their tween and pre-tween strategies are promoting empowerment and more democracy in the family.

"According to a leading expert on branding, 80 percent of all global brands now deploy a 'tween strategy,'" writes Ann Hubert in a 2004 *New York Times* article, "Tweens 'R' Us." Tweens, once referred to as preteens, is a marketing invention used to define a specific consumer demographic—children aged eight to twelve. These kids have more disposable income than ever before; in 2003, tweens had a total income of $42.3 billion. And they influence $300 billion in family spending annually.

Marketers recruit tween-aged kids to help create marketing buzz, hone campaigns, and create top-selling images. One marketing firm, GIA (Girls Intelligence Agency), attracts girls to sign up to be cultivated into a "special agent." The special agent, who has to be approved by GIA, has been identified as the alpha, or peer influencer, in her group. They number 40,000 to 50,000 across the United States and are specialized, too, for technology products, movies, fashion, and music. In exchange, the secret agent girls think it's a privilege and makes them cool.

Among other activities, secret agents host slumber parties. For example, to get a buzz going about a new pop star for one of their clients, Capitol Records, the GIA used their secret agents (7,000 girls at 500 slumber parties) to reshape the singer's look, video, and website, and choose what the first and second singles would be off her new CD.

One critic of these over-the-top marketing tactics, Juliet Schor, says the host girl is "being taught that her friends are an exploitable resource... She needs to get these friends over there, get that information out of them." GIA CEO Laura Groppe counters, "Marketers are obviously going to try to push the boundaries as much as possible."

And pushing they are. Right into the privacy of kid's homes under illusions of privilege and cool and inserting themselves into the secret agent's peer group. To these marketers, our kids healthy emotional and social development are worth risking and exploiting when there are hundreds of billions of dollars to be made from manufactured desire.

When marketers and commercial advertising infiltrate our kids' private spaces, why should their public spaces be any different? Public schools are no stranger to commercialization. The resistance to Channel One; soda and snack vending machines; contracts for exclusive-rights soda deals and with fast food corporations; advertising and logos in classrooms, in instructional material including textbooks, on sports uniforms, and on school facilities are all fights that have made local and national headlines for decades.

Prior to Emma-Joy starting public school kindergarten (Oh, just wait until you get to the next chapter—"Mom, I Wanna Go to Real School!"—to read how that happened!), she'd called McDonald's "Donald Ducks" and I wasn't about to correct her. The longer she went without knowing the McDonald's name, the better, even if she could recognize the Golden Arches whenever we passed them. One day when I picked her up from school, I saw a McDonald's sticker on her shirt and casually asked where it came from. Excitedly showing me a free coupon for a small fry (she doesn't even like french fries) and another for a free ice cream cone, she told me that Ronald McDonald had come to school that day for an assembly, "He was funny and he taught us a song!" Ugh, that song. She and her friend Kai sang that damn "da da da da da, I'm lovin' it" jingle a million times over.

Kai's mama, Adriana, and I made our objections well known to the school, rallying more parents on board to voice their opposition to Ronald's visit as well. And we let the kids know that Ronald McDonald was like a commercial, wanting them to learn that song so they would want to come spend money to eat at his junk-food restaurant. Emma-Joy started to get it, "Why don't they care about kids eating junk and want to just make money?" Before I could answer, she followed up her question with, "Well, I think it would be OK if we went there only sometimes, not every day."

By then, we'd had many conversations about junk food and their related commercials. (One third to one-half of the $15 billion spent on advertising to children in 2004 was spent on food advertising, mostly for sugary breakfast cereals, fast food, soft drinks, snacks, candy, and gum.) Because the junk-food commercials' messages are so clear, *Eat a lot of food and snacks, pester your parents to buy it, there's no difference between meals and treats, and gain fame, fun, and friends while eating our crap*, Ernesto and I, along with our modeled healthy food choices, felt it was our duty to teach Emma-Joy that people make a lot of money by selling a lot of unhealthy food and drinks. Without our guidance, we knew there was little competition with the overwhelming lack of quality nutrition messages that saturate culture's food arena; the encouragement for children to eat fresh fruits and vegetables is little compared to the massively funded campaigns to encourage children to want junk food. According to Yale University's Rudd Center for Food Policy and Obesity website, "In the year that funding peaked at $3 million for the main government nutrition education program (5-a-Day), McDonald's spent $500 million dollars on a single campaign ("We Love to See You Smile")." In June 2007, however, the Kellogg Company—maker of Froot Loops and other junky cereals and snacks—announced it would voluntarily phase out advertising products that did not meet specific nutrition guidelines for calories, sugar, fat, and sugar to children under age twelve; it also said it would stop using licensed characters or branded toys to promote these foods. Of course, this was not an altruistic move; Kellogg caved when threatened with a lawsuit by two advocacy groups.

Put simply, marketing to children is a predatory practice. While most funding is given to child-psychology research that is focused on education, on cognitive learning processes, not social and emotional processes, marketing researchers have spent gynormous amounts of dollars to better understand children. This

Don't Wait to Educate!

Children are never too young to start hearing you talk about marketing, consumerism, commercials, and advertisements of all kinds. Even when a child's TV/screen time is limited, kids still need savvy media skills. Forced to diversify their methods as a way to fight back against calls to limit their advertising, the industry describes their new methods with names like guerilla, viral, and stealth marketing. These methods show up in magazines, over the Internet, in schools, with product placement in movies and subsequent tie-ins with food products and fast food chains, and much more. "With new cell phones equipped with a GPS (Global Positioning System) chip, companies can identify the location of the user. The child marketers boast that tens of millions of children power up a cell phone when they leave school each day and can (and will) be beamed advertisements to local food establishments," according to the Yale/Rudd Center website.

1. Go through the day's mail with your child and explain the junk mail: how much of it there is in relation to the "real" mail, how it wastes resources, why and how it shows up unsolicited in your mailbox. Having your kid help take the junk mail to the paper recycling bin will enable them to make a connection with what you're teaching them by putting their hands on the advertising waste.

2. Limit commercial TV time at home; mute the commercials. A 1982 study confirmed that before the age of eight, children could not, on their own, distinguish between a commercial and a television show. Marketers know this and take advantage of the fact. Teach children the difference. Play "spot the commercials."

3. Critique commercials and advertising together. After your child has mastered the "spot the commercials" game, talk about what the commercial is selling, its persuasion, how the it makes them feel, how it entertains and makes them remember the product with slogans and catchy jingles. Use a stopwatch to compare how much time is dedicated to commercials and to programming. Dare to flip through a mainstream magazine together and count how many ads there are compared to how much actual content. Are the ads disguised as content? Help them recognize "articles" that are promoting products. Examine what kind of ads are in certain kinds of magazines. Which TV channels and magazines have more advertising than others?

child-development research that is essential to parents, educators, and the general public is not available because it's private data, called proprietary research. Toy companies like Nintendo, which runs at least 1,500 kids per week through their research center, understand more about kids and their culture than do the psychologists whom parents hire to help them understand their ten-year-old Johnny's fascination with playing Gunstar Super Heroes alone for hours on his Game Boy. Stephen Kline said in a 1997 interview, "Some very very important observations about the fate of childhood in the increasingly globalized consumer culture are simply not open to examination and debate!"

The advertising industry overall has not only increased its kid-aimed advertising, but private research-based marketing methods have changed to become more insidious, too; the toy industry is known for teaching its members how to market to "pre-moral youth," thusly taking advantage of the very innocence of the children without whom they'd have no business. The American Psychological Association (APA) published a statement in 2004 reflecting their view that such advertising efforts are fundamentally unfair because of young children's comprehension of the nature and purpose of television advertising, and that action to protect young children from commercial exploitation is warranted.

In addition, the February 20, 2004 Report of the APA Task Force on Advertising and Children makes the following recommendation: "We recommend that television advertising be restricted during programming directed to or seen by audiences primarily composed of children 8 years of age and under." Seven pages of the nine-page report call for and explain why there is a critical need for more child-psychology research that can be used for the public good: the field of psychology has provided sparse data to inform public discussion of the qualitative and quantitative changes in advertising that targets children; there is a need to understand how children comprehend and are influenced by new media advertising because "many of the traditional boundaries between advertising and entertainment content are blurred in new and unique ways;" there is a striking absence of psychological research on children's advertising that considered issues of gender, race, ethnicity, and culture given that much advertising is highly segmented along these target audience lines; media literacy research done by psychologists will assist in the development of effective media literacy curricula for students at different grade levels; psychologists need to engage in research on the impact of advertising and commercialism in schools; and "psychologists [must] weigh the potential ethical challenges involved in professional efforts to more effectively advertise to children."

It is impossible to protect all children from commercial exposure; advertising is reaching children in ways that we parents are unaware of. Yet, it is incumbent on us to help our children resist being unduly influenced by advertising pressures.

4. Fight back against pester power! When your kid starts with the begging, make him/her perfectly aware of what they are doing and why. Model behavior of not buying a product just because you saw it advertised. Or do an experiment: before a request turns into begging, buy something together that your kid wanted after seeing it on a commercial. Ask if the something you bought lived up to your kid's expectations. How long were they happy with the new thing before wanting another new thing? Ask your kid if they think the commercial told the truth about the product. After repeating this experiment with Emma-Joy a few times, the results were nothing short of amazing. Disappointed by all but one product, she'd firsthand felt misled by junk-food and toy commercials aimed at her.

5. While out shopping together, explain why you choose to buy one product over another (and one store/shop/market over others), why you don't buy some products at all (teach the difference between want and need), and why people choose to buy (or get for free) used things over buying them new. In addition to media education opportunities, these kinds of conversations plant seeds of personal finances/economics, environmental awareness, and health consciousness.

6. Make "Buy Nothing Day" a family holiday to celebrate together! In the United States, Buy Nothing Day is observed on "Black Friday," the day after Thanksgiving, known for being the biggest shopping day of the year. Remember that no one was born to shop! Instead, consumers are conditioned to do so. Celebrate by buying nothing, participating in a mall protest, or organizing your own event like a free community meal or coat exchange. Visit www.adbusters.org/bnd/ for more information.

40.

Interview with Rocker Mamas Eileen and Rachael

My mama friend, Tracey, told me about a mom-band compilation CD being put together. I was really curious to find out what a mom-band CD would be all about, so I got in touch with Eileen Alden, who's involved with the project. In addition to filling me in on the CD project, she also told me about her band, Placenta, and other on-fire projects she has her irons in. My mind started reeling with a ton more questions than I had already asked her, so it turned into this interview with not only her but also Rachael Huang, one of Eileen's bandmates in Placenta.

Before getting in touch with Eileen, I had no idea there had been a recent explosion of the mom-band phenomenon. Yes, I'm a mom, and yes, I play music, but I'm not one to pay much attention to the mainstream press or to frequent new websites. So it was pretty weird that while this interview was in progress (in September 2004), one of the midwives I work with (who had absolutely no idea that I was in the midst of this interview) happened to mention to me that she had just seen a band called The Mom Band, from Detroit, on TV. She said it was hilarious because they looked like hell and could really wail on their guitars, but what they were wailing were rock versions of kid songs, like a more-obnoxious-than-it-already-is version of "Twinkle Twinkle Little Star."

This particular Detroit mom-band would fall into what Eileen describes in this interview as a category A mom-band while hers, Placenta, falls into category C. Read on to find out what it all really means.

Jessica Mills: *Originally, your band was called The Lactators, then Junkbox, now Placenta. Can you give us some band herstory and how where you're coming from, your personal life experience, informs what doing this band is all about for you?*

Rachael Huang: Three years ago I was living with my two children (Elcy and Tilly) in a twelve-by-twelve room in a friend's house. My ex had quit his job and moved away to escape paying child support. I had been "let go" from my job because the boss's son didn't like me. I had a broken arm. I spent a good deal of time on the now-defunct *Hip Mama* message boards, mostly talking to other single moms, and I thought, *Fuck, it ain't just me.* The system supports deadbeat dads, the system scapegoats single moms, poverty is the norm for single moms. Most men, kid-free or not, have freedom to do what they want, when they want, and women (moms) are left to shoulder the burdens of childrearing, in a society that "eats" its own children while lip-servicing "family values." Isolation, exhaustion, scapegoating, poverty, disenfranchisement, no future, this made my high school mohawk experience seem like stringing daisy chains with the Maharishi. I wondered why people weren't talking in the media about this. I wondered why this huge group of people had no voice at all. I wondered why the media "norm" for women was Britney Spears. And I knew it was all fodder for punk rock.

So I decided to start an all-mom punk band. I found people through *Hip Mama* and Craigslist, and the old fashioned way—by talking. We became The Lactators, went through a lot of stuff that other bands go through (change-up in members, good gigs, bad gigs), but the other songwriter in the band really wanted it to be a pop-punk, borderline-joke-band response to the scrapbooking suburban moms she knew through her son's playgroup. I felt confined by the genre, and by the "oh-we're-moms-complaining-about-being-moms" aspect, so I quit, and the band split up.

In 2003, at the Big Shut Down the System war protest the day after The Village Idiot illegally invaded a sovereign country to pillage her oil fields, I ran into Kjetset (ex-Lactator), and we talked. Shortly thereafter, she suggested we start playing again, but not with the intention of re-forming The Lactators. In fact, we wanted a non-gender-specific name, because we wanted to be judged on the merit of our rock 'n' roll, not on being a "girl band" (Avril Lavigne having replaced Britney as the new norm for "girl rocker"). Junkbox. We played a couple gigs with our new, fabulous drummer, Mistress Linda, and in January, Appolonia the Mysterious (also an ex-Lactator) became our bassist. Then we realized that we wanted to reembrace the fact that we're moms. It's who we are, it's what we do, it colors every aspect of our lives, and we wouldn't want it any other way.

In what ways do you think it is different being in an all-mom band?

RH: 1. We can't spend a lot of time schmoozing at bars or clubs.

2. We don't have a lot of time to wank off at practice, so we show up ready to go. (I am the band slacker.)

3. We don't have to explain why we can't just hang out at practice or at the bar.

4. The idea of "all-mom" might make people take notice, on a novelty level, but we have to do a good job to keep them interested, and to have them take us seriously as rockers.

How do you manage to play out on average of twice a month on top of everything else you do—practice, work, have children, political involvement?

Eileen Alden: Fear of death? Punk version of supermom syndrome? Everyone asks me that and I have no idea. I just try to do a million things I want to do all at once, and hopefully one or two of them will turn out OK.

RH: Sleep? What's that? Really, it's a running joke. I have two kids, run two businesses (housecleaning and violin lessons), and am in two bands (Placenta and The Whoreshoes, a Bay Area all-female country band). My kids go with me just about everywhere I go, and my day planner is my best friend.

What are your shows like?

EA: We're big on audience participation, some dancing, a lot of inspiration from *Hedwig and the Angry Inch*. Rachael makes the women in the audience chant, "I own my own pussy."

Can you describe your own music?

RH: We do not perform songs complaining about being moms. We do not do cutesy "tweaked" covers like we used to. We perform songs about turning the tables on accepted societal norms of women being objects, of being weak, of being nurturing to assholes who treat us like shit. We have a message of empowerment to women, and to anybody who suffers under the sick, sick dominant societal, hierarchical paradigm, that, really, we all suffer under. And we do it by rockin' our (and our audiences') asses off. We work hard to craft each song into a musical entirety in and of itself. We are a musically tight band; we put on a great show. If you're going to have a soapbox, you might as well play the music so well that people have to listen to the message, instead of tearing apart the messengers.

EA: We have very few musical boundaries (except that I refuse to play any Southern rock), but somehow it all just winds up sounding like "us," whatever that means. When we were calling ourselves Junkbox, we thought it might make sense to say we played junk rock, but we don't know what the fuck it is. We have some songs that are punk rock, some bluesy funk, some hard rock, an acoustic emo-type thing, and a pop song.

RH: Southern rock all the way! Ha ha, not really. I write songs about whatever is going on at the moment in my life. Sometimes I try to reimagine the situation to make me look cool. Sometimes I just tell it like it is. Sometimes, the song won't come out because it's too close. I try to write about simple things, a slice of life (even if it is really weird)—I think Eileen takes on the bigger subjects. Re: Eileen's aversion to Southern rock, just wait, we'll sneak one in.

EA: What comes into our music is lots of emotional content about relationships, society and about being moms. A lot of our songs are about being RE-ALLY PISSED OFF! But they are also sometimes funny and ironic and everything in between.

Mostly I think we try to make the songs match the content of the song. There's this pop song Rachael wrote called "I'm Ugly" and it has a part that goes "la la la la I'm ugly," so it's a Green Day-sounding song with these fucked-up lyrics like, "I'm ugly and I'm stupid, never had any luck with Cupid, maybe if I was thin and pretty, then my life wouldn't be so shitty." That one also has the perverse thing where we enjoy having the audience sing "I'm ugly."

Then there's another one I wrote which is about domestic violence. It's got this kind of Jackie Brown revenge element happening, talking about "You better watch your back muthafucka" and "Bitches bounce back after the beatdown, battered and bruised and used and abused, beware of the women with nothin' to lose," and there's a lot of wailing guitars and Rachael screaming.

Assuming you don't bring the kids to all of your practices and shows, what role do your partners and/or support system play in helping Placenta be able to happen?

EA: Some of our close friends are also fans. We like to call them our band's "doulas." Amanda has come over to kid-watch. Melissa and Catherine ran a daycare for years and they do some kid-watching. Sometimes we just put them in a room with the TV and a box of cereal and tell the older kids to watch the younger kids and let chaos ensue like a white-trash version of *Lord of the Flies*. Just kidding. Sort of.

I've got it the easiest because we perform at my house in the performance room of our studio, but generally we just need all the support we can get. Trying to hook up babysitting can be just a nightmare.

RH: My kids are older, so they stay at home sometimes when we rehearse (10 a.m., Sunday mornings, Church of Rock). Sprint is very supportive by letting them call me in the middle of practice to ask where the pancake syrup is. Or, if they come to practice, they help watch Rock and Zen, Eileen's kids. My ex lives in West Virginia, my family is in Colorado. I have friends, but I try to spread out the requests for help. I piece it together—there isn't a very good support system in this society for single mothers to be able to pursue anything other than crappy jobs, least of all system-skewering rock bands. Honestly, Jay [Eileen's husband] and Ana [partner of Karen, another Placenta band member] are the most helpful, most reliable people for me to lean on to be able to perform, since they are already looking after their own children.

What's the age range of your kids?

EA: I have two boys. Rock just turned five, and Zen just turned two.

RH: Karen and her partner, Ana, have a son, Marcello, eight. My two girls, Elcy and Tilly, are twelve and ten.

What are their lives like? Where are they, what do they do, what are they into while you mamas are working, rocking, and helping change the world for the better?

EA: Mine don't want me to go to gigs. They just want me to stay home with them ALL THE TIME. That might just be a boy/mom thing, I don't know, but they are both in preschool so I'm sure it gets to be a drag when I go to rehearse or to a gig or if I'm working on stuff on the computer. They're just into normal stuff like breaking pieces off of action figures and jumping off of the couch.

RH: E and T are super intelligent, creative, media-savvy, analytical, spiritual human beings. I am constantly amazed at how quickly they can tear apart a media message and figure out the motives behind it. They are very good students in school. They study hip-hop dance, music, and now they want to play soccer outside of school. They have friends, pets, bikes, the usual kid stuff. Elcy is very bookish; Tilly is much more physical. They both meditate, write a lot, cook, make gigantic messes in the abyss known as their room.

What do the band's kids think about their rockin' moms? Are they embarrassed or supportive?

RH: E and T really like Rock and Zen, and they look forward to seeing them when we have band practice. For my kids, it's a way of life. It's one of the things that we do that makes us a family. They are proud (right now; we'll see when the new year starts) of having a mom in a rock band—a mom with pink-blue-green shaved hair. They are very creative and unusual kids, so it's part of each of their identities to be a little "different."

So what's Placenta all about anyway?

RH: Hey, the name... We wanted something that was going to be strong, woman-centered, a little controversial, but not in any way tied to PORN.

EA: Something we'll be working at for the rest of our lives, I'm sure. As an artist, for me, when I became a mother, it was like the lid of the box was opened and I became emotionally reconnected with myself like I hadn't been since I was maybe sixteen, and it doesn't feel like the switch is just going to suddenly turn off or something.

Our band is coming from a mama-activist/mama-feminist view of the world because we're very tuned into the political meaning of being moms and being women, and so naturally we have a punk antiestablishment orientation. What I'm finding is that the mom-bands out there are ranging from A—"I'm tired of changing diapers!" mom-angsty living room bands—to B—women who have been in bands for years who happen to be moms—to C—women who are moms and in bands whose music has a lot of content that comes from being moms because their music is feeding off of who they are.

We are right upfront about being moms and our music reflects that just like it reflects the facts that we are sex-positive women, left-wing, pro-breast-feeding, etc. Our music is personal and that makes it also political because being a mom and a woman is inherently political. So we're in the C category. But we really want to get BEYOND the condescending and patronizing "Mom's got a new hobby!" tone of the mainstream press.

What mainstream press has been taking notice of mom-bands?

EA: Stuff like *The Wall Street Journal*, *People*, CNN, and the *Today Show*. It's weird because at first we were like, "Cool! *The Wall Street Journal*!" Then we looked at each other and we were like, "No one who reads *The Wall Street Journal* is going to like our music!" We're singing, "We are dying a slow death at the hands of the corporation" and we're in *The Wall Street Journal*. Very surreal.

Why do you think that's happening right now? I know there's been an explosion in the mom-made zine scene over the last few years; is the mom-band thing an extension of that?

EA: I think the reason behind the mainstream press is from a lot of really hard work, mainly from Joy Rose and the Mamapalooza festival that she started. Her band is Housewives on Prozac. But I've been down with *Hip Mama* for years, and I give Ariel Gore a huge amount of respect for putting out the flavor that connected hip mom = political mom = artist mom, and Bee Lavender did it with the online version. So I think the mom-bands, whether they realize it or not, get a tremendous amount of support from what other mamas have done and are doing with the mama zines and books.

You trace the explosion, in part, back to Ariel Gore. Her print zine, Hip Mama, *started in 1993, years before the* Hip Mama *online community became really well known. What role has the Internet played? Do you think the Internet has been largely responsible for this popularity explosion? Can you trace what's evolved from* Hip Mama *(zine or website) to what you've gotten yourself involved with and were able to connect with in real life? Has real-life community been created through online community?*

EA: The zine and the online versions of *Hip Mama* are two different things, but I think the zine definitely set the tone for the online version, at least at the beginning. And the online community has definitely enabled real community to happen. Placenta is an example that proves that. But I also don't think it actually *creates* community. It just fast-forwards it. And I think that's particularly true for moms, because if you're a woman who is redefining or exploring womanhood in your life, when you become a mother, you can feel really isolated. You might find yourself looking for some kind of model of motherhood that's different than what you grew up with, or you might feel the pressure of society's standards of motherhood, or you might be trying to reconcile the fact you're a mom with your past abortions. Stuff like that. When you're a mom, you feel like a lot more is on the line when you're struggling to figure yourself out because it's not just about you anymore. You're trying to really get your act really fucking right because you're responsible for someone else. Those kinds of discussions online, at least for me, created deep and powerful connections really fast.

RH: I don't think that any of the bands in the *WSJ* article had anything other than passing knowledge of each other. I look at it this way—we are musicians. My mom is a musician—she sings in the church choir. For a woman her age, in her community, it is a perfectly reasonable musical expression. I am a child of rock 'n' roll—of punk rock. I am a mom and an activist. It simply makes sense for me to pursue rock 'n' roll as a reasonable musical expression. Is it a "scene" for other people in the same boat to do the same thing? I don't think so. Post-*WSJ*-article, the bands have chosen to come together to create some kind of community. Through e-mail, mostly.

Eileen and I met through *Hip Mama*. Karen found Linda via Craigslist. A lot of our equipment and gigs (and song fodder about icky men, I'll admit it) come to us via Craigslist as well.

Is the recent mainstream attention inherently good or bad?

EA: So what if *People* magazine wants our picture. I know if they put our story in there, they'll probably just write something about us with a catchy title like "Women on the Verge of a Nervous Breakdown," and they'll think the song is about housework. But it's about domestic violence. And I'm torn, though, too, because we would like to reach more people. I just don't think the mainstream press is going to be a real help. People will find out about us more from just word of mouth or through talking to people like you who are already on the same page.

You're working on a compilation CD of mom-bands. Is this project coming out of the network of mom-bands called The Mamalition? What exactly is The Mamalition anyway and how did it form?

EA: The Mamalition is just a name for this loose association of mom bands who have been talking to each other since the mainstream media blitz started. Part of it is the bands who did the 2004 Mamapalooza event in NYC, part of it is other mom-bands who I've been connecting with to try to get people together. I see it as a real artist collective where we could really make a huge statement as a group. So the compilation CD is part of that.

I'm trying to get together with other mom-bands who own the fact they are moms and who want to put a strong musical vision and artistic integrity out there to support the idea that what moms have to say is fucking important. So I want to use some of the publicity to spin things toward a message that's not condescending toward moms or part of a self-deprecating image that the mom-bands are a joke. I want the mom-bands involved to own their part in the group. I don't want to run the show. I want it to be a collective.

Tell us about your label, Soulmine Records. Does it pay the bills or do you have to work elsewhere?

EA: The label usually creates more bills than it pays for, but I also suck at being tight with money. Right now I probably have two credit-card collectors calling, but fuck them. I need to make T-shirts. It comes and goes in cycles with the label, but I will never let it die, so help me. I'm actually really psyched right now because we have an amazing compilation CD coming out in September called *Live Sound Warriors*, which is all live house music performed using old-school gear, no laptops or records or DATs or MP3s, just live performances. It's the most raw form of house music, like back in the day. So that's totally exciting. I pay bills by doing research on woman- and minority-owned investment managers. And we have a P.A. system that we rent out for parties.

You can see, hear, and read more about Placenta at www.placentamusic.com, and check out Eileen's record label at www.soulminerecords.com. The Mom-Aid 2005 compilation CD came out in September 2005 and features sixteen tracks by sixteen bands from across the United States and one from the United Kingdom. It's powerful, catchy, pop, punk, alt rock, slow grooves, and more. The songs cover topics relevant to moms and the people who love them. The proceeds from the CD go to UNICEF to aid the victims of the 2004 Indonesian tsunami.

41.

Mommy's Alone Time Starts
on the Greyhound

The last time I rode the Greyhound was September 1999. That time, I was four months pregnant and heading to Richmond, Virginia, to meet up with Citizen Fish for their U.S. tour. Over five years later, I climbed aboard again. This time, I was dashing back to be at work on Monday morning at the birth center after a weekend in Cocoa Beach with five-year-old Emma-Joy and Daddy Ernesto.

I could have just spent the weekend at home alone and saved the $39.50 bus ride, but why? This way I got a weekend warrior-style vacation with my famdamily fun troupe, and since they were staying in Cocoa Beach for four more days, I got plenty of wondrous alone time, too.

Heading to the Cocoa Greyhound station, already guessing I might miss the bus, I realized that just getting there and onboard was just as much part of the experience as the bus ride itself. I had gotten the station's address from Greyhound's automated phone service and Ernesto thought he remembered where it was from having grown up around there. But his dad told us he thought it was damaged in the previous season's hurricanes and that it was temporarily located elsewhere. We drove in frustrated circles for a while, even after having stopped to ask three different people if they knew where the station was. When we finally found it, it was five minutes past the scheduled departure time. It looked like a bombed-out, abandoned building and there was no bus in sight.

A call to Greyhound yielded me some guy's advice to wait there twenty-five minutes and if the bus didn't arrive by then, to call back and they'd be able to give me the bus's time status then. Ernesto said that sounded completely retarded, so I called them back to ask if this abandoned shithole was even the current Cocoa station. I got a woman this time and she told me no, that it's temporarily at an Exxon station about four state roads away.

Huh? Why'd they tell me, twice even, to be at the old station?

By now, I'm thinking I've really missed the bus. We had to stop twice to ask for directions, but finally found it. And there was no bus in sight, again. The Exxon clerk told me there is no 8 p.m. bus, that there's only a 9 p.m. bus.

Huh? Why did the Greyhound schedule tell me 8 p.m. all along?

Weird, but lucky. Not only had I not missed the bus, but I also had about a half-hour to eat some pizza with my sweethearts before I dogged it home. I enjoyed every minute, etching their images and imprinting their voices in my mind, feeling lucky and in love.

I wasn't done with my eggplant pizza roll when Ernesto spotted the bus pull in a few minutes early. I dashed through the store to grab my backpack from the car. The clerk told me I could relax because the driver always comes in before departing. I still went out to grab my backpack and it's a good thing I did, because from across the football field-length parking lot, I saw the door being pulled closed.

Scramble! No time to say goodbyes, I took off, until I heard my girl calling for me to come back to kiss her. And of course, I did, but so fast, I think I missed her mouth. I ran as fast as I could and the driver let me on, telling me I could pay up at the station stop in Vero.

Will someone who's involved with the bus arrangements please get the story straight? Or like I said before, is just catching the bus where the story actually starts?

Not many minutes into the trip, some guy a few rows back complained, "Somebody's ass rotten!" It must be true what they say about a rat not being able to smell its own hole. I'm not bothered in the least by the rot. I settled in with the fifth anniversary issue of *Clamor* and was only bothered by the strange, underwater gargling sound (or was it a neglected, crackling bus speaker?) that I soon discovered was a guy's snoring.

In Vero, the driver said we'd be taking a fifteen-minute lunch break when we got to Ft. Pierce. It was already 10 p.m., so I guess that's why laughter burst out all around the bus. That's when the woman next to me took the opportunity to let me know what she thought about the driver. I couldn't make out most of her French West Indies English, but I did make out "reckless driving," "swerving," "he got lost," and "not on time." I tried to show a little empathy, but I really didn't care. I thought he was driving just fine.

At our fifteen-minute break in Ft. Pierce, another woman became dissatisfied with the driver. He couldn't give her any helpful information about what stop in

Miami would be closest to her hostel in South Beach. So she asked me. I was a little more helpful, but not enough for her to be able to make a sound decision. I wondered if I should ask her to get off at my stop so I could get my car from home and take her there myself. Before I could decide, another woman offered me her lighter when she witnessed my match-lighting efforts repeatedly blow out. So far, only interactions with other women. That was good. The guys were all pretty much creepy.

Back onboard, rolling south on I-95, right around West Palm Beach, a bump jolted me to attention and a quick crunch sound had me whirling around to try to see what the fuck just happened. A damn car hit the bus! Or was it the other way around? Whichever way it was, I knew we were fine, so I started rooting for whoever was in the car to be fine, too. Evidently, they were because they kept going.

Remember the worried woman? You should have seen her silent panic attack, her eyes bulging, and the way she grabbed at her chest. She was silent when she caught me staring at her, but her thoughts were screaming at me, "I told you so!" I still didn't care. We were all fine.

And so began the peanut-gallery commentary. Just like the majority of my fellow passengers busted out laughing at the driver earlier over a silly little thing, the majority of them this time whipped out their cell phones to urgently tell someone about our interstate hit and run. I learned a lot from their frantic conversations: there'd already been a flat tire in Tallahassee and something else in Jacksonville, and the driver got lost in Cocoa, driving around in circles for a while. (Huh? Even the driver hadn't been informed about the Cocoa station's closure and temporary relocation!) From what I gathered, it sounded like I missed a pretty funny episode of the driver trying to explain to the passengers, "I know it's around here somewhere. I just know I can find it; I grew up eighteen miles from here."

The worried woman wanted me to borrow a cell phone so I could call Greyhound to complain, on her behalf, for what she thought was the driver's incompetence. She topped off her argument with, "And I haven't seen him eat anything all day!" I pretended I didn't understand and told her to relax, that he was at least giving an appearance of handling the most recent incident appropriately. After all, he'd pulled over, called both the cops and the company to report the accident, and had all of us fill out a chintzy passenger report of the accident for Greyhound.

After that, she kept glancing my way, still complaining. I wondered why, out of all the other passengers available to her, she'd picked me? Couldn't she see I didn't care? I was trying to read, for once without a kid to take care of, and didn't want to get caught up in looking after her wound-up ass.

We sat and sat on the side of I-95 and the cops eventually got there. Some more sitting and sitting, and we eventually got back on the road. When we finally made it to West Palm Beach, the worried woman switched seats away from me. Good riddance.

Another hour and we finally made it to my final Hollywood destination. I decided against waking the woman who needed to get to South Beach to offer her a ride with me. It was already 3 a.m.

What takes three hours by car took six hours on the bus. I didn't mind, though. And all the Greyhound schedule and station location misinformation was luckily comical. The ride was beyond a literal trip, I spent less on the ticket than I would have on gas, and I was safer having been in a bus for that interstate swipe than I would have been alone in my car.

I retrieved my bike that I had locked up there at the Young Circle bus stop beforehand and pedaled home through the not-quite totally empty downtown streets, but empty enough to give me a prelude of what I'd feel the next four days—just me, mama—free. I breathed it all in deep with each push of the pedal and felt more than fine.

42.

Discipline Notes:
Communication Is #1

The #1 trait of a healthy family is the ability to communicate and listen. Good communication is hard; you have to get comfortable with strong emotions and be willing to talk about anything. Just like any other healthy exercise, becoming a better communicator takes time and practice. Alongside Emma-Joy's emerging voice, mine grew and changed as well.

1. USE NONVIOLENT COMMUNICATION. Nonviolent communication matches nonviolent discipline. Practicing it and getting good at it is like learning a new language; it forces you to consciously reframe your feelings into words that will reflect respect, cooperation, and compassion instead of coercion. Beyond just words, nonviolent communication is all about attitude, belief, and demeanor. It includes stating your observations, feelings, needs, and requests. Nonviolent communication uses "I" statements instead of "you" statements: "I feel frustrated because I need help," instead of "You frustrate me because you don't help me." Tone of voice is everything; be aware of yours and make your child aware of theirs. Kid giving you 'tude? Invite them to have another chance: "Rewind. Start again." Don't verbally attack your child into good behavior. Don't raise your voice, asking, "What did you do?!" and expect to get a 100% honest answer. Tones like that invite defensiveness. Poor, not necessarily violent, communication blames, shames, accuses, calls names, threatens, commands, lectures, warns, compares, coerces, is sarcastic, prophesies or evokes martyrdom, guilt, or fear. This kind of poor communication might yield a reluctant offer of help from a child, but not until after s/he has mentally focused on defending themselves. Another example of poor communication with a child can happen during an intense discussion. Generally speaking, be-

cause kids need it to be lighter, they will change the subject and start talking about butterflies any second to get out of the intense discussion. When this happens, be willing to let go because your kid needs you to. When Emma-Joy used to do this, I at first thought she was just being clever and dismissive. But then I paid closer attention and realized that the way I was talking to her was just too much for her to process and I needed to back off.

2. PRACTICE ACTIVE LISTENING. Don't accuse your kid, "You're not listening!" You know darn well they *can* hear you. Stop to ask yourself if you might be speaking in such as a way as to cut off communication; that is, speaking in such as way that doesn't invite you to be listened to. A parent needs to model "listening" in order to be "listened to." While kids explore, listen, don't instruct. Show rather than tell. Be quiet long enough to hear their pure, honest, and heartfelt feelings. Show them that there are adults who listen and who take them seriously. Don't take your child's outbursts personally. They're really not about you. Harsh words, tantrums, storms of emotion, and other outbursts are simply communication. Learn to listen between the lines. Is this outburst "My blood sugar is too low!" or is this "I'm so tired I can't admit that I am!" or is this "It sucks I can't get what I want/need right this very minute!" After you've gotten good at actively listening to your child and hear what they're *really* saying, help them learn more acceptable behavior than flipping out and having outbursts. For example, if your four-year-old flips out because her baby sister's crying overstimulates her, help her learn how to cope by showing her how to use earplugs or listening to headphones in her room.

3. BE SELF-AWARE AND TAKE RESPONSIBILITY. Parents need to be aware of their own problems and tensions that they are bringing into the relationship with their child. Parents should acknowledge that their own attitudes and beliefs might be contributing to a problem. If Emma-Joy says we are arguing because of me (putting all the blame on me), I say it's both of us instead of putting all the blame on her—doing this accepts part of the responsibility for the argument. Sometimes, parents might need to give themselves a timeout, like in the bathroom or anywhere else where you can be alone for a little while. Explain your feelings to your child, what you were feeling to make you need to take a timeout, and why you needed one. Being self-aware means you can catch yourself before you lose your cool and gives you a little warning, "OK, I'm feeling frustrated and am about to lose my patience. Give me a second." When a parent is self-aware and can acknowledge a weakness that is making it difficult for them to act just and right towards their child, they should seek help.

4. DEVELOP A THICK SKIN. Get over your concern for your image in public—it can affect your actions towards your kid. You can't let yourself care what other people's perceptions are about how you handled a particular situation that they witnessed; chances are they have no idea about what variables are at play. Don't buy into other's view of a situation. Be aware that criticisms of your parenting will affect your confidence and self-esteem and fuel insecurity. Be more concerned about your child's welfare. Lose your pride so you don't risk damaging the trust you have with your kid. Trust yourself over another parent who you see bullying or exerting illegitimate authority or their elder status; be confident that there's no need to survive parenting a free-child by conforming, by changing how you do things in public versus private. And when you see another parent having a difficult time, for example, with a melting-down kid in public, be charitable and nonjudgmental.

> A NONVIOLENT COMMUNICATION
> TECHNIQUE FOR PARENTS
>
> 1. Stop reacting impulsively.
> 2. Take deep breaths.
> 3. Recognize your frustration.
> 4. Talk out how you are feeling in your head.
> 5. Get to source of problem through empathy with child.
> 6. Respond with cool head and loving way.

5. TEACH EMOTIONAL INTELLIGENCE. Reflect your feelings, reflect your child's feelings. Build empathy. Tell your kid how you feel: "I love you so much, it really upsets me when we argue." Validating feelings ("It's OK to be angry, but not OK to hurt me or yourself") without shame or bad feelings towards your child shows respect, and, at the same time, sets a legitimate boundary. Children need to hear the names of feelings and the names of desires because they often can't figure those out for themselves. Teaching this is the beginning of emotional intelligence. Encourage your child to tell you how something makes them feel. Genuinely acknowledging their feelings (and in turn, telling kids how what they said or did makes you feel) shows them you are not only a parent, but also an individual person. Kids resent when their show of emotions and feelings are met with lack of emotion and feelings, or worse, when they are dismissed as invalid or ridiculous or criticized. Sharing feelings builds mutual empathy and respect, a foundation to take with them out in the world—reflecting how their actions impact others and world, in positive and negative ways.

6. VALIDATE YOUR CHILD'S "ALTERNATIVE REALITY" COMMUNICATION. When you communicate to your child that you need her to pick up her art supplies from the middle of the living room floor, but you are met with "But if I clean up, my stuffed animals will be hungry because the colored pencils are their feast," give respectful credit for her creativity. "Oh, well, then clean up their leftovers when they are done eating, OK?" Doing so will validate her. If

A TEN-POINT CHEAT SHEET FOR GOOD COMMUNICATION

1. Be extra-aware of your own mood to prevent overreacting and calling out orders.
2. Ask for help instead of giving orders.
3. Be calm in your voice, not urgent.
4. Speak so kids can listen.
5. A loving and tender tone is better for serious moments.
6. Learn to say "I'm sorry."
7. Explain why you were "off" after an "off" time.
8. Be a good and fair negotiator.
9. Hear your own thoughts by listening to your kids'.
10. Listen closely and you will hear your children honestly express their needs.

it's really important to get cleaned up right then, explain why it needs to be done: "I'm afraid that if it stays there, it can get stepped on and broken or cut someone's foot." When you kid then says the pencil is her imaginary dog's bone and that's why it's on the floor, suggest your kid act like a dog and pick up "the bone" in her mouth and "bury it" in the drawing box. Also, kids will learn by example. Help each other clean up. Or help her assert her independence—let pickup be her idea.

43.

Playing Mamapalooza 2005

I'd originally gotten in touch with Soulmine Records' Eileen Alden about a mom-band compilation CD she was putting together called *Mom-Aid*, the proceeds of which were going through UNICEF to aid the victims of the 2004 Indonesia tsunami (see "Interview with Rocker Mamas Eileen and Rachael"). Since my band Molotonic contributed a song to the CD and I'd interviewed Eileen and Placenta bandmate Rachael Huang for one of my *Maximum Rock N Roll* columns, I thought it would be great for us to meet in person if we ever had the chance. I made the chance happen the next time I found myself in the Bay Area, and met up with Eileen and Rachael for a couple of hours.

We hit it off pretty well, and by the end of my visit, I had been invited to play with them at the Mamapalooza NYC show in May 2005, an annual nationwide cultural event honoring moms in music and art, to which Placenta wanted to bring a more subversive presence. (Their lead guitar player had finals and wouldn't be making it.) I'm by no stretch of the imagination a guitar player. The guitar lessons I'd taken when I was twelve were long forgotten, except for one song, "Dust In the Wind," and I don't think the one time I did play guitar in a band counts; it was a Bikini Kill cover band for Halloween 1999 when I was pregnant with Emma-Joy.

Nonetheless, the absurdity alone made the invitation even more appealing to me. The initial appeal of course being my already-established love of their band, Placenta, and a desire to join them in bringing some subversive presence to a "festival" that was looking to be a questionable, executively produced, mainstream-media convention. I promised I'd try my best to learn enough guitar in a month's time to pull it off and if I didn't feel confident after that time, I'd let them know so they'd still have a month to wrangle someone else to do it.

A month of trying got me not even able to strum through the Ramone's "Sheila is a Punk Rocker" due to my un-cooperative fingers' inability to make a complete F chord. Realizing that the Ramones' songs are definitely more simple than most of Placenta's, I told the Placenta mamas thanks for inviting me, but there was absolutely no way I'd be pulling it off. They came back and said no sweat, they'll have Eileen's husband play guitar instead, and why don't I still come along and play sax.

Hell, yeah! They pony expressed their latest practice recorded to CD so I could start coming up with sax parts for the four songs they'd be playing at the show. The absurdity reached new heights and I was practically giddy with excitement. *Placenta hasn't ever even had a sax player and I'm being handed over four songs to saxify?* My guitar dreams of dread and embarrassment quickly turned to the good kind of anxiety you get when faced with a challenge that, given a lot of enjoyable, concentrated effort, you know you'll be able to pull off.

I snapped to and set about a practice schedule for myself. In hindsight, it was too ambitious (as usual) and didn't resemble reality in terms of available free hours in my busy working mama days. But I got a necessary and well-timed break when Ernesto finished his finals and decided that he and Emma-Joy would take off on a week-and-a-half daddy-daughter team road trip. I tightened my self-assigned practice schedule and even passed on much-needed nights out to see the Collapsing Lungs and Southern Flaw. I just worked my shifts at the birth center and came home to play.

It was a hella good time. (Though I did start to miss me sweeties around day three.) And perhaps the most entertaining part about the Placenta sax seclusion was the one "band practice" we had via phone with them in Oakland, California, and me in South Florida—me playing my little handheld recorder into the phone receiver so they could hear what I'd come up with so far, recorded with their CD playing in the background. They said it was perfect and we proceeded to sing and hum more ideas to each other, and that was perfect, too.

The next time we practiced was the first time we met up with each other on W. 24th Street in Manhattan. I had flown there the day before and was staying with my friends Luci and Scott in Brooklyn, who helped hook us up with a place to practice for an hour before the show. I was sweating it, thinking we needed at least two hours. But things went so well, like we had always played together, and we only needed forty-five minutes.

We dashed back to Manhattan and proceeded to enter a celebrity hangout (according to my local friends) bar world called the Cutting Room, owned by some famous actor dude I'd never heard of, full of major mainstream parenting magazine sponsorship and a self-promoting Mom Rock Movement press conference. My natural buzz killed, reality hit me that the event was going to be less of a show and more of a showcase for some sort of discovery game, playing to win industry sponsorship and press coverage instead of playing for fans. I heard the founder-turned-executive producer say to the press something like, *We're here tonight to build Mamapalooza momentum and success, blah, blah, blah* countless times throughout the evening. It was a corporate-style schmooze fest. Far from a rock show environment, important so-and-sos and sponsors sat at tables, ordering food and talking shop, networking, promoting product, and maintaining respectable wine buzzes. There were far more press people and performers than actual audience members. I'd never been to a music festival where there wasn't a real audience. Where were the normal people who come to rock shows for fun? Were they even invited, or were they scared off by how the festival had been promoted? Even Whoopi Goldberg must have thought it was too weird to hang out at because she came in the front door, saw the media-heavy scene, asked what was going on, turned right around, and left.

Days beforehand, Rachael, Eileen, and I had brainstormed via phone and e-mail trying to come up with independent media folks we could try to pack the "press conference" with. Some did come, and one in particular, Vikki—for whom we got a press pass for *Hip Mama* zine—was bold enough to question the organizers and other participants, "Where are the people of color?" (Out of nineteen performers/bands totaling over 100 participants, there were only three individuals of color, one of whom was playing in Placenta.) And, "If this is a 'movement' building event for mothers, why is there no organized childcare?" Vikki's questions received a rather predictably lame response. Something along the lines of, "Well, everyone is invited to get involved," which completely dismissed necessary outreach efforts and ignored addressing race and class barriers.

The show itself ranged from painful to full-on fun. Though painful (read: Guinness and free wine required!) reigned, there were three other bands (besides Placenta of course, heh heh) that were heavy-hitters and totally rocked: Frump, the Mydols, and the Mothers (from Derby, United Kingdom).

> ### RACHAEL'S MOM-SONG
>
> When I was younger, I danced in the mosh pit
> Now, when I think of it, I go to the toilet
> When I was younger, I used to slam dance,
> Now if I jump at all, I have to pee my pants
> Up, Down, Up, Pee
> Up, Down, Up, Pee
> Up, Down, Up, Pee
> Incontinence Pogo!!!
> Up, Down, Up, Pee
> Up, Down, Up, Pee
> Up, Down, Up, Pee
> Incontinence Pogo!!!

There's just so much schtick I can take with songs about telling your kids to eat their damn spaghetti, wearing your stay-at-home-mom fuzzy house slippers instead of your corporate power pumps from the pre-kid corporate job days, and nagging kids to pick up their socks. And even though there's some schtickiness to the three bands I liked, I most certainly can get into a remake of the Ramones' "I Wanna be Sedated" that now demands, "Get a Vasectomy!" and thanks to the Mothers, an early-80s English punk sound that inspired a new dance from Rachael and me, called "The Incontinence Pogo." (We both learned too late that pogo-ing is out until we make a firmer commitment to Kegels exercises.)

As for our ten minutes of the show, we had so much fun playing and I really loved how it sounded. Plus, we were the only band there throwing out free hand-screened and Sharpied shirts between songs, and while introducing and playing songs, raising issues of violence against women, beauty standards, the public school system, and domestic violence.

We were definitely the most colorful and diverse band (racially and multigenerationally), with Rachael's crazy tall bright-green liberty-spiked mohawk, Eileen's multicolored extensions swingin', Jaswho's striking looks and ass-length locks, and Karen (a mother of three daughters, one of whom was in the Yeastie Girlz, and grandma of four, yeah!) wearing her bad-ass '80s checkerboard necktie. Though by comparison I was the most plain looking with only my freshly dyed two-tone hair, I guess I did add my own two cents to the diversity ante since I was the only sax player all evening.

On a personal level, the whole musical experience was nothing like I'd ever done. It's not every day a band who lives over 3,000 miles from you, and who's never had your particular instrument in their band before, invites you to come along just for fun, handing over their songs for you to come up with pretty much anything you want—and like it!

But on a whole mom-band "movement"/explosion/Mamapalooza festival level, the experience was alienating and disappointing. Leave it to the corporate, business-building-minded to take something with consciousness-raising, grassroots movement-building potential and try to mold it into a marketing scheme and sell it.

44.

"Mom, I Wanna Go to Real School!"

I never thought I'd send my girl to school. I remember shrugging off comments like, "Oh, just wait and see how fast she'll grow up. Next thing you know, she'll be in kindergarten." And I can still hear Ernesto saying to his dad, "I'm not sending her to the indoctrinating, crap public school system I went to."

So when we were driving down the road and Emma-Joy announced out of the blue, in a matter-of-fact tone, "I'm not going back to the co-op skool; I want to go to real school," I was caught off guard. I should have known by then that just because I had my parental sights set on a certain plan, that didn't mean it would happen. There are greater forces at work than just my own idealistic desires; five-year-olds are great forces unto themselves.

Befuddled, I asked, "But why? I thought you liked our co-op skool." She evidently had been thinking about this skool-versus-school thing for a while, because she answered, "We play too much at co-op skool. No one teaches me anything. I should be reading by now." I tried to explain the skool's unschooling philosophy: "The idea is that you're allowed to explore whatever you want and the teachers will help you learn about whatever you're interested in." Without missing a beat, she exclaimed, "That's the stupidest thing I've ever heard of! Why can't the teachers just teach me what I should know?"

I was crushed. And silenced.

I still hadn't thought of any response before she asked, "Well?"

"OK, fine," I conceded, "Daddy and I will talk with you more about it together. I'm sure you can go to kindergarten if you want to. But remember when you wanted to learn about snails and I took you to the library to get books about snails, and we looked on the computer to find all different kinds of snail pictures, and we went on snail hunts and found snails and made a snail terrarium?"

"Yeah, but I want to go to real school," she said.

No More Skool

Let me rewind a little. The co-op skool to which she referred is the one I cofounded with a handful of other "unschooling" parents I know. (See the "Cofounding the Village Cooperative Skool" chapter.) We met constantly for six months before we opened our doors in order to hash out all the logistical and philosophical details. To say it was hard work is an understatement. It was hard, fun, exhausting, constant, exciting, never-a-dull-moment, imaginative, nerve-wracking, dirty, beautiful, and peaceful work.

We operated as a collective, developed a general daily routine, created a stable environment by renting an affordable classroom space at a Unitarian Universalist church on five acres, let the kids make the rules as they were needed, and responded to their struggles with each other by teaching them conflict-resolution skills. We held skool four days a week and maintained a ratio of six to eight kids to one or two adults on any given day. Some days were practically magical, while a few others felt like a root canal *sans* Novocaine.

What it came down to for my daughter, I think, is that there just weren't enough kids, structure, or challenge. She and I are quite different in that department. I thrive with little structure, but it makes her unravel. She thrives in a structured environment, but it strangles me. Skool wasn't meeting her needs and she was bored.

I decided to quit busting my ass over something that wasn't working for her. After all, it was her education. And just because she'd be going to school didn't mean she'd stop learning at home and out in the world with us.

But I wasn't looking forward to the early bedtimes and wake-up times that would now be necessary, the uniforms, the Pledge of Allegiance, the standardized tests, the state curriculum, and the lessons about illegitimate authority, punitive punishments, and oppressive rules and policies. I was really uneasy about how my girl would—or wouldn't—adjust to all these changes. I was worried about how Ernesto and I would adjust to them, too. I hadn't dealt with them so well when I had been a public high school teacher a decade earlier.

Doing Our Homework

After weeding through the Broward County public school options, we finally decided to send her to a brand-new charter school that promised to offer curricula in a multicultural context. We did our homework to make sure the school wasn't going to be run by some for-profit business like Charter Schools USA, whose board of directors reads like a who's-who list of Republican Party speech writers and fundraisers.

We liked that the charter was instead held by a nonprofit group of educators who said they were fed up with the way things were operating in the traditional public schools. We also liked that it was bike-riding distance from home, that the maximum enrollment for the school was 125 students (grades K–5), and that the student population itself was multicultural. (It's rarely anything other than diverse in South Florida, except at private schools.) Although the classrooms were very small, I was excited that they were promising smaller numbers of students in each class, two-full time teachers for the kindergarten class and a Waldorf-ish kindergarten approach.

Our first experience, two weeks before the first day of school, started out on a punk rock note. Ernesto took Emma-Joy in for the requisite testing so the school could determine her "school readiness." In an attempt to get Emma-Joy to warm up to her and cooperate, the tester resorted to flattery, "My, what a pretty flowered skirt you're wearing." Still not getting anything from my girl, she leaned in closer, "And what's this on your shirt? Harum Scarum? And a pentagram?" At this point, the tester's voice trailed off, she leaned back and gave a little nervous fidget to the "I Love Jesus" key holder around her neck. Emma-Joy then proceeded to pass the test with flying colors. She had been asked to identify shapes, colors, numbers, upper and lower case letters, and personal information such as her birthday, address, and phone number. Unschooling thus far had apparently served her well by public school readiness standards. A proud dad, Ernesto left the school with Emma-Joy, certain that her outfit had made the school organizers happy about their uniforms-required dress code.

The first day came, and our girl woke up early, eager to go to school. Given her history of being hesitant in any new situation with strangers, I anticipated needing to give her a little coaxing into the room. I couldn't have been more wrong. Still twenty feet from her classroom door, she sprinted into the classroom without looking back to blow me a kiss, let alone even say goodbye. She was already sitting on the floor among her classmates by the time I reached the door to poke my head in to say goodbye. But before I could, the teacher was shooing me away with, "Bye, mom." So much for the classic teary-eyed kid on her first day of school; the tears were all mine.

The night after the second day of school, walking past the bathroom, I heard Emma-Joy mumble a few lines of the Pledge of Allegiance while in the bath. I

STUDENT RIGHTS AND THE PLEDGE

Under the First Amendment of the U.S. Constitution, children may not be compelled to say the pledge. States that require children to recite the pledge do so in violation of U.S. Supreme Court precedent. For details, see www.firstamendmentcenter.org/speech/studentexpression/topic.aspx?topic=pledge.

poked my head in and casually asked, "What's that you're saying?" She said, "You know what it is." I told her, "Yeah, you're right. I was just wondering if you knew." She replied, "It's just some stupid prayer we have to say at school and I don't even believe in God." Stifling my giggles and feeling validated, I ran to tell Ernesto what she had just said. Two reasons for us opposing the pledge in schools are that it is a tool of nationalistic indoctrination and seems too close to being a prayer. He, in turn, ran to the computer to look up the state statutes governing the pledge in school. He found just what he was looking for—that no child is required to say the pledge and that in Broward County, this right to opt out was required to be posted in each classroom—and was armed for battle if she ever reported being forced to say it against her wishes. We explained to her that there are lots of things she does have to do to cooperate at school with the teacher and her classmates, but saying the pledge isn't one of them. That, we explained, was her choice and that if she chose not to say it, she was allowed to remain quiet so she wouldn't disturb the others.

On the morning of the third day of school, we had to drag Emma-Joy's ass out of bed. The honeymoon already over, I couldn't help myself from giving her a lame, classic, I-told-you-so: "I told you that you wouldn't like having to get up early in the morning." Of course, this didn't help the situation, but I just couldn't hold my tongue. I am not a morning person, either.

By the fourth day, we were receiving reports that the teacher was "mean" and that she was withholding recess from the kids for not finishing their morning work or for talking too much. It seemed counterintuitive to me to withhold an energy-burning activity when the kids obviously had energy to burn.

When she came home from her fifth day of school with a Shining Star Behavior Report that revealed she had lost a star that week for "talking," I was convinced we had made the wrong choice. A former public school teacher myself, I was surprised to find out that an elementary-level teacher still used a negative-behavior reinforcement program. What was the rationale for giving kindergarteners four stars at the start of each day (they did nothing to earn them), with the threat of taking the stars away for "breaking a rule"? Didn't this supposedly experienced teacher know that kids love attention, even if it meant breaking a rule to get it? Emma-Joy proved this point when she told me, "It's fun to have to go in front of the class and draw a star out of the bag and hand it to the teacher," and, "My friends and I dare each other to take stars out of the bag when the teacher's not looking."

That night at home, Ernesto made up a parody report of the teacher's behavior. On his report, she had lost stars for such things as not letting kids be kids or play on the playground and taking kindergarten too seriously, among others. Our girl made her own parody, a purse full of paper cutout stars she made us draw from all weekend if we said or did something she didn't like.

There were a few other things on the grievance list. One time when Emma-Joy had a stomach ache, the teacher told my girl that she'd lose a star if she didn't "do as the teacher says and stop crying and be quiet"—that really got my mama growl on. With the kids sitting at individual desks and required to raise their hands before talking or getting up for any reason, I felt like the school's website had been misleading. Its kindergarten description promised incentives and materials provided for creative free play, and said that after a gentle welcoming circle, "The remainder of the day features activities presented in a weekly rhythm, including beeswax modeling, watercolor painting, creative movement, cooking, puppet shows, and storytelling. Seasonal festivals and nature outings are woven into this basic framework." None of that description fit how the kindergarten was being run. More unfortunately, Emma-Joy was communicating about her school experience in terms of behavior modification. It's sad to hear your kid say, "Mom, it was a perfect day. I didn't lose any stars, we got to play on the playground, and we didn't have to put our heads down on our desks one time all day." I wondered what exactly the charter school's educators were fed up with in the traditional public schools, because in practice, they didn't seem too different in their approaches to academics or discipline.

After digging around the state statutes and county school-board policy, we gathered enough information to dispute the teacher's methods, and sent a few letters and held conferences with the teacher and school principal. Our actions apparently succeeded in forcing some changes. We did not receive a Shining Star Behavior Report after the first one, and the kids were allowed recess every day.

I'm sure we became "those parents" the school authorities hated to see coming down the hall. The principal once said to me, "You really do your homework, don't you?" The principal probably did cringe when she saw us, but the truth is that we weren't the only ones who spoke up and questioned what the hell was going on with the kindergarten crabapple teacher. There was solidarity among the ranks. And apparently the second teachers in the kindergarten class weren't satisfied either. The first one quit after two weeks. The next one quit after two days. (The rest of the school year was spent with a half-day assistant, instead of two full teachers as promised.)

A month into it, the kinks were getting worked out. Though my girl didn't reveal much about her school experience other than reporting if her teacher had a "mean" or "almost nice" day, she wanted to stick with it. This was most definitely a good thing, as Ernesto and I agreed that teaching her commitment would be a valuable life lesson, that she couldn't just quit after having a bad day, and that working out problems is more responsible than running from them. We wanted her to learn to seek to create change where change is desired.

She was totally into the navy blue and red plaid jumper uniform, and believe it or not, loved doing homework *every* night. (I thought it was too much.) She was excited about her role in the first monthly cultural-showcase program, and designed her own Caribbean clothing. And you should have seen my jaw drop at the first term's awards assembly, where my girl walked away with not only the Most Responsible Kindergartner certificate, but also the engraved plaque award for Most Responsible Student in the entire school. My kid? After the awards ceremony, Emma-Joy asked me what the awards meant. I walked her over to her teacher and asked, "Can you please explain to Emma-Joy what she did to earn these awards? She doesn't know." Her teacher told her that she had come to class every day ready to learn and that she had always completed all her homework and assignments. Emma-Joy walked away very proud of herself, eager to hang her plaque on her bedroom wall.

For her sake, I hope she does continue to get out of school what she wants and that her genuine, burning desire to learn more isn't squelched. I also hope she doesn't learn too much how to bow to authority and just accept the bullshit. There's no telling whether she'll be happy or pissed about us getting involved in things we think need to change. But at least we'll be setting the example that you can stick up for what you think is right.

Resources

Pregnancy and Birth

Active Birth by Janet Balaskas

American Pregnancy Association http://www.americanpregnancy.org

The American Way of Birth by Jessica Mitford

Baby Catcher (www.babycatcher.net) by Peggy Vincent

The Birth Book by William Sears & Martha Sears

The Birth Partner: Everything You Need to Know to Help a Woman Through Childbirth by Penny Simkin

Birth Without Violence by Frederic Leboyer

Birthing From Within by Pam England & Rob Horowitz

Gentle Birth Choices by Barbara Harper

Gentle Birth, Gentle Mothering: The Wisdom and Science of Gentle Choices in Pregnancy, Birth and Parenting by Sarah J. Buckley MD.

Heart & Hands: A Midwife's Guide to Pregnancy & Birth by Elizabeth Davis

Immaculate Deception by Suzanne Arms

In the Way of Our Grandmothers: A Cultural View of Twentieth-Century Midwifery in Florida by Dedra Anne Susie

Ina May's Guide to Childbirth by Ina May Gaskin

A Midwife's Story by Penny Armstrong & Sheryl Feldman

Midwifery Today http://www.midwiferytoday.com

Midwives Alliance of North America http://www.mana.org

Natural Childbirth the Bradley Way: Revised Edition by Susan McCutcheon-Rosegg, Erick Ingraham, & Robert A Bradley

Obstetric Myths Vs. Research Realities: A Guide to the Medical Literature by Henci Goer

The Pregnancy Book by William & Martha Sears

Prenatal Yoga & Natural Birth by Jeannine Parvati Baker

Rediscovering Birth by Sheila Kitzinger

Sisters on a Journey: Portraits of American Midwives by Penfield Chester
Special Delivery by Rahima Baldwin
Spiritual Midwifery by Ina May Gaskin
The Thinking Woman's Guide to a Better Birth by Henci Goer
Wise Woman Herbal for the Childbearing Year by Susan S. Weed.

Breast-Feeding

Breast-Feeding by Mary Renfrew
Breast-Feeding: Your Priceless Gift to Your Baby and Yourself by Regina Sara Ryan & Deborah Auletta
Fresh Milk: The Secret Life of Breasts by Fiona Giles
How My Breasts Saved the World: Misadventures of a Nursing Mother by Lisa Wood Shapiro
Kellymom (Evidence-based information on breast-feeding & parenting issues) http://www.kellymom.com
Le Leche League International http://www.lalecheleague.org.
The Milk of Human Kindness: Defending Breast-Feeding from the Global Market and The AIDS Industry by Solveig Francis.
Money, Milk and Madness: The Culture and Politics of Breast-Feeding by Naomi Baumslag M.D. & Dia L. Michels
Nursing Mothers Companion by Kathleen Huggins
Womanly Art of Breast-Feeding by LLL International

Snacks and Food

Mash and Smash Cookbook by Marian Buck-Murray
My Child Won't Eat! by Carlos González, MD
Pregnancy, Children, and the Vegan Diet by Michael Klaper.
Sugar-Free Toddlers by Susan Watson
Tracking Down Hidden Food Allergy by Dr. William G. Crook
Vegetarian Baby by Sharon K. Yntema
Whole Foods For the Whole Family by Roberta Johnson. Second Edition.
Whole Foods For Kids to Cook by Le Leche League International
Whole Foods for Babies and Toddlers by Margaret Kenda

Baby Care and General Health

The Baby Book: Everything You Need to Know About Your Baby: From Birth to Age Two by William Sears, M.D. & Martha Sears, R.N.
Baby Signs: How to Talk with Your Baby Before Your Baby Can Talk by Linda Acredolo, Susan Goodwyn & Douglas Abrams
Bullying: The Bully, the Bullied and Bystander by Barbara Coloroso
The Fluoride Deception by Christopher Bryson
The Happiest Baby on the Block by Dr. Harvey Karp
How to Raise a Healthy Child In Spite of Your Doctor by Robert S. Mendelsohn
Natural Family Living: The Mothering Magazine Guide to Parenting by Peggy O'Mara

"Plain Talk About Spanking" by Jordan Riak (http://nospank.net)
Smart Medicine for a Healthier Child by Janet Zand, Rachel Walton, & Bob Rountree

Cool Stuff, in General

Becoming the Parent You Want to Be by Laura Davids & Janice Keyser
Children and Feminism by Lee Mackay (Editor), et al.
The Continuum Concept: In Search of Happiness Lost by Jean Liedloff
The Essential Hip Mama by Ariel Gore
Kids: How Biology and Culture Shape the Way We Raise Young Children by Meredith F. Small
Mamaphonic: Balancing Motherhood and Other Creative Acts edited by Bee Lavender & Maia Rossini
The Mommy Myth by Meredith Michaels & Susan Douglas
The Mother-Daughter Project: How Mothers and Daughters Can Band Together, Beat the Odds & Thrive Through Adolescence by SuEllen Hamkins & Renee Schultz
Mother Daughter Revolution by Elizabeth Debold, Marie C. Wilson, & Idelisse Malave
TheMotherhoodProject.org—working to build a mothers' renaissance
Mother Nature: A History of Mothers, Infants, and Natural Selection by Sarah B. Hrdy
Mother Shock by Andrea Buchanan
The Mother Trip by Ariel Gore
Our Babies, Ourselves: How Biology and Culture Shape the Way We Parent by Meredith F. Small
The Price of Motherhood by Ann Crittenden
The Second Shift by Arlie Hochschild
Sexy Mamas: Keeping Your Sex Life Alive While Raising Kids by Cathy Winks & Anne Semans
Mother Warriors Voice, a quarterly newspaper by, for, and about mothers in poverty http://www.welfarewarriors.org

Media

Campaign for a Commercial Free Childhood http://www.commercialfreechildhood.org.
Center for Commercial-free Public Education http://www.ibiblio.org/commercialfree
Center for Screen-time Awareness http://www.tvturnoff.org (home of TV-Turnoff Week)
Commercial Alert http://www.commercialalert.org
Commercialism in Education Research Unit http://epsl.asu.edu/ceru/
Ethical guidelines for advertising to children http://www.bbb.org/advertising/cauguid.html.
Hey Kidz, Buy This Book: A Radical Primer on Corporate and Governmental Propaganda and Artistic Activism for Short People by Anne Elizabeth Moore
Media Education Foundation, a nonprofit organization devoted to media research and the production of resources to foster analytical media literacy. http://www.mediaed.org
National Institute on Media and the Family http://www.mediafamily.org
Out of the Garden: Toys and Children's Culture in the Age of TV Marketing by Stephen Kline
Stay Free! Issue #13, April 1997: "Marketing to Kids" http://www.stayfreemagazine.org

What to do when there's nothing to do by Boston Children's Hospital & Elizabeth Gregg

Art & Creativity

Don't Move the Muffin Tins by Bev Bos
How Children Make Art by George Szekely (Lessons in Creativity from Home to School)

Gender

Beyond Guns and Dolls: 101 Ways to Help Children Avoid Gender Bias by Susan Hoy Crawford
Growing a Girl: Seven Strategies for Raising a Strong, Spirited Daughter by Dr. Barbara Mackoff
My Gender Workbook by Kate Bornstein
X: A Fabulous Child's Story (text available at http://www.trans-man.org/baby_x.html)

Anarchist Parenting

Anarchist parenting email list—http://lists.mutualaid.org/mailman/listinfo/a-parenting
Anarchist Parenting Community on LiveJournal http://community.livejournal.com/anarchoparents/profile
www.infoshop.org/faq/secj6.html
m*A*m*A* (NYC)(mothers alliance for mutual aid) is a grassroots collective of radical mothers and kids http://lists.interactivist.net/mailman/listinfo/mama
RAMBL (Revolutionary Anarchist Mom and Baby League) http://www.ainfos.ca/ainfos336/ainfos05566.html
Radical/Anarchist Parenthood/Motherhood articles http://www.anarcha.org/sallydarity/moms.php

Gentle Discipline

Between Parent and Child by Dr. Haim G. Ginott
Howtoparent.net, parenting with positive discipline
How to Talk So Kids Will Listen & Listen So Kids Will Talk by Adele Faber & Elaine Mazlish
Kids Are Worth It! by Barbara Coloroso
Kids, Parents and Power-Struggles by Mary Sheedy Kurcinka
Liberated Parents Liberated Children: Your Guide to A Happier Family by Adele Farber & Elaine Mazlish
Mothering.com, gentle discipline forum found with "discuss" tab
Noncoersive Discipline by William Glasser
Playful Parenting by Lawrence J. Cohen, Ph.D.
Positive Discipline for Single Parents: Nurturing, Cooperation, Respect and Joy in Your Single-Parent Family by Jane Nelsen, Ed.D., Cheryl Erwin, & Carol Delzer
Raising Self-Reliant Children in a Self-Indulgent World: Seven Building Blocks for Developing Capable Young People by H. Stephen Glenn, Ph.D. & Jane Nelsen, Ed.D.
Raising Your Spirited Child by Mary Sheedy Kurcinka
Siblings Without Rivalry by Adele Faber & Elaine Mazlish

Taking Children Seriously http://www.tcs.ac
Traits of a Healthy Family by Dolores Curran
Unconditional Parenting: Moving from Rewards and Punishments to Love and Reason by Alfie Kohn

Co-Sleeping

The Benefits of Bed-Sharing by Dr. Helen Ball, Sally Inch, & Marion Copeland. Documentary at http://www.platypusmedia.com
The Family Bed by Tine Thevenin
The No-Cry Sleep Solution by Elizabeth Pantley

Education

Chomsky On MisEducation by Noam Chomsky
Creating Learning Communities: Models, Resources, and New Ways of Thinking About Teaching and Learning edited by Ron Miller
Deschooling Our Lives edited by Matt Hern
Deschooling Society by Ivan Illich
Dumbing Us Down: The Hidden Curriculum of Compulsory Education by John Taylor Gatto
Field Day: Getting Society Out of School by Matt Hern
Guerilla Learning: How to Give Your Kids a Real Education With or Without School by Grace Llewellyn & Amy Silver
Have Fun.Learn Stuff.Grow: Homeschooling and the Curriculum of Love by David Albert
Homeschooling and the Voyage of Self-Discovery by David Albert
How Children Learn by John Holt
The Modern School Movement: Anarchism & Education In The United States by Paul Avrich
Parenting a Free Child: An Unschooled Life by Rue Kream
A Primer of Libertarian Education by Joel Spring
Rethinking Schools magazine http://www.rethinkingschools.org
Summerhill School: A New View of Childhood by Alexander S. Neill & Albert Lamb

Websites and blogs

Babble.com
Birthonlaborday.com
Bloggreen.wordpress.com/tag/radical-parenting/
daddy-dialectic.blogspot.com
DiaperFreeBaby.org
Diaperpin.com
EquallySharedParenting.com
Hip Mama zine and HipMama.com
KirstenAnderberg.com
Leahbowe.com/embassy/
Mamaphiles.com
Mamaphonic.com

Mamazine.com
Momsrising.org
Motheranarchy.blogspot.com
Mothering magazine and Mothering.com
Mothersmovement.org
Parentsconnect.com
Piratepapa.blogspot.com
raddadzine.blogspot.com

Essays

"Who's in Control? The Unhappy Consequences of Being Child-Centered" by Jean Leidloff
"Five Reasons to Stop Saying 'Good Job!'" by Alfie Kohn
"On the Care and Feeding of Humans" by Retta Fontana
"Instead of Hitting" by Peggy O'Mara
"Parenting for Youth Liberation, an interview with Cynthia Peters" by Tim Allen
"Raising our kids in the anarchist community," *Off Our Backs*, Jan/Feb 2002

Kids books we love!

Alia's Mission: Saving the Books of Iraq by Mark Alan Stamaty
As Soon As You're Born They Make You Feel Small: Self Determination For Children, anonymous classic collection of liberation articles for kids
Brown is Black is Tan by Arnold Adoff & Emily Arnold McCully
The Color of Dissent, Book One—Jay Moreno (Illustrator) & Nicole Waugh (Editor)
Come Back Salmon by Molly Cone
Crossing Bok Chitto by Tim Tingle
The Daddy Machine by Lynette Schmidt & Johnny Valentine
The Dumpster Diver by Janet S. Wong
Freedom Summer by Deborah Wiles & Jerome Lagarrigue
Girls are Not Chicks coloring book by Jacinta Bunnell & Julie Novak
Girls will be boys will be girls will be..., a coloring book by Jacinta Bunnell & Irit Reinheimer
Have Fries Will Travel!: The Adventures of a Veggie-Powered Car and an Eco-Rap Star by Kathy Dotson (Illustrator) & Linda Hempel
Heather Has Two Mommies
The Honey Jar by Domi (Illustrator) & Rigoberta Menchu
I Can Make a Difference by Marian Wright Edelman
I Love Animals and Broccoli: A Children's Activity Book by Debra Wasserman & Charles Stahler
It's So Amazing: A Book about Eggs, Sperm, Birth, Babies and Families by Robie H. Harris
Kid Blink Beats the World by Don Brown
Let's Talk About Race by Julius Lester
A Little Piece of Ground by Elizabeth Laird
The Librarian of Basra: A True Story from Iraq by Jeanette Winter
The Little Squatters' Handbook by Cordelia & Ziggy

Monsters are Afraid of the Moon by Marjane Satrapi

One Dad, Two Dads, Brown Dad, Blue Dads by Melody Sarecky & Johnny Valentine

Peace, Peace, Peace: A Peace Coloring Book from Around the World by Karan Porter

A Place Where Sunflowers Grow by Felicia Hoshino (Illustrator) & Amy Lee-Tai

Playing War by Kathy Beckwith

Questions and Swords: Folktales of the Zapatista Revolution by Subcomandante Marcos

Selavi, That is Life: A Haitian Story of Hope by Youme Landowne

A Shelter in our Car by Monica Gunning

Should We Burn Babar? Essays on Children's Literature and the Power of Stories by Herbert Kohl (this one's for the parents)

Si, Se Puede!/Yes, We Can!: Janitor Strike In L.A. by Diana Cohn

Skateboard Mom by Barbara Odanaka & JoAnn Adinolfi

Skin Again by bell hooks

Snark Inc.: A Corporate Fable by Brian Gage

A Spoon for Every Bite/Una Cuchara Para Cada Bocado by Joe Hayes & Rebecca Leer (Illustrator)

Stories for Free Children edited by Letty Cottin Pogrebin

The Story of Colors (La Historia de los Colores) by Subcomandante Marcos

The Tree of Life: The Wonders of Evolution by Ellen Jackson

Uncle Aiden by Laurel Dykstra

The Wicked Cool Sustainable Solutions Activity Book for Radical Kids and Everyone! By Becky Johnson

Wild Children: A Zine For Kids Age 0–18 by Peter Lamborn Wilson (Editor)

Online

Anarchist Stories for Children by Stephen DeVoy http://melbourne.indymedia.org/uploads/childrensstories.pdf

Anti-bias Literature for Young Children http://www.KingStreetCoopPreschool.org

The Amelia Bloomer Project http://libr.org/ftf/bloomer.html

IndyKids! http://www.indykids.net

Girlsnotchicks.com

Coop Childcare Form

CHILD CARE REGISTRATION

Parent/ Guardian Information:
    Parent or Guardian Name:_____
    Parent/ Guardian Address and Telephone:_____
    Local Emergency Contact Name and Tel. No.:_____
    Additional Emergency Contact Name and Number:_____
Information About Your Child:
    Name of Child:_____
    Date of Birth:_____
    Blood Type:_____
    Primary Physician: [name and contact information]_____
    Medical Insurance Information: [name, group plan, identification number]__

_____
    Food Preferences and / or Allergies: _____
    Current Medications:_____
    Directions for Administration:_____
    Potty Trained: Yes No [please indicate]_____
    Language Needs:_____
    Favorite Game[s] or Toys: _____
Any other comments:_____
_____
_____

Authorization for Emergency Medical Treatment:
    By signing this agreement, the parent/ guardian affirms that he/she is the person authorized to enter into this agreement, and authorizes the childcare volunteer on duty to seek and obtain emergency medical treatment for my child if circumstances appear to warrant such treatment. The parent/guardian agree to reimburse the person or persons who obtain such emergency medical treatment for any expense reasonably incurred. The parent/guardian agree to indemnify the person or persons who obtain such emergency medical treatment from any and all claims for payment by medical service providers arising from the incurring of reasonable medical expenses._____

Skool Proposals and Brochure

Proposal for The Village Cooperative Skool

Mission Statement:

Because we share a vision for our children's development and education that none of us feel can be met through already-established institutions and traditional models of education, we will strive to provide an engaging environment as to facilitate a community of learners whose exploratory learning needs and desires will be met.

We will achieve this by drawing from various contemporary, progressive, child-centered educational philosophies such as unschooling, free schooling, Waldorf, and Montessori.

I. Who are we?

A. We are a collective who makes decisions by consensus and who will make a commitment to The Village Cooperative Skool in the following ways:

1. Monetary

2. A signed Letter of Commitment

3. Attendance at regularly scheduled meetings

4. Active participation

a. teachers/ facilitators

b. rotation of jobs

B. We will operate 4 days a week from 9:30 a.m. – 2:30 p.m.

C. Age ranges will be from 2 years, 9mos/ pottytrained to 6 years.

D. Facilitator to child ratio will not exceed 1 to 5.

II. Discipline

A. A child can choose not to participate in any group activity.

1. s/he must stay within a caring distance of the facilitators

2. s/he behaves within the Behavior Guidelines, to be drafted by co-op

B. Transgressions will be learning opportunities—no rewards/no punishments.

1. conflict resolution

2. natural consequences

3. cooperation and sharing

4. mutual respect

C. Facilitators will always treat children with respect and never use bodily force as punishment.

III. Snacks and Lunch

A. Snacks provided by the co-op will be healthy, vegetarian choices.

B. Lunches will be brought from home.

C. Each child will have on file a signed Dietary Form that will include allergies and restrictions.

IV. Location Proposal

A. The Unitarian Universalist Church in Fort Lauderdale.

B. Beautiful location on 5 acres.

C. Ideal outside area for nature exploration and organic garden.

D. Satisfies our co-op space requirements (2 classrooms, kitchen and bathroom access, and outside playground and ground labrynth).

V. UU requirements for The Village Preschool co-op
  A. Insurance?
  B. Medical release forms?
  C. General safety guidelines?
  D. What are the restrictions/limitations on the rented space?
  E. Deposits and monthly rent?

The Village Cooperative Skool Brochure

"Trusting in our kids' innate desire to learn."

*Beautiful location	*Affordable
*Child-led learning	*Fun!
*Community Building	*Computers
*Art & Creativity	*Gardening
*Communication Skills	*Healthy Snacks
*Nature Exploration	*Puppets
*Cooperation	*Responsibility
*Singing & Body Movement	*Conflict Resolution Skills

*Mutual Respect with others & the environment

Mission Statement:

Because we share a vision for our children's development and education that none of us feel can be met through already-established institutions and traditional models of education, we will strive to provide an engaging environment as to facilitate a community of learners whose exploratory learning needs and desires will be met.

We will achieve this by drawing from various contemporary, progressive, child-centered educational philosophies such as unschooling, free schooling, Waldorf, and Montessori.

Days, times and location:

Monday, Tuesday, Thursday, and Friday from 9:30 a.m. until 2:30 p.m. at 3970 N.W. 21st Avenue in Ft. Lauderdale, approximately 2 miles north-west of Oakland Park Blvd. West and I-95.

Membership requirements:

  *Monthly tuition, approx. $100
  *3 years old & toilet trained
  *Snack rotation
  *Facilitate one day a week
  *Attend regular meetings
  *Commitment!

Daily routine:

9:00–9:30 = Facilitator meeting and set-up.
9:30–10:00 = Free play
10:00–10:20 = Circle Time
SONGS, BODY MOVEMENT, DISCUSSION, GAMES
10:20–10:40 = Snack
10:40–11:40 = Workshops, centers, activities
11:40–12:40 = Lunch and outside play.
12:40–1:10 = Quiet time
STORY TIME IS OFFERED FOR THOSE WHO WANT TO GET COMFY AND LISTEN OR NAP.
THE ADJOINING "IMAGINATION STATION" ROOM IS AVAILABLE TO THOSE WHO WANT
TO PLAY QUIETLY.
1:10–2:00 = workshops, centers, activities
2:00–2:10 = snack
2:10–2:30 = Clean-up and get ready to go home

Interested in becoming a member?

If so, we're interested in getting to know you! Please take the time to answer the following questionnaire. Cut it on the fold and return it to a member in person or by mail

1. How old is your child(ren) and are they toilet trained?

2. Are you available to be a facilitator at the skool one day a week from 9:30 a.m. – 2:30 p.m.?

3. Why are you interested in becoming a member of The Village Cooperative Skool?

4. Please describe your educational philosophy.

5. Please describe your philosophy of and/or active approach to "discipline."

About Us:

Founded in June 2004 and operating since December 2004, we are a collective of homeschoolers who make decisions by consensus.

We believe in each unique child's need and desire to grow and learn at his/her own pace and in the ways best suited to her/him.

We believe in redirecting behavior and modeling cooperation and mutual respect instead of punishing, coercion and authoritative indoctrination.

We are actively engaging in building a long-standing alternative institution for the educational needs of our children because we are passionate about education being allowed to happen beyond desks, raising hands, busy work, grades, bells, age segregation, curriculums and standardized tests.

References

Pregnancy: Month by Month, Inside and Out

Curtis, Glade B. *Your Pregnancy Week-by-Week*. Tucson: Fisher Books, 1989.
Davis, Elizabeth. *Heart & Hands: A Midwife's Guide to Pregnancy & Birth*. Berkeley: Celestial Arts, 1987.
Goer, Henci. *The Thinking Woman's Guide to a Better Birth*. New York: Perigee, 1999.
Hotchner, Tracie. *The Pregnancy Diary*. New York: Avon Books, 1992.

Epilogue: Reflections on My Birthing Experience

"Group B Strep FAQs/Induction/Intervention." http://cl-cathiemac-ivil.tripod.com/gbs/interventions.htm.
International Chiropractic Pediatrics Association Research Foundation, "FDA Alert on Cytotec." http://www.icpa4kids.org/research/pregnancy/induction.htm.
Oxorn, Harry. *Oxorn-Foote Human Labor and Birth*. New York: McGraw-Hill Medical Publishing, 1986.

Breast-Feed Your Baby

Bonyata, Kelly. "Engorgement." http://www.kellymom.com/bf/concerns/mom/engorgement.html.
———. "Healing Tips for Nipple Cracks or Abrasions." http://www.kellymom.com/bf/concerns/mom/nipplehealing.html.
———. "Latching and Positioning Resources." http://www.kellymom.com/bf/start/basics/latch-resources.html.
Infant Feeding Action Coalition (INFACT) Canada. "Nestlé Boycott." http://www.infact-canada.ca/Nestle_Boycott.htm.
La Leche League. "Breast-Feeding Remains Best Choice in a Polluted World." http://www.llli.org/Release/contaminants.html.

———. "Is Thrush Causing My Sore Nipples?" http://www.lalecheleague.org/FAQ/thrush.html.

———. "What Are LLL's Guidelines for Storing My Pumped Milk?" http://www.lalecheleague.org/FAQ/milkstorage.html.

National Conference of State Legislatures. "50 State Summary of Breast-Feeding Laws." http://www.ncsl.org/programs/health/breast50.htm.

Neville, Margaret C. "Milk Secretion: An Overview." http://mammary.nih.gov/Reviews/lactation/Neville001/index.html.

O'Mara, Peggy. *Natural Family Living: The Mothering Magazine Guide to Parenting.* New York: Atria, 2000.

Prentice, Ann. "Constituents of Human Milk." *Food and Nutrition Bulletin*, vol. 7, no. 4 (December 1996).

Smith, Linda J. "How Mother's Milk Is Made." *LEAVEN*, vol. 37, no. 3 (June–July 2001): 54–55.

The Family Bed Controversy

American Academy of Pediatrics. "Policy Statement: Changing Concepts of Sudden Infant Death Syndrome: Implications for Infant Sleeping Environment and Sleep Position." *Pediatrics* vol. 105, no. 3 (March 2000): 650–656.

———. "Policy Statement: The Changing Concept of Sudden Infant Death Syndrome: Diagnostic Coding Shifts, Controversies Regarding the Sleeping Environment, and New Variables to Consider in Reducing Risk." *Pediatrics* vol. 116, no. 5 (November 2005): 1245–1255.

Brant, Martha, and Anna Kushment, "The Little One Said Roll Over." *Newsweek* (May 29, 2006).

Col, Jeananda. "Enchanted Learning." http://www.EnchantedLearning.com.

Consumer Product Safety Commission. "CPSC Warns Against Placing Babies in Adult Beds; Study Finds 64 Deaths Each Year from Suffocation and Strangulation." http://www.cpsc.gov/cpscpub/prerel/prhtml99/99175.html.

Gilbert, R.E., R.E. Wigfield, P.J. Fleming, P.J. Berry, and P.T. Rudd. "Bottle Feeding and the Sudden Infant Death Syndrome." *British Medical Journal* no 310 (1995): 88–90.

Heinig, M. Jane PhD, IBCLC and Jennifer Banuelos, BS. "American Academy of Pediatrics Task Force on Sudden Infant Death Syndrome (SIDS) Statement on SIDS Reduction: Friend or Foe of Breastfeeding?" *Journal of Human Lactation.* 2006 February 1; 22(1): 7–10.

O'Mara, Peggy. *Natural Family Living: The Mothering Magazine Guide to Parenting.*

O'Mara, Peggy. "Sleeping With Your Baby." *Mothering* no. 41 (March–April 2007): 10–14.

Palmer, Linda F. *Baby Matters: What Your Doctor May Not Tell You About Caring for Your Baby.* San Diego: Baby Reference, 2004.

Sears, William, and Martha Sears. *The Baby Book: Everything You Need to Know About Your Baby from Birth to Age Two.* New York: Little, Brown and Co., 2003.

Thoman, Evelyn B., "Co-Sleeping, an Ancient Practice: Issues of the Past and Present, and Possibilities for the Future." *Sleep Medicine Reviews.* 2006 Dec; 10(6): 407–17.

Babywearing

O'Mara, Peggy. *Natural Family Living: The Mothering Magazine Guide to Parenting.*

Sears, William, and Martha Sears. *The Baby Book: Everything You Need to Know About Your Baby from Birth to Age Two.*
Liedloff, Jean. *Continuum Concept: In Search of Happiness Lost.* Boston: Addison-Wesley, 1986.

The Virtues of Cloth Diapering

Biobottoms Diapering Resource Center. "What's Wrong with Disposable Diapers?" http://www.borntolove.com/wrong.html
Cancer Prevention Coalition. "Risks of Talcum Powder." http://www.preventcancer.com/consumers/cosmetics/talc.htm
Ecobaby Organics. "Diapers! Disposable or Cotton?" http://www.ecobaby.com/cloth.htm
Gore, Ariel. *The Hip Mama Survival Guide.* New York: Hyperion, 1998.
Harlow, B.L., D.W. Cramer, D.A. Bell, W.R. Welch. "Perineal exposure to talc and ovarian cancer risk." *Obstetrics & Gynecology,* 80 (1992): 19–26.
Lehrburger, Carl, and Rachel Snyder. "The disposable diaper myth." *Whole Earth Review.* Fall, 1988.
Real Diaper Association. "Diaper Facts." http://www.realdiaperassociation.org/diaperfacts.php
United States Code. Title 42, The Public Health and Welfare. Ch. 82, Solid Waste Disposal.
U.S. Consumer Product Safety Commission. http://www.cpsc.gov

The Baby Gender-Coding Phenomenon

Carmichael, Carrie. *Non-Sexist Childraising.* Boston: Beacon Press, 1978.
Mackoff, Barbara. *Growing a Girl: Seven Strategies for Raising a Strong, Spirited Daughter.* New York: Dell, 1996
Rosenberg, Debra. "(Rethinking) Gender." *Newsweek* (May 21, 2007): 50.

Battling Isolation

Calkins, Lori. "Thoughts on the Isolation of Motherhood." *Birth Issues* vol. 14, no. 4 (Spring 2000).

Going Back to Work

Aloi, Daniel. "Mothers Face Disadvantages in Getting Hired, Study Says." http://www.news.cornell.edu/stories/Aug05/soc.mothers.dea.html.
Boushey, Heather. "Are Women Opting Out? Debunking the Myth." http://www.cepr.net/documents/publications/opt_out_2005_11_2.pdf.
Heymann, Jody, Allison Earle, and Jeffrey Hayes. "The Work, Family, and Equity Index: How Does the United States Measure Up?" http://www.mcgill.ca/files/ihsp/WFEIFinal2007.pdf.
Warren, Elizabeth, and Amelia Warren Tyagi. *The Two-Income Trap: Why Middle-Class Mothers and Fathers Are Going Broke.* New York: Basic Books, 2003.

First Foods

Kenda, Margaret, and Phyllis Williams. *The Natural Baby Food Cookbook.* New York: Avon Books, 1988

O'Mara, Peggy. "A Quiet Place." *Mothering* no. 41 (March–April 2007): 10, 12.

Toddler Chomps

Horodynski, Mildred A., and Manfred Stommel. "Nutrition Education Aimed at Toddlers (NEAT): An Intervention Study." *Pediatric Nursing* vol. 31, no. 5 (Sept–Oct. 2005).

Sears, William, and Martha Sears. *The Baby Book: Everything You Need to Know About Your Baby from Birth to Age Two.*

Roberts, Susan, and Melvin B. Heyman. *Feeding Your Child for Lifelong Health: Birth Through Age Six.* New York: Bantam, 1999.

Never Join the "MOPS"

Bianchi, Suzanne M., Melissa A. Milkie, Liana C. Sayer, and John P. Robinson. "Is Anyone Doing the Housework? Trends in the Gender Division of Household Labor." *Social Forces* vol. 79, no. 1 (September 2000): 191–229.

Cinamon, Rachel Gail, and Yisrael Rich. "Gender Differences in the Importance of Work and Family Roles: Implications for Work-Family Conflict." *Sex Roles: A Journal of Research* vol. 47, nos. 11–12 (December 2002): 531–541.

Rubenstein, Carin. *The Sacrificial Mother: Escaping the Trap of Self-Denial.* New York: Hyperion Books, 1998.

Snell, Marilyn. "Home Work Time." *Mother Jones* (May/June 1997).

"Survey Confirms It: Women Outjuggle Men." *The New York Times* (September 15, 2000).

U.S. Department of Labor, Bureau of Labor Statistics. "American Time Use Survey: 2004 Results Announced by BLS." http://www.bls.gov/tus/home.htm.

The Great TV Debate

American Academy of Pediatrics. "Television: What Children See and Learn." http://www.aap.org/pubed/ZZZNKWJGQ2D.htm?&sub_cat=1.

Center for Screen-Time Awareness. "Screen-Time Fact Sheet." http://www.tvturnoff.org/factsheets.htm

Dennison B. A., T. A. Erb, and P. L. Jenkins. "Television Viewing and Television in Bedroom Associated with Overweight Risk Among Low Income Preschool Children." *Pediatrics.* vol. 109 (2002): 1028–1035.

Federal Communications Commission. "Annual Assessment of the Status of the Competition in the Market for the Delivery of Video Programming, 12th Annual Report." http://hraunfoss.fcc.gov/edocs_public/attachmatch/FCC-06-11A1.pdf.

Rideout, Victoria J., Elizabeth A. Vandewater, and Ellen A. Wartella. "Zero to Six: Electronic Media in the Lives of Infants, Toddlers and Preschoolers, Fall 2003." http://www.kff.org/entmedia/loader.cfm?url=/commonspot/security/getfile.cfm&PageID=2275

The Gender-Coding War Continues

Beattie-Moss, Melissa. "Are Gender Differences Predetermined?" http://www.rps.psu.edu/probing/gender.html.

Campbell, Anne. "I Had to Smack Him One." *New Scientist* (May 23, 2003).

Mackoff, Barbara. *Growing a Girl: Seven Strategies for Raising a Strong, Spirited Daughter.*

Discipline Notes: Relationship Is Everything

Bakunin, Mikhail. *The Political Philosophy of Bakunin.* New York: Free Press, 1964.

Setting Up an Art Center

Amabile, T. M., and B. A. Hennessey. "The Motivation for Creativity in Children." In *Achievement and Motivation: A Social-Developmental Perspective,* edited by A.K. Boggiano and T. Pittman. Cambridge: Cambridge University Press, 1992.

Bos, Bev. *Don't Move the Muffin Tins: A Hands-Off Guide to Art for the Young Child.* Roseville, CA: Burton Gallery, 1978.

Goleman, Daniel, Paul Kaufman, and Michael Ray. *The Creative Spirit.* New York: Plume, 1992.

Guiding My Kid Through the Marketing Madness

Adler, Richard. *The Effects of Television Advertising on Children.* Lanham, MD: Lexington Books, 1980.

"Ads Seek Kids' Grip on Family Purses." *Minneapolis Star Tribune* (December 4, 2006).

Center for a New American Dream. "Kids and Commercialism." http://www.newdream. org/kids.

———. "Thanks to Ads, Kids Won't Take No, No, No, No, No, No, No, No, No for an Answer," Center for a New American Dream website: www.newdream.org/kids/poll.php.

The Early Show. "Marketing To 'Tweens' Going Too Far?" (May 14, 2007).

Hulbert, Ann. "Tweens 'R' Us." *The New York Times* (November 28, 2004).

Kline, Stephen. "Babysitter's Club: Stephen Kline on Character Toy Marketing." *Stay Free!* (Spring 1997): 8–12.

———. *Out of the Garden: Toys and Children's Culture in the Age of TV Marketing.* London: Verso, 1995.

Linn, Susan. *Consuming Kids: The Hostile Takeover of Childhood.* New York: The New Press, 2004.

Paris Committee on Consumer Policy, Organisation for Economic Co-operation and Development. "Advertising Directed at Children: Endorsements in Advertising." *Paris: Organisation for Economic Co-operation and Development,* 1982.

Rudd Center for Food Policy and Obesity, Yale University. "Food Advertising & Children." http://www.yaleruddcenter.org/default.aspx?id=37.

Schor, Juliet B. *Born to Buy: The Commercialized Child and the New Consumer Culture.* New York: Scribner, 2004.

Wilcox, Brian, Joanne Cantor, Peter Dowrick, Dale Kunkel, Susan Linn, and Edward Palmer. "Report of the APA Task Force on Advertising and Children, Recommendations, February 20, 2004." http://www.apa.org/releases/childrenads_recommendations.pdf.

Friends of AK Press
Help sustain our vital project!

AK Press is a worker-run collective that publishes and distributes radical books, audio/visual media, and other material. We're small: a dozen individuals who work long hours for short money, because we believe in what we do. We're anarchists, which is reflected both in the books we publish and in the way that we organize our business: without bosses.

AK Press publishes the finest books, CDs, and DVDs from the anarchist and radical traditions—currently about 18 to 20 per year. Joining the Friends of AK Press program is a way that you can directly help us to keep the wheels rolling—and these important projects coming.

As ever, money is tight as we do not rely on outside funding. We need your help to make and keep these crucial materials available. Friends pay a minimum of $25/£15 per month (of course we have no objection to larger sums!), for a minimum three month period. Money received goes directly into our publishing funds. In return, Friends automatically receive (for the duration of their membership), as they appear, one FREE copy of EVERY new AK Press title. As well, they are also entitled to a 10% discount on EVERYTHING featured in the AK Press distribution catalog—or on our website—on ANY and EVERY order. We also have a program where individuals or groups can sponsor a whole book.

PLEASE CONTACT US FOR MORE DETAILS:

AK Press
674-A 23rd Street
Oakland, CA 94612
akpress@akpress.org
www.akpress.org

AK Press
PO Box 12766
Edinburgh, Scotland EH8 9YE
ak@akedin.demon.co.uk
www.akuk.com